972.98 Adkin, Mark
AD
        Urgent fury

        $24.95

© THE BAKER & TAYLOR CO.

Urgent Fury

Issues in Low-Intensity Conflict Series
Neil C. Livingstone, consulting editor

Beyond the Iran-Contra Crisis
*The Shape of U.S. Anti-Terrorism Policy
in the Post-Reagan Era*
Neil C. Livingstone and Terrell E. Arnold, editors

The Complete Security Guide for Executives
Neil C. Livingstone

**The Handbook for Effective Emergency
and Crisis Management**
Mayer Nudell and Norman Antokol

Low-Intensity Conflict
The Pattern of Warfare in the Modern World
Loren B. Thompson, editor

The Road to Kalamata
A Congo Mercenary's Personal Memoir
Mike Hoare

The Safe Travel Book
A Guide for the International Traveler
Peter Savage

Special Operations and National Purpose
Ross S. Kelly

Urgent Fury
The Battle for Grenada
Major Mark Adkin

URGENT FURY

The Battle for Grenada

by

MAJOR MARK ADKIN

Lexington Books

D.C. Heath and Company • Lexington, Massachusetts • Toronto

This book is published as part of the Lexington Books
Issues in Low-Intensity Conflict series
Neil C. Livingstone, consulting editor.

Library of Congress Cataloging-in-Publication Data

Adkin, Mark.
Urgent fury : the battle for Grenada / by Mark Adkin.
p.   cm.
Bibliography: p.
Includes index.
ISBN 0-669-20717-9 (alk. paper)
1. Grenada—History—American invasion, 1983—
Personal narratives, American.
2. United States. Marine Corps—History—20th century.
3. United States—Military history—20th century. 4. Adkin, Mark. I. Title.
F2056.8.A35   1989   88-38718
972.98'45—dc19   CIP

Published simultaneously in Canada
Printed in the United States of America
International Standard Book Number: 0-669-20717-9
Library of Congress Catalog Card Number: 88-38718

The paper used in this publication meets
the minimum requirements of American National Standard
for Information Sciences—Permanence of Paper
for Printed Library Materials, ANSI Z39.48-1984.

∞™

90 91 92 8 7 6 5 4 3

To my son, Robert

Contents

Maps

Acknowledgments

A host of people and organizations, from the United States, Antigua, Barbados, the United Kingdom, and Grenada, assisted me. I thank them all most sincerely; without them, this book could not have got beyond the wishful thinking stage. Of Americans who deserve particular thanks, at the top of the list must be Stan and Alice Lucas, whose son, Captain Keith Lucas, was killed piloting the helicopter that was shot down after the attempted attack on Richmond Hill Prison. Robert Jordan, a staff member of St. George's Medical School, and Christine Gigliuto and Kathleen Major, both students in Grenada at the time, have supplied much useful information and answered numerous queries. Similarly, I must single out Jiri Valenta, director of the Institute for Soviet and East European Studies, for his patience and generosity in explaining the political implications of the Bishop-Coard split. Finally, Brigadier General E.H. Simmons, director of Marine Corps History and Museums, assisted with the supply of photographs from the 22d Marine Amphibious Unit and clarified details of the marines' operations.

In Barbados, Brigadier Rudyard Lewis, my boss for five and a half years in the Caribbean, gave me a frank and fascinating account of events before, during, and after the intervention, as he had seen them. Lieutenant Commander Peter Tomlin and Major Mike Hartland contributed substantially to my knowledge. Without Peter Tomlin's expertise and contacts in many places, including Grenada, this book could certainly never have been finished.

On the island itself, I must mention several former People's Revolutionary Army officers. Major Einstein Louison kindly discussed the military aspects of the PRG up to his own arrest by Coard; Second Lieutenant Raeburn Nelson played a critical part in the actual fighting, participated in the assault on Fort Rupert just prior to Bishop's execution, and was later found not guilty of murder after an endlessly prolonged trial. To them I must add Sergeant Fabian Gabriel, the former logistic noncommissioned officer at Fort Rupert, who witnessed Bishop's death and was compelled to assist in his burial. I thank all of these people for helping so willingly to set the record straight concerning such traumatic events in their country.

It was Joe Gaylord, the American owner of the delightful hotel, Twelve Degrees North, who was the only person to take a video film of the Rangers as they jumped on Salines. He gave me every assistance, permitted me to watch and rewatch his film, and put me in touch with several other witnesses of events on the island. My grateful thanks.

My own personal knowledge of Urgent Fury has been extensively supplemented by others who for various reasons do not wish to be identified. I salute them for their enormous help in fitting together many key pieces in the puzzle.

My final debt is to my wife, Sandhira, who struggled, successfully, to master the intricacies of a word processor in order to spend count-less hours converting my awful writing into an immaculate manuscript.

The comments and opinions expressed in this book are entirely my own. They represent nothing more than a personal assessment by a soldier who had the good fortune to be there when it was all happening.

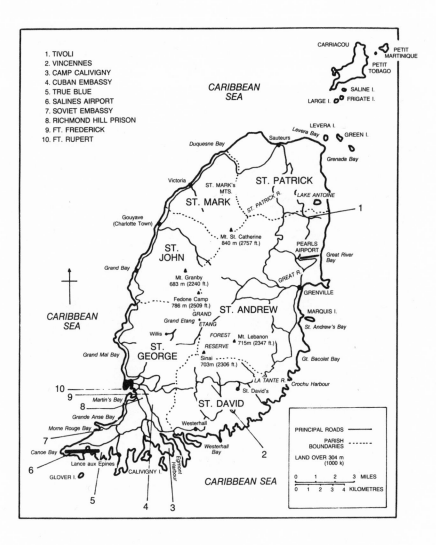

1. TIVOLI
2. VINCENNES
3. CAMP CALIVIGNY
4. CUBAN EMBASSY
5. TRUE BLUE
6. SALINES AIRPORT
7. SOVIET EMBASSY
8. RICHMOND HILL PRISON
9. FT. FREDERICK
10. FT. RUPERT

GRENADA

Introduction

T ucked away in a St. George's back street is the Grenada
museum. Inside, among more typical exhibits, is a dark, scruffy,
blood-soaked pair of jeans, alongside a pair of boots. A note ex-
plains that these were presented by the People's Revolutionary
Government (PRG). The jeans were worn by leading revolutionary
Maurice Bishop when he was beaten up by then prime minister
Gairy's police on Bloody Sunday, November 18, 1973, while the boots
were on the feet of future PRG general Hudson Austin, when he
led the attack on Gairy's Defence Force barracks on March 13, 1979.
For all I know they are still there, a pathetic reminder to the curious
of the beginnings of the only Marxist regime in modern times to
suffer invasion and military destruction by a Western power.

The execution of Prime Minister Bishop on October 19, 1983, together with seven close supporters, on the orders of his former deputy,
Bernard Coard, gave the U.S. president a unique opportunity for
decisive action. He took it. A communist nutmeg was smashed by
an enormous American sledgehammer. It was all over in a few days.
Protests were heard around the world. The U.S. invasion was roundly
condemned from all sides, by democratic as well as dictatorial governments. The United States had invaded a foreign country; it was likened
to the Soviet's attack on Afghanistan; international law had been
flouted. Such reaction was predictable, even understandable, but it
ignored the thousands of Grenadians who took to the streets waving,
smiling, holding up "God bless America" signs, or eagerly pointing
out the hiding places of their erstwhile communist bosses and their
weapons. Coard, had he been handed over by the U.S. Marines after
his arrest to the jeering crowd, would have been lynched. He probably
still would be if he avoids the gallows and was ever freed.

The political decision to launch Urgent Fury, as the intervention was
code-named, was proved by events to be a sound one. A democratically

elected government was subsequently restored to an island that for a decade had suffered grievously under autocratic, corrupt, and ruthless regimes. The intervention cost lives, but it saved far more. The spread of the communist revolution in the Caribbean was set back for years. For Cuba and the Soviet Union, it was a serious blow; for the Grenadian people, it gave them another chance, a chance to live their lives without fear. Sergeant Kenneth Landry, formerly of the 2d/75th Rangers, expressed the views of most participants when he said he was "glad we did it. . . . It's about time we showed we had some backbone left."

The United States could not have lost militarily. It wielded a sledgehammer; the target was a nut. Until now the full story of how the sledgehammer was used has not been told. The press was excluded from Grenada until the third day of the invasion, by which time all serious fighting was over. The U.S. forces achieved a victory, for which they can rightly claim credit, but their success in Grenada has been used as proof that they have reestablished their military competence, lost in Vietnam, Tehran, and Beirut. "We blew them away," said Vice-Admiral Metcalf, the overall on-scene commander.

This may be true, but no military operation ever has been, or ever will be, flawless. Battles are fought by people, and people err. After Urgent Fury, the U.S. military became sensitive to criticism, some of it ill informed, about how the operation had been conducted. There had been a spate of newspaper articles based on a report charging ineptitude compiled by William Lind, a legislative aide and adviser on defense to Senator Gary Hart. Lind's research was largely based on bar talk. "If you are willing to hang around bars and keep your ears open, there's a lot you can find out," was how he described it. When asked how many bars he visited, Lind replied, "A significant number; I've been researching this for some months."

General John Vessey, chairman of the Joint Chiefs of Staff, responded in writing to the Armed Services Committee of the U.S. House of Representatives. Lind's twenty allegations of ineptitude by the military in Grenada were listed, and Vessey replied to each with facts and comments. This report, with a covering letter dated June 6, 1984, and signed by Vessey, was sent to Congressman James Courter, who was requesting a committee investigation into what had really happened in Grenada. Courter claimed that a hearing the committee had held the previous January "was absolutely one sided" and a "rosy assessment." But with this report, an unclassified document that could be released to the public, the critics had to be satisfied unless Courter was prepared to insist on a full-scale official investigation. He was not. (For readers interested in forming their own opinion, Vessey's analysis of Lind's barroom allegations appears in Appendix A, but I suggest this be read after the rest of the book rather than before.)

I participated personally in the planning and execution of Urgent Fury with the Caribbean contingents, and it has long been my wish to set down an account of what happened from the military point of view. The Grenada story is a fascinating one. Its political significance has been thoroughly documented and analyzed; not so the military. I have spent many months researching the facts and interviewing participants, many on the island. If I have made errors, the fault is mine. I deliberately waited several years before writing to allow the dust of battle to settle and heated emotions to cool. This pause has had the added advantage that the murder trial of Coard and others has been concluded, thus allowing me to interview key witnesses and one accused.

I am a great believer in the use of maps to explain events, particularly military ones, so I make no excuse for the number in the text. Although the situations they portray are as accurate as possible, troop dispositions, scale, contours, and locations of some buildings and tracks are sometimes only approximate.

Many quotations have been used from PRG documents, speeches, and letters, as well as from other participants. In the case of Grenadians, I have made no attempt to alter spelling or grammar, so there are occasions when errors of both are fairly obvious.

For the sake of simplicity all timings are local.

Principal Participants

T HE people who played a prominent part or who feature frequently in the story of the struggle for Grenada in 1983 are set out below for convenience and ease of reference. Any rank shown is that held at the time; nicknames, where known, are given in parentheses.

Grenada

Abdullah, Iman ("the Butcher"), Lieutenant. Commanded Bishop's execution squad and burned the bodies. Sentenced to hang.

Austin, Hudson ("G Man"), General. Minister of defense, interior, and construction. Commander (under Bishop) of the People's Revolutionary Armed Forces and a member of the Central Committee. Sentenced to hang.

Bain, Fitzroy ("Fitzy"). Central Committee member and Bishop supporter. Executed with Bishop.

Bishop, Maurice. Prime minister; commander in chief of the armed forces. Seized power in a 1979 coup against Gairy. Executed October 19, 1983, on the orders of Coard and the Central Committee.

Coard, Bernard. Deputy prime minister; minister of finance; leading Marxist ideologist. Led the anti-Bishop power struggle and ordered Bishop executed. Sentenced to hang.

Coard, Phyllis. Wife of Bernard. Central Committee member; ardent Marxist. Sentenced to hang.

Cornwall, Leon ("Bogo"), Major. Ambassador to Cuba; later on the Central Committee; Coard supporter. Sentenced to hang.

Creft, Jaqueline ("Jackie"). Bishop's mistress, minister of education, youth, and culture. Executed with Bishop.

Gahagan, Basil ("Akee"), Major. Operations staff officer in the army; Coard supporter. Narrowly escaped prosecution after Urgent Fury. Now works on yachts.

Gairy, Sir Eric ("Uncle G"). Flamboyant and dictatorial prime minister at independence. Ousted by Bishop's coup in early 1979.

James, Liam ("Owusu"), Lieutenant Colonel. Deputy secretary for interior under Austin; responsible for security and secret police. On Central Committee; Coard supporter. Sentenced to hang.

Layne, Ewart ("Headache"), Lieutenant Colonel. Deputy secretary for defense under Austin; responsible for army affairs. On Central Committee; Coard supporter; ambitious. Sentenced to hang.

Louison, Einstein, Major. Army chief of staff under Bishop; the only Bishop supporter among senior military officers. Narrowly escaped execution on October 19, 1983.

Louison, George, brother of Einstein. Minister of agriculture; strong Bishop supporter. Narrowly avoided execution with Bishop by being previously detained in Richmond Hill Prison.

Mayers, Conrad ("Connie"), Officer Cadet. Commanded the attack on Fort Rupert, with orders to kill Bishop, on October 19, 1983. Killed in the assault.

Nelson, Raeburn, 2d Lieutenant. Commanded the Motorised Company at Fort Frederick; participated in the attack on Fort Rupert. The only person out of eighteen subsequently tried for murder to be acquitted.

Noel, Vincent ("Vince"). Prominent trade unionist and supporter of Bishop. Removed from Central Committee. Died in the attack on Fort Rupert.

Prime, Cecil ("Dumpy"), Lieutenant. Chief of all artillery within the army; opposed Bishop; present at his execution. Sentenced to hang.

Redhead, Lester ("Goat"), Captain. Commanded the regular Security Company in the army. Coard supporter who organized Bishop's execution and burial. Sentenced to hang.

St. Bernard, Ian ("St. B"), Major. Commissioner of police under Bishop; supported Coard in his power struggle. Narrowly escaped prosecution. Now free in Grenada.

St. Paul, Cletus, 2d Lieutenant. Head of Bishop's personal security guards; arrested just prior to Bishop's execution. A key witness at the trial of Coard and his supporters. Now a taxi driver.

Scoon, Sir Paul, Governor-General. Represented Queen Elizabeth in Grenada under Gairy, Bishop, the Revolutionary Military Council, and after Urgent Fury. Still governor-general.

Stroude, Christopher ("Chris"), Major. The political commissar of the armed forces. Strong Coard supporter; present at Bishop's execution. Sentenced to hang.

Whiteman, Unison ("Uni"). Minister of foreign affairs under Bishop; strong Bishop supporter. Executed with Bishop.

Caribbean

Adams, Tom. Prime minister of Barbados. Staunch advocate of the need for military intervention after Bishop's death. Died of a heart attack in 1985.

Adkin, Mark, Major. British contract officer with Barbados Defence Force; operations staff officer responsible for the planning of the Caribbean participation in Urgent Fury. Now in the United Kingdom.

Barnes, Kenneth ("Ken"), Colonel. The Jamaica Defence Force officer who commanded the Caribbean Peacekeeping Force during Urgent Fury. Still serving.

Castro, Fidel. President of Cuba. Supporter of the Grenadian communist revolution under Bishop. Personal friend of Bishop; refused to cooperate with Coard and Austin after Bishop's death.

Charles, Eugenia. Prime minister of Dominica and chairperson of the Organisation of East Caribbean States. Strong advocate of military intervention by the United States in Grenada. Still prime minister.

Hartland, Michael ("Mike"), Major. British citizen serving with the Barbados Defence Force. Lived in Grenada under Gairy and Bishop; knew the island well. Still serving in Barbados.

Lewis, Rudyard E.C. ("Rudy"), Brigadier. Chief of staff–Commander of the Barbados Defence Force, and coordinator of the Regional Security System. The Caribbean's senior military representative in Urgent Fury. Still serving.

Rizo, Torres. Cuban ambassador in Grenada under Bishop and at the time of Urgent Fury. Later disciplined for his failure to predict the climax of the Bishop-Coard conflict.

Tomlin, Peter, Lieutenant Commander. Served on the staff of the Regional Security System during Urgent Fury. Extensive knowledge of Grenada; attempted to capture Austin during the operation. Still serving in Barbados.

Tortolo Comas, Pedro, Colonel. Sent by Castro to Grenada less than twenty-four hours before Urgent Fury started to organize the Cuban work force. Controlled the Cuban defense of their positions.

United States

Civilian

Bush, George, Vice-President. Member of the National Security Council. Chaired the Special Situation Group for some of the planning for Urgent Fury. Now U.S. president.

McFarlane, Robert. National security adviser during Urgent Fury. Later resigned as a result of his involvement in the Iran-contra scandal.

Motley, Langhorne. Assistant secretary of state for inter-American affairs. Initiated planning for an intervention in Grenada as early as October 13, 1983. Still serving.

Reagan, Ronald, President. Made the ultimate political decision to intervene militarily, despite considerable overseas pressure not to do so.

Army

Hagler, Ralph, Lieutenant Colonel. Commanding officer of the 2d/75th Rangers. Dropped at Salines on D day, his battalion rescued the U.S. students from Grand Anse campus and then attacked Camp Calivigny. Still serving.

Henry, Terence M., Colonel. Commander, Task Force 160, the helicopter unit that flew in the Special Forces on D day. Promoted to brigadier general; still serving.

Lucas, Keith J., Captain. Pilot of the only Black Hawk helicopter to crash during the assault on Richmond Hill Prison. Killed during the attack.

Scholtes, Richard A., Major General. Commanded Task Force 123 (the Special Forces units) during Urgent Fury. Now retired.

Schwarzkopf, Norman, Major General. Deputy commander and army adviser to Admiral Metcalf at Task Force 120's headquarters on the *Guam*. Retired.

Scott, Steven, Colonel. Commanded 3 Brigade in the 82d Airborne Division; in control of the attack on Camp Calivigny. Still serving.

Silvasy, Stephen, Colonel. Commanded 2 Brigade in the 82d Airborne Division. His command post was strafed by U.S. aircraft on October 27. Still serving.

Taylor, Wesley, Lieutenant Colonel. Commanding officer of 1st/75th Rangers. Dropped at Salines on D day and secured the airfield. Still serving as a colonel commanding the 75th Ranger Regiment.

Trobaugh, Edward, Major General. Commanded the 82d Airborne Division and Task Force 121 during Urgent Fury. Retired.

Vessey, John W., General. Chairman of the Joint Chiefs of Staff during Urgent Fury. Retired.

Navy

Berry, Richard, Rear Admiral. Commander of the USS *Independence* Carrier Battle Group (designated Task Group 20.5), which provided air and surface support for Urgent Fury. Still serving.

Erie, Carl, Captain. Commanded Amphibious Squadron Four with his headquarters on the USS *Guam*, carrying the 22d Marine Amphibious Unit to Lebanon when it was diverted to Grenada. Still serving.

McDonald, Wesley L., Admiral.   As commander in chief Atlantic his naval headquarters staff was given the responsibility of planning and controlling Urgent Fury. Still serving.

Metcalf, Joseph, Vice-Admiral.   Commander of the navy's 2d Fleet when he took over the detailed planning and on-scene control of Urgent Fury as commander of Task Force 120. He had his headquarters on the USS *Guam*. Retired.

Marine Corps

Amos, Granville R. ("Granny"), Lieutenant Colonel.   Commanded the Marine Medium Helicopter Squadron 261 with CH-46 and CH-53 heavy-lift helicopters. His squadron was heavily engaged in the initial landings and during subsequent operations. Still serving.

Faulkner, James P., Colonel.   Commanding officer of the 22d Marine Amphibious Unit, with almost 2,000 marines. Initially deployed in the north of the island. Still serving.

Giguere, John P. ("Pat"), Captain.   Pilot of a Cobra gunship during fierce actions over St. George's on D day. Shot down and killed over St. George's harbor.

Howard, Timothy B., Captain.   Pilot of a Cobra gunship during fierce action over St. George's on D day. Badly wounded when shot down.

Scharver, Jeffrey R., First Lieutenant. Copilot to Giguere; killed in the crash.

Seagle, Jeb F., Captain. Copilot with Howard; survived the crash and pulled Howard out of the wreckage but was shot and killed while seeking help.

Smith, Ray L., Lieutenant Colonel.   Commanding Officer of 2d/8th Battalion Landing Team, the unit that carried out all the marine ground operations during Urgent Fury. Still serving.

Air Force

Couvillon, Michael, Major.   Piloted the first AC-130 Spectre gunship over Grenada on D day to drop the Ranger pathfinders. Subsequently flew vital ground support missions. Promoted; still serving.

Meyer, Richard L., Brigadier General.   Commanded Task Force 126 based at Roosevelt Roads in Puerto Rico. His F-15s were used to deter overseas Cuban interference and his Airborne Warning and Control Systems (AWACs), for aerial reconnaissance. Still serving.

Patterson, Robert, Brigadier General.   Military Airlift Command officer with responsibilities for controlling and coordinating the air flow into the island on D day. Still serving.

Simms, David, Lieutenant Colonel.   Pilot of AC-130 Spectre heavily involved in firing in support of ground units on D day. Still serving.

Military Symbols
Used on Maps

UNIT SIZES

⊡	A platoon, 20–35 men
⊡	A company, 100–150 men
⊡	A battalion, 450–800 men
⊡	A regiment, 800–1,500 men
⊡	A brigade, over 1,500 men
⊡	A division, over 8,000 men
⊡	A corps, over 20,000 men
(—)	An understrength unit

TYPES OF UNIT

⊠	Infantry	⬭	Tanks
⊡	Artillery	⊠	APCs or amphibious vehicles
⊠	Rangers	⊠	Armored cars
⊠	Airborne	⊡	Engineers
⊠	Marines	CPF	Caribbean Peacekeeping Force
⌐	A U.S. headquarters	⊠	Artillery used as Infantry
◁	A Cuban or PRA headquarters		

AN EXAMPLE

C ⊠ 1/75   C Company 1st Battalion, 75th Rangers

WEAPONS

⊥	75-mm recoilless rifle
⊥	82-mm mortar
⊥	Antiaircraft gun

MILITARY SYMBOLS USED ON MAPS

Prologue

Last March 13th the Grenada People had their fairest election ever; that is ONE MAN, ONE GUN! Nobody can dispute the fairness of that!

— Selwyn Strachan, PRG minister of mobilization at a public meeting in November 1979

I F you stand in the market square of St. George's, Grenada, and look eastward and upward, to where the long, green ridgeline meets the sky, you will see on the highest point of the ridge an enormous steel crucifix cross. Standing within the old walls of Fort Frederick 20 meters high, it is bare, gaunt, and uncared for. Its rusting struts and spars, broken electric lights, and twisted wiring make an ugly contrast with the tropical beauty that surrounds it. It is a monument to "Uncle" Gairy's reckless spending of the 1960s and 1970s, a typical example of the wasteful expenditure that was the hallmark of Gairy's government in the years before and after Grenada's independence. Ablaze with light, it was visible to Grenadians on many distant parts of the island—a symbol that "Uncle G" was there, watching over them. When Gairy went into enforced exile in 1979, the lights were switched off, never to be relit. The symbol of Gairy's dominance remains today, sharing the solitude with a radio mast, as a forlorn reminder of yesterday.

Grenada is the southernmost of a chain of tiny islands that runs for 400 miles from the east of Puerto Rico to the coast of Venezuela. They bar the passage from the Atlantic to the Caribbean Sea (map 1). Like most of its neighbors, the Spice Island, as it is often known because of its export of nutmeg, mace, and cloves, is blessed with

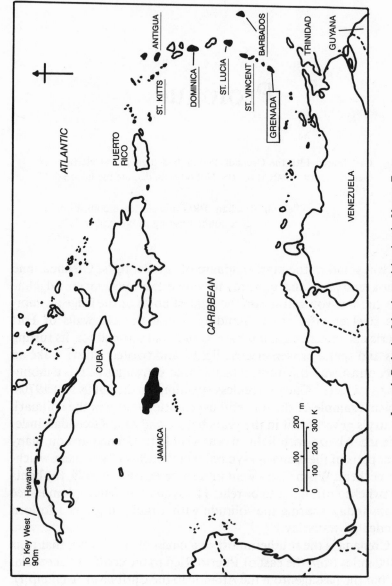

Legend: <u>Barbados</u>-Islands participating in Urgent Fury

Map 1. STRATEGIC LOCATION OF GRENADA

lush vegetation, green-clad mountains in the central areas, and superb white sand beaches in the bays and inlets around its coast.

Nature has been generous to Grenada. Heavy tropical rain, falling on rich volcanic soil, has provided its 90,000 people with an abundance of fruit and vegetables. Grapefruit and guavas, limes and lemons, tamarinds and tangerines, refresh Grenadians with a minimum of effort, as do bananas, pumpkins, cassava, tomatoes, and yams. To own one of the 50-foot-high nutmeg trees ensures economic security. A mature tree bears upwards of 3,000 nuts a year; the island industry supplies a third of the world's demand for this aromatic spice. Many Grenadians are fishermen. The seas abound with dolphins, flying fish, and red snappers, which today, with an expanding tourist industry, find their way onto the plates of thousands of appreciative visitors.

Grenada's history has been bloody. Discovered by Columbus in 1498, the original Carib Indian inhabitants were slaughtered by the French colonists in the mid-seventeenth century. The cliff north of Sauteurs is still called Carib's Leap, after the unfortunate Indians who leaped to their death rather than submit to their pursuers. Another 150 years of war and rebellion followed as France and England struggled for supremacy, and the plantation slaves for freedom. Britain finally secured the island in 1803 and held it until Sir Eric Gairy obtained full independence in 1974.

By this time Britain was grateful to go. The run up to independence in Grenada was marked by strikes and vicious political rioting that cost several lives. The New Jewel Movement (NJM), led by Maurice Bishop, was behind the opposition. Gairy's response was to turn the police and his Mongoose Gang loose on the people, to hound them and, if necessary, kill them.[1] Independence was celebrated in the middle of a general strike on February 7, 1974, only sixteen days after police had shot and killed Bishop's father.

Never before or since has a British colony achieved its independence in such miserable circumstances. The island was in turmoil; businesses were shut, power was cut off, people were going hungry as dockers in Trinidad and Barbados refused to load cargoes destined for the island, and the governor, Dame Hilda Bynoe, a medical doctor, had resigned a few days before the celebrations. The British government refused to consider delay; they wanted out. A rich white Grenadian, Major Leo de Gale, was persuaded at the last moment that it was his duty to become governor and the country's first governor-general.

Queen Elizabeth was to have been represented by Prince Richard of Gloucester, but it was so obvious that the ceremonies were going to be a farce, if not actually dangerous, that his attendance was cancelled. Instead a lowly parliamentary under secretary at the Foreign and Commonwealth Office, Peter Blaker, flew out. On the day itself, the Holiday Inn on the Grand Anse beach had been chosen for the evening's gala dinner, but the management abandoned the hotel at the last moment, leaving the chef to his own devices.

Bishop was unable to watch the proceedings. He had been locked up the day before, charged with attempted assassination after the police claimed they had found arms and bombs in his house. He was released on bail two days later.

Eric Gairy had returned to his home island in 1950 after being thrown out of the oil refineries of Aruba for union agitation within the work force. Ambitious, bright, and brash, he was soon organizing Grenada's poor into the powerful Grenada Manual and Mental Workers Union. As its name indicates, virtually everybody was eligible to join. It was not long before Gairy and his union clashed violently with the colonial authorities. The resultant arson, bloodshed, looting, and riots forced the governor, Sir Arthur Grimble of Gilbert Islands fame, to call in Royal Navy warships with troops.[2] Gairy was placed under house arrest in Carriacou, but the violence escalated. The governor backed down. Gairy returned in triumph to Grenada; tranquility was gradually restored. From then on he used his union power and popularity to further his political ambitions. He formed the Grenada United Labour party (GULP), which soon became a force to be reckoned with throughout the islands.

In 1961 Gairy became chief minister, and what became known as squandermania began in earnest. A commission set up in 1962 to investigate lavish expenditure on his official residence found that substantial sums had been spent without authority. Britain suspended the constitution, and Gairy was thrown out of office, but he was skillfully able to manipulate the situation to his future advantage. To the people, it appeared as though the white colonial government was persecuting their black leader, not allowing him to live in the style they themselves enjoyed.

In the 1967 elections, Gairy was back as chief minister—back to stay, until he was forcibly removed by Bishop twelve years later. These years saw him consolidate his position as an autocratic ruler, conferring upon himself some thirty honors, decorations, degrees, and titles. Fastidious about his appearance, he spent hours in front of his mirror, admiring the sight of himself covered with medals. He developed a passion for psychic phenomena, mysticism, and UFOs, which he coupled with apparently strong religious convictions. He hosted a visit from Jim Jones from the United States, who was looking for a site to set up his People's Temple. Luckily it was not to be in Grenada, but Guyana, where Jones later organized the mass murder or suicide of 800 men, women, and children.

Gairy began to amass a considerable personal fortune. Patronage and nepotism became rampant, with Gairy infiltrating his henchmen and informers into all branches of government. Nothing of significance could be done without his knowledge or personal approval. He acquired substantial business interests and property, including the Tropical Inn, Rock Gardens, and Evening Palace hotels. In 1976 his government introduced a law requiring banks in Grenada to put 5 percent of their deposits in the treasury; two years later, this was increased to 10 percent. Bernard Coard, Bishop's finance minister in the PRG, was later to think this was an excellent idea and upped it to 20 percent.

By the early 1970s, many Grenadians had had enough. It was at that time that Bishop, a young lawyer, returned to organize the political opposition. The NJM was formed as a direct threat to Gairy, who reacted predictably—with violence. Law and order collapsed. Protests were broken up by Gairy's police, his Mongoose Gang, or the green uniformed soldiers of the Defence Force (the so-called Green Beasts), wielding batons and often firing guns. People were injured; some were killed. A special Commission of Enquiry under Sir Herbert Duffus was appointed in 1973, just before independence, to report on the allegations of police brutality. The findings confirmed what everybody knew: that the beatings and killings were unjustified and unlawful. The Mongoose Gang was described as "an unlawfully constituted body of men paid from public funds"—legal words for a bunch of thugs. Voices were raised calling for Gairy's resignation, but he ignored them. The resultant nationwide strike, which started on New Year's Day 1974, was to drag on for months, continuing through the formal granting of independence in February.

Nothing improved with independence. Gairy became increasingly determined to crush opposition by bullying and intimidation. But by

1977 he was worried by the inroads the NJM was making into his traditional union support. On one occasion he called a meeting of all commercial workers in St. George's to harangue them on what he had done for their betterment. Afterward a young NJM militant, Vincent Noel, who was destined to die with Bishop, stood up to respond. Noel recalled:

> I noticed as I spoke that I was being surrounded by his Mongoose men. One came and stood right behind me, and another sat down directly facing me, staring at me hard and patting his side pocket menacingly, as if he had a gun in there. I carried on outlining to the workers the steadily increasing prices of sugar, saltfish, transport to and from work, school fees, and the general cost of living. He [Gairy] then interrupted me, clearly flustered, and announced: "Mr. Noel will now lead you all in prayer! Ah, but no, communists don't like praying, so I'll lead the prayer." And after that he simply closed the meeting.

On the evening of March 12, 1979, after Gairy had left the island to endeavor to get a full debate in the United Nations on UFOs, a band of men huddled together in the darkness in the small village of Mardigras, 2 kilometers east of St. George's. Gairy apparently had left instructions that a final rounding up of NJM leaders was to take place during his absence. Vincent Noel was among those seized. To the group of conspirators, many of them on the run and facing jail or worse, now was the time to act. They had been planning this moment for some months, their original plot in January having been postponed. They were armed with a few antiquated weapons, some ammunition, homemade petrol bombs, and cutlasses, and they had three or four trucks. That night they were to attack the camp of the Green Beasts, located in the south of the island, near a place called True Blue. Some twenty-four men were involved in the operation, among them Hudson Austin, the leader, Basil Gahagan, Einstein Louison, Ewart Layne, Kenrick Radix, John Ventour, and Straughan Phillip. Maurice Bishop did not participate in the actual assault but had helped plan the operation, overruling the hotheads, Austin and Gahagan, who wanted to liquidate as many as possible of the opposition. Bishop shrewdly sought a bloodless coup. He was to get it—almost.

The Defence Force had some ninety members, of whom forty or fifty might be expected to be sleeping in their barracks that night.

Allies among the soldiers had tipped off the attackers as to camp routine and security, or rather lack of it. So when the twelve men detailed to surround the buildings did so in the early morning of March 13, no sentries were encountered, no alarm given. Petrol bombs were thrown, the buildings caught fire, the Green Beasts fled, nobody was shot, nobody was caught. The only casualty occurred when somebody telephoned the home of a Defence Force officer, Lieutenant Brizan, to tell him the camp was on fire. Dutifully, but rather foolishly, he leaped into his car to investigate. About 1 kilometer from the camp, his headlights picked out a party of armed men on the road, signaling him to stop. He did so. One of the group approached, carrying a .303 rifle, calling out to him to freeze. Brizan may have tried to draw his pistol; that's what he was alleged to have done. A shot was fired through the car door, killing him instantly. His body lay in the road for a long time.

The coup was welcomed by most Grenadians. They saw it as the start of a new era—one without Gairy, without corruption, and without brutality. What they could not know was that they were escaping from the frying pan, only to jump into the fire.

1

Heavy Manners

You get detained when I sign an order. . . . Once I sign it, like it or not it's up to the hill for them!
— Maurice Bishop, PRG prime minister in his secret Line of March speech to party members, September 13, 1982

W INSTON "Broko"Simon, a Grenadian farmer and fisherman, was screaming, screaming horribly. Although still in shock and pain from what had already been done to him, it was knowing what was about to happen that caused Simon to squirm so desperately against the hands that gripped his hair and arms and forced open his legs. Simon was "ketching arse," the local phrase for undergoing harsh treatment. He was suffering far more than harsh treatment, however, he was being tortured in a most horrific way. He was being put under "heavy manners," which was originally a Jamaican expression, later adopted throughout Grenada, meaning discipline, punishment, or control. To "manners" somebody meant to imprison, beat, or otherwise discipline the person. It was June 1980, and after fifteen months of the Maurice Bishop revolution, Grenada was under "heavy manners."

Simon lived and worked in the small village of Tivoli, some 3 kilometers north of the airport at Pearls. The area had been, and still was to some extent, Gairy country. As such it came under close scrutiny from the PRG's security service. This parish was supposedly a hotbed of counterrevolutionary activity; the people were bourgeoisie and petite bourgeoisie farmers and therefore not yet part of what Bishop described as "a dictatorship of the entire working people."

At about 10:30 A.M. on June 18, Simon had received a message that People's Revolutionary Army (PRA) soldiers had surrounded his home and were asking for him. On arrival at his house a soldier called "Ronnie" Bubb told him he was wanted for questioning. He was driven to the PRA camp at Pearls Airport, where Captain Ewart "Headache" Layne opened the car door. As Simon got out, he was handcuffed by a PRA lieutenant, Lester "Goat" Redhead. Layne then put his arm around Simon's shoulders saying, "Let's walk," and led him to a hut full of soldiers, explaining that he had been sent to clean up the Tivoli area. When they reached the door, the group halted while Redhead bent to handcuff Simon's feet. On straightening up, Redhead kicked him hard in the small of the back, jackknifing him to the ground, whereupon Layne, Redhead, Bubb, Leon "Bogo" Cornwall, and others started to beat him with rifle butts and boots. It was the start of three weeks of hell for Simon.[1]

His most terrifying ordeal was when Layne asked him if he knew how they altered pigs. Simon knew only too well. Redhead brought out a packet of razor blades while a soldier fetched a knife and some peppers, which he cut up into chunks. Redhead stamped and crushed the peppers before putting them in a tin with some water. Simon was stripped naked and held down by several soldiers, two of whom pulled open his legs. Layne took a razor blade and began to slice Simon's testicles and penis while Redhead rubbed in the peppers. At the same time Simon was beaten about the head with a pistol butt by the others. Simon told his tormentors nothing.

Taken outside, Simon heard Redhead shouting for a hot cutlass, which he proceeded to use to brand his victim all over the body. Simon did not even notice the kicking and beating that continued in between the sickening agony of the red-hot cutlass blade. After a while, Layne became concerned at the amount of blood, and, thinking Simon might die on them, ordered a halt. The broken, bleeding body was thrown in a cell.

The interrogation was not over yet. During the course of the next three days, Simon continued to suffer appallingly. He was beaten frequently. Redhead tried drowning him in a drum of oil, and a number of soldiers tried to lynch him by holding his arms and legs and pulling. He was buried in a hole, sand put over his body, and eight heavy concrete blocks placed on top of him. When it seemed he might be dead or dying, he was hauled out. After a short respite, they tried again. This time it was Layne who had him staked out on the ground by his arms and legs, lying on his stomach. The heated cutlass was applied again and a red-hot iron pushed up his rectum. He was left tied to a stake for several days.

It is not certain whether Simon was a man of almost unbelievable courage or whether he genuinely knew nothing—perhaps both. After three weeks at the airport, he was imprisoned in a tiny cell at Fort Rupert for six months, before finally ending up in Richmond Hill Prison. It took the PRG authorities fifteen months to bring a charge of withholding information against him, and the magistrate eventually dismissed the case for lack of evidence. Not that that helped Simon; he was sent back to the prison on the hill. There "I remained until the rescue mission in October last year," Simon told the senior government official who prepared the special report to the governor-general, dated May 14, 1984, on torture allegations. Heavy manners indeed.

The outcry at the time against the perpetrators of this horrendous crime could not be ignored, even by Bishop. Layne, Redhead, and Cornwall were brought before a PRA court-martial, dismissed from the party and the army, and made to confess to the error of their ways in a number of public apologies. But they were all key supporters of the revolution and had been closely associated with the Gairy overthrow. They could not be under "manners" for long. Within a few months, they were all reinstated in the party and the PRA—with higher ranks. Bishop and the party looked after their own.

Simon's case was not the only one of torture under Bishop's regime. According to Richard Pascal, a detainee in Richmond Hill Prison in December 1980, Justin Roberts, the officer in charge of the prison, and Victor Husbands, Bishop's special investigator, took him and another prisoner in a jeep, blindfolded, with his hands tied behind his back. He was punched, beaten, and tied to a post. Pascal states that Husbands said, "What a fucking noise you make in the night. We killing you, but we see what you know first." Roberts returned; Pascal was untied, thrown to the ground, and held down by his long hair. Allegedly Roberts almost choked him to death by pressing his foot on Pascal's throat. He was kicked repeatedly in the stomach and passed out. He woke up back in his cell with a badly damaged eye and urinating blood.

"Heavy manners"—in the prison, Fort Rupert, some PRA camp, or a police cell—was something to be avoided. A wide variety of tortures have been described, among them the use of an electric prod, burning with cigarettes or matches, standing at gunpoint next to a hornets' nest or all night long in a courtyard. In jail access to a toilet was often at the whim of the guard, food was revolting, washing often impossible. In Fort Rupert prisoners often spent many days in a concrete cell with a barbed-wire roof exposed to the elements.

Torture, however, was the extreme example. Bishop was to institute more subtle ways of putting Grenada under manners, to ensure absolute control of the country in the name of the revolution. He was to follow Marxist-Leninist principles, mirroring the Soviet system exactly, in both the PRG and PRA.

‡   ‡   ‡

There is no doubt that Bishop's almost bloodless coup in March 1979 was popular with the great majority of Grenadians. Most people had had more than enough of Gairy, his Mongoose Gang, and the Green Beasts, who had persecuted and harried unmercifully the NJM. On Bloody Sunday, November 18, 1973, Bishop, with several close supporters such as Hudson Austin, Unison Whiteman, Selwyn Strachan, and Kenrick Radix, had been savaged by the Mongoose Gang and police under an inspector called, rather inappropriately, Innocent Belmar.[2] Bishop had to go to Barbados for private hospital treatment. Two months later, on January 21, 1974—Bloody Monday—during a prolonged general strike, Rupert Bishop, Maurice's father, was shot dead during mass protests in St. George's by Gairy's police while he tried to prevent their access to a building in which NJM members were sheltering.

Had Bishop held an election within a few months of his coup, the PRG would have been swept to power and his regime legitimized, at least in the eyes of most of the outside world. But there was no election, although Bishop half-promised to have one after suitable rewriting of the constitution. Whether one would ever have been held, or if it had, whether it would have been free, is doubtful. Communists do not have national elections, and by 1979 Bishop was a Marxist, although his skillful maneuvering enabled him to keep this fact from the majority of the people. Four and a half years later when he was executed, most Grenadians did not understand their hero was a communist or what he and the PRG had done to their country. To them he was still the leader who had freed them from Gairy. Considering what Bishop did, or sanctioned, this was quite an achievement.

Bishop resolved that although the NJM was now in control, a subtle working relationship, or alliance, must be established with prominent Grenadian institutions and the business community. They must tread softly in some areas at first to bring about necessary improvements for the masses, with the assistance of the bourgeoisie if necessary. Over a period of time the PRG would entrench itself without the people realizing what had happened; then it would not matter if Grenadians understood they were trapped. Bishop recapitulated on this plan clearly in September 1982 in a secret speech to party members now referred to as his "Line of March" speech: "We need the alliance, comrades, because we don't have enough managers, because we don't have enough capital, because we don't have enough international contacts, because we don't have enough markets. For all these reasons, we need the alliance."

The original ruling council of the PRG contained a number of capitalists and businessmen, or, in Marxist terminology, "petite bourgeoisie, upper petite bourgeoisie, and national bourgeoisie." As Bishop said, "This was done deliberately so that imperialism won't get too excited and would say 'well they have some nice fellas in that thing; everything all right.' And as a result they wouldn't think about sending in troops." Norris Bain, described as a middle capitalist, and Lyden Ramdhanny, a big capitalist, were both PRG ministers who remained loyal to Bishop to the end. Bain was eventually shot with him.

Like the Soviets, the Grenadian system of controlling the masses was based on the party. It was an elitist system whereby real power was held by a few full party members. From full members, the majority of the top governing bodies of the PRG were formed; the Central Committee, the Politburo, and to a lesser extent the cabinet. While founder members of the NJM such as Bernard and Phyllis Coard, Austin, Layne, James, Strachan, Cornwall, and others, automatically assumed full membership, it was an exclusive group of people. By May 1983 there were only eighty full members.

The method of selection for party membership was rigorous. Like the Soviets the PRG initially had three grades: applicants, candidates, and (full) members. Shortly after the coup, an additional grade of membership was introduced: the potential applicant. To rise up to full membership took time, plus much hard political study and work.

Bishop insisted on a tight screening process, from recruitment up to all levels. He defined four basic requirements for party membership:

1. Regular collective ideological study organized by the party.
2. Consistent political work under the guidance of the party.
3. Regular payment of 5 percent of gross salary into party funds.
4. Understanding, accepting, and implementing the principles and program of the party, which included accepting party discipline in many areas of one's private life.

The minimum period to be served as an applicant was a year, with another year as a candidate, before being considered for full membership. In May 1982 there were 160 applicants and 83 candidates. Thus, after three years of the revolution, only 323 Grenadians—of a population of 90,000—were actually in the party system.

Within the party the governmental organization reflected that of the Soviet Union. The supreme body was the Central Committee under the chairmanship of the prime minister, Maurice Bishop. It had between fifteen and seventeen members, right up to just before the Bishop-Coard split. Normally it met about once a month to decide policy matters or give overall directions. Next in importance was the Politburo, with a membership of seven or eight. Also under the chairmanship of prime minister, this body was the executive arm of the Central Committee, charged with implementing its decisions. It convened weekly, having particular responsibility for party affairs. Invariably its members were also on the Central Committee, so there could be no dissension over their tasks. Next was the cabinet, consisting of some twenty ministries, with appointed ministers in charge. It was here that Bishop allowed some leeway with appointments. A few "capitalists" became ministers for the sake of appearances. Lyden Ramdhanny became minister of tourism, although he was never allowed on the Politburo or Central Committee. The majority in cabinet were full party members, with almost half being Central Committee members as well. The cabinet was merely a respectable front, a rubber stamp, for the Central Committee.

Because it was possible for one person to be a member of all three government bodies, the individual concerned could spend all his time attending meetings, rarely having enough left to get work done in his ministry—particularly during crises, when Central Committee meetings alone could go on for days. A good example was Austin, who was ridiculously overburdened and complained about it on several occasions. He was on the Central Committee, the Politburo, and had two ministries: Defense and Construction. He also sat on the Security and Defense Committee. Add to these his overseas tours, bouts of sickness, and it was hardly surprising that Austin was difficult to find in his office.

To oversee political indoctrination, a special Ministry of National Mobilization was set up. Its work had nothing to do with military mobilization as such. Its primary task, as Bishop himself put it, "must be to sink the ideas of Marxism/Leninism amongst the working people." This critical ministry was headed by Selwyn "Sello" Strachan.

Add to the above apparatus the Organising Committee, the Discipline Committee, the highly secret Security and Defense Committee, the Workers' Committee, the Economic Bureau, the Propaganda Department, and the complexity of the higher organization of the PRG becomes obvious.

‡   ‡   ‡

The system was designed to give control to the state, or more particularly to the party. In Grenada this objective of state control was all part of ensuring Grenadians were under party "manners." Bishop made it clear to his party comrades in his Line of March speech,

> That the state sector must be built to be the dominant sector. . . . We must assume total control over all financial institutions over a period of time. . . . We must assume total control of all foreign trade, and also of some aspects of internal trade. . . . We must assume total control of all public utilities—electricity, telephone, water, transport."

A comprehensive nationwide organization was gradually set up to sink Marxism-Leninism into the minds of the people under the guise of "is freedom we making." Euphemistically called people's power in the party's propaganda, this organization had, at its center, the Politburo. The next outward stage was the party, then the parish coordinating bodies, parish councils, zonal and village councils, and finally community groups. In communist jargon, this system was termed democratic centralism. With party officials supervising the activities of these bodies with personal responsibility to the Politburo, the "centralism" is clear, but the "democratic" aspect remains somewhat of a mystery.

To all this must be added the other national organizations set up to indoctrinate and mobilize the masses behind the revolution, including the People's Revolutionary Militia (PRM), the National Women's Organisation, the National Youth Organisation, and the Young Pioneers (for children from 5 to 14). All officials must be addressed as "Comrade" or "Brother" or "Sister" depending on their sex. The 23-year-old commissioner of police, Ian St. Bernard, who was given his job without any training or experience, insisted nobody called him "Sir" but always "Comrade." Those who forgot, through force of habit, he threatened to send "up the hill."

Promotion or appointment to a senior post within any PRG organization was dependent on political reliability. Everybody was compelled to attend study periods, or party propaganda sessions, at least once a week. These could be held in a community or village center or at the workplace. Some form of party membership was essential for anybody with ambition. Any sign of "imperialist" characteristics in a person weighed heavily against him or her, both in the village and at work. In the PRA every officer had to be of a working-class background and at least an applicant party member. Bishop boasted, "When you look at the officers in the army it is Working Class comrades or petty-bourgeois revolutionary democratic, or communists, who are the officers in the army—that's the situation in our army."

Even the PRG felt it necessary to operate under some sort of law, but the previous imperialist legal system was considered totally inappropriate. This meant abolishing the majority of the existing statutes and rewriting their own. Because there was no way for laws to be debated in a parliament or a congress, they were issued as proclamations. A series of People's Laws were drawn up, all signed by Bishop. People's Law No. 2 established the PRG; People's Law No. 10 (Declaration and Effect of Laws) gave the prime minister his all-embracing powers; and People's Law No. 46, the Terrorism (Prevention) Law, was the proclamation under which "heavy manners" were imposed. Under this law terrorism was defined as "the use or threat of violence for political ends," which in effect was saying that the

PRG themselves were terrorists. The PRA or police could arrest a suspect without a warrant, and he or she could then be detained (no bail was allowed) without trial more or less indefinitely.

Bishop's words express the position of the PRG with great clarity:

> One thing we do have is political control. . . , so we can decide on how much taxes to charge, we can decide who get credits, we can decide on who gets concessions and pioneer incentives, we can decide on what laws to pass and when, we can decide who to "manners" and when. In other words we can use the apparatus of the State in order to effect those controls.

The Propaganda Department brought in experts from Cuba to train Grenadians in the use of slogans and placards that could be used to remind everybody of their responsibility to work for the revolution. Hundreds of these slogans were posted on notice boards, scrawled on walls, or carried on banners in the numerous marches held to celebrate revolutionary anniversaries. Outside Fort Rupert two prominent notices proclaimed "Forward to Political and Academic Education for 1983" and, with a more military flavor, "Political Discipline and Combat Readiness Equals Victory." Political graffiti was evident everywhere. In the villages, in the streets, in the schools, and in the workplaces, the revolution was hammered home.

‡   ‡   ‡

Political indoctrination was of far greater importance to the PRG than academic education. According to the plans of the mobilization minister, Strachan, political indoctrination must be all embracing; no part of Grenadian society must be exempt. But there were problems. There was resistance in some schools. Boredom with political lectures led to extensive absenteeism from classes. The teachings of the church, and many people's religious beliefs, ran contrary to the new communist theories. In September 1981 Strachan expressed concern to the Politburo at the lack of political education in the army. A meeting of party members in the PRA had called for the setting up of a Department of Politics within the army. This was agreed, and the Grenadian equivalent of political commissars was created. Captain Christopher Stroude was appointed chief of politics and academics.

The party was to be paramount, so it was agreed that a prestigious headquarters building was essential. This project, first mooted by the Politburo in May 1981, was to be sited at Mount Royal, which the Politburo minutes described as "a fantastic spot, and should be of tight security." A huge complex was envisaged for the party elite. Facilities included offices, a library, printing and darkrooms, four bedrooms, living quarters for visiting VIPs, a cafeteria, a radio room, an auditorium for 500 people, classrooms, committee rooms, a gymnasium, and two secret rooms plus a bunker (the former presumably for highly confidential meetings or interrogations and the latter as a refuge for the party faithful if things went wrong). The cost was prohibitive without aid, so the Soviet Union was approached for finance. Drawings were prepared, but work had not started before the 1983 crisis. The concept is indicative of the party's priorities for giving members privileges or entrenching their bureaucracy at the expense of economic development.

Hand in hand with the establishment of the party and the necessary organizations for spreading Marxism went suppression of opposition. People who in any way appeared unenthusiastic about the government were branded counterrevolutionaries and fair game for "manners."

The press especially was a target. The two independent newspapers in the country, first the *Torchlight* and then the *Grenadian Voice,* were soon closed down. To quote Bishop, "When they want to put out a newspaper, and we don't want that, we close it down. . . . When they want freedom of expression to attack the government, we crush them and jail them."

In June 1981 twenty-six Grenadians, including journalist Alister Hughes, had formed Spice Island Printers Ltd. for the purpose of publishing the *Grenadian Voice,* a newspaper they intended to be totally nonpolitical and within all PRG laws. However, when U.S. officials showed an interest in it, Bishop responded. American expressions of support gave him an opportunity to brand it as CIA inspired. The predictable result was instant closure, followed by a huge anti-imperialist rally in Queen's Park at which Bishop warned, "When the revolution speaks, it must be heard, listened to. Whatever the revolution decrees it must be obeyed; when the revolution commands, it must be carried out; when the revolution talks, no parasites must bark in their corner." The so-called Gang of 26 was broken up, several jailed, and their businesses confiscated.

The Security Service under Lieutenant Colonel Liam "Owusu" James was tasked with infiltrating any suspicious organizations, including the church and the St. George's University, a United States offshore medical school. Its authority was virtually unrestricted, being answerable only to the Central Committee or Bishop, as prime minister and chairman of the Defense and Security Committee. Scores of people were detained without charge or trial, sometimes for years. Many, like Winston Whyte and Winston Simon, remained in their cells until Urgent Fury rescued them; others were released after months in prison when repeated efforts by the Security Service had failed to produce any evidence against them. Even after release, they were invariably placed under rigid restrictions as to travel or activities. All detention orders went to Bishop for approval; he was not averse to signing them. Records reveal some 183 political detainees held in Grenada in January 1982.

The PRG quickly realized the importance of politically influencing the young at school or through the Young Pioneers. A Pentecostal pastor described the situation:

> In our elementary schools the national anthem had been substituted by a new song, "The Forward March against Imperialism." They would sing it at the start of the day, and at the end. As they sang they would have to march. . . . Obviously the brain-washing was successful, as the children who lived near me, who were involved in the Pioneer movement would jeer at us when we had Sunday School at our home. And they would sing songs of the revolution and shout out the slogans they had been taught.

Josephine Romain, who worked for the Inter-Schools Christian Fellowship, said, "They had little children walking the streets and speaking enthusiastically about the revolution. . . . The Marxists have learned how important their impressionable minds are."

A section of the community quickly singled out for "manners" were the Rastafarians. With their long hair, strange ways, close knit family way of life, and lack of interest in the revolution, they were quickly labeled counterrevolutionaries. The Security Service argued that they were actively involved in antigovernment plotting and were a threat to the PRG.

In June 1981 James reported to the Politburo that the Rastas were supposedly planning to attack a PRA camp. Major Einstein Louison stated that a "place" was under construction to house 300 of them. The suggestion was that they be seized by the army and their hair cut. James argued that in order to legitimize the operation, the Rastas be allowed to go ahead with their attack before being arrested. Bishop, however, opposed the idea because people on both sides could be killed. Nevertheless, Louison was to continue constructing the camp, James was to focus his efforts on identifying the leaders, and the Rastas' camps were to be infiltrated. The Central Committee's minutes of June 24, 1981, record Vincent Noel as recommending that "the army should prepare a programme for the Rastas that will be picked up—wake up time, eat time, books, films, pacifying music, etc.—a rigid programme."

In fact a special detention center, Hope Vale, was set up at Vincennes for Rastas. Magistrates sentenced them to prolonged periods of "rehabilitation" at this camp. Hard labor and large doses of indoctrination were the basic ingredients of the regime, interspersed with beatings. Although many Rastas were vegetarians, they were forced to eat meat or nothing. The actual regime was a substantial advance on Noel's somewhat gentle suggestions. Over 300 persons, including women and children, served sentences at Hope Vale.

Rasta leader Naa Naa was arrested by the PRA as early as October 1979, suspected of being a CIA agent. After eighteen months in Richmond Hill Prison, he attempted to escape. He was shot deliberately three times, in the foot and legs. Seized again in July 1981, he was shot in the stomach and through his leg, with the bullet grazing his penis. He also spent months at Hope Vale.

‡   ‡   ‡

Despite the PRG's insistence that it had come to power as a result of a revolution and despite the incessant propaganda to the masses to support the revolution, there had been no such thing. Bishop and the NJM had seized power in an anti-Gairy coup. A small group of armed men, with covert advice from Cuba, accompanied by at least one officer from the Guyana Defence Force, attacked Gairy's Defence Force barracks and within a few hours had taken over the country. Clearly this was no people's revolution. The leaders of the coup later called themselves the People's Revolutionary Government, but it was a misnomer.

The new leadership immediately began to set up the infrastructure for the People's Revolutionary Armed Forces (PRAF) in its effort to establish a people under arms. Under Bishop as the overall commander in chief, an elaborate military organization evolved. General Hudson "G man" Austin became the secretary for defense and commander of the PRAF. Although the size of the PRAF was justified by the PRG as being required to counter invasions by imperialist-backed mercenaries or the United States, in reality it was needed to place Grenada under "manners."

The PRAF consisted of all the bodies permitted to carry arms or involved in internal or external security. The PRA was the most significant. Its members, full-time soldiers, had the same powers as the police in terms of arrest or search and took over most normal policing duties. The Grenada Police Service was part of the PRAF but under Bishop shrank in size to a small rump of its former self. Its morale was low, its pay and conditions of service the worst in Grenada, and its responsibility confined to providing a few guards, such as at the governor-general's residence, plus traffic or firefighting duties. Police were confined during curfews. Deputy Commissioner Luckey Bernard, who went out in his car during a curfew in 1980, was shot and left for dead by PRA soldiers when he refused to get out of his car despite their recognizing him.

Most "crimes" were political or counterrevolutionary ones, investigated by the Security Service, with the assistance of the military. Typically the PRA arrested people, interrogated them, confined them, and took them to jail. At Richmond Hill detainees were handed over to the custody of the Prison Service, itself a part of the PRAF.

The largest organization within the PRAF was the People's Revolutionary Militia (PRM). It numbered several thousand and was scheduled for extensive expansion between 1984 and 1986. Its members were volunteers in a part-time military-political organization, expected to turn out for training each week.

With this extensive military infrastructure, Bishop and the PRG set about turning Grenada into an armed camp. By October 1983 they had only partially succeeded, yet the militarization of this country of 90,000 people (the population dropped substantially under Bishop from over 100,000 as many Grenadians fled overseas) was blatant and excessive. Tom Adams, prime minister of Barbados, called Grenada "one of the perhaps dozen most militarised states in the world in terms of population under arms."

For military assistance, initially Bishop turned to those close neighbors that had encouraged and supported him in the early days of the NJM: Cuba and Guyana. Guyana had secretly assisted with the actual coup, but its support afterward was confined to sending its Defence Force training teams to the island. The first substantial military assistance came from Havana, although military and security help was available elsewhere. Britain tried to provide some, for example. The overseas police adviser from the United Kingdom, accompanied by a senior military adviser from the Ministry of Defence, arrived in St. George's to discuss assistance, but they were ignored and after a few days departed.

As early as April 1979, shipments of arms, with military specialists, were arriving from Cuba. According to Major Einstein Louison the weapons included 3,400 rifles (Soviet AK-47s, U.S. M-16s, and British .303s), 200 machine guns, 100 pistols, 100 rocket launchers, 12 82-mm mortars, and 12 12.7-mm antiaircraft machine guns, together with ample ammunition. All of these weapons were old or reconditioned (the .303 rifles and 12.7-mm AA guns were ancient) but still serviceable.

In late 1981 or early 1982 a protocol of military collaboration was signed by Cuba and the PRG. It established the twenty-seven-man Cuban military mission in Grenada, tasked with training the troops and staff of the PRA, plus the PRM. The Cuban specialists in infantry, engineering, communications, logistics, and exploration (reconnaissance) would be based at the mission headquarters in the southwest of the island, traveling out to work at the various PRA or PRM camps and headquarters. Grenadians do not speak Spanish, however, so a high proportion of the team were translators. The Cubans were also responsible for coordinating training requests, along with arms deliveries received from the Soviet Union.

Although the Soviet Union had been sending massive supplies of military equipment to Grenada for many months previously, it was not until October 1982 that their embassy was set up in the old Flying Dutchman Hotel near Quarantine Point. By then the Soviets were confident that the PRG could not survive without them, and they intended to exert direct influence from within Grenada itself. Grenada was now considered an important post. Governor-General Sir Paul Scoon was surprised to see the new Soviet ambassador dressed in the full uniform of a major general, complete with decorations, when he came to present his credentials. That Gennadiy Sazhenev, an experienced military intelligence officer in his mid-sixties, had been sent from a senior position in Argentina to this tiny Caribbean island underlined the growing significance the Soviets now attached to Grenada. With an initial staff of twenty-six and two large white Mercedes cars, Sazhenev quickly established himself. A priority task was the setting up of an office of the Soviet news agency, Tass, in a room next to Bishop's at Butler House. A year later the Soviets were on the verge of establishing a strategically placed satellite, second only to Cuba, in the Caribbean.

There were three formal military agreements signed between Moscow and St. George's: in 1980, 1981, and 1982. A fourth had been drafted before the intervention. On October 27, 1980, Austin went to Havana to finalize and sign a treaty for the delivery to Grenada of "special" (military) equipment: "The USSR shall ensure in 1980–81, free of charge, the delivery to the Government of Grenada of special and other equipment . . . in the amount of 4.4 [U.S.$5.85 million] million rubles." The annex listed the items: 12 82-mm mortars, 24 RPG-7s, 1,054 machine guns, 1,500 carbines, 18 23-mm ZU antiaircraft guns, and 28 Gaz trucks, all with ample ammunition or spares. The agreement was to be kept secret so, like subsequent shipments, it was to be sent via Cuba on Cuban vessels. Bishop and the PRA went to elaborate lengths to conceal the arrival of military supplies from the population. All deliveries were made at night, and for each there was a convenient power failure in St. George's while the equipment was offloaded onto trucks to be driven south to the warehouses at Frequente. Nevertheless, the blackout, coupled with the rumble of heavy vehicles through the night, did not fool many Grenadians.

The following February Major Basil Gahagan went to Cuba, where he signed a protocol to the first agreement providing another U.S.$6.65 million worth of arms and assorted military supplies. Included this time were 8 BTR-60PB Soviet APCs, 2 BRDM-2 armored cars, 1,000 submachine guns, 1,000 grenades, 60 radios, 47 vehicles, 12,600 uniforms, compasses, binoculars, blankets, field kitchens, generators, excavating equipment, and spares, plus more ammunition. Most of these items were in place by the time Urgent Fury was launched.

Bishop was enthusiastic about these agreements. In writing to Brezhnev in November 1981 about his planned meeting with the Soviet leader the following year, he stated: "The visit of the Grenadian delegation has as its objective first, additional requests for means that we consider vitally necessary in our defence plan for the country and, secondly, to request the speeding up [ahead of schedule] of delivery of means and resources already agreed in a previous protocol."

The third treaty for military aid, dated July 27, 1982, was the largest, totaling some U.S.$13.3 million. It was this agreement that provided for increasing numbers of Soviet personnel to accompany the equipment to train Grenadians in its use. It was to be implemented during the period 1983–1985. Of particular significance were 50 BTR-152VI APCs, 30 76-mm guns, 30 57-mm antitank guns, 50 GRAD-P portable launchers, 60 82-mm mortars, and 2,000 AK-47s.

Just what was the PRG going to do with all this weaponry? The answer appears to be contained in an unsigned letter from the PRA to the Armed Forces of the Soviet Union, dated July 2, 1982, which spelled out a three-year development plan for the PRAF. It called for the Soviets to equip and assist in training, "further consolidation of one permanent Infantry Battalion [INF BN] and five reserve INF BNs." Additionally support was required to create three more regular infantry battalions and nine reserve (PRM) battalions. Also requested were 65 more trucks, tents, medical supplies, uniforms, a military workshop, cameras, infrared equipment, TV alarm systems, sniper rifles, and pistols, the last probably destined for the Security Service.

These were enormous requests, sufficient to equip 10,000. Virtually none of the items listed in the July agreement reached Grenada before the end of October 1983. The extent of the deliveries, and the expansion plans, were highly secret; many officers of the PRA were unaware of what was happening. 2d Lieutenant Raeburn Nelson, when shown the evidence in 1987, was shocked; according to him, there was no way Grenadians would, or could, have supplied the manpower to use the arms. They would have rusted away in the stores.

Clearly the PRG spared no effort to ensure Grenada was militarized. In addition to Cuba and the Soviet Union, Czechoslovakia, Libya, North Korea, and North Vietnam were asked to assist. Had their plans ever been realized, one adult Grenadian in four would have been under arms.

‡   ‡   ‡

On August 15, 1979, 40-year-old Antonio "Clem" Langdon was working on the foundations of his house at Happy Hill north of St. George's. Langdon, a native Grenadian, had lived in New York City for sixteen years, where he ran a boutique, which also sold newspapers and magazines, of which he was subsequently told the PRG disapproved. He had come to Grenada with his 5-year-old daughter just a week before for a vacation.

While he was working, two PRA soldiers arrived and told him, "The big man wants to see you for a couple of minutes." When Langdon refused to go, he was seized at gunpoint and pushed into a car in front of his screaming daughter and hysterical sister. He was taken to Fort Rupert.

Langdon was not charged with anything. He fasted for twenty-one days in a cell, refusing to eat until somebody told him what was going on. When he shouted at a guard, his head was banged against a wall until he fell down. Later he told an officer to "shut his stupid mouth." A soldier shot him with his AK rifle several times in the left side. He was thought to be dead, covered with a sheet, and taken to the hospital to be put in the mortuary. When an orderly found him coughing blood, he was rushed to surgery. After the operation, the doctor declared him dead, but again an orderly saved him by pointing out that his heart was still beating. He survived, but with a frozen left shoulder and without the use of his left hand. According to Langdon, Bishop refused to allow him medical treatment in Barbados because it would be dangerous to the revolution.

At one stage he was not allowed to wash for over 250 days, causing worms to infest his legs and groin. He was refused hospitalization and instead chained hand and foot and fed intravenously. That part of Fort Rupert where he was kept was later nicknamed "Langdon Hospital."

Langdon was freed from Richmond Hill Prison over four years later, on the afternoon of October 26, 1983. He was evacuated to Bardados prior to returning to the United States to find his American wife and salvage what was left of his life.

Clem Langdon was another victim of "heavy manners."

2

Bishop versus Coard

I have heard many options, but the best one is for him [Bishop] to go to Cuba and cool it for a few years.

— Bernard Coard, deputy prime minister and minister of finance to George Louison, four days before ordering Bishop shot

O PPOSITION to the PRG surfaced in early 1980, before the revolution was a year old. It was centered around the Budhlall Gang, Tivoli-area residents led by Kenneth and Kennedy Budhlall. Both brothers had been keen supporters of the PRG but had quickly become disillusioned, largely because they believed Bishop had reneged on his promises of advancement. Kenneth was in the army, the chief of the PRA detachment at Pearls, and as such a powerful local figure who had the people of nearby Grenville under "manners." The Budhlall Gang was associated with some dissident Rastas and Muslims. They talked of how to put an end to the PRG. Another former Bishop supporter who was now a dissident was Straughan Phillip. He was a man with military experience; he had served several years in the British Army and recently had been a leader under Austin in the night attack on Gairy's Defence Force camp.

The PRG quickly focused its attention on the Tivoli–Mt. Rich area. Kenneth Budhlall was transferred to St. George's but failed to turn up for duty. He was arrested and jailed in Richmond Hill. A PRA crackdown in the area was only partially successful; a number of gang members were able to go into hiding, some of them armed. The army's methods were anything but gentle, as Broko Simon's story showed.

On the afternoon of June 19, 1980, one of the PRG's interminable rallies was to be held at the Queen's Park sports ground, just north of St. George's. As usual, the party leadership was scheduled to address the crowd. Shortly before 3:00 P.M., a portion of the stands erupted in a shattering explosion. Two schoolgirls died (a third, injured, died later). The bomb had been placed well away from the leaders and in such a way that the main force of the explosion was downward into the ground. If it was an assassination attempt, it was a badly bungled one, with tragic consequences for the innocent people nearby.

Retribution was swift. Within an hour the PRA had surrounded Straughan Phillip's home at Mount Airy and gunned him down. Nineteen bullet holes were counted in his body. His girlfriend claimed Phillip had surrendered after being wounded but was then shot again and again at close range. Phillip had been effectively prevented from answering any charges as to the bombing. Arms were found in his house, so it was announced he was responsible for the outrage at Queen's Park.

Speculation continues to this day about the incident. The fact that Radio Free Grenada was announcing that the bomb was a sophisticated one with a timing device within a few minutes of the explosion, the immediate killing of Phillip, the lack of party casualties, and the poor positioning of the bomb have fueled rumors that it was a PRG plot to allow them to eliminate counterrevolutionaries.

Bishop made a lengthy, emotional speech to the nation that evening over the radio. He ranted on and on against imperialism and for the need to safeguard the revolution. He finished with the usual slogans, adding a new one for this occasion: "Their blood must be further manure and fertilizer to push our revolution forward." A curfew was imposed. PRA "manners" were intensified in the NE; their efforts dragged on for the rest of the year.

‡   ‡   ‡

On October 12, 1982, the Central Committee of the NJM was convened in an extraordinary plenary to discuss a letter of resignation from Bernard Coard, deputy party leader, and to examine the issues raised in the letter related to the state of the party and the crisis in the work of the higher organs. The PRG was in a mess. Coard, with considerable political cunning, had made his first move in a bid for power.

Coard's letter came as a shock to his colleagues. He did not have the courtesy to explain personally his resignation to the Central Committee but sent his close associate, Selwyn Strachan, as his spokesman. Apart from Coard, it was a full meeting, with seventeen members attending, and it lasted four days. By the end, it was Bishop, not Coard, who was under attack. Pro-Bishop members were savaged. Radix was sacked from both the Central Committee and Politburo; Caldwell Taylor (the PRG representative at the United Nations) lost his place on the Central Committee; Fitzroy Bain was put on probation for six months; and Unison Whiteman was "severely warned for his weak performance." McBarnette was the only member, eventually to side with Coard, who was disciplined; he was put on probation.

The meeting had started with two hours of heated debate over Coard's resignation and the manner in which he had done it. There were many calls for him to be forced to appear and to discipline him for his arrogant behavior, but nothing was agreed except for Strachan to summarize Coard's reasons for resigning. Strachan explained that Coard had privately considered leaving both the Central Committee and Politburo six months earlier. His final decision had been made as a result of a combination of factors: his workload was too heavy (the economy was collapsing); his authority as chairman of the Organising Committee was being undermined; he was concerned about the slackness of the Central Committee in its lack of preparation and unwillingness to study; and, if he remained, there would be personality clashes with the chairman of the Central Committee. Strachan ended by stressing that the resignation was not negotiable; Coard could not remain and tolerate the present inefficiency. In Coard's view, what was needed was "the introduction of Leninist measures including a change of chairmanship of the Central Committee, chopping of dead weight, putting all members to actually do some work on outside committees, and expansion of the Politburo."

The rest of the meeting was largely an orgy of self-criticism in true Marxist style. Phyllis Coard, Cornwall, Layne, Ventour, and James all pitched in with the view that the party failings were the main issue, not Coard's resignation. One after another they attacked Bishop for his lax working habits, softness, taking a "right opportunist course," and generally poor leadership of the party. Austin hoped Bishop's hand would become "a Marxist-Leninist-Stalinist hand." More "manners" were needed.

Bishop accepted most of the criticism and made excuses—he was tired, overworked, personal problems were worrying him, there had been differences of approach over policy matters with Coard. Although some of his friends, such as Radix and Whiteman, attempted to defend him, their remarks merely diverted the wrath of the others onto themselves. Day after day the rantings continued until, as a climax, they all graded themselves from 1–5, under the headings of discipline, ideological level, work performance, relations with the masses, character, analyzing ability, dues, and functional ability. A special appendix to the minutes records the illuminating results of this exercise. Top scorers were George Louison and Strachan with 4.5 each. Lowest were Radix and McBarnette, with a miserable 1.5; Radix collected a zero for discipline. The result was that Coard was to organize an eight-week crash course in Marxism-Leninism for those members whose knowledge of communist theory was considered shaky—Austin, Bain, Bartholomew, Taylor, and Whiteman. Radix was finished. The minutes record: "The Central Committee had taken note of his lack of political work, his extremely bad attitude to study and deep seated individualism and petty bourgeois opportunist attitude to criticism. The concensus was that his performance was exceedingly below that befitting a Central Committee member."

The knives were out, with the battle lines beginning to emerge for the struggle for party control that was not to end until Bishop's murder. The first round went to Coard. All the long hours spent within the Central Committee arguing about the need for more Leninist discipline was a clever way of obscuring Coard's personal takeover bid. He had skillfully used the communist obsession with self-criticism to attack Bishop's leadership of the party. Within the party, this "failure" of Bishop was eventually believed by the majority; it was his weaknesses that were the cause of the state of disarray in the country and the revolution. This was never believed by the masses, but Coard's bid for control came from within the party; it was dependent on the support of party members, not the people.

Bishop had no inkling at this stage that a leadership struggle had started. In fact he was so concerned when, after the meeting, Coard retreated to the island of Carriacou that his deputy was contemplating suicide that he sent a security man to watch him.

It had been a well-orchestrated, well-timed move by Coard. He had removed himself from the two top party committees at the time when the economy and the revolution were foundering. But although he had left the limelight personally, his faction still formed the majority, and he would be kept well informed—his wife was still a member. When things got worse, Bishop would get the blame, so he could then play the part of savior of the revolution.

‡ ‡ ‡

Born in 1944, Maurice Bishop was 39 years old when he faced the firing squad, the same age as the man who ordered the execution, Bernard Coard. Two avowed communists who had built a revolution, a Marxist state in Grenada, clashed in a bitter struggle for leadership that was to be fatal to Bishop and the revolution. Bishop's death was the final act that triggered Urgent Fury. The revolution had destroyed itself. Although with entirely different personalities, Bishop and Coard were both Marxist-Leninists whose ultimate aims for Grenada were identical.

Bishop was a charismatic man. He had saved Grenada from Gairy, so for many this made him a hero. As the economy soured, as "manners" were increasingly used to crush opposition, as the military became more powerful, as arms poured into the country, and as first Cubans and later Soviet advisers appeared in many organizations, Bishop escaped censure from the masses. He had been beaten by Gairy's thugs; his father had been shot by Gairy's police, while Coard had never suffered in this way. Bishop was adept at making the most of this advantage, often genuinely seeking to improve the lot of Grenadians, although improvements were to be brought about in a Marxist manner. He tolerated no opposition. Most Grenadians did not understand what was happening to their country or why. Those who did were unable or unwilling to do anything about it. People did not understand that their leader was a communist or what this meant for Grenada. Maurice Bishop was their prime minister, and thousands of Grenadians would rally to him up to the moment of his death— and after.

Bishop was, like Coard, well educated. He had been brought up in a Catholic family, attending a Catholic primary school before going to Presentation College for his secondary education. In 1963 he went to London to study law at Grey's Inn, qualifying in 1966, although he never completed his postgraduate studies. In that year he married an attractive young nurse, Angela Redhead. They had two children, John and Nadi. They stayed on in Britain for another four years, Bishop working in the civil service as a surtax examiner but involving himself with voluntary work with the Legal Aid Clinic in Nottinghill Gate.

After his return to Grenada in 1970, Bishop became caught up in Grenadian politics, largely as a way in which to help people combat "Gairyism" and the corruption associated with it. He did a lot of free legal work, and his efforts in the courts were often successful. The Gairy government singled him out as a troublemaker. In 1972 Bishop formed the Movement for Assemblies of the People (MAP), while Unison Whiteman, another Gairy opponent, led the Joint Endeavor for Welfare, Education, and Liberation (JEWEL). In 1973 these two bodies merged to form the New Jewel Movement (NJM), which became the main opposition to Gairy, eventually toppling him in the March 1979 coup.

Bishop was the leader of the NJM from the outset. He was a good speaker, a good lawyer; he was willing to suffer for his beliefs, while his outgoing style of leadership won him an enduring popularity. He was tall, good looking, youthful—a person to whom everybody could relate. It was not until some years later that other characteristics became more obvious. He was an avid card player but a poor loser. He would become angry and stop playing a game of squash if he felt he could not win. He liked the trappings of power. No expense was spared on his overseas travel, his private plane, domestic entourage, or security at his official residence. He, who had often stated that one house was enough for everybody, owned at least three houses at Parade, plus four apartments at the Quarantine Station. He had other human failings; he smoked incessantly and was fond of women. He appointed his mistress, Jackie Creft, minister of education. (Angela had separated from him and moved to Canada.)

In behavior, if not beliefs, Coard was the opposite of Bishop. Physically he lacked Bishop's appeal; he was flabby and round faced, with glasses. His wife was not slim and attractive but a rotund woman who took little apparent interest in her appearance. Phyllis Coard was a pale-skinned Jamaican by birth. Although she came from a wealthy background, being an heiress to the Tia Maria liqueur fortune, she was a hard-line Marxist who fully supported her husband in his bid for party leadership. There has always been suspicion that Phyllis's ambition was greater than her husband's and that it was she who pushed him into his plot to oust Bishop. She was certainly an arrogant, convinced Marxist, well versed in communist terminology and theory.

Coard joined the NJM later than most others. He had returned to Grenada in 1976 from a lecturing job at the Trinidad campus of the University of the West Indies. An economist, he had studied at Brandeis University in the United States and then at Sussex University in Britain. It was at Sussex that he developed his communist beliefs. Before returning permanently to Grenada, he had visited his home island frequently from Trinidad, but he had missed the violence, the personal danger of the anti-Gairy conflict.

Coard had founded a key organization, the Organisation of Revolutionary Education and Liberation (OREL). From the start he held meetings and indoctrinated members in his dogmatic, unrelenting Marxist-Leninist principles. The meetings were training sessions, where people like Layne, James, Cornwall, Gahagan, and Stroude learned their creed and cemented their personal loyalty to Coard, who controlled the organization. A vital part of Coard's subsequent bid to topple Bishop depended on his getting OREL members into key positions in the top echelons of the party and PRA. When he later sought their active support, he got it. It was members of this group who eventually turned on Bishop.

Coard was an industrious, competent, ruthless economist. As minister of finance, he was renowned for his capacity for hard work. Bishop himself acknowledged the debt the government owed to his deputy in his budget day speech in 1982. After praising the zeal and industry of the Finance Ministry, he called Coard "the greatest worker of them all, a comrade who sleeps regularly two or three hours a night." He finished by calling for an ovation: "I ask you to recognise the tremendous, outstanding work of Comrade Bernard Coard, our Minister of Finance."

Although not a lawyer himself, Coard had the good lawyer's capacity to debate, to argue. Highly intelligent, he was able to convince people by his reasoned oratory. He lacked Bishop's charm, but he was a great talker. In 1985 I recall vividly listening for 40 minutes to Coard's monologue through the bars of Richmond Hill Prison as he sought to convince the officer in command of the Jamaican guards that he was being deprived of his visiting rights. He was most convincing. Although surrounded by several of his former Central Committee henchmen, they said nothing; as always, Coard was their spokesman, their leader.

There is little doubt that Coard's growing dislike of Bishop was fueled by jealousy, linked to his personal ambition. He was an unyielding man, inclined toward military solutions. It was Coard who had advocated executing some of Gairy's senior supporters, including his deputy prime minister, immediately after the 1979 takeover. When things started to go wrong in Grenada, Coard's solution was more disipline, more rigid application of Marxist-Leninist dogma. He saw in the difficulties facing the party and the economy a way to remove Bishop. As Radix was later to say, "The pretext of ideological differences was merely applied to provide the ammunition to murder Bishop."

Despite the enthusiasm that had greeted the NJM's coup, by the following year, revolutionary zeal was dwindling. The story of gradual collapse is vividly described in the minutes of the Central Committee and Politburo from 1981 to 1983, as are Coard's clever maneuverings to get himself into position to strike, and his faction onto the committees, or into senior army posts.

As early as May 1981, the seriousness of the cash flow crisis is recorded in a Politburo meeting. With only two days of fuel left, the Grenada Electricity Service had been told that Esso's fuel tanker would bypass Grenada unless they were paid EC$478,000. Worse, the electricity company had not been able to issue bills to consumers because the computer had broken down.

By April 1982 the lack of progress in agriculture and fisheries under pro-Bishop George Louison came under heavy attack in the Central Committee: "The levels of chaos in the Agro Industries and Fisheries were really frightening." What was required were "systems which the relevant minister [Louison] needs to implement but has failed to do so even though he has been criticised time and time again."

As early as mid-1981 compulsory socialism classes had lost their appeal to many Grenadians. Vincent Noel, who had been sacked from the Central Committee but was still on the Politburo, reported that workers claimed "that the classes are not related to our situation and [are] uninteresting." Politburo members attributed this boredom in part to too much use of Marxist jargon.

By October 1982 things had become "dread" in Grenada; then Coard resigned. The revolution had exactly a year to run.

‡　‡　‡

From July 1983 until Bishop's execution on October 19, the party hierarchy had virtually ceased to govern Grenada; the day-to-day business of running a country in collapse was left to a handful of civil servants. The political leaders spent these weeks in interminable meetings, most of which lasted for days on end, leaving the participants drained physically and mentally. During this period, Coard's plan to seize control became clear. The followers of both Bishop and Coard had no time for anything other than to argue or plot the next move in the rapidly approaching crisis. Toward the end, the meetings verged on violence, with pistols being brandished and members shouting that others were talking "shit."[1]

The first of these marathon sessions lasted for six and a half days. "The first full scale wholistic plenary of the Central Committee" was held July 13–19, with no less than "54 hours assessing all areas of Party, Mass and State work." For hour after weary hour, members rose to describe how all the key sectors of the revolution were failing. There was an emergence of "petty bourgeoisie manifestations" characterized by a lack of response to all aspects of party work in the field. The Propaganda Department's activities were in a "state of deep crisis," with their efforts among the people on the verge of collapse. "Consumerism" was identified as rampant. The parish of St. Andrew was castigated as being "a major source of counter-revolution." Membership of the PRM was declining, and the PRA itself lacked proper party control. Students showed a depressing lack of enthusiasm for the revolution, with many teachers remaining backward politically. It was the same story with the economy. It had become increasingly difficult to obtain foreign aid; that promised did not always materialize. The economy was not growing, some capital projects were being halted uncompleted, and plans for marketing of exports had not come to fruition. It was a miserable catalog of failure. The meeting concluded that the answer must lie in greater ideological training. The Leninist path must be followed more strictly.

Coard was putting on the pressure. On August 25, at the insistence of his OREL clique, an emergency meeting of the Central Committee was summoned to assess progress since July. Bishop called the meeting to order at 8:00 A.M. with a request for Cornwall to summarize the situation. Cornwall stated that his feedback from party members was that the Central Committee was responsible for many of the problems and that some Central Committee comrades were not functioning properly. There was a feeling that the Central Committee did not criticize itself enough before general meetings. Others supported Cornwall. Tan Bartholomew made the minor but interesting point that the East German technical delegation had nothing to do and were complaining about their unsatisfactory housing and security. This, said Bartholomew, "can tarnish our image in the eyes of fraternals." Both the police and army came under attack. There was a lack of respect for the party within the police, too many right-wing elements held positions of authority, and the morale of recruits was low. Austin painted a gloomy picture of the PRA, with many wanting to leave. He recommended that the Central Committee devote an entire day to examining army problems. He also felt he should be working full time with the military. Layne believed that "we are seeing the beginning of the disintegration of the Party."

Bishop, who as party leader was beginning to understand that much of the criticism was aimed at him, had said little. He summarized the need for more discussions within the party and with the people before another full-scale review in September. By way of conclusion Bishop urged members to study the history of the Communist party of the Soviet Union, reread *Standards of Party Life* by Pronin, and reflect on the individual strengths and weaknesses of all Central Committee members.

Coard, this time through Liam James, was to reveal his intentions at the next month's extraordinary meeting of the Central Committee scheduled for September 14–16. The attack started with Layne's dismissing Bishop's proposed agenda as "lacking in focus. It is not consistent with what was agreed in the [previous] emergency meeting." He went on to insist that the function of the present meeting "is to discuss the state of the Party and revolution and the work of the Central Committee." Bishop agreed to alter the agenda. Layne continued to analyze the gravity of the situation. It was a long speech, peppered with a mixture of colorful Grenadian expressions and Marxist phraseology. He stressed that "the internal state of the Party is very dread. There is wide protest against the higher organs." Finally he concluded that the main problem was the Central Committee (implying its leader), which he described as being "on a path of right opportunism."

Even Bishop's followers like Fitzroy Bain, Whiteman, and George Louison joined in the orgy of criticism, carried away by the mood of the meeting and not realizing where it was all going to end. Phyllis Coard was the first to speak out directly against the prime minister. In her view, "The Comrade leader has not taken the responsibility, not given the necessary guidance, even in areas where he is directly in charge the guidance is not adequate. He is disorganised very often, avoids responsibilities for dealing with critical areas of work."

Shortly after James stood to deliver the coup de grace, which would reveal Coard's plot: James proposed joint leadership. The strengths of Comrades Bishop and Coard should be married. Bishop should retain his position on the Central Committee with responsibility for work among the people and regional or international work, while Coard should return to the Central Committee and become chairman of the Politburo, responsible for all aspects of the party.

This bombshell provoked further rounds of heated debate. Whiteman and Louison foresaw practical difficulties, as did Bishop himself; he felt that Coard should be called in to give his views before a decision was taken. Most members disagreed; they knew this was Coard's proposition. Bishop stated his personal concerns: how to explain joint leadership to the party and the masses. It would (correctly) be seen as a power struggle, the image of his leadership would suffer, and it could indicate imminent collapse of the revolution. He did not see how he could "inspire the masses when he had to look over his back, or feel that he does not have the full confidence of the Comrades." The criticisms leveled at him "indicated a clear note of no confidence."

George Louison saw the implications. Forcefully he asked, "How will it evolve? What would it evolve to? Is it a temporary feature or a permanent feature?" De Riggs rebutted Louison. Then Layne joined in provoking Louison to lose his temper, shouting that he "regarded Layne's comments as shit."

An unprecedented procedure was then taken: the question was put to the vote. Always previously the Central Committee had decided by consensus, never using the vote. On the formalization of joint leadership, nine voted for, one voted against (Louison), and three abstained (Bishop, Whiteman, and Austin). The meeting also voted to inform party members through the use of written minutes at two separate meetings—for members and then for candidate members and applicants. The vote as to whether to tell the masses what they were up to was nine against, three abstaining; Louison refused to participate.

Bishop needed time to consider the implications. He and Whiteman were to leave the country the next day to attend the St. Kitts–Nevis independence celebrations, and Louison was to fly to Eastern Europe to prepare the way for Bishop's visit there in October. Bishop agreed to return by September 24 in time for a general meeting of full party members the next day. In the meantime the Central Committee would reconvene the following day to put their decisions to Coard.

‡ ‡ ‡

Cletus St. Paul, Bishop's chief security officer, was worried. He was peering out of the window of the plane as it taxied to a halt in front of the small terminal building at Pearls Airport. It was October 8, and the prime minister was returning from official visits to Hungary and Czechoslovakia and an unscheduled stop in Cuba. He had been away for twelve days. What concerned St. Paul was that he could not see the usual Central Committee welcoming delegation on the tarmac. This was highly suspicious and alerted him to possible trouble. These suspicions were not allayed when he noticed the solitary figure of Strachan emerge from the building dressed scruffily in a yellow T-shirt, jeans, and slippers. St. Paul instructed all the passengers to remain on board while he went out to check the situation. After finding nothing untoward, the official party disembarked without incident except that Strachan's greeting was noticeably cold. Twelve days was a long time to be out of the country. Whiteman and George Louison had been away on the visit as well, giving Coard ample opportunity as acting prime minister to advance his position. During the next few days, Bishop's misgivings were reinforced when none of the Central Committee members contacted him to report, as was customary. Bishop was officially ignored for two days, until October 10, when Austin and Einstein Louison visited him. In the past, Layne and James had always briefed him on what had been happening during his absence.

The Coard faction wanted a showdown. Since receiving a telephone call from Havana alerting them that Bishop had changed his mind again and did not now accept joint leadership, Coard was determined to expose Bishop as a counterrevolutionary and depose him.

It had been the day before his departure overseas, September 25, that Bishop, choked with emotion, had embraced Coard in front of party members, accepted joint leadership, and joined in the singing of the "Internationale." Things had moved decidedly in Coard's favor. On the day Bishop had left for St. Kitts–Nevis, nine Central Committee members met to explain formally to Coard Bishop's reaction to the joint leadership suggestion. All nine were Coard's supporters (Bishop, Louison, and Whiteman were out of the country, and Fitzroy Bain was sick). Although Coard was not a member and the minutes record him only as attending, he quickly took control. Instructions were given to inform all the party members of the proposals at a series of meetings for each category of member. The most critical one was scheduled for full members on September 25.

At this gathering Liam James was in the chair, but the Central Committee's report to the membership was presented by Layne. At the start, with Bishop and Coard absent, Layne pulled no punches. The report stated that "the Central Committee's main problem is that of the weak quality of leadership provided by Comrade Maurice Bishop." Bishop's qualities were acknowledged, but they were insufficient to overcome the present crisis. What was needed "was a leader who had a high level of Leninist discipline, great ideological clarity, was brilliant in strategy and tactics, with the capacity to exercise Leninist supervision." In other words, Coard.

After hearing the report, James called on the members to be "frank, open, cold-blooded, and objective in their deliberations." He went on to explain that Bishop was absent because he still needed time to consider the joint leadership idea and that Coard felt he could not attend if Bishop was not there but that he would come if the members so wished. The reaction of the meeting was to insist both attend; the feeling was that Bishop had had plenty of time for reflection; his absence was attributed to arrogance. After two hours of Bishop character assassination, a delegation headed by Ian St. Bernard went to fetch him and Coard.

By 11:10 A.M. Coard had arrived. At 12:42 P.M. St. Bernard announced that although Bishop was still reluctant, he stated that he would, in his opinion, attend. Bishop arrived over an hour later to face a decidedly hostile gathering. Realizing the precariousness of his position, Bishop spoke carefully, explaining that he did not see how he could motivate the masses if the Central Committee lacked confidence in him. He was considering resigning from his position but needed more time. When he sat down, member after member spoke out for Bishop to accept the joint approach. Only Whiteman and Fitzroy Bain expressed reservations, George Louison being already overseas. Coard rose; he praised the membership for their "genuine commitment to struggle for socialism and lay the basis for the eventual building of communism." He pledged to put all his efforts into this process, and he knew Bishop would do the same. Both owed it to the party.

Bishop, by now emotionally moved by the situation, stood to embrace Coard. He admitted his attitude to criticism had been petit bourgeois, stating, "I sincerely accept the criticism and will fulfill the decision [joint leadership] in practice." The "Internationale" was sung; Coard was smiling broadly.

Bishop's spur-of-the-moment decision to accept joint leadership had been made by his heart, not his head. His difficulties with the concept remained. He was well aware that much, if not all, of his authority would go to Coard. When he discussed what had happened with George Louison while overseas in Eastern Europe, Louison was horrified. Away from the charged atmosphere of the meeting, away from the daily pressure to decide, to which he had been exposed, Bishop realized his mistake. He would reopen the whole issue on his return.

On his way home, he decided to spend a few days in Cuba, but not, as was assumed by many at the time and later, to discuss his difficulties with Castro. It was from Havana that his change of mind was relayed to Coard.

Although neither of the two protagonists realized it, when Bishop arrived at Pearls on October 8, he had only eleven days to live. The final rounds of the political battle for Grenada were about to be fought.

‡   ‡   ‡

At last Bishop understood the danger he was in. While the Central Committee conferred in Coard's house for the next three days, he was virtually ignored. Efforts by St. Paul to contact Coard, James, and Strachan by phone or visits proved fruitless. Vincent Noel came to see him late on the evening of October 11. Bishop confided to him that his primary concerns were how joint leadership could work in practice (there was no historical precedent for such an arrangement) and his treatment by the Central Committee since his return. His reception at Pearls had shaken him. Noel was stunned when Bishop said that he had heard talk of an "Afghanistan solution" (where the moderate prime minister had been assassinated in a coup by radicals). While Bishop had been overseas, Noel himself had heard that Chalkie Ventour had stated, "There would be a solution like Afghanistan if the Chief fucked around on the question of joint leadership." Bishop and Noel both fully understood what that sort of talk could mean in terms of violence and bloodshed. Before leaving, Noel urged Bishop to bring up all these matters at the Politburo meeting the next morning.

Not only was Fort Rupert to be the scene of Bishop's actual death a week later, but on Wednesday, October 12, it was to be the setting for his political destruction.

In the early hours of the morning, Major Keith Roberts, the security service chief, held a clandestine meeting of security guards at which they were told that Bishop had betrayed the revolution so their primary loyalty was now to the Central Committee. At around 7:00 A.M. party members of the PRA assembled in the operations room at the fort to agree they too were behind Coard. They went so far as to prepare a written statement of their solidarity, which ended with the prophetic sentence, "The People's Revolutionary Armed Forces Branch of the NJM awaits the decision and orders of the Central Committee."

This gathering was just ending when Bishop was driven up by St. Paul to attend the Politburo meeting. This meeting was to last, with a short lunch break, until late that night, merging into a Central Committee session in the afternoon. Coard had lined up the party, the army, and even most of the personal security guards against the prime minister. Earlier Strachan had expressed deep concern about Bishop's surprise visit to Havana when he told Noel, "Maurice has now compounded the problem by taking the Party's business to the Cubans in an unfraternal and unprincipled way, using his personal friendship with Fidel." Strachan claimed, erroneously, that the extra days in Cuba were for this purpose and "that as a show of support for Maurice, Fidel had given a reception for Maurice at which eight members of the [Cuban] Politburo had been present including Fidel and Raoul."

During the morning, attempts were made to discuss the PRA's resolution, but these were defeated on procedural grounds because this item was not on the official agenda. They then attacked George Louison, who bore the brunt of the blame for having persuaded

Bishop to change his mind. He was dismissed from both the Central Committee and Politburo. It was then announced that a rumor was circulating that Bernard and Phyllis Coard were plotting to murder Bishop and that this had been spread on the instructions of Bishop himself, to arouse the masses. Errol George, one of the prime minister's personal security guards, had confessed after interrogation. St. Paul was arrested later in the afternoon and, despite denials, confined at Camp Calivigny, handcuffed to a bed.

The mood of the meeting became more murderous when news arrived of a minor uprising in support of Bishop by some militia personnel at St. Paul's. Arms had been taken from the armory; plans were made to move on Mount Weldale to protect Bishop from the Coards. The army command reacted quickly, ruthlessly crushing and disarming the St. Paul's and St. David's militia.

Bishop fervently denied starting any rumors to kill Coard, but he was not believed. The meeting got out of control to such an extent that the chairman, Ventour, threatened the gathering with his pistol. Bishop did not return to his house until after midnight, a shaken man, having been compelled to make a short radio broadcast stating that rumors concerning the Coards were totally false and that the party was united.

Early on October 13, the Central Committee gathered at Coard's house and quickly decided to put Bishop under house arrest. That morning the platoon commander of the PRA detachment on Carriacou received a radio message to return at once to St. George's. There were no suitable flights, so a Coast Guard vessel was sent to pick him up. At around 1:00 P.M. Lieutenant Callistus Bernard, better known as Iman Abdullah, reported to the duty officer at Fort Rupert. Abdullah was briefed that Bishop was to be placed under house arrest and that he was to be responsible for the security of the prime minister. Abdullah took charge immediately, briefing the men to be vigilant "and not to allow any person to come to see Bishop unless they consulted me; and that I would always be around."

Later that afternoon Bishop, under guard, was escorted to Butler House to attend a party meeting. He looked exhausted and ill; indeed Noel had tried to send a doctor to him earlier but on leaving Bishop's home had been put under house arrest himself. Noel had felt that Bishop looked suicidal.

Some 250 members were assembled to witness Bishop's downfall. Noel, who was allowed to attend, described the meeting as "a horrendous display of militarism, hatred, and emotional vilification." Ventour, again in the chair, announced that the main purpose of the meeting was to inform them of the arrest of Bishop and to get their views on that and the situation in the country. Strachan stated that George Louison had been dismissed from the Politburo and Central Committee, which led to shouts for his arrest as well. Bishop spoke in his own defense, again stressing he had not started the rumor to kill the Coards. It was no use, the party was out for blood. Layne stated categorically that Bishop was a traitor: "History had already condemned Maurice Bishop, he was already removed as leader of the Party and country, and the only thing left was whether to court-martial him."

Coard was conspicuous by his silence. Louison urged him to speak, but he refused, adding, "What the Party needs now is a psychiatrist." No final resolution was agreed; Ventour closed the meeting by repeating that the Central Committee had wanted to hear members' views and that Bishop would remain under arrest, stripped of his positions in the PRG.

It was not until that Thursday, October 13, that the Cuban ambassador, Torres Rizo, was informed of the internal strife within the NJM, together with Bishop's detention. Rizo was staggered, as was Havana. They had not appreciated the critical nature of the situation.

The battle for leadership was now in the open. People, initially disbelieving, soon began to demonstrate against Coard and his Central Committee. In St. George's on the following day, Strachan foolishly announced publicly that Coard had taken over the prime ministership. He was howled down, manhandled, and chased away by furious Grenadians. This violent reception of the news prompted Coard to declare his own resignation as deputy prime minister. He was replaced as minister of finance by another ardent Marxist, Nazim Burke, who until then had been Coard's permanent secretary. Phyllis Coard resigned with her husband. From then on they kept well out of public view.

The news soon spread internationally. The *Barbados Sunday Sun* of October 16 carried the headline, "Day 2 of Turmoil: Grenada Remains Quiet But Tense—Army Dumps Bishop." The previous day it had been Radix who had led demonstrators through the streets of the capital, shouting that although in poor health he would have to take up his gun again if Bishop was not freed. By evening Radix was in jail. Journalists from overseas were having problems getting into Grenada. On October 15, nine, including some from Britain and the United States, were refused entry at Pearls. Some had managed to slip in, such as Barbadian reporter Neville Martindale and photographers Charles Hackett and Willie Alleyne. Although arrested by the PRA, subjected to rough handling and body searches, both photographers were able to smuggle film out when they were later put on an aircraft leaving the island.

On Saturday, Fidel Castro reacted. He wrote personally to the NJM Central Committee, expressing his horror at what was happening and emphatically denying the allegation that Bishop had sought his assistance during his recent visit. Castro referred to this as "a miserable piece of slander." He stressed that there was great respect and admiration for Bishop in Cuba: "Even explaining the events to our people will not be easy."

Later the same day Major "Bogo" Cornwall, summoned back from his ambassadorial post in Havana to be in at the kill, went on the radio in an attempt to justify the Central Committee's actions. Speaking on behalf of the PRA, he stated that Bishop had refused to accept firm decisions on internal party changes, "even though he had himself agreed them at a meeting of the Party." He continued, "Much as we of the PRA love and respect Comrade Bishop, we will definitely not tolerate this development." Cornwall emphasized that Bishop was implicated by his security personnel in the rumors circulating that the Coards had planned to murder him. The overwhelming public reaction was disbelief. Grenadians wanted to see their prime minister, to hear his version themselves.

Over the next few days pro-Bishop protest marches were commonplace. Shops and businesses stayed shut. On October 18, Tuesday, five ministers formally resigned: George Louison, Whiteman, Norris Bain, Ramdhanny, and Jackie Creft. Whiteman telephoned the media in Barbados to tell of the resignations. He stressed, "Comrade Coard, who is now running Grenada, has refused to engage in serious talks to resolve the crisis. Coard is running the show from his house." He and Bain went into the streets to organize the demonstrations. On that day hundreds marched in the northeast, many of them women and students. For a while they closed Pearls Airport.

Between October 15 and 17, four men met and argued almost continuously, desperately trying to resolve the crisis. Early on Saturday, October 15, Coard had telephoned George Louison to come to his house for discussions. Louison went, accompanied by Whiteman. There they met Coard and Strachan. These four tried in vain to break the deadlock. Coard and Strachan insisted the arrest and removal from office of Bishop had been fully justified. It was during these meetings that Coard suggested Bishop "cool it" in Cuba and that if the masses wanted to march, he would let them: "They can stay in the streets for weeks, after a while they are bound to get tired and hungry and want peace." After all, the party and the army were behind him. Louison and Whiteman stuck out for Bishop's reinstatement, or the revolution was dead.

On October 17, after another three hours of going over the same ground again, Coard agreed to take their views to the Central Committee and to give Louison an answer by 10:00 A.M. the next day. The following morning McBarnette rang to say there was no decision yet but to call back at 2:00 P.M. At that time Strachan said try again at 4:00 P.M. At four Coard came on the line to say it would now be 2:00 P.M. on October 19. An angry Louison protested strongly, but Coard was adamant and slammed down the telephone. That evening after returning home, George Louison was detained by the PRA; he was taken first to Butler House, then to a cell at the Park in St. Paul's, before finally ending up in Richmond Hill Prison. Now Bishop, Radix, Creft, and George Louison were under arrest, as were Vincent Noel and Einstein Louison. Only Whiteman, plus Fitzroy and Norris Bain, among the leading Bishop supporters, had avoided detention.

Selected party members of the PRA met on the morning of October 18 at Butler House. A delegation consisting of Austin, Layne, James, and Bartholomew would put the Central Committee's final proposals to Bishop that evening. If he did not accept them, martial law would be imposed. Apart from Abdullah, who was keen to bring in martial law at once, the majority of the officers had grave reservations as to whether the PRA would be willing, or able, to impose military rule on the masses.

October 19 had the makings of a difficult day. As a precaution, Ventour instructed all civilian party members to report to Fort Rupert by 7:00 A.M.

3

Bloody Wednesday
The Morning

We get we leader, fuck Coard.
— Grenadian crowd after freeing Maurice Bishop
on the morning of October 19, 1983

I T was not until 1:00 A.M. that Austin, Layne, James, and Bartholomew left Bishop's house. They had completed several hours of seemingly fruitless, bitter argument over Coard's final proposals for a compromise. The best they could offer was that Bishop would remain prime minister and a full party member, but he was not to be allowed real authority. He was to lose his role as chairman of the Central Committee; indeed he would no longer be on the committee at all. He would be removed from his position as commander in chief of the PRAF. He was expected to broadcast to the nation announcing these changes, accepting personal responsibility for the Coard assassination rumors, and agreeing to the setting up of a special team of negotiators to smooth over the divisions in the party. Exhausted though he was, it was clear to Bishop that acceptance meant he would be finished. He was to be a figurehead, used by the Coard faction to placate the masses or sensitive foreign governments. Playing for still more time, Bishop agreed to consider the proposals, although he insisted he had never plotted Coard's murder. He needed to discuss everything further with Whiteman, George Louison, and, significantly, the Cuban ambassador, Rizo. Then he would be able to give his answer.

Although Radix and George Louison were imprisoned and Major Einstein Louison under house arrest, some prominent Bishop supporters were still free. Bishop was aware that mass demonstrations in his favor were planned for that morning. With people like Whiteman, Fitzroy, and Norris Bain to lead the crowds, perhaps he still had a chance.

After six days, Bishop was haggard and weak. Fear of poisoning had prevented him from eating properly; incessant smoking, lack of sleep, and the endless mental turmoil had sapped him physically. He felt isolated and powerless. Although still in his own home, still surrounded by his bookshelves stacked with Marxist literature, still sleeping in his own bed with the steel plate on the floor underneath, he was confined night and day by the PRA soldiers of whom he was supposed to be the commander in chief. He had been disarmed, his personal bodyguards dismissed, his telephone cut off, and his visitors rigidly restricted by the ever watchful Abdullah.

From early on, October 19 had the makings of an eventful day. But it was to be more than that; it was to be a momentous day in the history of the Caribbean. The climax of the struggle between the two Marxist leaders would push the United States into mounting its largest military operation since Vietnam.

‡   ‡   ‡

One person in a good position to watch the events of the day was Tony Buxo, a Sandhurst-trained former army officer of the West India Regiment, now an optician.[1] Anticipating an interesting morning in St. George's, he was located in the house of a Dr. Bierzynski on top of Old Fort Hill, some 500 meters north of the Careenage. He had equipped himself with a powerful telescope and had an unrestricted view down into the town, across to Coard's residence only 400 meters away to the east, and over to Fort Rupert to the southwest. He had picked a perfect observation spot, although he could not have appreciated that it would eventually make him, somewhat reluctantly, into a key witness at the most sensational murder trial ever held in the Caribbean.

After watching the crowds gathering in the town for a while, Buxo noticed several hundred people moving up toward Mount Weldale where the governor-general, Bishop, and Coard had their residences.

Focusing his telescope on Coard's house, he was able to see clearly right into the living room.

A meeting between Coard and his close supporters was in progress. Apart from the Coards, Austin, Layne, Cornwall, McBarnette, James, Strachan, St. Bernard, Ventour, and later Redhead were present. Buxo spotted an Indian and a white, balding man with glasses in a Texaco T-shirt, neither of whom he recognized. It is quite possible the latter was from the Soviet embassy. The group had been assembling since early morning, to be briefed by Austin and Layne on their late night meeting with Bishop.

Austin was not able to tell them much except that Bishop had said he would give an answer later that day after more discussions with Whiteman, George Louison, and Rizo. Whiteman was out whipping up the crowds, and there was no way Bishop was going to be allowed to talk with the Cuban ambassador. That left George Louison, who, Austin explained, had been escorted from his cell to Bishop's house at around 7:30 that morning. The two of them had spent nearly an hour and a half going over the same problems.

Not long after Louison's departure back to jail, some of the crowd began to assemble on the road that led past Coard's house to Bishop's. This was around 9:30 A.M. Coard and his companions were moving in and out of the living room to the veranda, talking excitedly and watching the activities of the crowds gathering below in the town.

It had been Whiteman who announced to the crowd that they must march to Bishop's house to rescue him. Since early morning, he had been haranguing the people as they built up from hundreds to thousands in Market Square (map 2). As more and more people began to assemble outside the gates on the approach road, there was mounting concern. Pro-Bishop agitators were pointed out. Whiteman, Fitzroy Bain, and Vincent Noel in particular were marked down as leaders of the demonstrators, whose purpose was clearly to get to Bishop. The demands and shouts were plain: "We want Maurice, we want Maurice." As the numbers outside increased to hundreds, all inside Coard's house realized their growing danger. Not only might the people release Bishop, but equally they could turn on them. Although all Central Committee members or PRA officers carried pistols, there were no soldiers between the crowd and themselves. In this situation, Layne was the first to act. He telephoned the duty officer at Fort Frederick, ordering him to send three armored personnel carriers

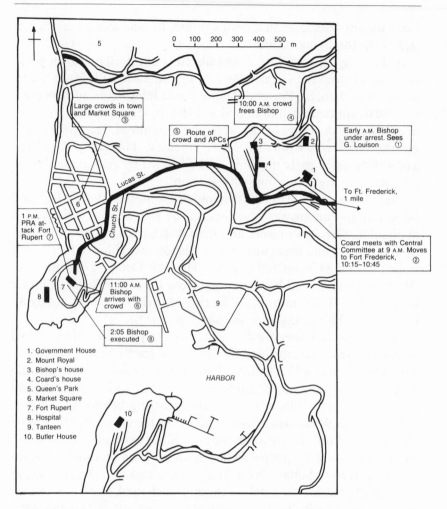

Map 2. EVENTS IN ST. GEORGE'S, OCTOBER 19, 1983

(APCs) at once. Major "Akee" Gahagan, the operations chief of the PRA, arrived with the vehicles shortly before 10:00 A.M.

Bishop's and Coard's houses were adjacent to each other, but with only one narrow approach road, so the people and APCs had to pass Coard's house in order to reach Bishop's. Gahagan had to force his way through the people jammed in the road. There was only room for one APC to advance at a time. The situation was serious, with the crowd chanting, shouting for Bishop, pressing right up to the gates and fence of his house. Placards denouncing Coard were prominently displayed. One said, "Only a monster has two heads," referring to the joint leadership idea. At the front was a blue pickup with Vincent Noel sitting on top.

Inside the grounds Abdullah had deployed his men, mostly at the gates, where they were pushing back people who were trying to force their way through. The APCs were a welcome reinforcement for Abdullah, who although he had secured Bishop and Creft, realized that there was no way short of shooting that he could prevent the crowd's bursting in. Gahagan was now the senior military officer present, and responsibility for making on-the-spot decisions passed to him.

Two APCs got as far as Coard's gate; the other was dropped off at the southern fork in the approach road. None of the vehicles presented a particularly warlike appearance. On halting, hatches were opened while commanders and crew stood or sat on top of the vehicles. People were all around, milling past; soldiers and civilians exchanged shouts. Indeed Buxo, watching through his telescope, described the crews as relaxed, patting hands or "touching five," with the crowd. Gahagan spoke with Layne inside Coard's residence. What was he to do?

From Coard's point of view, the position could hardly have been worse. The masses clearly detested him and were determined to release Bishop. His own life was in jeopardy. At any moment they might rush in on him. He decided on one last attempt at compromise: Layne was to get through to Bishop, persuade him to speak to, and calm, the crowd, and then continue their discussions from the previous day. He shrank from ordering the APCs into action. They were not hand-picked crews or commanders, merely men detailed in a hurry from the motorized company at Fort Frederick. Would they obey orders to save him with hundreds of pro-Bishop supporters all around them? As it turned out, Coard made the correct decision: there was no bloodshed, and he was able to retrieve the situation later in the day.

Nevertheless, it was far too late and too difficult for Layne, or anybody else, to get to Bishop. Abdullah and his men could not hold the crowd any longer without violence. He raised his submachine gun to fire two short bursts into the air. Gahagan spoke to the gunners in the two APCs at the gate: "Fire in the air." Several long bursts from the heavy machine guns momentarily hushed the crowd. For a few seconds it was quiet as people sought to discover the effect of the shooting. When it was realized that the firing was over their heads, the people booed, shouting "Shoot us. Kill us," before surging forward again. They could not be stopped. They swept through the gates into the house. They found Bishop and Creft tied to their beds, Bishop in shorts and light green T-shirt and his companion in a blue smock.

‡   ‡   ‡

Bishop had won—almost. At ten o'clock that morning when he was freed, there can be no doubt that he was within a hairsbreadth of defeating Coard. He had been released by the masses; the army had not stopped them, indeed had seemed almost friendly to some. Coard was virtually defenseless only a few meters away. Voices clamored to seize Coard and those with him, but it seems Bishop stopped them. He made a decision that was to cost him his life. Perhaps he lacked the ruthless streak necessary to survive in those circumstances, or possibly his dazed and weakened condition had befuddled him. Whatever the reason, he let the opportunity slip. Fortune was not to favor him again. Ironically, in Barbados at this moment Prime Minister Tom Adams was debating with his cabinet how they might mount a military rescue operation to free him.

Watched by the PRA, Bishop was assisted from the house to a waiting truck for a triumphal entry into St. George's. He hesitated, preferring a car, then agreed to the truck, before finally opting for the car. Surrounded by his Grenada, his people, Maurice Bishop moved slowly down toward the town.

Whiteman, Noel, Creft, and the Bains were to die with him, so it remains impossible to be sure what he hoped to achieve immediately following his release. Some decisions were taken, but whether they were his entirely is uncertain. Having declined to arrest Coard, where was Bishop to go? St. George's was one possibility; thousands of people had gathered there to see and hear him. Market Square, the traditional meeting place, was packed. However, if that was his original destination, it was changed en route to Fort Rupert, the PRA headquarters. From Bishop's point of view, occupying Fort Rupert would be a shrewd move. In the eyes of most Grenadians, he was certainly still the commander in chief of the PRAF and so had every right to be at the headquarters. It might influence doubters within the military, at least not to support his rivals actively. Headquarters would give him communication facilities, together with arms and ammunition, at the same time depriving Coard of the same. Finally, it would give him security. Fort Rupert is atop a dominating position with only one narrow approach. Up there Bishop might be safe for a while with food, water, weapons, and radios. Such a place would give him time—time to recover, time to think, time to organize, time to mobilize assistance. Provided Fort Rupert could be occupied without a fight—and Bishop and his followers had every reason to think it could—the decision to go there instead of Market Square made sense.

It is not clear whether the idea of asking the Cubans for assistance was taken during Bishop's march through St. George's or later at the fort, but an approach for help was apparently made. Bishop needed military support quickly, before there was any chance of the PRA being used against him. Although it had not yet attacked the masses, the military leadership was virtually all committed to Coard. Bishop was well aware political power came from the barrel of a gun. He himself had seized power with a gun, and now he needed more guns to retain it. The Cubans were armed. Although Cuban military personnel were few, there were hundreds of construction workers with weapons only 6 kilometers away at the new airport site. Castro was his friend; surely he would come out in support of Bishop at this time of crisis. If armed Cubans could be seen as protecting Bishop, then the PRA would be checkmated. A messenger was sent hurrying to the embassy.

Ambassador Rizo could not take that sort of responsibility on his own shoulders; he radioed Havana for instructions. Within the hour Castro replied, telling Rizo that under no circumstances were Cuban personnel, civil or military, to become involved in the internal turmoil of Grenada. Bishop had been turned down. The situation was too confused, and changing by the minute, for Havana to risk taking a decision that might necessitate Cubans shedding Grenadian blood. Castro made an oblique reference to this request, and its rejection, in his November funeral address to the nation for Cubans later killed in combat:

> It is to our Revolution's credit that, in spite of our profound indignation over Bishop's removal from office and arrest, we refrained from interfering in Grenada's internal affairs, even though our construction workers and all our other cooperation personnel in Grenada—

who did not hesitate to confront the Yankee soldiers with the weapons, Bishop himself had given them for their defense in the case of an attack abroad—could have been a decisive factor in those internal events. Those weapons were never meant to be used in an internal conflict in Grenada.

Whether Bishop learned of his friend's refusal to help before he died is doubtful. At around 11:00 A.M., accompanied by hundreds of enthusiastic supporters, he arrived at Fort Rupert.

‡ ‡ ‡

The PRA headquarters had been alive with activity since dawn. All in the fort, built over 100 meters above the sea, had been able to watch with considerable excitement as events unfolded in St. George's. As the army headquarters, the fort was the normal workplace of more than sixty soldiers. It contained offices for Austin and Layne, although they were more often found at Butler House some 800 meters across the harbor to the southeast. The chief of staff, Major Einstein Louison, worked there, as did Major Chris Stroude, the PRA's political chief (or commissar); Major "Akee" Gahagan, the operations chief; Lieutenant "Dumpy" Prime, chief of artillery; and Lieutenant "Porgie" Cherubin, the finance officer. The officer responsible for day-to-day security was Captain "Goat" Redhead, with a platoon of men from his security company based at Camp Boney on Quarantine Point. Of these, Stroude, Redhead, Prime, and Cherubin were at the fort that morning, together with two other officers, 2d Lieutenants Andrew and Hypolite. Apart from the detachment providing the guards, the personnel stationed there were administrative soldiers required to staff the communications facilities, stores, armory, kitchen, canteen, and registry. These permanent garrison troops had barrack accommodations on the upper level of the fort, while the headquarters offices were situated in the two-story operations room building lower down, facing the narrow access road.

Redhead had been awake since 5:00 A.M. He was well aware that it was likely to be a difficult day, and his duty was security. This responsibility seemingly extended to the town as well as the fort, as by half past eight he had become alarmed by the size and activities of the crowd.

Redhead decided that an attempt should be made to contain them or at least to arrest some ringleaders. Taking Andrews and another soldier in a truck, he sped downhill toward the Careenage. He soon realized the impossibility of his task and wove his way through the streets to Coard's house for instructions. He arrived in the middle of a heated debate as to what should be done and whether Fort Rupert was endangered. It was agreed it was. While someone went to the fire station to get trucks to block the approach road, Redhead was told to obtain tear-gas shells from Grand Anse police station some 3 kilometers away. Even at this late stage, Coard and his Central Committee members drew back from ordering troops to fire on other Grenadians. Fort Rupert's access should be barricaded and defended, if necessary, by tear gas in the first instance.

As it turned out, neither the fire trucks nor the tear gas arrived in time. Redhead drove at high speed to Grand Anse, only to discover that no tear-gas ammunition was held there. He dashed back to St. George's, making for the police headquarters at Melville Street on the sea front just north of Fort Rupert. The crowds slowed his progress, and although he stocked up his vehicle with the tear gas at the station, by the time he reached the fort again, Bishop was already in occupation.

Stroude was the senior officer in the fort that morning. He too had watched with Redhead and the others as thousands of men, women, and children flocked into the streets below. He saw the people massing in Market Square; he saw them pressing up around Coard's and Bishop's houses; he saw the APCs arrive in that vicinity; and he heard the bursts of firing. He was nervous. Civilian party members had been arriving since 7:00 to seek shelter on instructions they had received the previous night at the party meeting. Redhead had disappeared. The crowds were enormous, and now troops had opened fire. Clearly he should do something.

Stroude got a situation report from Cherubin, who as the fort's duty officer that day was in telephone contact with Fort Frederick. He now knew that Bishop had been freed. The party members present were getting agitated, so he called a meeting of all the soldiers in the mess hall. At this meeting Stroude told Sergeant Fabian Gabriel, the senior logistics noncommissioned officer, to issue weapons to all the civilian party members. He announced that Bishop had been released by the crowd and might come to the fort. Orders were issued to strengthen the guards and for the garrison to take up defensive positions. They were not to open fire without specific orders to do so. However, before these arrangements could be properly implemented, a soldier burst into the mess hall to announce that Bishop and the crowd were at the operations room.

‡   ‡   ‡

The soldiers on duty in front of the headquarters building did not know what to do. Coming up the short, steep access road to the fort was an overwhelming sight. The approach was solid with people. Men, women, and small children, all shouting, chanting—"We get we leader, fuck Coard"—waving placards, and pressing around the car containing Bishop. Their former prime minister and commander in chief was free and, judging by the massive support being demonstrated, perhaps back in control again. Senior PRG leaders such as Whiteman, Noel, Fitzroy, and Norris Bain were in the forefront. There was no physical barrier to block their progress. The guards hesitated.

Whiteman shouted out that they came in peace. Bishop descended from the car and confronted the soldiers. After a slight pause, he recognized one of them, a Corporal Bogman, and called his name, telling him that he was responsible for ensuring that nobody opened fire. Bishop and his followers moved toward the building where one soldier was reluctant to let them pass; she had to be thrown to the ground before she would relinquish her rifle. Apart from this small incident, Bishop's entry into Fort Rupert was unopposed.

Bishop was escorted up the stairs to the first floor balcony. Several soldiers did nothing to prevent entry into the operations room, despite the fact that the door had to be kicked in. Once inside, a table and chairs were organized for a conference. There was no knowing how long they had before Coard reacted. Certain matters called for urgent action, and despite the hundreds of supporters waiting and watching from the parking lot below, Bishop did not attempt to address them. He was still weak, confused, and surrounded, almost overbearingly hemmed in, by the dozens of people in the room. He recognized Sylvia Belmar, a former area president of the National Women's Organisation, as she approached and asked her for a drink of water. She left the room with Cherubin, who as finance officer had keys to the canteen, to fetch some. She was away for some time; the press of people made progress slow.

After his mess hall meeting broke up in confusion, Stroude hurried down toward headquarters. At the top of the steps, leading up from the parking lot, Stroude met Officer Cadet David Francis with two soldiers struggling to push people back. He told them to prevent entry and to block the nearby tunnel, which also led to the upper level, with wire. At this moment Fitzroy Bain appeared. Bain told Stroude that Bishop was free and that now was the time to settle the joint leadership dispute. They came in peace, he said, adding that Coard and his faction of Central Committee members had surrendered. Stroude went back to explain matters to the anxious party members and soldiers. He announced what Bain had told him, adding that he was in command as the senior officer present. There was no point now in opening fire on the masses as there were too many, and the garrison would be overwhelmed in the end, at the needless expense of civilian lives. He ordered the soldiers to hand back their weapons to the armory and then change out of uniform. Most of the men refused to return their arms but agreed to put them in an armorer's workshop inside the tunnel, where they would be more accessible.

During this time Bishop, Creft, Whiteman, Noel and others had agreed on some immediate priorities. First, the PRA garrison should be disarmed, and weapons should be distributed to some people at the fort for self-defense. Second, it was critical that contact be made with all Grenadians and the outside world, including the Cubans. This necessitated radio and telephone communications. Third, Coard and his followers must surrender and accept their fate.

Bishop sent for Stroude and subjected him to a lengthy harangue. Bishop told him that the Grenadian people had released him; Coard and his followers must submit to the will of the masses. Negotiations must take place now, in the operations room. Coard was to be arrested and jailed at once. Similarly Layne, whom Bishop described as a "bloodthirsty maniac" for wanting him expelled from the party and court-martialed, and Cornwall were to be seized. Bishop emphasized that there was to be a new type of army; the PRA was to lay down its arms. Stroude was personally told to hand over his pistol, which he did. He was then ordered to explain the situation to the other officers present—Redhead, who was back from his mission to collect tear gas, Prime, Cherubin, and Hypolite. Next Bishop demanded the armory keys. Stroude replied that Gabriel held them and was told to get them in order to distribute more weapons for the defense of the fort if necessary. Bishop also wanted to know the whereabouts of Major Einstein Louison, whom he intended to appoint army commander immediately. Stroude collected the keys with Bain and handed them to Bishop.

Among the people crowding around in the room were Peter Thomas, an immigration officer, and Don Rojas, Bishop's friend and formerly his press secretary. They were both to assist in establishing communications, particularly telephone links. Thomas was given a list of telephone numbers and instructed to go to the telephone company in St. George's to ensure certain lines were cut and others secured. Bishop wanted to prevent Coard from using his two hot lines to coordinate any counterattack, from either his house or Fort Frederick. These lines were to be severed; those to Fort Rupert were to be kept open. Bishop went so far as to specify that the independent journalist Alister Hughes's telephone be kept open to facilitate his passing information overseas.

Rojas was also to go to the telephone company to establish communications with the outside world. Bishop wanted the rest of the world to know what had happened but that Grenadians could handle their own affairs; he wanted no outside interference. Nevertheless, he also wanted Grenadians abroad, and Caribbean leftist organizations, to express support and solidarity.

A group of supporters, including several telephone employees with militia training, were assembled and armed with weapons taken from the garrison. They escorted Thomas and Rojas into the town. The telephone company building was locked and barricaded when they arrived; however, the workers soon opened up when they knew the purpose of the crowd outside. Thomas was able to get Coard's lines disconnected, including those to Fort Frederick. He then collected some spare weapons held in the building before making his way back to Bishop. Rojas had a longer task trying to make contact overseas but eventually was successful. He placed three or four overseas calls before heavy firing from the direction of the fort interrupted him. Rojas was able to give an eyewitness account over the telephone to the Caribbean News Agency in Barbados.

Meanwhile at the fort, Einstein Louison had appeared, having also been freed from house arrest. Bishop told him that he was to take over as army commander; he handed him the armory keys with instructions to issue weapons and organize the defenses of the fort. Louison, Stroude, and several others headed for the armory.

It was now just after 1:00 P.M. The first floor room was still jammed with people; outside, the balcony was crowded; below in the parking lot, several hundred more waited for their leader to appear. It was two hours since they had occupied the fort.

‡   ‡   ‡

In those two hours Coard and the Central Committee had been spurred into action. Incredulous at their good fortune in not being arrested at Coard's house, they agreed that for security reasons they must move at once to Fort Frederick. Layne climbed onto one of the APCs and went ahead to alert the fort and obtain reinforcements. Arriving at around 10:30 A.M., he immediately had the alarm sounded.

Fort Frederick, on a dominating ridge some 2 kilometers by a twisting road southeast of Coard's residence, was normally the head-quarters of Military Region I. As such there was a number of PRA permanent staff, and it was also the base of Nelson's motorized company with two of its three platoons mounted in six Soviet BTR-60 APCs. This fort was also immediately south of the mental hospital, with which it shared a main entrance.

It was clear to Coard that he would need the full support of the army before the day was over, but at this stage, he was still not certain in exactly what circumstances it might be deployed. Layne for one realized they needed to have a reliable unit in reserve. The APC crews and commanders were a well-trained force, but they had been exposed that morning to the influence of the crowds, they had seen Bishop freed, seen the massive support for him, and had been ordered to fire in the air, not at civilians. Young Nelson, their commander, was a good soldier, but was he politically reliable enough to obey orders and compel his men to kill other Grenadians if required? Layne felt that fresh reinforcements, with different commanders, might be needed. To this end, he ordered the duty officer to telephone Abdullah at Bishop's house to get him to report immediately. Then he set off in a car at high speed for Camp Calivigny, some twenty minutes away to the south.

Cletus St. Paul, still under arrest at the camp, saw Layne arrive at about 11:00 A.M. Layne dashed into the office of the acting chief of the camp, Officer Cadet Conrad "Connie" Mayers. Within moments Mayers was banging vigorously on the old piece of iron that was the alarm. The troops ran to the parade ground and quickly assembled in front of Layne and Mayers. Layne spoke first. He announced that civilians were causing massive disturbances in town, that they were threatening to "turn back the revolution." The troops were to be prepared for combat; they might have to retake Fort Rupert. Mayers asked, "Are you ready to fight for your country?" "Yeah, yeah," came the response. He then added, "Some have to die for some to survive. Every soldier should see blood in the eyes."[2] Layne departed while Mayers led his men in the Grenadian revolutionary chant: "Forward ever, backward never." The soldiers got dressed in full combat gear, and a platoon of some twenty-five men, with Cletus St. Paul onboard, left in a truck for Fort Frederick shortly after 11:30.

Layne arrived back at Fort Frederick around 11:45, with Mayers and his men some fifteen minutes later. By this time it was known that Bishop was in control at Fort Rupert. The situation was worsening by the minute as far as Coard was concerned. Cletus St. Paul, who although still handcuffed had been more or less forgotten, was able to sit on the veranda of the Fort Frederick office building and watch the crisis building. Even at that time the Central Committee had not fully assembled. James, head of the security services, was among the first to arrive. The PRA soldiers saluted, and James took the opportunity to address them. He told them that the masses had freed Bishop and taken him to the town. In consequence, "Things are getting dread in the country, and as a result the Central Committee will be arriving shortly to take a serious decision." All shouted, "Long live the Central Committee. Long live the revolution."

Coard and his wife arrived, driven up to the fort in Bishop's former car. He carried a briefcase and was openly wearing his Makarov pistol. The others soon followed—Austin, Bartholomew, Cornwall, McBarnette, and Ventour. A meeting was held, punctuated by much argument, raised voices, shaking of heads, and waving of arms. Was there any possibility of compromise left? Despite the cutting of the telephone lines, it had been possible, by using the water works telephone on top of the old fort, to speak to Fort Rupert. They had been told that Bishop had taken over the operations room, and that the garrison had been disarmed. Whiteman had been fetched and renewed negotiations requested. Whiteman's reply was allegedly, "No negotiations; is manners for all you."

Up to this moment, no decision had been taken to kill Bishop. Bishop's popularity with the people had made Coard hesitate to use the PRA in earnest. Despite the support of the military leadership, despite the soldiers' seeming loyalty to his version of the revolution, the troops were, after all, Grenadians, with families in the crowds. Would they attack their own former prime minister and commander in chief? Negotiations, firing in the air, the use of tear gas—everything short of shooting to kill had been considered or tried. But now it was a simple matter of Bishop's life or theirs. If Bishop triumphed, and it certainly looked as if he was going to, they were all dead men. Up to this moment they could claim they were fighting for the Grenadian revolution. Now they were fighting for their lives.

The Central Committee took the decision to retake Fort Rupert and kill Bishop with his close supporters at around 12:30 P.M. Cornwall came to inform the troops. He told them, "Because of vicious rumours spread by Maurice Bishop, counterrevolutionaries and big businessmen had freed him. As a result these elements must be liquidated." Raising his arms, he yelled, "Central Committee orders." The soldiers responded, "We obey. We obey."

The plan was that Mayers's platoon with three APCs would attack to retake the army headquarters and that Bishop and the others should die in the fighting. The troops would storm the fort to hunt down and kill Bishop. That way their deaths could more easily be explained away to the people, and indeed to the rest of the world, later. The army was retaking its own headquarters, and Bishop was killed resisting.

Layne went to brief Mayers, Abdullah, and Nelson.

4

Bloody Wednesday
The Afternoon

It was a unanimous decision that all had to die.
— Major Chris Stroude, PRA political chief, in
a statement to the police in November 1983

I NSIDE Richmond Hill Prison, close to the entrance to the women's
compound, was the goat pen—a small building, some 2 meters
by 4, with dirty brick walls and a corrugated iron roof. The outer
wall faced west, down the hill, and through the gaps in the ventila-
tion blocks it was possible to see most of St. George's. The view was
its only redeeming feature. It had no amenities, having been originally
used to accommodate goats. In more recent times, it had been used
as an extra cell, frequently containing up to twenty prisoners on a
temporary basis.

On the afternoon of October 19, four men sat sweltering on the
floor: two former PRG ministers, George Louison and Kendrick
Radix; the ex-manager of the airport project, Bob Evans, who was
also a cousin of Bishop; and Anthony Munroe. All recently had been
arrested on the orders of the Central Committee as being counterrevolutionary supporters of Bishop. Shortly after 1:00 P.M., a violent
explosion brought them to their feet, and, peering through the holes
in the wall, they saw a cloud of gray smoke rising up above Fort
Rupert. Long bursts of automatic firing and more explosions followed.
They could see dozens of people running and leaping off the walls.
The noise of firing continued intermittently for some minutes. Then

there was silence. Nothing further happened for nearly an hour before the detainees were brought back to their feet again by more long bursts of machine-gun fire. They could see nothing this time except, when it ceased, a white flare curving gracefully above the fort.

The far-reaching significance of what they had witnessed was not apparent to the men in the goat pen.

‡　‡　‡

The morning had belonged to Bishop. His ace was the people, the masses who had marched to free him. Coard was to play his trump in the afternoon, the PRA. Thousands of young Grenadians had taken to the streets, making it quite clear where their loyalty lay. The people did not believe that the soldiers would fire on them. At the confrontation at Bishop's house that morning, shots had been fired but over their heads. They were confident that so long as the crowds kept together and were composed of men, women, and children, they were safe. It was a reasonable assumption, based on their experience that day and the knowledge that the PRA had been trained to respect the masses. However, the PRA had not, as yet, been ordered to shoot civilians. Coard was gambling that he had secured the army's support to the extent that they would gun down their own people if so directed. If the soldiers failed, then he, and his Central Committee followers, were finished. By noon there could have been no doubt in the minds of the two protagonists that the climax of their struggle had arrived or that the loser would surely die.

A platoon of three Soviet armored personnel carriers, from the motorized company based at Fort Frederick, were detailed for the attack. Each vehicle mounted a heavy 14.5-mm machine gun in its turret. They were far from being the latest Soviet APC, and their length of 24 feet and width of over 9 feet rendered them slow and hard to maneuver in the narrow streets of St. George's or along twisting rural roads. Nevertheless, they were more than adequate to overcome any Grenadian opposition. A driver and gunner normally made up the crew, and on this occasion there was an officer in each, with an infantry squad of about eight to ten men in the rear compartments. The infantrymen carried the usual AK-47 rifles, PKM machine guns, grenades, and one or two RPG-7 rocket launchers. In all there were some thirty-five men in the force. This was the unit that was going to make history.

A military unit is as good as its leader. In this case, no fewer than three officers were present, but with the usual commander of the motorized company, 2d Lieutenant Raeburn Nelson, relegated to a supporting role in the third APC. The man in overall command of the assault was an officer cadet and therefore the most junior of the three; nevertheless, he had been selected with care. Officer Cadet "Connie" Mayers was the acting chief at Camp Calivigny, the training depot of the PRA and base for the mobile infantry company of which he was the commanding officer. He held a key field command in the PRA, one that in any other army would have ensured much higher rank. Mayers was a professional soldier who, in addition to his Cuban training, had spent several years in the U.S. Army, serving for a while in Berlin. It was this factor that had delayed his promotion. There was a lingering suspicion in the political hierarchy of the PRG that Mayers's spell in the United States might have tainted him in some way. However, Coard, or more particularly "Headache" Layne, was confident he would obey orders. He had more military experience than most others and was deemed the best available leader for this particularly difficult operation. Mayers armed himself with an AK-47 before climbing atop the leading vehicle.

Immediately behind, in the second APC, came Lieutenant Iman Abdullah, the erstwhile commander of the platoon guarding Bishop while under house arrest. Abdullah was the ranking officer in the attacking force but was second in command to Mayers on this occasion. He had been chosen for his reliability and ruthlessness. He was an avid Coard supporter and hard-liner, with little love for Bishop, who, he was now convinced, was a counterrevolutionary. During Bishop's arrest, it was Abdullah who had rigidly restricted access, personally lecturing his men on the need for vigilance and security. He turned away Bishop's mother on at least one occasion and told Jackie Creft, Bishop's long-time mistress, that she could visit him but that if she went in, she must remain under arrest herself. It was he who had given orders that Bishop and Creft be tied to their beds on the approach of the crowd earlier that day. Had it not been for the explicit instructions of Gahagan, Abdullah would almost certainly have ordered the troops to fire at, not over, the people clamoring at the gates. He had cast his lot with Coard and Layne. If Bishop now regained power, Abdullah was lost. The powerful motive of self-preservation would ensure Abdullah followed orders. He carried a U.S. .45 caliber M-3 submachine gun, originating from stocks captured in Vietnam, and traveled in the back of his APC.

Bringing up the rear was Nelson, with a squad of ten men from his own unit. Nelson was a regular soldier with extensive training in Cuba and the Soviet Union. Although a candidate party member, he lacked the fanaticism of Abdullah. Nelson was destined to play a key role in the events of the next seven days, and eventually, after three years in prison, he was the only one out of eighteen accused to be acquitted of murder. He chose to go into action with an AK-47 rifle.

A few minutes before one o'clock, the three APCs were waved out of the gates of Fort Frederick by the commissioner of police, Major Ian St. Bernard. They roared off on their 2-mile journey through the center of St. George's. Not a man in the unit had ever seen shots fired in anger before, and on this, their first occasion, they would be required to kill civilians—their own fellow Grenadians.

‡　‡　‡

The drive did not take long. With gears grating and engines screaming at the sharp bends, the three vehicles hurtled along the road to the rotary outside the governor-general's residence, then down Lucas Street, turning left at the crossroads just before the Market Square into Church Street, and finally up the steep, narrow approach to Fort Rupert. The trip took not more than 10 minutes.

The troops, although in full combat gear and wearing steel helmets, did not appear to be expecting serious opposition. The leading two APCs had soldiers sitting casually on top, including Mayers himself. Certainly it was hot inside, and having to exit through roof hatches instead of via a rear door was awkward and, if being shot at, highly dangerous. Nevertheless, had they anticipated coming under heavy fire, military prudence would have kept them all behind the armor plate.

The crowds that hastily moved aside to give them passage were dense but friendly. Thousands of people were in town. About 4,000 milled around in the Market Square, fixing up microphones, awaiting Bishop's arrival to speak. Their mood was generally happy and excited; their leader was free. Few, if any, noticed the rude shouts of some soldiers at a group of youths who were slow in getting out of the way. Those who saw the APCs did not comprehend what was about to happen; some said afterward they thought the army was coming to help Bishop.

At about 1:05 P.M. Mayers's vehicle nosed its way up the sharp incline to the fort and halted a mere 30 meters from the headquarters building. Strangely, there was (and still is) no gate or barrier of any sort to prevent direct entry. Abdullah's APC pulled up behind, 4 feet to the rear and on the other side of the road. Nelson, who had left Fort Frederick about a minute later than Mayers, stopped farther back opposite the church and the St. James Hotel, out of sight of the fort. His men dismounted to double down the two branch roads to form a cordon. His APC moved up behind the others but was not far enough forward to see the headquarters building. The decisive moment had arrived.

The PRA headquarters was located on top of the foundations of the old British fortifications of Fort George, renamed Fort Rupert after Maurice Bishop's father, Rupert Bishop, who had been gunned down by Gairy's police nine years before. Because of the steepness of the ground within the old walls, the buildings were constructed on two levels, centered around the bottom and top squares (map 3). The bottom square was in fact the parking lot, on the northern edge of which Mayers was poised. Facing him across the square was the two-story headquarters building with an outside balcony running along the first floor. Up there were the PRA operations room and offices; the command post and telephone exchange were housed below on the ground floor.

There was only one way to get from the bottom to the top square, and that was up the steps on the right (west) side of the building. Once up, access to the top square was either through a tunnel or up more steps and then down a short slope onto the square itself. It was enclosed completely by high stone walls to the north and west and by long two-story buildings to the south and east. It was used for parades or drill and occasionally as a basketball court. Bishop himself was familiar with the top square; as commander in chief of the PRA, he had inspected detachments there on several occasions.

Except for the narrow approach up from St. George's, the high walls prevented entrance or exit through 350 degrees. The other ten degrees belonged to Mayers.

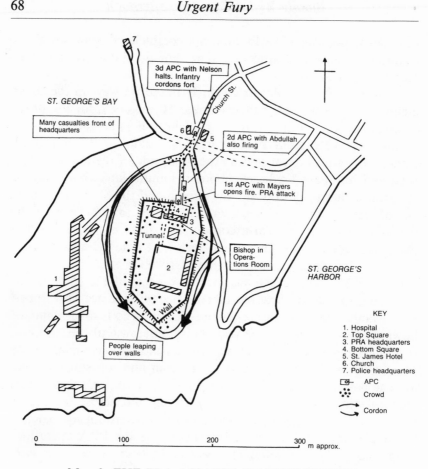

3d APC with Nelson halts. Infantry cordons fort

ST. GEORGE'S BAY

Many casualties front of headquarters

2d APC with Abdullah also firing

1st APC with Mayers opens fire. PRA attack

Bishop in Operations Room

ST. GEORGE'S HARBOR

Tunnel

Wall

People leaping over walls

KEY

1. Hospital
2. Top Square
3. PRA headquarters
4. Bottom Square
5. St. James Hotel
6. Church
7. Police headquarters

APC

Crowd

Cordon

0   100   200   300 m approx.

Map 3. THE PRA ASSAULT ON FORT RUPERT

‡   ‡   ‡

The view confronting Mayers at that moment was hardly hostile. The bottom square had some military and civilian vehicles parked on it; nobody was shooting, although a few had weapons; and the square was filled with scores of men, women, and children expecting Bishop to address them. Of the former prime minister there was no sign, and he was rightly assumed to be in the headquarters building. The balcony was thronged with people, one of whom was Vincent Noel, the prominent trade unionist.

There was to be no hesitation on the part of commanders or men. A survivor recalled Mayers shouting, "Concentrate fire on the fort."

One of the first soldiers to jump down carried a rocket launcher, the plan being for one round to signal the assault. His shot went low, and with a deafening roar, one of the vehicles in front of the building disintegrated in a mass of flames. Almost simultaneously the heavy caliber machine gun in the turret of Mayers's APC opened fire, the barrel swiveling left and right as the gunner raked the crowd and building. Abdullah's gun joined in moments later. The soldiers from both APCs, including Mayers and Abdullah, dismounted and opened up with their personal weapons; grenades were thrown; the rocket launcher fired again; and the troops advanced toward the right of the building.

The effect of this volume of fire at such close range was devastating. The heavy bullets literally chopped people to pieces. There was indescribable panic as people sought to escape. The APCs blocked the only exit, so demented fugitives, some grievously injured, sought to throw themselves over the walls or scramble up the steps leading to the top square. Even there many were compelled to leap 20 feet or more onto rocks, breaking bones in the process. Women and children were cut down with the men. In the first few moments, pandemonium reigned. Within two minutes, the bottom square and headquarters balcony were deserted except for the dead or crippled. The firing became more intermittent, though still heavy. Some soldiers had run up the stairs behind the headquarters and were shooting into the rear of the building.

The thin walls of the operations room offered no protection from the streams of bullets that smashed both people and furniture indiscriminately. The attack caught Bishop and those with him completely by surprise. Inside the room everyone hurled themselves to the floor or scrambled to get out of the windows. Bishop was heard to cry, "Oh God, oh God, they've turned their guns on the masses." Among the first to fall was Vincent Noel, who collapsed on the balcony, not dead, but with both legs shattered. When the rocket exploded, Sylvia Belmar was with her daughter, Gemma, and Mrs. Bain drinking soft drinks. She threw herself down and was horrified to see Gemma struck on the head and fall, blood pouring from her wound. Dumpy Prime was quick off the mark and at the first burst leaped from a window, making his way to the top square. Goat Redhead followed, successfully escaping through the tunnel out of the immediate danger area. Not so fortunate was the noncommissioned officer in charge of communications, Sergeant Darset Peters. He, like the other PRA soldiers in the fort at the time of Bishop's arrival, had been disarmed. As he clambered through a window, several shots struck him, and he crashed to the ground, dead.

Nevertheless, despite surprise, despite the weight of fire, despite their trained soldiers, the attackers did not have it all their own way. After the initial shock, some defenders courageously started to return fire. A few men in the building had weapons, mostly AK-47 rifles and Makarov pistols, which had been taken off the PRA guards. Judging by the results of their shooting, had the fort been put into a proper state of defense, the day might have ended differently. A burst of four rounds from an AK struck Mayers in the groin as he ran forward. He was dragged clear and carried to the nearby hospital, but his wounds proved mortal. He was dead within an hour. Abdullah was now in command. Equally unlucky was Warrant Officer Raphael Mason, a platoon leader from Camp Calivigny, who was shot and killed while advancing across the open ground. Finally 20-year-old Lance Corporal Martin Simon was severely wounded in the chest and died later in the hospital. Only one of the attackers survived his wounds: Sergeant Byron Cameron, who had his legs smashed as he was preparing to lob a grenade.

The defenders had killed three and wounded one of their attackers. Of the persons caught in the cross fire or those who hurled themselves over the walls, no accurate statistics were ever recorded. The number of dead is not known, but estimates of eyewitnesses put it between thirty and forty. The main hospital was located just behind the fort. Its records indicate over a hundred people were treated for injuries sustained that afternoon, thirty-nine of which were serious. The day fully justified its "Bloody Wednesday" title.

‡   ‡   ‡

Such an unequal struggle could not last long. After about 10 minutes, during a lull in the firing, those inside the operations room surrendered. One man took off his shirt to use as a flag and told Bishop he was going outside to surrender. Bishop, who, along with his hard-core supporters, had miraculously escaped injury, agreed. The man yelled, "Comrades, we surrender," and then, "We have a person dying here," referring to Gemma Belmar. A voice responded from outside: "Bring out the fucker; and let the others come out with their hands in the air.'' Slowly the terrified survivors crawled from beneath the conference table, picked up Gemma, and emerged onto the balcony, past one woman softly moaning on the floor with her buttocks shot away and her intestines bursting out. On the balcony itself, three or four men lay still, dead or unconscious, while on the bottom square, bodies were sprawled everywhere, and two vehicles burned furiously.

It was obvious to Bishop, Creft, Whiteman, and Norris Bain as they filed down with their hands on their heads that they personally were still in extreme danger. Uninjured people were coming out from behind buildings or walls, but there was no way to get out unless the troops let them pass. Most people were allowed through, but Bishop and the other three were quickly halted and turned about for the brief walk up the steps, through the tunnel, out onto the top square.

A little before one o'clock Sergeant Fabian Gabriel, the senior logistics noncommissioned officer at Fort Rupert, was in his kitchen in a building adjacent to the top square when a party of men approached him headed by Stroude. Stroude was accompanied by Major Einstein Louison, the former chief of staff of the PRA. Gabriel was told to issue weapons to all the men in the group. This was an order from Bishop. Having passed on these instructions, Stroude disappeared, leaving Gabriel to take the six men to the armory on the ground floor of the building on the south side of the top square. It faced the entrance to the tunnel opposite. Gabriel proceeded to give out Makarov pistols, AK rifles, and ammunition to each person, including Matie Maitland and Pumphead Hayling, both prominent businessmen and strong Bishop supporters. Just as Gabriel was finishing this task, a shattering explosion interrupted them, followed by heavy automatic firing. Gabriel, Maitland, Hayling, and another man sought refuge inside the armory, slammed and locked the heavy door, then lay flat on the floor. Outside the battle raged.

One of the key pro-Bishop clique, in fact his only senior ally in the PRA, Major Einstein Louison, was not intended to survive the attack. He was to be shot on sight, and he knew it. When firing started, he was armed with an AK-47 and near the armory. At first he considered joining the defenders, but the impossibility of descending to the headquarters building and the speed with which the attackers gained supremacy deterred him. Instead he sheltered on the top square. As the attackers began to infiltrate up the steps, through the tunnel, he decided his only option was to jump over the nearest wall. He landed awkwardly on the stones, damaging his leg and hip, but was able to drag himself away, not daring to go to the hospital nearby. He remained in hiding for two days in the vicinity of the fort and was not found until the pain from his injury forced him to the hospital. There he was treated and later detained in Richmond Hill Prison. By that time, however, the Revolutionary Military Council was trying to improve its image, both internally and internationally, so his life was spared. Unsuccessful attempts were made by Ian St. Bernard and others to persuade him to join the Coard faction.

As the firing died away, Stroude, Redhead, and Prime emerged from hiding and headed for the bottom square. Redhead, moving quickly, was heard to shout, "Bishop playing bad. I going for he mother cunt now. Is execution time," as he dashed through the tunnel. On reaching the bottom square, he was confronted by Abdullah, holding in his hand a grenade from which the pin had been removed. Abdullah did not seem to know what to do with it, so Redhead told him to throw it over a nearby wall. It exploded with a roar.

Redhead set about ensuring that Bishop, Creft, Whiteman, Norris and Fitzroy Bain, and "Brat" Bullen (another friend of Bishop) were escorted up to the top square under heavy guard. Fitzroy Bain, in a state of shock and terror, had reached the top of the stairs when he met Stroude coming down. He called out to beg for his life, but Stroude replied that this was a decision for the Central Committee to take. Bain was hustled on up. Stroude was later to brag about this incident.

On the top square, Prime was busy organizing the reissue of arms to some of the PRA garrison. He found the armory locked. Hammering on the door he shouted, "Gabriel, Gabriel, open up." Gabriel, Hayling, Maitland, and the other man emerged onto the edge of the square, with Hayling and Maitland still armed. Prime was furious with Gabriel: "Gabriel, what the fuck you doing here? Mayers and Mason and Vincent Noel got killed on bottom square, and you up here? You up here?" Gabriel was then ordered to reissue weapons to the soldiers outside. He allowed them in to collect their own.

Coming out of the tunnel at that moment were Bishop, Creft, Whiteman, the two Bains, and Bullen, all with their hands on their heads, surrounded by Corporal Vincent Joseph and Privates Cosmos Richardson, Andy Mitchell, and Keith Noel. Arriving with them were

Redhead and Stroude, now armed, together with Abdullah. Redhead seemed to be giving the orders; it was he who got the prisoners lined up against the west wall. It was obvious to all that Bishop and those accompanying him were about to die. Maitland and Hayling, still just outside the armory, started to inch their way slowly toward some steps leading to the kitchen between the two buildings. If they could get out of sight, they might survive. They were out of luck. Redhead spotted them. "You Hayling, join the fucking line, and you Maitland, join the fucking line too. You also a bourgeois?" Turning to Mitchell, Redhead said, "Look, Pumphead has a Makarov. Take it off him." Mitchell, who stammered, said to Hayling, who still had a rifle as well as the pistol: "Drop the fu- fu- fucking gun." He then removed both Hayling's and Maitland's pistols, handing them to Gabriel. Like the others at the wall, with the exception of Jacqueline Creft, they were forced to remove their shirts. There were now seven men and one women, expecting to be shot at any moment. But it was not to happen—not yet.

‡   ‡   ‡

Enthusiastic as he was to get on with the killing, Redhead hesitated to take that responsibility on himself entirely. Although he was the officer directly responsible for the security of the army headquarters, he was outranked at that moment by Stroude, and he had not been present when Mayers received his orders. Mayers, the commander of the attack, was dying, and Abdullah was the next in line. Their orders had been to retake the fort and liquidate Bishop with his followers in the process. They were supposed to have been hunted down and killed in the assault so it could be announced they had died in the fighting—not so devastating to the public and the rest of the world as an execution.

Things had gone wrong: Mayers had been shot, the building in which Bishop was sheltering had not actually been assaulted by soldiers, and now the prime minister, ministers, and close associates had emerged unscathed. Vincent Noel, lying bleeding on the balcony, was the only battle casualty among the Bishop hierarchy. Stroude, Redhead, Abdullah, and Prime conferred. As Stroude had said minutes before to Fitzroy Bain, it was up to the Central Committee to decide the next move.

They left the prisoners against the wall. Joseph and Noel, overlooking the scene from the top of the tunnel wall, watched, with a PKM machine gun; so did Mitchell and Richardson, also with PKMs. The four officers left the top square. Stroude, Redhead, and Abdullah, and possibly Prime, were on their way to Fort Frederick.[1] The journey took only a few minutes.

Coard and the other Central Committee members were not pleased with Abdullah's report to Layne. Bishop was not dead; if he was to be killed now, the method used would be hard to conceal. Coard and ten other Central Committee members—Austin, Layne, James, Strachan, Cornwall, Ventour, McBarnette, Bartholomew, Ian St. Bernard, and Coard's wife, Phyllis—met to agree on a decision. Details of the hasty deliberations are still unknown, but the decision was unanimous: Bishop and the other seven were to be shot at once. Redhead was to organize the execution, and Abdullah was to command the firing party. It was almost 2:00 P.M. when they returned to Fort Rupert.

‡ ‡ ‡

The condemned prisoners had stood waiting for nearly three-quarters of an hour. All realized that short of a miracle, they were going to be shot. Nevertheless, there was no pleading, no obvious emotional breakdown, and no attempt, on the part of Bishop or the others, to talk their way out or make a break. They appeared resigned. The only sign of their inner turmoil and tension came from Bishop, the heavy smoker, who called out to Gabriel, "Gab, I want matches for a cigarette." Gabriel made to give him some but was abruptly stopped by Mitchell. As he pointed his machine gun at Gabriel, he said, "No fu-fucking light." Gabriel's response that this was the prime minister provoked Mitchell to shout, "No fu-fucking PM at this time." Bishop did not get his light.

A minute or so after 2:00 P.M., Redhead and Abdullah strode out of the tunnel onto the top square. Bishop, Creft, Whiteman, Norris and Fitzroy Bain, Bullen, Hayling, and Maitland still faced the dirty, white, 4-meter-high west wall. Slightly to the left, over their heads, some faded lettering read, "THE PRA THE PEOPLE IN UNIFORM," and farther right were the words "TOWARDS A HIGHER DISCIPLINE IN THE PRA." In front of the group stood a dilapidated basketball post with a net.

There was no more delay. Abdullah positioned his firing party (map 4). He himself, still with his M-3 submachine gun, was in the center of three firers. On his left stood Mitchell with his PKM, and to his right Richardson, also with a PKM. Both soldiers had long belts of ammunition hung over their shoulders. They were all standing opposite the west wall, some 20 meters from the prisoners. To their right, on top of the north wall, also part of the firing squad, was Joseph with a third PKM. Alongside him was Keith Noel. Several others are known to have been watching: Gabriel from the square itself, Redhead probably from just inside the tunnel, Stroude from the top of the

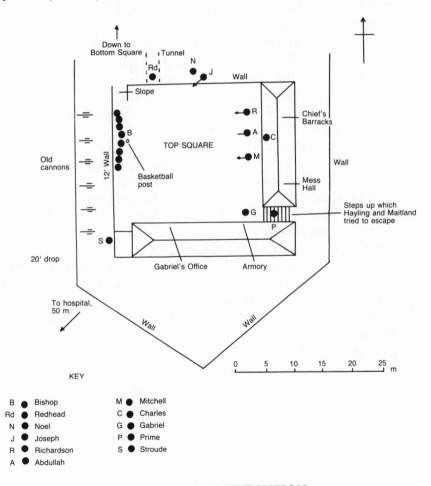

KEY

B	● Bishop	M	●	Mitchell
Rd	● Redhead	C	●	Charles
N	● Noel	G	●	Gabriel
J	● Joseph	P	●	Prime
R	● Richardson	S	●	Stroude
A	● Abdullah			

Map 4. BISHOP'S EXECUTION

west wall at the southwest end, Prime from the stairs at the southeast corner of the square, and Privates Walter Charles and Beverley Ann-Marie Charles from the first floor of the building behind the firing party.

Abdullah called out, "Comrades, turn round." The eight at the wall did so. Abdullah took out a piece of paper, saying: "This is an order from the Central Committee, that you shall be executed by fire. It is not my order, it is the Central Committee's." They were ordered to face the wall again. Jackie Creft half-turned to plead, "Wait, wait, hold on; I'm pregnant," just as Abdullah started to give his orders to fire. It was useless. The ever aggressive Mitchell replied: "No fu- fucking Comrade at this time."

Abdullah shouted out, "Prepare to fire." Weapons were cocked and raised; Joseph lay down behind his machine gun. "One, two, three, FIRE!" Bishop, in the center of the group, was hit a split second before the others, probably by the heavy bullets of Abdullah's M-3. Virtually simultaneously three machine guns opened up with long, continuous bursts. The firing went on and on, well after all the bodies had collapsed in a heap. Abdullah described it thus: "The bodies fell backward. Some fell down slow, and some fell down fast." Gabriel expanded: "Bodies tripe open. Fitzroy Bain tripe was out, Maurice Bishop back, belly, and neck was cut, Jacqueline Creft hand fly off. The bodies were lying there, virtually in bits and blood. Pieces of flesh of the bodies were also stuck on the wall."

After a minute or so Abdullah yelled, "Cease fire," and went forward to inspect the mangled remains for signs of life. Incredibly there was movement. Abdullah told Gabriel, "Look Gab there's a body over there not well dead; finish it off." He was pointing to Fitzroy Bain. Gabriel, fearful of refusing, fired one shot into his head.[2] Next Abdullah gave Gabriel instructions to issue blankets and get the corpses taken to the bottom square and loaded onto a truck. When Gabriel expressed great reluctance to handle the bodies, Abdullah snarled, "I gave you a fucking order Gabriel." Gabriel complied.

The deed that was to set in motion Urgent Fury was done. A white flare soaring up over the fort signaled the fact to the Central Committee.

‡   ‡   ‡

Fort Frederick, perched on top of a 750-foot-high ridge that dominated even Richmond Hill Prison, provided a grandstand view of the events to Coard and his Central Committee followers. They had all observed with mounting tension as the attack had gone in. Now, at 2:00 P.M., all eyes were watching for a flare. When it came, Austin shouted, "Mission accomplished," and on the upper level, the others joined in: "Long live the revolution. Long live the Central Committee." Later Redhead and Abdullah returned to report to Layne, followed by the APCs carrying the troops involved in the attack. Cletus St. Paul, who, although still under arrest, had been able to watch events, was later to ask Prime what had happened. He responded, with evident satisfaction, that Bishop had been killed on the orders of the Central Committee. Prime then passed his hand across his neck, saying, "We had to cut he fucking throat."[3]

Coard had won. Nevertheless, the difficulties confronting the new regime were enormous. There was feverish activity at Fort Frederick, which from that time on was to become the headquarters of the Revolutionary Military Council (RMC) and PRA. Suitable accommodation was scarce, so a large tent was erected to act as a command post or conference room. Telephone lines were out except for the water works telephone, so communications were a problem. The most critical immediate concern, however, was to ensure continuing control within Grenada. How could they carry on government and explain to the people the killing of their leader? There could be a massive revolution against the revolution; a civil war, with the PRA deployed against the masses, was not impossible.

Coard personally could not be seen as in control. He had to remain hidden at Fort Frederick, although this did not prevent his continuing as the decision maker. One of his first acts was to draw up the broadcast that must be made that evening. The people must be told that the army was in charge and that the RMC was formed. General Austin would head it because of his military rank, because of his popularity within the PRA, and because, until the last few days, he was well known as a long-standing Bishop supporter. Austin was the obvious choice for a figurehead. Coard and the other former Central Committee members who held military rank—Austin, Layne, James, Cornwall, Bartholomew, and St. Bernard—would continue to wield the power. This was the elite group, joined in their secret meetings by Strachan, Ventour, McBarnette, and Phyllis Coard, that would control Grenada until October 25. The junior officers of the RMC, like Nelson, were members on paper only and were never called to meetings. Kamau McBarnette was dispatched to Radio Free Grenada to ensure all was ready for the broadcast.

At about 5:30 that evening, after a long silence followed by some music, Radio Free Grenada started calling for retired nurses and Salvation Army personnel to report to the hospital "to assist with the care of patients." Free transport was to be made available for volunteers. The announcer went on to say that General Austin would address the nation at 8:30.

Austin was late. It was not until after nine that virtually the entire population heard his hesitant voice proclaiming the formation of the sixteen-man RMC. It was, he said, to govern the country, "until normalcy is restored." He gave his version of the events of that afternoon: "The Revolutionary Armed Forces were forced to storm the Fort, and in the process Maurice Bishop, Unison Whiteman, Vincent Noel, Norris Bain, Fitzroy Bain, and Jacqueline Creft were killed. . . . Maurice Bishop had declared his intentions to wipe out the entire leadership of the party, and the army. . . . The Revolution itself would have been wiped out." He went on to announce the imposition of a twenty-four-hour curfew for the next four days: "Let it be clearly understood that the Revolutionary Military Council will govern with absolute strictness. Anyone who seeks to demonstrate or disturb the peace will be shot. . . . Anyone violating this curfew will be shot on sight." He finished with the familiar phrases: "Long live the revolution, long live our people, long live Grenada. Forward ever, backward never." Grenada, its people stunned, was under martial law.

Up at Fort Frederick, Coard and his followers issued a host of instructions. The curfew that night was to be used to cloak the cleaning up of the mess made during the day. The bodies of Bishop and those killed with him must be disposed of, a responsibility given to the industrious Redhead, who detailed their executioner, Abdullah, for the task. The corpses littering Fort Rupert must be got rid of, and leading pro-Bishop Grenadians must be hunted down by PRA patrols. The goat pen was to be full. Alister Hughes and Cletus St. Paul were among those deposited in the pen that night. Some, like Einstein Louison and Sylvia Belmar, were lucky to avoid capture, although the net was spread wide. Even one man in agony from a bullet in the groin received on the bottom square was imprisoned.

The four men who had started the day in the goat pen were moved out at around 4:00 P.M. George Louison, Radix, Evans, and Munroe were taken to Fort Frederick. They thought they were finished. Indeed, had they been free to do so, they would undoubtedly have been with Bishop that day and ended up against the wall. Ironically their arrest had saved them. But at that moment they were again in deadly danger. St. Bernard went so far as to tell them they were going to be shot. They were kept in suspense until 10:00 P.M. when Abdullah appeared, not to form another firing party but to incarcerate them in a dark, wet tunnel at the top of the fort. There they remained for two days before being again sent to the goat pen, from which they escaped on the morning of October 27.

‡ ‡ ‡

The mess at Fort Rupert was appalling. There were bodies, bits of bodies, and blood everywhere; vehicles continued to burn. The fire service had been summoned and quickly extinguished the flames, only to be given the task of assisting the soldiers in washing away the pools of blood that lay all over the bottom and top squares. Hoses were put to use, together with a whole crate of disinfectant bottles. Major Keith Roberts had been arrogantly keeping dozens of relatives and friends away, near the St. James Hotel, by firing his AK into the air. When the people did not move, he instructed the senior fire officer, Inspector Williams, to turn the hoses on them. Williams ignored the order and left.

Meanwhile, Vincent Noel had been brought down from the balcony of the headquarters building to be placed, still alive, on the ground. He was seen by several people, including Nelson, who had returned from checking his men on the cordon. Noel was being given a drink from a soft drink bottle. Shortly afterward Abdullah noticed he was still moving and was about to shoot him in the head when Nelson pushed the gun away saying, "No." Noel did not survive much longer, however. He died of either shock and loss of blood or was finished off.

Immediately after the execution, Stroude confined the fort, ordering the guards to shoot any PRA attempting to leave. He then summoned a meeting for the garrison in the mess hall. He had some explaining to do. Redhead, Abdullah, Prime, and Gabriel, along with the soldiers, heard him say:

> The purpose of this meeting is to outline to you the incident you saw here this afternoon. Maurice Bishop was not true to the Revolution. He was a fucking traitor. That is why he had to be executed. Have no fear, be of good courage. The welfare programme will continue. The house repair programme will also continue, and tomorrow we shall select a committee called the Military Council that will run the country. We shall inform you.

It was not until late afternoon that Gabriel completed moving the bodies from the top square to the bottom one. In the process of this gruesome task, one soldier, a woman, fainted. The mangled remains, including those of Vincent Noel, were heaped onto the surviving Public Works Department truck under blankets. Austin then telephoned Redhead to confirm that under cover of darkness and the curfew, the bodies of Bishop and the others who had been executed were to be burned in a large pit, conveniently located behind the latrines at Camp Calivigny. The other dead civilians were to be disposed of by the undertaker, Eric La Qua, and others. All must be gone by morning. No proper identification or registration was permitted.

At around 11:00 P.M. that night, Austin arrived at Fort Rupert to check on progress. Gabriel met the black Honda on the bottom square and saluted as Austin descended. "Gabriel, where are the bodies?" he asked. Gabriel pointed, and Austin walked across, lifted a blanket and peered down. Turning to Gabriel, he said, "These fucking trouble makers were supposed to dead long." They then went to the top square, where Gabriel pointed out the site of the execution. Austin's comment was, "Maurice bring that about for himself because he was not true."

Some time after 1:30 the following morning, Gabriel was awakened in his office by a soldier telling him he was wanted on the bottom square. On arrival, Abdullah ordered him onto his jeep with some other soldiers; they were going on a mission. Of the yellow PWD truck there was no sign. Eventually the jeep stopped near Camp Calivigny in marshy ground. The truck with the bodies had bogged down. Abdullah and the soldiers were forced to transfer the remains to the jeep to get them to the pit. It was an unpleasant business. As Gabriel was later to say, "It was so stink." Having got the bodies to the hole, Gabriel and the others were sent back to Fort Rupert, leaving Abdullah to carrry out the actual burning.

The job was not completed until around midday on October 20; Abdullah worked alone and was short of wood and old tires, which he used to line the grave. The only known witness was a camp cook, Private Christopher Bowen, who described seeing the bodies, including those of Bishop, Whiteman, Creft, and both Bains, "frying as if you frying eggs in a frying pan."

5

The Revolutionary
Military Council

Long live martial law!
> — Lieutenant Cecil Prime on the establishment
> of the RMC, October 19, 1983

M ARTIAL law lasted six days, until October 26, when the hierarchy of the RMC scuttled into hiding on the second day of Urgent Fury.

Sixteen military officers of the PRAF made up the council. Headed by General Hudson Austin, a former prison warder, the membership consisted of the bulk of the regular PRA command. Joint vice-chairmen were Lieutenant Colonels Layne and James who, together with Majors Bartholomew, Cornwall, and St. Bernard, made up the former Central Committee military faction. Then came the key officer of the political department, Major Stroude; the security service, Major Roberts; and the operational staff officer of the army, Major Gahagan. The remaining seven—Captains Redhead and Hughie Romain, Lieutenants Prime, Rudolph Ogilvie, and Abdullah, and 2d Lieutenants Kenrick Fraser and Nelson—held senior executive or administrative posts in the PRA. Although officially on the council, this last group did not participate in formal meetings and thus played no part in policy decisions. Keeping well out of the limelight, as advisers, were Coard, Strachan, and Ventour.

The situation facing the council was daunting. To survive, they had to contend with several monumental problems. The first, and probably the most immediately pressing, was internal security. Most Grenadians had no love for the RMC, or Coard, who had just executed their heroic leader. Unless draconian measures were applied at once, before people recovered from the shocks of the last few days, it was quite possible the masses would turn on their oppressors. The answer was the curfew, enforced, so the council hoped, by the army.

To confine the entire population to their houses for twenty-four hours a day is certainly draconian, but to enforce it requires a large and dedicated security force. The RMC did not have sufficiently large a force, in terms of manpower or vehicles, to maintain patrols around the clock in all parts of the island. And whether the PRA was dedicated remained to be seen. Certainly the militia, with its high proportion of Bishop loyalists, could not be utilized. Although the curfew was a shoot-on-sight one, hundreds broke the curfew while furtively searching for food or water after dark throughout the island; none was shot.

Nevertheless, Grenadians were frightened and stunned by events. Since very few houses had refrigerators, perishable food must be bought daily, so at night people with hungry families would sneak out, listening for the sound of any approaching vehicle, to find a store that would slip some food to them through a back window. Eugene Pursoo, a Grenadian-American who spoke with many people later, has described how a group of men crept to the back entrance of a rum shop for some drinks and a chat. Within a few minutes, a jeep load of soldiers burst in with rifles raised. The military, who probably knew the men inside anyway, gave everybody five seconds to disappear. They disappeared.

Many Grenadians feared arrest more than the curfew. They fled into hiding in the woods or to a friend's house. Scores dreaded the arrival of a PRA patrol at their door, followed by the trip "up the hill." Typical was a taxi driver, who told Pursoo, "On the night they killed Bishop I saw an army jeep pull up at my gate. I suspected they came for me. I dove through the back door and made for the high woods. I spent five nights and five days in the woods—I knew nothing of any shoot to kill curfew."

Unless there is to be a total breakdown in every aspect of life, certain people must be exempt from curfews. But who? As the RMC soon discovered, if they wanted to keep the country running, the number of people to whom a pass must be given was vast. Virtually all government workers, those in state-controlled enterprises and hospitals, and those supplying power, water, and communications needed to be at their jobs. And as those responsible soon appreciated, the effort required to institute a curfew at short notice was daunting.

The strains of applying the curfew soon showed. What was announced as a four-day curfew was relaxed on the second day, Friday, from 10:00 A.M. to 2:00 P.M., to allow shopping. Pandemonium reigned at banks and food shops as hundreds of people clamored for cash or to make purchases, while soldiers on the streets of St. George's kept shouting out how much time was left before they would start shooting. On Monday, October 24, everybody, including the RMC, had had enough. The daytime curfew was lifted entirely.

‡   ‡   ‡

Stroude went to the Radio Free Grenada studios on October 22 to announce the RMC's plans for the immediate future, with emphasis on how the military would tackle the next crucial problem: imminent economic collapse. He confidently declared that a new, civilian cabinet would be appointed within ten to fourteen days with a broad-based composition, thus "ensuring that all social classes and interests in our country are represented." In all seriousness Stroude spoke of building up agriculture, manufacturing, and tourism. With the last, he stressed the need to complete the airport at Point Salines and build more hotels, restaurants, and other facilities. If anything had died with Bishop, it was tourism, and yet here was the RMC blithely announcing "that in order to ensure the most rapid development of the tourism industry, and also manufacturing, there is need to encourage much more positively the need of private investment, including both local and foreign investment."

Turning to foreign affairs, Stroude made it plain that the RMC was desperate to reduce the massive buildup of overseas resentment and horror that had erupted:

> Efforts would be made to immediately explain the real situation in Grenada to the many countries and organisations, as well as to our Caribbean neighbours, to counter the lies being told in the foreign press. Efforts made recently [referring to Bishop's visit in June to the United States] to better relations with the United States government would continue.

The final appeal was for national unity: "Let us now, in an atmosphere of calm, and of love for one another, unite as one people." All this within three days of massacring at least fifty Grenadians. Little wonder it fell on deaf ears, at home and abroad. If, in its first few days, the RMC was guilty of ignorance of its image, both within the country and without, it did not lack for industry. There was a frenzied attempt to deal with the difficulties confronting it on all sides. Nazim Burke, under the guidance of Coard, became the chairperson of a nine-man Economic Council working to an Emergency Economic Commission. All the councillors were also commissioners, given the overriding responsibility to keep Grenada functioning.

Economic Report No. 1 spelled out the tasks and priorities. Lists of work to be completed within three, seven, and ten days were highlighted. Under the topic of energy, for example, some thirty tasks were identified, including ascertaining existing stocks of fuel, monitoring consumption, rationing, locating countries willing to make further deliveries, making special arrangements for essential services, and working out a shutdown plan for power. With fuel and electricity supplies, top priority was given to military installations. After their needs had been satisfied, other recipients, in order of priority, would be cold storage facilities, essential communications, Radio Free Grenada, vital security areas such as lighting for food storage, key local production areas, the hospital, and St. George's Medical School.

With the announcement of sanctions by the Organisation of East Caribbean States (OECS) on October 22 and the Caribbean Community's (CARICOM) measures of economic pressure on October 23, Grenada's situation was critical. OECS governments cut all sea and air links until further notice. The implications of this move, coupled with a substantial dependence for overseas telecommunications on Trinidad and Cable and Wireless, were well understood by the Economic Commission. The tasks to be completed within three days included identifying all aircraft that could be seized by the state, "including doing what is necessary to put [the] Russian plane [aircraft] in full operation," and applying for money on Monday, October 24, in the usual way. Cash was likely to run out, and the OECS had specifically stated that the East Caribbean Central Bank would not make any new issues of currency.

Transport shortages were acute. As with food, fuel, and power, preference was given to the army, which was responsible for coordinating and commandeering as necessary. Cornwall issued a public notice on October 22 instructing all persons who had state-owned vehicles to deliver them to the RMC by noon. The notice gave three delivery points and guaranteed the drivers safe conduct during the curfew, together with a lift home after delivery. Cornwall signed off by stating, "Anyone who resist in any way or another this directive of the Revolutionary Military Council (RMC) will be dealth with in the strickest manner." Whatever other attributes the former PRG ambassador to Cuba had, spelling was not one of them.

‡   ‡   ‡

When Austin announced the shoot-on-sight curfew on the evening of October 19, it caught Dr. Geoffrey Bourne some 4 kilometers from his house. It was dark, and he was unable to telephone his wife because his phone was not working. With some apprehension, he decided to risk the drive. He arrived safely.

Dr. Bourne was the vice-chancellor of St. George's University School of Medicine, which had opened in early 1977, primarily to teach medicine to American students who had failed to obtain places at similar schools in the United States. It had been a great success. In 1983 some 600 Americans were studying medicine in Grenada. Bishop and the PRG had had a sort of love-hate relationship with the school. The PRG fully appreciated the material benefits it brought to Grenada —primarily in the form of foreign exchange, U.S. dollars. Direct annual payments included a general fee of U.S.$75,000, plus rent for the True Blue facility, U.S.$100,000 for upgrading work to the hospital, U.S.$300,000 in wages for local employees, together with, as Dr. Bourne put it to the U.S. House of Representatives' Foreign Affairs Subcommittee on the Eastern Caribbean, "colossal gas, electricity, telephone, and water bills." He estimated indirect payments of EC$60,000 for postage and EC$100,000 for air travel and that students spent U.S.$2.5 million locally each year. Grenada could not afford to lose the school.

The hate side of the relationship stemmed from the fact that the Marxist-Leninist regime felt uncomfortable, even embarrassed, being so financially dependent on the United States. The PRG officials who had to come, cap in hand, to ask the school to pay its general fee and True Blue rental early so that they could make a down payment to the British firm Plessey to start work at Salines Airport were acutely embarrassed.

Then there was the PRG's fixation with security or, more precisely, with their belief that the CIA had an agent within the school. In view of their generally unfriendly relationship with the U.S. government and President Reagan's anti-Grenada pronouncements, this suspicion was understandable. Dr. Bourne's insistence that the school harbored no CIA agents and that it was entirely nonpolitical was unconvincing. Roberts's security personnel kept a close but unrewarding watch on the school. In the light of later events, it is almost certain that Dr. Bourne was correct. At the time immediately preceding Urgent Fury, no CIA agent was in place at the school.

When Dr. Bourne opened the door of his house early on the morning of the day following Bishop's death, he was startled to see a man and a woman, both armed, from the security service. But they were not coming to make an arrest, only checking on whether the campuses at True Blue and Grand Anse had sufficient food and water to last a four-day curfew. Dr. Bourne told them that True Blue was short, and he was given a curfew pass authorizing him to travel anywhere on the island but with a police escort. Later the same day, more water was made available, although it was delivered by a fire truck and proved undrinkable.[1]

Bourne's next visitor was a PRA officer who told him that Austin wanted to meet him at 11:00 A.M. at a place designated by himself. Bourne suggested his own home. Austin arrived

> in a small red car with a driver and with a soldier with what appeared to be an AK-47 sitting in the back. The soldier patrolled around the house while General Austin was talking with me. General Austin himself was dressed in uniform and was carrying a pistol. When he came into the house he threw himself onto a chair, spreading his arms and legs, and looked completely exhausted. He looked like a man completely overwhelmed by what he had done and the world-wide reaction it had caused, and that he was looking for help.

The RMC chairman proceeded to give Bourne a highly inaccurate account of Bishop's killing, ending up by disclosing how sorry he was about Maurice's death as they had been close friends since their school-days; now even his own daughter refused to speak to him. Turning to the current situation, Austin expressed his concern that he had had no contact from the United States or any other Caribbean countries. Dr. Bourne urged him to admit the press and to allow American diplomats in for talks. Austin insisted that Pearls Airport was not closed, merely that Leeward Island Air Transport had stopped flights. Finally Austin queried the position of the students. He wanted to know their reactions to recent events and whether many would want to leave. He gave his personal assurance that the students were in no danger, leaving Bourne with his home telephone number in case of difficulties.

There is no doubt that, from the start, the RMC made the decision not to harm U.S. students. Purely on the grounds of self-interest, they had determined that this would be the best way to avoid U.S. intervention in Grenada. The council was well aware of U.S. hostility and military power and their own inadequate defenses. Above all they wanted to avoid antagonizing the United States further, to avoid a military confrontation they could never win. They deduced, quite rightly, that U.S. citizens in danger would be an overriding factor with President Reagan when he decided appropriate action. The correctness of their thinking was later reinforced by Havana, which strongly urged the RMC to leave the students alone and not to interfere with any who were evacuated or wished to leave.

This policy might have worked. It failed because President Reagan had other pressing reasons for intervening, besides the safety of the students. Also he could not know whether a regime such as the RMC would not suddenly change its mind. Even the remotest possibility of a hostage situation caused understandable panic in the Pentagon and at the White House.

‡ ‡ ‡

On October 20 the Palace of the Revolution in Havana issued a decree proclaiming the official three days of mourning to be observed in Cuba for Maurice Bishop. Signed by Fidel Castro as president of the Council of State, it instructed all ministers of the armed forces and foreign affairs to ensure that national flags flew at half-mast on public buildings. It was intended to underline to the RMC Cuban abhorrence with what had happened in Grenada.

The RMC had few friends. Instinctively the council turned to Cuba for support, but it was rebuffed. Castro, and Cubans generally, had been horrified by the execution of Bishop within eleven days of his recent visit. Bishop and Castro had been personal friends. Cuba had supplied numerous specialists, technicians, and workers for the Salines Airport project and acted as the staging point for all shipments of arms and supplies from the Soviet Union. Grenadian diplomats and officials had signed treaties with the Soviets at Havana. Cuba had nurtured the Grenadian revolution, along with its leader.

Castro had been caught by surprise: surprised at the depth of the divisions within the NJM, surprised that Bishop had not mentioned these problems to him personally, surprised at the speed at which events unfolded and reached a bloody climax in a matter of days. He was far from pleased with the performance of his ambassador in St. George's. Had Rizo been doing his job properly, the Cuban president might not have been caught so obviously off balance. Rizo was to be severely disciplined for his failure later.

Nevertheless, Havana stuck to the principle of not getting involved in the internal political affairs of Grenada. On October 15, Castro had sent a letter expressing "deep concern over the division that had emerged and that in Cuba itself, where Bishop enjoyed high esteem, it would not be easy to explain events." But that letter was prompted by arrest, not execution. The actual killing of Bishop was not anticipated in Havana; when it happened, it caused shock and profound consternation. On October 20, Castro personally wrote to the RMC:

> No doctrine, principle, or position proclaimed as revolutionary, nor any internal division can justify such brutal procedures as the physical elimination of Bishop and the prominent group of honest and worthy leaders who died yesterday.
>
> The death of Bishop and his comrades must be clarified; and had they been executed in cold blood, those responsible for it deserve exemplary punishment. Imperialism [the USA in particular] will now try to profit from this tragedy. . . . After yesterday's tragic outcome, we shall closely follow the course of events; we shall strictly abide by the principle of non-interference in the internal affairs of Grenada and shall, above all, take into account the interest of the Grenadian people concerning economic and technical cooperation, where it is possible in the new situation, but our political relations with the new Grenadian leadership must be subjected to a serious and profound analysis.

The RMC was far from happy with this reaction. Even the penultimate sentence, which seemed at first to offer a ray of hope—"however, if the Grenadian revolutionary process is preserved, we shall do our best to assist"—in reality referred to continuing economic help if the RMC survived, not assistance in ensuring its survival.

Meanwhile the regular Cuban air link was cancelled, and Cuban workers at the Salines site stopped work to protest the detention of Bob Evans. Vehicles and equipment were parked on the runway, and the labor force was confined to its nearby camp. Although Cuba would do its utmost diplomatically to prevent outside, especially U.S., intervention, that was all.

Coard, rather than Bishop, had the backing of the Soviets. Although perhaps an oversimplification, it is not far from the truth to say Bishop looked to Castro and Cuba for support and revolutionary guidance, while Coard favored direct Soviet alignment. The killing of Bishop did not provoke the same outraged response from Moscow as it did from Havana. Tass stated:

> A tense situation has formed in the country following sharp differences and a split in the leadership of the New Jewel Movement.
>
> An armed clash took place which claimed the lives of the Prime Minister and several ministers. The Revolutionary Military Council assumed full power in the country. It stated its determination to uphold the cause of the revolution.

Coard had been a frequent and favored visitor to the Soviet Union. It was he who had led the PRG's first official visit in 1980, and, unlike Bishop, he returned every year thereafter. During early 1983 he was invited with his family for a long vacation on the Black Sea. The Soviets preferred Coard's hard Leninist style and were suspicious of Bishop's personal popularity. In May 1982 Daniel Ortega, the Nicaraguan leader, visited Moscow and met with Brezhnev, Tikhonov, Gromyko, Chernenko, and Ponomarev; two months later, Bishop was only able to see Tikhonov and Ponomarev, although he did meet Gromyko at the Kremlin in April 1983. But in June that year, the Soviets took a dim view of Bishop's visit to the United States to try to improve relations. They were displeased that this gesture had been made without prior consultation with Moscow. This sort of initiative was not appreciated; it was typical of Bishop's behavior, not Coard's.

While the Soviets intended, with the huge arms shipments due in the post-1983 years, the proposed influx of more advisers and the use of the powerful radio transmitter at Beausejour to strengthen their grip on Grenada, there is no direct evidence that they were part of the plot to overthrow Bishop. They certainly felt happier dealing with a man like Coard; they certainly had masterminded a similar coup in Afghanistan; they certainly knew what was happening long before Havana did (with a senior military intelligence officer as ambassador, this is not surprising); and they certainly did not condemn Bishop's death the way others did. They reserved their condemnation for U.S. imperialism after Urgent Fury was launched, with no public acknowledgment that without Coard's gunning down of Bishop, there would have been no intervention.

The RMC could expect no physical support from Moscow. Grenada was a tiny island thousands of miles from the Soviet sphere of influence and comparatively unimportant. The probable loss of a potentially useful Caribbean satellite was deplorable, but Moscow's means of preventing it happening were nonexistent.

‡   ‡   ‡

On October 16, Major Mark Adkin, the staff officer of operations and training of the Barbados Defence Force, received a summons to report to the chief of staff's office. On arrival Colonel Rudyard Lewis, looking rather pleased, put in motion the military planning that, ten days later, was to put Caribbean troops into Grenada. Lewis instructed Adkin to put together an outline plan to rescue Bishop from house arrest. Adkin was told to assess what troops and transport would be required and to allocate tasks. He was not to concern himself with where they were coming from, merely to define the requirement, but both officers understood that any airlift would be provided by U.S. planes or helicopters.

Adkin immediately obtained one of the few Grenada maps and consulted the Regional Security System intelligence officer, Lieutenant Commander Peter Tomlin, who had a lot of information on Grenada and the NJM. He knew the islands well and had met Bishop several times, including on March 14, 1979, the day following Bishop's coup. Tomlin had skippered a Barbados Coast Guard vessel into St. George's harbor with a CIA man and a Canadian representative on board to assess the situation, with particular reference to any foreign nationals wanting to leave.

The information available to these two officers was supplemented by the detailed knowledge of the island, and its personalities, of Major Mike Hartland. Hartland, a former British regular officer, was then serving with the Barbados Defence Force but had spent eleven years in Grenada, 1968–1979, as the manager of Point Salines estate. He had lived on the hills overlooking the ground on which the new runway was being constructed.

Within a few hours, a draft plan for Bishop's rescue was completed. It assumed a hostile reception and was based on a surprise coup de main operation. The first phase would occur during darkness, with the troops arriving by helicopter. Key targets were Bishop's house, the governor-general's residence, Pearls and Salines airfields, the radio station, and a series of blocking or ambush positions to the north and south of St. George's. Initially it was thought two battalions would be sufficient, with a third being flown in later on D day. No major PRA military installations or headquarters were to be attacked. The object was to get into a number of suitable strategic positions from which to block PRA troop movement when they realized what was happening. The onus for initiating attacks would be put on the PRA or Cubans.

Adkin gave the plan to Lewis, who agreed with the concept and took it to the prime minister, Tom Adams. It was this plan that was under discussion by the Barbados cabinet on the morning of October 19 when Bishop was rescued by the people. The idea of a rescue mission to release Bishop had come from the U.S. embassy in Bridgetown, on October 15, to a senior official in the Barbados Defence and Security Division of the prime minister's office. It never got further than a first draft, and no decisions were taken as to the exact composition of the force. Nevertheless, the military headquarters in Barbados continued to press ahead with updating information on the island.

Just two days before the RMC took over, a young Barbadian man and his girlfriend were undergoing a lengthy questioning by the immigration officials at Pearls Airport as to why they wanted to visit Grenada. They were on vacation, having just arrived from St. Vincent, as their tickets showed. The young man said he was an accounts clerk who had been to the island several times before. It was probably his knowledge of Grenada that finally persuaded the immigration officer to let the couple through.

Their cover secure, 2d Lieutenant Alvin Quintyne and Lance Corporal Marita Browne of the Barbados Defence Force, who had volunteered to infiltrate covertly into the island to report on the situation to Colonel Lewis back in Barbados, traveled by taxi to the Skyline Guest House south of St. George's. They noted no AA guns or armed PRA at Pearls.

As they wandered around the streets of the town later that day, they found people reluctant to talk, particularly to strangers, and they were surprised at the number of schoolchildren about. They could not get near Fort Rupert without arousing suspicion, since no other civilians were going that way. They started to walk south toward Point Salines to look at the new airport. After a while a truck drew up, and the Cuban driver offered them a lift. He was friendly but had an AK-47 rifle in the cab. They were taken as far as the area of the Cuban mission headquarters north of Salines. They were unable to reach the airport but noticed numerous military vehicles at Frequente.

That night they became concerned whey they discovered a man peering through the door of their room. Quintyne decided they should leave the next day. They had some anxious moments when the immigration officer queried their cutting short their vacation. They were lucky to get out on October 18; had they delayed one more day, it might have been a different story. Later Quintyne was awarded the Barbados Service Star and Browne the Barbados Service Medal for their daring.

On the afternoon following Bishop's murder, a small Cessna 402 took off from Grantley Adams International Airport in Barbados and headed toward Grenada. On board the aircraft, which belonged to the Barbados Defence Force, were Tomlin and Major Robin Keaney, a contract officer who had recently retired from the Royal Air Force. They were armed with nothing more offensive than binoculars. Their mission was to have as close a look as possible at the island, particularly the PRA camp at Calivigny.

In less than an hour, they were flying down the east coast at 2,000 feet, about a mile from the shore. They peered through the starboard windows and found Pearls Airport quiet, with no activity, but an AN-26 aircraft was parked on the apron in front of the terminal. The Cessna continued steadily down the coastline, banking to the right, still over the sea, as it turned toward Calivigny. The south coast presented a beautiful sight, with numerous tiny bays and inlets, all washed by creaming white surf. The island looked peaceful and idyllic as they flew south of Westerhall Point, with its red- and white-roofed bungalows of the expatriate exiles who had retired to the sun. The camp at Calivigny was unmistakable with its neat lines of barrack huts in the center of an otherwise deserted peninsula. Although occupied, there appeared to be little of significance happening.

As they flew south of the new airport under construction at Salines, they noticed that work had stopped and that the runway was obstructed with vehicles and yellow fuel tankers parked across it. Turning north, they continued past the magnificent mile-long white sand beach of Grand Anse. Then came St. George's, with its harbor guarded on the south by the huge white building of Butler House and to the north by Fort Rupert. They saw nothing of military importance except that a Cuban ship, the *Vietnam Heroica,* was anchored in the harbor. The Cessna flew up the west coast before returning home after circling the island.

While these two officers were airborne, Commander Roger Porteous, who was on secondment from the Royal Navy to the Barbados Coast Guard and the Regional Security System, was compiling a comprehensive report on all the beaches and bays around Grenada. The object of his study was to select areas that might be suitable for landings. Porteous recommended Grand Anse and Grand Mal bays on the west coast as being ideal, free from reefs or heavy surf. To the south, Prickly Bay and several of the tiny coves would be suitable for limited small boat operations, but the whole east coast was decidedly unsuitable. The reefs were numerous and the coastline exposed to heavy seas and wind.

When Bishop was killed, the possibility of some sort of military option was already under consideration by the planners in the Regional Security System and Barbados Defence Force. Whether it ever got beyond a paper exercise depended on many factors, one of which was the reaction to the situation of the other Caribbean countries.

‡   ‡   ‡

Late on the afternoon of Friday, October 21, anybody approaching the Dover Convention Centre on the south coast of Barbados was subjected to strict security screening. As ministers from other Caribbean countries arrived, several driven by Barbadian soldiers, there was no formal welcome, no fluttering flags or guard of honor. Police and troops guarded all entrances, and a few hundred meters offshore, a Coast Guard vessel, the *George Fergusson,* patrolled slowly.

The emergency meeting of the OECS had been convened after thirty-six hours of frantic calls and messages between Caribbean leaders. Prime Minister John Compton of St. Lucia was the first to react to events in St. George's. He telephoned Tom Adams early on Thursday, October 20, to express his views forcefully. He proposed nothing less than multinational intervention to restore law and order. He felt that all Caribbean nations must be invited to participate, and, once they agreed, assistance should be sought from outside the region. The Barbados cabinet later met to endorse this course of action in principle.

Compton undertook to arrange a meeting of Caribbean heads of government. He contacted Prime Minister George Chambers of Trinidad and Tobago, chairman of CARICOM, to ask him to call an urgent meeting in Barbados. Chambers agreed to the need but not the venue, preferring Trinidad. There followed some confusion as to the location of the meeting, which was finally settled as Trinidad, on Saturday.

Meanwhile OECS leaders, who had to fly to Trinidad via Barbados anyway, decided to meet there the day before.

The situation was complicated by the composition of OECS and CARICOM. The former was a small grouping of seven islands: Antigua and Barbuda, Dominica, St. Kitts–Nevis, St. Lucia, Montserrat (still a British dependency), St. Vincent, and Grenada. Barbados and Jamaica did not belong. The chairperson was Eugenia Charles, prime minister of Dominica. CARICOM was a far larger organization. It had thirteen members: the OECS countries, plus the Bahamas, Barbados, Belize (another British dependency), Guyana, Jamaica, and Trinidad and Tobago.

The likelihood of these nations' reaching a unanimous decision on effective action in so critical a crisis was remote. A major stumbling block was that both organizations required a consensus on all important matters; the treaties under which both the OECS and CARICOM were established did not permit action on a majority vote. Another complication was Grenada's membership; it would not be present and, in any case, would not be likely to approve action against itself. These were legal problems that could not be removed at short notice. But they could be ignored.

Within CARICOM, at least one country, Guyana, could be expected to oppose any effective moves against Grenada on principle. Although not a communist country, Guyana had for years encouraged the Grenadian revolution. It had provided practical assistance for the 1979 coup and army training teams for the PRA. If military action was to be proposed, more countries would be certain to opt out. Even ignoring Grenadian membership, even assuming the United Kingdom or the United States would provide the military muscle to intervene, total agreement was an impossibility.

Adams, who had been contemplating military action for several days, fully understood that he would never get all CARICOM nations behind him. He also faced the problem that neither Barbados nor Jamaica, the hawks among the CARICOM doves that had some military forces, belonged to the OECS.

With OECS assistance, Adams was able to circumvent these difficulties. He would ignore CARICOM and work with the OECS and Jamaica. The OECS agreed to meet in Barbados on the evening of October 21, the day before CARICOM.

Knowing that both the United Kingdom and United States would require a formal request for assistance from a recognized international organization, and indeed from Grenada itself if possible, Adams conceived a plan. It envisaged OECS agreeing to intervene, then requesting assistance from Barbados and Jamaica, and then deputing Barbados to invite the United Kingdom and the United States to participate. The Saturday CARICOM meeting in Trinidad would not be allowed to effect the plan; indeed Adams excused himself from attending, sending his attorney general instead.

The question of obtaining a plea for help from Grenada posed real problems. The RMC was not recognized by anybody else as a government so the only constitutional authority remaining on the island was the governor-general, Sir Paul Scoon. If he could be persuaded to request intervention, that should weigh heavily with the United Kingdom and the United States.

On Thursday, while Compton and Chambers were trying to put together the CARICOM summit, Adams held a noon meeting in Barbados with the U.S. ambassador, Milan Bish. Forcefully and eloquently he argued the case for military action, even hoping the PRA would resist so they could be swept away, thus clearing the ground for a fresh democratic start in Grenada. He thought there was a chance the

Cubans on the island would not fight. Bish, who had already alerted the State Department to the possibility of some sort of military option, stressed that U.S. intervention would largely depend on unequivocal written requests to do so from Caribbean nations.

The next day, before the OECS ministers assembled at Dover Convention Centre, Adams set to work. First he told the Trinidian high commissioner that he could not attend the CARICOM meeting because a military solution was being considered, and he was needed in Barbados. This information was passed in strict confidence. At 12:30 P.M. Adams saw Giles Bullard, the British high commissioner, telling him the same thing and that the United Kingdom would be asked to participate. Next he went to the U.S. ambassador, who again agreed to convey the message to the president while awaiting a formal request. At 5:00 P.M. Adams discussed the situation with the Canadian high commissioner, although Canadian participation was never contemplated.

Meanwhile at Dover, the OECS had agreed to invoke Article 8 of their Treaty of Association. The text, not completed until two days later, read, "The Authority proposes therefore to take action for collective defense and preservation of peace and security against external aggression by requesting assistance from friendly countries to provide transport, logistic support, and additional military personnel to assist the efforts of the OECS to stabilize this most grave situation within the Eastern Caribbean."

Adams was called to the meeting to be given his invitation to join the operation. Later the same evening he spoke with the Jamaican prime minister, Edward Seaga, who also accepted his invitation to participate. Adams, Seaga, and Eugenia Charles presented the OECS decision to Bish on Friday night. On that night in the United States, the chairman of the Joint Chiefs of Staff instructed Atlantic Command to include plans for a military option to neutralize the PRA.

On Saturday the CARICOM meeting started late; delegates had to await the arrival of President Forbes Burnham of Guyana. At 8:30 P.M. discussions began. Little was achieved, as expected, and the meeting dragged on into the small hours of Sunday morning. It recommenced later the same day. Eventually, with the exception of Guyana, it was agreed to expel Grenada from CARICOM and impose economic sanctions. The military option was opposed by the Bahamas, Belize, Guyana, and Trinidad.

Before boarding his aircraft to return home, Burnham telephoned Havana to inform the Cubans about the OECS military planning. Later Sunday, Radio Free Grenada announced that invasion was imminent.

The safety of foreign nationals in Grenada was of great concern to the U.S., British, and Canadian governments. On Saturday Ken Kurze and Linda Flohr, from the U.S. embassy, together with David Montgomery, the deputy British high commissioner in Barbados, flew by charter flight to Pearls to ascertain the number of their citizens wishing to leave and to discuss methods of evacuation with RMC officials. Montgomery had the additional task of visiting Sir Paul Scoon. Adams was to claim that it was during this visit that Sir Paul Scoon verbally requested outside military assistance to restore law and order. If this was correct, then it was good news for the hawks but not quite good enough. Such a request must be in writing. The State Department obliged by drawing up a draft of the sort of letter it would like to receive and sent it to Barbados, unsigned and undated. Copies of this letter were carried into Grenada on October 25 by Brigadier Lewis (he was promoted for the operation), Colonel Ken Barnes of the Jamaica Defence Force, the Caribbean forces commander, and the Jamaican company commander. On October 26 Lewis was able to give his copy to Sir Paul to sign, which he did, at Point Salines. The letter was backdated to October 24.

Invasion plans were going ahead in Barbados. On Saturday Lewis had told the other participating islands to send their contingents of police or soldiers to Barbados the next day, although nothing could actually happen until the United States gave the final order to proceed. On Sunday, President Reagan sent a special envoy, Francis McNeil, and Major General George Crist, U.S. Marine Corps, to Barbados. In his briefcase, McNeil had the State Department's drafts of Scoon's and the OECS's requests for intervention.[2] That afternoon they were briefed on the military situation by Adkin and Tomlin. They were given all the information on Grenada available to the Caribbean planners, but Crist remained silent on U.S. intentions. He was not able to confirm that the operation would go ahead.

That evening McNeil, Crist, Bish, and Charles Gillespie met with Adams, Seaga, and Charles in the Barbados cabinet room. There was a touch of farce in the proceedings. The United States wanted a formal written request from the OECS to intervene; the Caribbean leaders did not want to send it until they knew for certain Reagan would agree. The Americans could not reveal that a Sea, Air, and Land (SEAL) team was already winging its way to Grenada or even confirm that Urgent Fury was on. The meeting devoted most of its time to finalizing the draft of letters requesting assistance for an operation that had already started. In the end both the OECS letter, to which Eugenia Charles signed a cover note, and the one supposedly coming from the governor-general were agreed.

It was almost twenty-four hours later, at about 7:00 P.M. on Monday, that Bish was allowed to tell Adams that Urgent Fury was being implemented. Simultaneously Reagan cabled Prime Minister Margaret Thatcher confirming the military intervention.

‡ ‡ ‡

In Grenada the RMC, whose suspicions of impending attack were confirmed on October 23 beyond any doubt, redoubled their efforts to prevent an event they knew they could never survive. They were shocked at Cuba's refusal to come to their assistance and began to understand that Coard was a liability to the regime. Most people detested him; Havana had rejected his appeals for help; and the outside world regarded him as a dedicated Marxist in the Soviet camp. Within two days of Bishop's death, Coard and his wife withdrew completely from events in Grenada. It was rumored that they left Fort Frederick for a house on the outskirts of St. George's. Certainly Cornwall, who became the chief negotiator and spokesman for the RMC, told Montgomery that he had no idea of Coard's whereabouts. From then until the Coards were captured by the U.S. Marines, they were never seen or mentioned.

The RMC leaders devoted considerable effort to trying to convince everybody that foreign nationals, particularly the U.S. students, were in no danger. They agreed to meet diplomats to discuss how many wanted to leave and how they could do so. They were anxious that Grenada should appear to be calm and functioning normally. On Monday, the daytime curfew was to be lifted, and shops, businesses, and offices were to open again.

When Kurze, Flohr, and Montgomery arrived on Saturday, they were met by Cornwall and allowed access to their citizens. A meeting was arranged at the Ross Point Inn just south of St. George's at 11:00 A.M., which was attended by the British and U.S. officials, Cornwall and, at the RMC's request, Dr. Bourne. Cornwall repeatedly pledged that the students and foreigners were not in danger and that transport would be authorized to evacuate those wishing to leave. Difficulties arose as to the means. Cornwall stressed that Pearls would be open to civilian charter aircraft, but the U.S. diplomats argued that because the runway would take only small planes carrying fewer than fifty people, the evacuation would take too long, particularly in view of the distance over poor roads from St. George's. Also they felt that maintaining security in such an operation would be impossible. Kurze suggested instead evacuation by a U.S. warship. Cornwall refused to consider this, which would look like an invasion, but he did agree that a large cruise liner might be an alternative.

As far as the British were concerned, Montgomery estimated that between thirty and forty citizens, mostly tourists, wanted to leave immediately. The U.S. officials were talking about getting all 600 or so students out, although at that stage, Dr. Bourne insisted that only sixty or seventy wished to go. Bourne visited both campuses to keep the students informed during this period. It was not until Sunday, when invasion rumors circulated and then Radio Free Grenada started announcing imminent attack, that alarm for their own safety became widespread among the students. After this the majority wanted to leave.

On the next day, Sunday, a chartered aircraft carrying U.S. envoys James Budeit and Gary Chafin arrived at Pearls on their second attempt at landing. An internal communications foul-up had caused the airport authorities to refuse landing permission on their first attempt, and Dr. Bourne had been asked to untangle the mix-up. Budeit and Chafin had arrived to relieve Kurze, whose mother had died, and their aircraft would take him and Montgomery back to Barbados. They were destined to remain on the island until after the invasion.

While Bourne felt the students should stay and was inclined to accept Austin's assurances of safety, the U.S. officials urged them to leave. Budeit met with them on Sunday night to advise evacuation but later agreed that even then many had not made up their minds. On Monday afternoon Budeit visited the homes of some married students who lived in cottages near the radio station and warned them of the risk of a counter-coup. He admitted that he and his colleague "scared the hell out of those people." Later when he saw some of the same wives again at the campus, now crying, he said, "I stayed the hell away from them. I had done my bit, and gotten them out of there."

Both Budeit and Chafin agreed that Cornwall was in a friendly and conciliatory mood on Sunday. Chafin even recalled Cornwall's asking for their advice on which Grenadians should be appointed to their new civilian government—a genuine request or the ploy of desperate men? Evacuation proposals were still being discussed up to the evening of October 24. Even at this late stage Budeit was able to telephone his embassy in Barbados.

From Sunday onward the RMC realized that little short of a miracle would prevent an invasion. Nevertheless, they continued to try to forestall it. That evening they sent out two telexes. One went to the U.S. embassy in Barbados appealing to the United States not to attack. It arrived but was ignored. The second, with a copy of the first, was dispatched to the British Foreign and Commonwealth Office in London. It contained an urgent request for the United Kingdom to take action to prevent military intervention. This telex did not arrive at its intended destination. Because Grenada was using an old telex number, the message ended up on Sunday night on the telex machine of Scanplast, a West End plastic bag firm. Scanplast officials found it on Monday and telephoned the Foreign and Commonwealth Office. They were told that the telexes had probably already been received and to put them in an envelope and send them across. When Scanplast asked to whom they should be given, they were told to leave them at the door. Scanplast put the telephone down in disgust and posted them that afternoon.

Back in Grenada Austin tried again. On Monday afternoon another telex was fired off, urging the British government to raise the question of invasion in the United Nations. On Tuesday, the day of the attack, Scanplast discovered this message awaiting them—and made another telephone call. This time, as Scanplast tried to dictate the text, the woman at the Foreign and Commonwealth Office desk complained that she could not take shorthand and that somebody would call them back. By the time they did Urgent Fury was under way.

‡   ‡   ‡

At around 5:30 A.M. on October 25, 1983, listeners to Radio Free Grenada heard a male and female hysterically announcing the assault.

FEMALE VOICE. . . . You should report to your militia bases immediately. . . . Why? . . . Because we are under attack. . . .

MALE VOICE. . . . Defend our homeland! We shall win! We shall beat them back! We shall bury them in the sea! Them have to get a beating!

FEMALE VOICE. . . . At 5:30 this morning, foreign troops began landing in our country! Our armed forces are engaging them in fierce battle. . . . All doctors, nurses, medics, report to the hospital immediately.

MALE VOICE. . . . We shall beat them back. . . . Militia come out now! Together with the People's Revolutionary Army, we will save our country. . . .

FEMALE VOICE. . . . The Revolutionary Military Council is calling on all friendly countries to condemn this act of aggression, and immediately come to Grenada's aid.

Nobody came.

6

Reagan Resolves

Well, if we've got to go there, we might as well do all that needs to be done.

— President Reagan, in a telephone conversation with George Bush, October 22

"GOD bless America"; "Thank you USA for rescuing us"; "Darling, if it wasn't for the Almighty and Mr. Reagan we would not be here." These words, used by Grenadians to express their feelings to U.S. forces after the successful completion of Urgent Fury, were the president's reward for making a momentous political decision. Young American troops had been greeted as their grandfathers had been when they liberated Europe almost forty years before. Some 85 percent of Grenadians welcomed the intervention not as an invasion but as a rescue mission. They were adamant that they had been saved from a fearful fate.

Flag waving, embracing, kissing, crying, offering cold drinks were the ways hundreds of people expressed their gratitude. Coupled with scenes of U.S. students kissing American soil on their arrival back home, they were enough to convince all but the most hardhearted that President Reagan had made the right decision—at least, with those most personally affected by it.

Invasion, forceful extraction, predawn vertical insertion, nonpermissive evacuation, intervention, and *rescue* are all words that have been used to describe Urgent Fury; all in their way are correct depending on the viewpoint of the user. Stanley Arthur, a former British high commissioner in Barbados, summed up the results of Urgent Fury in a paper to the Institute for the Study of Conflict:

The joint US–Caribbean intervention in Grenada removed, not the People's Revolutionary Government of Maurice Bishop, which, although it had not strict constitutional validity, was at least initially popular, and was internationally recognised, but a totally unrepresentative and highly unpopular armed faction, which had no claims to legitimacy, and could only be described as having hijacked the island in the wake of Bishop's murder. The temporary occupation of Grenada restored the right of the people to choose their own government, and at the same time removed what was seen as a major threat to the stability of the region.

Urgent Fury was a military operation, although the decision to mount it was political. Reagan, as president and commander in chief of the armed forces, was the man who had to take the ultimate responsibility. Because of the need for speed and secrecy, he was unable to consult with Congress before committing the United States to armed conflict, albeit against a tiny adversary. He acted on his own, using the authority granted to a president under the War Powers Resolution of 1973, which allows military action in a crisis without congressional approval for up to ninety days.

At the end of one of the worst weekends of his presidency, during which he had slept little, been involved personally in a hostage-taking incident, received the shocking news of hundreds of marines blown to pieces in Beirut, Reagan finally signed the National Security Decision Directive (NSDD) for Urgent Fury on the evening of Sunday, October 23. He had scanned the papers, listened as Robert McFarlane, his national security adviser, briefed him on the latest information before picking up his pen. He signed with a single word: "Go."

Now it was up to the military. Although the final signature had not been obtained until less than thirty-six hours before the main assault was to go in, preparations had been under way for four days. Up until that moment, indeed for another twenty-four hours, it was still possible for the president to abort the entire operation—to turn back ships and aircraft already on their way. Reagan did not do that. Neither did he interfere with the military side of the operation.

Reagan had ordered an invasion of a foreign country, a country that was not the object of external attack. He intended, with token assistance, to occupy that country with U.S. forces temporarily and to crush any opposition. He was well aware of the international furor that would result, with the probability of almost worldwide condemnation, both inside and outside the United Nations. He did it in the knowledge that Britain, which had constitutional and Commonwealth links with Grenada, was strongly opposed. He did it knowing that his action would be likened by many to the Soviet invasion of Afghanistan in 1979. He did it without the support of Congress or, more important, the American people; they would learn about it after the event. He did it realizing that he was flying in the face of international law, which universally forbids interference in the internal affairs of nations. He launched the largest U.S. military operation since Vietnam in circumstances that could end his presidency and jeopardize U.S. international relations for years to come. It was a decision of enormous import and of enormous risk, not from a military point of view—the United States could never actually lose the shooting war— but from the political consequences.

What convinced the president that it was the right decision?

‡   ‡   ‡

With Bishop's execution, a fleeting opportunity presented itself to the United States to act dramatically in the Caribbean. The chance would exist for a few days, a week at most, before events and world opinion made intervention impossible. The circumstances of Grenada in October 1983 were unique. The opportunity for inflicting military defeat on a rigid Marxist dictatorship, establishing democratic government, and getting away with it virtually unscathed are unlikely to be repeated. Reagan grabbed the chance. The closest precedent for the United States was in 1965 when President Johnson sent troops into the Dominican Republic to restore order. They went ostensibly to protect U.S. citizens but also to prevent a communist takeover. As was to happen in Grenada, they stayed until a new government was installed.

The text of the president's announcement of the landings in Grenada gives three reasons for his authorizing such action:

> First, of overriding importance, to protect innocent lives, including up to 1000 Americans whose personal safety is, of course, my paramount concern.
> Second, to forestall further chaos.
> And third to assist in the restoration of conditions of law and order and of governmental institutions. . . .

> When I received reports that a large number of our citizens were
> seeking to escape the island, thereby exposing themselves to great
> danger and after receiving a formal request for help, a unanimous re-
> quest from our neighboring states, I concluded the United States had
> no choice but to act strongly and decisively.
>
> Let me repeat: The United States objectives are clear—to protect
> our own citizens, to facilitate the evacuation of those who want to leave,
> and to help in the restoration of democratic institutions in Grenada.

Although worded for public consumption and although the second
reason is really part of the third, this statement contains the two
primary grounds for Urgent Fury: humanitarian and strategic-political
considerations. To these should be added the intense desire of the
president, and his advisers, to improve U.S. prestige, particularly at
home and within the armed forces, where morale and self-respect had
fallen substantially since Vietnam. The United States needed a success, something to be proud of.

Whether the hundreds of U.S. students on the island were in serious
danger is debatable. With hindsight the answer is almost certainly
no. There can now be little doubt that the RMC and Cuba had no
intention of harming foreigners. Austin was solicitous of the students'
welfare and was anxious to agree to arrangements for their evacuation. His motive was self-preservation; he desperately sought to avoid
giving the United States a pretext to invade. Most of the students
themselves were content to remain—that is, until imminent invasion
was announced over the radio on Sunday. This announcement,
coupled with Budeit and Chafin's efforts to scare the students into
evacuation, caused many of them to opt for leaving.

But this is not how the president saw it at the time. He saw how
horrifyingly easy it would be for the RMC to change its mind and
seize hostages. How could he rely on the assurances of people who
had so recently murdered their own prime minister, along with
numerous others, including women and children? Reagan was haunted
by the fear of another Tehran-type hostage situation, with the United
States powerless in the hands of a small group of fanatics. He had
a horror of being caught, as had President Carter, in a no-win situation that would cost American lives and weaken U.S. prestige even more.

A shrewder adviser might have contended that invasion could precipitate the very thing the president wanted to avoid: hostage taking.
It was obvious to all that Grenada could not withstand military assault

by the United States. It was only a question of how quickly the RMC would succumb. With defeat staring at them, the only way they might survive personally was to take hostages. With fifty or so students locked up in Fort Rupert or Richmond Hill Prison, it would become a very different ballgame. Demands for the invasion forces to withdraw or at least for the RMC's safe conduct out of the country would be difficult and costly to refuse. With no military intervention, there was no reason to take hostages.

Scores of students' parents in the United States saw it this way. They appealed to the president not to take precipitate action that might endanger their children. Dr. Bourne in Grenada confirmed this on being queried by the RMC, and Radio Free Grenada broadcast it the same day.

The safe evacuation of citizens who wished to leave was another matter. Diplomats like Kurze, Flohr, Budeit, and Chafin from the U.S. embassy and Montgomery from the British High Commission were sent to make the arrangements, while at the same time the military planners put together their option.

Although announced repeatedly as the primary reason for launching Urgent Fury, the safety of U.S. citizens was really one of several pretexts for grabbing an unprecedented opportunity to halt communist expansion in the U.S. backyard—the Caribbean. Gary Colin from Chicago, the bursar at the medical school, summed up the situation neatly: "Our safety was never in danger. We were used as an excuse by this government to invade Grenada. They needed a reason to go in, and we were it!"[1]

‡ ‡ ‡

The underlying reason for military action lay in the politico-strategic field. Coard's bid for power, culminating in his killing of Bishop, opened the door, albeit briefly, for an easy victory.

Since Bishop's coup in 1979, the United States had felt uneasy about Grenada. The island sat on the American southern doorstep in an area through which flowed, each day, more petroleum than transits the Strait of Hormuz. It had become a Cuban satellite that was moving more and more toward Moscow. Although details of the huge Soviet armament shipments and other military aid were unknown to the United States at the time, it was common knowledge that Grenada was the most thoroughly militarized island in the region. The danger that it would be used to export revolution and to train Caribbean subversives and would be the first of a number of island dominoes to fall was very real to watchers in the United States and elsewhere. That this reaction was justified was later revealed in the minutes of a meeting held in Moscow in March 1983 between the chief of staff of the Soviet armed forces, Marshal Ogarkov, and the PRA counterpart, Major Einstein Louison. Ogarkov stated, "Over two decades ago there was only Cuba in Latin America, today there are Nicaragua, Grenada, and a serious battle is going on in El Salvador."

One PRG project that seemed particularly unsettling to the United States was the construction of the international airport at Point Salines. Why did Grenada need such an airport? The obvious answer, and that given by the PRG, was tourism. Certainly Pearls Airport could never handle anything other than small aircraft and was located in the northeast of the island at the end of a tortuous and poorly maintained road. But the United States was suspicious, and understandably, because Cuba was doing the building; Havana provided the bulk of the materials, plant, and the labor force. Also a tourist industry needed hundreds, if not thousands, of hotel rooms. These were not being built. U.S. observers watched with some alarm as the Cuban work force climbed from 150 in 1979 to 650 in 1983 in a determined effort to complete the project by March 13, 1984, the fifth anniversary of Bishop's takeover.

But Cuba was not the only aid donor. By May 1983 Libya, Finland, the United Kingdom, Iraq, Algeria, Venezuela, and Syria had contributed or pledged to do so. Even a U.S. company had been involved with the filling in of Hardy Bay. Certainly Point Salines was not designed or constructed as a military airfield. Fuel was to be stored above ground, and no facilities were built to withstand military attack. But like any other airfield, there was nothing to prevent military aircraft using it, just as the airport at Barbados was used by the U.S. military during Urgent Fury. The likelihood of this facility's being available to the Cubans and Soviets, coupled with the strategic position of the island, was what was worrying officials.

The U.S. administration made no secret of its fears. At the time of the large-scale U.S. military exercise "Ocean Venture 1983," in March of that year, on the Puerto Rican island of Vieques, which precipitated an island-wide anti-invasion mobilization in Grenada,

American leaders and officials publicly stated their concern. Defense Secretary Caspar Weinberger, in the 1983 edition of *Soviet Military Power,* claimed that the PRG was engaged in a rapid military buildup. On March 9, he told the Voice of America that Cuban and Soviet military assistance to Grenada had no other explanation than the projection of Soviet power in the region. The president himself, on television on March 23, referred to a rapid military buildup on the island and its threat to U.S. oil supplies.

Perhaps U.S. feelings were best expressed by Ludlow "Kim" Flower, the U.S. chargé d'affaires in Barbados at the time, when in response to questions he replied:

> It isn't the airport per se that bothers us. Lots of islands around here have airports of comparable size. It is that the airport in Grenada was primarily financed and built by the Cubans, who tend not to do these things out of a sense of Christian charity. . . . With the completion of the Point Salines airport next year, and the additional military development in the Calivigny and Egmont harbor areas, there will exist a complex that would make deployment of Cuban and other hostile forces to Latin America and African points easier.
>
> Indeed the complex could be thought of as a stationary aircraft carrier.

U.S. worries were reinforced by the obvious foreign policy alignment of the PRG with Havana and Moscow. In the United Nations, Grenada faithfully voted in support of the Soviets time after time, including the invasion of Afghanistan.

Bishop's visit to the United States in June 1983 had not allayed suspicions. He had wanted to meet the president, but this was not allowed, so he was forced to content himself with senior State Department officials and congressional leaders. He expressed a tentative wish for Grenada and the United States to exchange ambassadors and for a lessening of tension. What he really wanted was cash because by then the Grenadian economy was crippled. All he got was agreement in principle to improved relations, but this would be dependent on Bishop's toning down his anti-American propaganda and distancing himself somewhat from his Marxist allies. Whether he really wanted, or would have been allowed, to achieve warmer relations will never be known; within four months he was murdered. Certainly the Soviets (and Coard) did not appreciate the visit.

What finally tipped the balance in favor of the hawks—what weighed heavily with Reagan and most of his senior advisers—was that this was a chance for the United States to redeem itself, not only in the eyes of the Western world but in its own eyes. Given a quick political decision and even mediocre military response, here was an easy-win situation. The United States, and more particularly the military, had become accustomed to failure. Since the traumatic withdrawal from Vietnam, on almost every occasion where U.S. forces had been deployed in combat, things had gone alarmingly wrong.

The *Mayaguez* incident in 1975, where the crew of a U.S. merchant ship was seized by Cambodians, had ended with an ad hoc marine battalion landing team's being badly mauled as they carried out a helicopter assault on a tiny island where the crew was thought to be held. The tragedy was that the Cambodians had already responded to diplomatic pressure and released the crew, who were not on the island the marines attacked. Even worse, the military commanders knew the crew were free before the assault team went in. They could have been recalled; the operation was unnecessary.

This was followed by the disastrous attempt to rescue the U.S. hostages in Tehran in 1980. Then, in the middle of the decision-making process for Urgent Fury, 241 marines died in Beirut. Grenada could, and did, restore self-respect as far as the public was concerned. As the president was later to say in New York when addressing the Congressional Medal of Honor Society, "Our days of weakness are over. Our military forces are back on their feet, and standing tall."

‡   ‡   ‡

Splendid opportunity though it may have been, there were grave problems, political difficulties, and repercussions to be considered. If the operation could be mounted in great secrecy and carried through with speed, the world would be presented with a fait accompli. All very well—but how would invading another country square with U.S. obligations under the U.N. Charter and the Organization of American States treaty, which categorically condemns interference in any country's internal affairs?

The president was anxious to have as strong a case as possible to argue in the international forum afterward. First and foremost was the need to protect U.S. citizens. This would certainly justify some sort of intervention involving the military, if only for transportation or as escorts, but would it stretch to justifying an assault with the aim of taking over the whole island? Hardly—particularly because initially many students did not see themselves in danger and wished to remain. The RMC was discussing peaceful evacuation with U.S. and British officials for those wanting it.

Some better legal arguments were essential. The first of these came early: the appeal from the Barbados prime minister Adams for the United States to use military force to restore law and order. If this could be reinforced with similar requests from other Caribbean countries, it would strengthen the case for intervening immeasurably. The OECS obliged, for sound reasons of their own future security. However, they were somewhat dilatory in putting it in writing, and a State Department's draft was not agreed to by Caribbean leaders until late at night on October 23.

The chairperson of the OECS, Eugenia Charles of Dominica, became an instant heroine in the United States as a result of her request for help. She was secretly flown in a U.S. government plane to Washington on October 24 to make an appearance alongside the president at the announcement of the invasion to the press the following morning. Viewed as a hard-hitting, uncompromising anticommunist, she was a great success.

Whether the OECS acted strictly in accordance with its own treaty is outside the scope of this book, but the United States was content to accept its interpretation. But even this was not quite enough justification for the invasion.

The situation was complicated by the fact that Grenada still had a governor-general, Sir Paul Scoon, who represented the queen. Grenada was part of the Commonwealth; the queen was head of the Commonwealth; and Sir Paul was, in the circumstances prevailing, the only constitutional authority on the island. There was no government, only the self-appointed military regime; therefore the governor-general was the only link with legality. Britain made plain early on its opposition to a military solution. It had spent many years disengaging from Caribbean defense or security obligations. With independence, responsibility for these matters passed to the islands themselves. Although prepared to send a warship in case an evacuation of British citizens was necessary and a diplomat to assess the situation (Montgomery), the United Kingdom urged negotiations, not fighting.

For the United States, this was awkward. If the governor-general were to ask for outside assistance to restore order, it would put the seal of legality on the entire operation. Such a request would carry great weight with international lawyers and might convince Britain to cooperate. But Sir Paul, isolated in Government House, was silent. He had been governor-general under Gairy; Bishop, and now the RMC, had seen it expedient to keep him in place.

A suitable letter, addressed to the prime minister of Barbados, was drafted in the State Department and brought to Barbados on Sunday, October 23, by McNeil, for onward transmission to Grenada for Sir Paul to sign. After dating the letter October 24, the governor-general signed it on the afternoon of October 26, when most of the fighting was over. There is no dispute about these facts. The written appeal came after the event. Was there a verbal request before? Despite the statement to the contrary by Adams later, the likelihood is no.

Adams, in addressing Barbadians after the conclusion of Urgent Fury, said:

> Now that Sir Paul Scoon is safe, I can reveal that by the kind offices of a friendly government, albeit a nonparticipating government, his views were sought well before the military operations commenced, on the issuing of an invitation to friendly countries to enter Grenada and restore order. According to my information Sir Paul agreed to do so as soon as possible.

The "offices of a friendly government" meant the United Kingdom. Specifically it referred to the British deputy high commissioner who flew to Grenada on Saturday, returning to Barbados next day. Montgomery met the governor-general but denies that Sir Paul asked for intervention. Sir Geoffrey Howe, secretary of state for foreign and commonwealth affairs, made a number of observations on a report on Grenada by the United Kingdom Foreign Affairs Committee in June 1984. Among other things he stated, "Early on the 24th October the Deputy High Commissioner in Bridgetown reported, following his brief visit to Grenada, that the Governor General (as the latter has subsequently confirmed) had made no request for Britain to intervene in Grenada."

Had Sir Paul made such a verbal appeal, even if it excluded Britain, he would have gone out of his way to confirm it after the event.

He never did. In fact when pressed on the issue later in a BBC interview, he stated he had not considered intervention necessary until late on the Sunday evening—well after Montgomery had left. A verbal cry for help from the governor-general, even if only to the OECS, would have featured prominently in Montgomery's report. It was not there. Finally, when the president spoke personally on the telephone to Thatcher in London on October 24, why was such a crucial factor never mentioned? The answer almost certainly is that the first Sir Paul knew of his appeal was when Brigadier Lewis asked him to sign the letter at Salines on Tuesday.

The decision to intervene in Grenada was made on the basis of seizing a fleeting strategic-political advantage, which had the added merit that inevitable military success would raise U.S. flagging morale. It was justified by a possible potential danger to U.S. citizens on the island and an urgent plea for help by OECS states, together with Barbados and Jamaica. That the governor-general had requested invasion was, in all probability, a fabrication to strengthen the shaky legality of the operation.

For all that, it was a bold decision, fraught with risks. It succeeded. Because of its success, the president is entitled to the credit and the enduring gratitude of Grenadians and other Caribbean communities who were saved from a grim future.

‡ ‡ ‡

Although under constant review, the U.S. system of international crisis management is little changed today from what it was in 1983. The president makes the final political decision. As commander in chief, he directs military forces to act. The constitutional requirement for congressional approval for the use of military force can be waived in an emergency under the War Powers Resolution for up to ninety days. As soon as possible, the president must justify his actions to Congress. He makes his decisions on the basis of considering advice and options presented to him by his advisers and staff, both civil and military.

If the decision required has security implications, the advice and options will be considered and fine-tuned by the National Security Council (NSC), whose membership in late 1983 comprised the president, the vice-president (George Bush), and the secretaries of state and defense (George Shultz and Caspar Weinberger, respectively), with the chairman of the Joint Chiefs of Staff (JCS) (General John Vessey) and the director of central intelligence (William Casey), also the head of the CIA, advising as necessary. The permanent staff of the NSC is headed by the president's assistant for national security affairs, more often called his national security adviser (Robert McFarlane). During Reagan's administration, however, this body was, for all practical purposes, replaced as the top decision-making body by the National Security Planning Group (NSPG), which differed from the NSC only in that the Joint Chiefs of Staff chairman and central intelligence director were members rather than advisers. To carry through a decision to execute an operation, the president must agree to an NSDD, a file of documents, compiled by the staff, which contains the details of the options available. In it will be intelligence briefs, diplomatic cables, readiness reports, maps, aerial photographs, and any other relevant information to be studied. As the crisis develops, the NSDD expands. The final version, the "smooth copy," requires the president's signature.

In a critical situation, the vast bureaucracies of State, the Pentagon, and the CIA are responsible for sifting information and producing workable solutions for consideration. A constant watch on all potential crisis areas needs to be maintained, and if developments escalate, special staff groups are assembled to assess the situation. An example, used in the Grenada crisis, of this type of restricted interagency group, was the one first called on the day Bishop was arrested, by the assistant secretary of state for inter-American affairs, Langhorne Motley. This was a meeting of middle-level staff from the NSC, State, Defense, CIA, and the JCS at the State Department. Its task—to take a preliminary look at developments on the island and possible implications for the United States with regard to evacuation of citizens— led to the JCS's being asked to dust off contingency plans for evacuation. The following day, October 14, the buck was passed down another step in the military chain of command. A "what-if" phone call from the JCS was received by the headquarters of Atlantic Command at Norfolk, Virginia.

U.S. planners had started to focus on Grenada on October 13, almost two weeks before Urgent Fury took place. The U.S. ambassador in Paris was later to get his knuckles severely rapped for alluding in an interview to plans being made two weeks before the invasion.

Invasion plans, no; but evacuation plans, yes; and possible rescue plans for Bishop, yes. Yet when Senator Claiborne Pell queried the ambassador's statement with Deputy Secretary of State Kenneth Dam on October 27 before the Senate Foreign Relations Committee, Dam's response was, "I can simply say that [the ambassador] was dead wrong, and he has so acknowledged."

On January 24, 1984, Motley declared to the House Armed Services Committee, "October 19, the day that Prime Minister Bishop was murdered, marked the beginning of serious planning for the possibility that a non-permissive evacuation—one in which the host government impedes the departure of foreign citizens—would prove necessary." But it was on October 14 that Atlantic Command had been alerted to start planning for possible noncombat evacuation operations. The U.S. representative in France was guilty of indiscreet, not inaccurate, comment.

The need for serious planning had been made clear by Bish, in Barbados, on October 13 when he sent a flash signal describing riots, the use of APCs, and firing in St. George's. His message ended, "Am Embassy Bridgetown recommends that the US should now be prepared to conduct an emergency evacuation of US citizens residing in Grenada."

As far back as Monday, October 17, as Quintyne and Brown from the Barbados Defence Force were arriving on the island, McFarlane, as a result of Motley's meetings, briefed Reagan on the need for contingency evacuation plans. The president agreed they should proceed. The next day, the military crisis action team at Norfolk started putting together various courses of action.

Nevertheless, it was the killing of Bishop six days before the intervention that lit the fuse making military involvement inevitable if the president gave the order. On that day the JCS provided Motley's interagency group with a list of the military resources immediately available. Late that night the JCS sent a warning order confirming to Atlantic Command that evacuation plans were required at once.

October 20 was a hectic day for the planners. By the early hours of the morning, staff at Atlantic Command had produced no fewer than six different options for an evacuation-type operation. Admiral McDonald's staff, assuming availability of forces, assuming no other hostile country (Cuba) would intervene, and assuming most of the evacuees were near Salines Airport, briefed Vessey later that morning when he visited Norfolk. Two of the plans evisaged evacuation in a friendly environment, three in a hostile environment, and the last one was merely a show of force.

At 8:00 A.M. McFarlane's deputy, Rear Admiral John Poindexter, chaired a meeting of the Crisis Pre-Planning Group (CPPG) in the White House.[2] This group had been established by Reagan shortly after taking office to assess a potential crisis in the early stages. It was composed of officials from State (Motley), the NSC (Lieutenant Colonel Oliver North of the Marine Corps and Constantine Menges, a hard-line, right-wing, former CIA officer whose nickname was, inevitably, Constant Menace), plus the CIA (Douane "Dewey" Clarridge). They gathered in room 208 of the Executive Office Building, which was equipped with the latest high-technology computer and secure communication systems.

The discussions largely revolved around Menges's forthright arguments for full-scale military intervention to destroy the communist regime. He went so far as to suggest that anything less could give the Soviets a base for nuclear weapons. The meeting agreed that the situation could get a lot worse. It merited consideration by the next-higher group, chaired by the vice-president, the NSC's Special Situation Group.

Meanwhile in the Pentagon, in the office of Under Secretary Fred Iklé, the logistical requirements of an evacuation were under examination. The NSDD was starting to take shape.

On the same afternoon the State Department received Prime Minister Adams's message urging military action not just to secure foreign citizens but to crush opposition, restore law and order and, in fact, overthrow the RMC. The idea of going all the way was now in the cards, and it began to look like an attractive proposition. Bish was told to inform Adams that for the United States to intervene under those terms would require a formal, written request from Caribbean countries. The OECS, Barbados, and Jamaica obliged verbally on October 21 and in writing on October 23.

At a quarter to five in the afternoon, George Bush convened the Special Situation Group. It soon became apparent that very little was known about Grenada. After all the fuss about the PRG, the meeting was shocked to hear that there was no CIA agent on the island, that nothing was known about the military situation, and that no aerial photographs had been taken of Salines for more than five months.

Strenuous efforts needed to be made to rectify these omissions, and the vice-president endorsed an overriding necessity for secrecy. The decision was taken to divert toward Grenada the amphibious task force that had sailed for Lebanon on October 18. Under the command of Captain Carl Erie, this group consisted of the amphibious assault ship USS *Guam,* with four accompanying vessels. On board was the 22d Marine Amphibious Unit (22d MAU) with some 1,900 marines. After the meeting, McFarlane took a first draft of the NSDD up to the president. At this stage the emphasis and planning was still focused on evacuation, although the possibility of going further had been mentioned.

On Friday Reagan initialed the draft of the NSDD, prepared by the dedicated workaholic marine officer North to allow planning to proceed, before boarding Air Force One at 4:00 P.M. with Shultz and McFarlane, for a golfing weekend at Eisenhower Cottage at Augusta, Georgia. Ultrasophisticated, secure communication systems allowed them all to remain in instant touch with Washington, even in the middle of their game. In Barbados Gillespie waited anxiously at the Dover Convention Centre for the outcome of the OECS meeting, and in Washington Poindexter called another evening conference to review the situation. It was agreed that the JCS should plan for a full-scale military operation to seize the island as an alternative option. Vessey alerted not only Atlantic Command but the Military Airlift Command (MAC), Readiness Command (REDCOM), and the recently formed Joint Special Operations Command (JSOC) at Fort Bragg, North Carolina. Even earlier in the day McDonald's staff had been anticipating a nonpermissive evacuation operation, and it was on October 21 that the marines at sea, the Ranger commanding officers, and, late that night, staff of the 82d Airborne Division were alerted to something more than a peaceful exercise.

With the arrival from the embassy in Barbados of the OECS's urgent plea for the United States to join them in restoring order and democracy on the island, planning switched to an all-out military operation. No plan could be executed without the president's approval, which could be withheld until the last moment. But while awaiting a signature, the complex operation had to be pieced together, made practical. The opportunity to act was brief; time, speed, and secrecy were critical. If the military waited for the president to sign before acting, it would be too late to put together a workable plan.

‡   ‡   ‡

Poindexter did not hesitate before disturbing the sleep of his seniors in Augusta. The OECS message was of vital importance. He called Secretary of State George Shultz with the cry for help at 2:45 A.M. on October 22. Shultz woke McFarlane. Then they called Bush and Weinberger from their beds for a secure radio-telephone conference in which all could participate simultaneously. They agreed the president should be roused. So at 5:15, still in his bathrobe and slippers, the president received Shultz and McFarlane in his quarters to hear the news. He stated that the United States should respond quickly and positively, and he called the vice-president, instructing him to set up a Special Situation Group meeting for 9:00 A.M. In order not to arouse suspicions, Reagan, Shultz, and McFarlane would continue with their golf.

That Saturday was another frantic day for the planners in room 208. Leaving aside the military activities for later, the Special Situation Group conference confirmed the invasion option. The president joined in the discussions from Augusta, with Bush explaining that the NSDD now contained an operation with three objectives: to ensure the safety of U.S. citizens; in conjunction with OECS forces, to restore democratic government on Grenada; and to eliminate current, and prevent further, Cuban intervention on the island—in other words, full-scale invasion, the crushing of resistance, and the takeover of the country. The president responded: "Well, if we've got to go there, we might as well do all that needs to be done." Again the need for absolute secrecy was repeated.

On that day, Castro, using the U.S. Interests Section of the Swiss embassy in Havana, formally notified the United States of Cuba's wish to cooperate in protecting all foreign nationals in Grenada. The message was ignored. On that morning, Kurze, Flohr, and Montgomery, oblivious of the hectic invasion activities, set off for Grenada to discuss evacuation with the RMC. At Augusta in the afternoon, a man demanding to see the president crashed through the gates of the golf course and seized several hostages. Reagan was rushed from his game to a place of safety, from which he spent some minutes trying to speak to the man on the telephone. Shortly before 5:00 P.M. the JCS issued their operation order code named Urgent Fury. That evening in Trinidad, CARICOM started deliberations. In the United

States, the press had got wind of the diversion of the marines to the Caribbean. On Grenada, the RMC was convinced that invasion was imminent.

Again the next morning, the president was woken early, this time at 2:27. McFarlane had appalling news: the marines' barracks at the airport in Beirut had been the victim of a suicide attack. A single truck, packed with explosives, had burst through into the compound where hundreds of marines were billeted and exploded. The results were devastating. McFarlane spoke of 100 dead, but this figure would soon climb to 241. It was an unmitigated disaster, probably the worst tragedy ever to strike the U.S. Marine Corps.

Reagan immediately returned to Washington, in darkness and pouring rain, the strain of the situation reflected in his drawn face. Another meeting of the Special Situation Group was called, with the president in the chair. All Sunday morning and into the afternoon, discussions revolved around Lebanon and Grenada. The main question was whether the awful events in Beirut should affect the decision to intervene in Grenada. For Reagan, it was the climax of a terrible weekend. However, the 73-year-old president revealed his determination and moral courage when he said, "If this [Grenada] was right yesterday, it's right today, and we shouldn't let the act of a couple of terrorists dissuade us from going ahead." As this meeting broke up, the JCS chairman briefed the president, along with Shultz, Weinberger, and a senior CIA representative, on the military plans so far. He explained the use of the Special Operations Forces in the operation, particularly the intention to put a small unit of SEALs ashore at Salines that night. The necessity for absolute secrecy was once again stressed.

On Sunday McNeil and Crist flew to Barbados with the State Department's draft of the letters for signing by the OECS and Sir Paul. The CARICOM meeting continued that morning. In Barbados contingents of troops and police started arriving from nearby islands. In Grenada the militia was being mobilized, the RMC was telexing in vain to Britain to halt any U.S. attack, and invasion warnings were being broadcast. That evening the president signed the "smooth copy" of the NSDD, and in the darkness the aircraft carrying the sixteen-man SEAL team that was to start Urgent Fury took off.

‡   ‡   ‡

Despite the fact that U.S. troops were on their way to Grenada, the president did not inform Adams that he had given the final go-ahead for another twenty-four hours. Similarly it was not until 1:00 P.M. on Monday that he cabled Thatcher regarding the written OECS request. At 6:00 P.M. the official "go" cable was sent to Bish in Barbados authorizing him to tell Adams; fifty minutes later, a second dispatch went to Britain stating that the United States, along with Barbados and Jamaica, had agreed to intervene. Thatcher's response, protesting military action forcefully, was received at 8:00 P.M. At 2:00 A.M. on October 25 the president sent his third cable thanking the British prime minister for her reply, but confirming that the United States was going ahead. A personal telephone call from Thatcher, who was furious, had no effect.

For the most part, the reluctance to inform even participants such as Barbados that Urgent Fury was to be launched, indeed had been launched, was due to the need to maintain secrecy, to prevent leaks. This was understandable but in reality ineffective. The United States succeeded in hoodwinking Britain as to its intentions, but Grenada had been expecting attack nightly since Sunday. The movement of ships, aircraft, and Caribbean troops had been seen and reported. Guyana had blown the OECS's intention to invade, if not the actual time. Within the Caribbean, Urgent Fury achieved no strategic surprise; it remained to be seen whether tactical surprise could be gained.

Thatcher was angry primarily because she was deceived by her American allies. They went ahead with an attack on a Commonwealth country with the queen's representative still in office, indeed the only remaining constitutional authority, without her knowledge. It was galling to say the least. Her government had been made to look extremely stupid, if not incompetent. Sir Geoffrey Howe, the secretary of state for foreign and commonwealth affairs, had, as late as 4:00 P.M. (in London) on Monday afternoon, been denying any knowledge of a likely U.S. invasion to the House of Commons. Surely his office knew what was going on in the Caribbean, certainly in Barbados, the center of activity, where Britain maintained a high commission?

In Bridgetown, Bullard and his staff had been desperately trying to keep in touch with events. Between October 19 and 24 they had sent no fewer than thirty cables to London concerning the crisis. They reported on October 21 that some Caribbean leaders were pressing for military action. The next day Bullard telegrammed to the Foreign and Commonwealth Office the results of the OECS meeting and that the United Kingdom had been invited verbally to join the intervention. A formal written request was to follow. It never did. The next day the high commissioner reported another conversation with Adams, in which he had been told once again that British participation in a multinational force was being requested.

Britain also maintained a high commission in Jamaica with a defense adviser, Colonel Pat Beaumont, on the staff. He had been active in alerting the Ministry of Defence in London as to what was happening and in seeking permission to go to Grenada personally.

Reaction in the Foreign and Commonwealth Office was slower than usual as it was a weekend. Cables arriving after normal working hours, or on Saturday and Sunday, went initially to the duty officer, who had to pass them to the third ranking official, Richard Luce, who was in charge. If the message was judged critical, copies had to be sent to Athens, where Howe was attending a European Community foreign ministers' meeting or to the prime minister's house at Chequers. Luce responded that Britain was opposed to military action, but the prime minister, as a precaution for the possible evacuation of British citizens, authorized the Royal Navy's West Indian Guard Ship, HMS *Antrim,* to leave Cartagena on October 23, to sail to Grenadian waters. All major cables from the Foreign and Commonwealth Office on the crisis were repeated to Bridgetown and the British embassy in Washington. On Monday Thatcher chaired a meeting of ministers to review events. They made it plain that Britain was against military action, listing legal, constitutional, and practical difficulties. This message went to Washington. Both Thatcher and her ministers were clearly unaware that Urgent Fury had been authorized the previous evening.

Britain was concerned about its citizens in Grenada, but neither John Kelly, the only British diplomat on the island, nor Montgomery on his return from his visit felt that foreigners were in immediate danger. The RMC had promised to allow evacuation of any wishing to leave; Pearls was to be opened on Monday and the curfew lifted. Additionally Scoon had not urged a military rescue when he spoke to Montgomery. Seen through British eyes, a military invasion was in no way necessary.

In Washington the State Department persistently told the British ambassador, Sir Oliver Wright, that the United States would act with caution and consultation, reiterating that its primary concern was the safety of its citizens.

The United States, however, had other motives for intervention. The safety of its citizens was indeed important, if they were at risk, but in this case it was a pretext. The need for secrecy dictated that the fewer who knew the better, and as Britain appeared opposed anyway, why risk further delay in a situation that demanded prompt action.

7

Urgent Fury

The Concept

We just did not have the time to get someone in. We had rough
estimates, but nothing more.
> — Admiral Wesley L. McDonald, commander in chief,
> U.S. Atlantic Command, in testimony before the Senate
> Armed Services Committee

A DMIRAL McDonald had his headquarters at Norfolk, Virginia.
In October 1983 he was 59 years old and had held this key naval
post for exactly a year. By training and background, he was a naval
aviator with a Distinguished Flying Cross plus a Gold Star in lieu
of a second award. He had been a midshipman at the U.S. Naval
Academy in 1943, graduating as an ensign in 1946. His career had
been highly successful, and he had held flag rank for twelve years.
He had spent most of his earlier service as a flyer, or commander
of flyers, with naval attack squadrons. Later he had commanded the
USS *Hermitage* and *Coral Sea.* After experience as chief of naval air
training and on the air warfare staff as deputy chief of naval operations (air warfare), he assumed his post as Commander in Chief of
the Atlantic Command, which was, and is, a critical NATO (North
Atlantic Treaty Organization) naval appointment.

McDonald commanded the U.S. Navy's Atlantic Fleet, as well as
being NATO's Supreme Allied Commander for the Atlantic Ocean.
His headquarters was, in theory, one of the six unified commands
in the U.S. strategic command system. (A unified command means
a shared command, with staff posts divided up among all the services.

This is different from a specified, functional command such as the Strategic Air Command, where the air force is in firm control at all levels, with other services being brought in only if needed.) In practice McDonald's headquarters setup was more specified than unified as naval staff were in the great majority. This was not surprising considering its primary role of winning naval supremacy in the Atlantic in a world war.

Urgent Fury came as a surprise. At very short notice, Atlantic Command, rather than the U.S. Forces Caribbean Command, Key West, Florida, became responsible for planning what was mainly a ground forces operation. The operation would involve techniques and tactics bearing no resemblance to maneuvering naval battle groups, convoy protection, or antisubmarine warfare, the normal day-to-day activities of the staff at Norfolk.

At 4:54 P.M. on Saturday, October 22, the JCS issued their Execute Order for Urgent Fury to McDonald. He was directed to "conduct military operations to protect and evacuate US and designated foreign nationals from Grenada, neutralize Grenadian forces, stabilize the internal situation, and maintain the peace. In conjunction with OECS/friendly government participants assist in the restoration of a democratic government on Grenada."

It was vital for the operation to be done quickly. The world must be presented with a fait accompli. U.S. forces must go in, crush any opposition, get the U.S. citizens out, hand over the job to a peacekeeping force of Caribbean units, and come home. The State Department and the JCS wanted it all over in days, not weeks or months—quite a tall order for a U.S.-NATO naval headquarters.

Atlantic Command had the responsibility for producing the overall military plan for the operation, which had to receive JCS approval before it went to the president as part of the NSDD. However, although Atlantic staff could, and did, provide evacuation options as early as October 20, as soon as the operation looked as though it might involve serious combat, and taking over the island, it was obvious they could not cope unassisted. The headquarters at Norfolk lacked the intelligence and communications capacity to handle the situation. Neither did the staff have the planning expertise for a large-scale ground operation.

Once invasion became an option, the JCS had to put together an operation involving the navy and air force—at the very least for transportation and logistic support—with the marines, and possibly the army, for ground combat. Because the operation demanded speed and surprise, with the possibility of hostages' being seized or the need to rescue U.S. citizens, there was a role for Special Operations Forces as well. It quickly became apparent to all the services that they must be in on the action. Urgent Fury would increase the prestige of the armed forces, so none of them could afford to miss out. To assist Atlantic, the commanders of REDCOM (Army), MAC (Air Force), and JSOC (Army) were designated as supporting commands to McDonald.

A large combined force had to be cobbled together at speed. An ad hoc joint headquarters was required to plan and coordinate the operation on or around Grenada. An on-scene commander was needed. The operation would require a Joint Task Force (JTF), under a task force commander. For Urgent Fury the task force was designated JTF 120, with its commander being Vice-Admiral Joseph Metcalf III.

Metcalf had been the commander of the 2d Fleet for three months. Fifty-six years old, he had been in the navy since 1946, alternating naval staff posts with command appointments throughout the previous three decades. He had commanded Cruiser-Destroyer Group 8 from 1979 to 1981 and had been director of the Department of the Navy's Program Information Center immediately prior to taking over 2d Fleet. His Vietnam Service Medal had four bronze stars.

To supplement Metcalf's naval team, a seventeen-man joint "fly away" staff was assembled. This group would fly out with the commander of JTF 120 to establish an operational headquarters on the *Guam*. It was all very rushed, with most officers never having worked together before. The short time frame also limited the army and air force representation. (Lack of staff who understood how to plan and coordinate joint fire support programs for ground forces on the island, by aircraft or naval gunfire, was an omission later much regretted.)

The planning of Urgent Fury was complicated by the requirement to include small units from Caribbean countries in a peacekeeping role. Additionally the final plan had to incorporate the involvement of both the State Department and CIA. It was an unusually complex operation.

To get Urgent Fury launched on October 25 required all concerned to work ceaselessly around the clock. The planning staffs at all levels were beset with problems, some insurmountable. By Sunday the final version of the plan had been given to the JCS by McDonald.

Vessey made some modifications, briefed Bush and Weinberger, JTF 120 was activated, and that night the president signed the NSDD. Urgent Fury, which was to involve some 20,000 servicemen, including sailors, soldiers, airmen, and marines, together with Special Operations Forces personnel from the army, navy, and air force, was conceived, planned, and launched in four days.

‡   ‡   ‡

To achieve all objectives, the plan required certain basic elements. The first and foremost of these was surprise. The operation had to be over quickly. Key targets had to be identified. Units needed to be selected to concentrate on these objectives and then be transported to them in secrecy. It required meticulous planning, complete security, flexible and reliable communications, firm command and control, a high standard of interservice cooperation, plus a huge logistical backup— no mean undertaking.

To ensure surprise, the planners had one need above all others: information. They needed intelligence on the Cuban presence on the island, the Cubans' and Soviets' likely reactions to attack, the PRA strengths, armaments, deployment, intentions, and morale. They needed to know what defenses had been set up at the airfields and where the PRA headquarters, communication centers, supply depots, and antiaircraft positions were.

Because a main objective of the operation was the safety of foreign citizens, they needed to know where such persons were living, whether they were guarded, whether they were at one location or several, and how many were at each. They needed information on the geography of Grenada: the suitability of beaches for landing, the type of terrain, the road system, the hills, the layout of St. George's, and the details of approaches to selected targets. These were all critical for tactical planning.

To the amazement—and consternation—of all who wanted information, virtually none was available. There were not even any proper maps with grid coordinates. From the military point of view, the lack of accurate intelligence was to be the most serious failure of the operation. Intelligence shortcomings were directly or indirectly responsible for Urgent Fury's delayed H hour, loss of surprise, slow development, tactical failures, and unnecessary casualties.

The U.S. intelligence community is vast. Billions of dollars are spent annually by the various intelligence agencies on obtaining, correlating, evaluating, and disseminating information. The president's principal adviser on intelligence matters is the director of the CIA, then William Casey. He is the chairman of the "supreme court" of the intelligence community: the U.S. Intelligence Board, which considers all major intelligence estimates going to the president. He also wears the hat of director of central intelligence, reporting to the NSC.

Although the CIA has some 20,000 employees in the United States and thousands more overseas, it is not the largest intelligence agency; it is exceeded in size and budget by the National Security Agency, probably the least-known agency, responsible for electronic espionage. From its headquarters near Washington, D.C., it controls a worldwide network of satellites and spies in the sky. Thousands of personnel are employed making and breaking codes or ciphers. The Defense Intelligence Agency has over 7,000 staff and a budget of hundreds of millions every year. Its director advises the defense secretary and the JCS. Each service also maintains its own intelligence organization, and the State Department's Bureau of Intelligence and Research collects and analyzes political, economic, and cultural intelligence. Completing the bureaucracy is the massive bulk of the FBI.

The U.S. government, including the president, had viewed with considerable alarm the Marxist regime of Maurice Bishop. They had publicly expressed their concern at the possible military uses of Salines Airport, at the growing Cuban presence, at the Soviets' establishment of an embassy, and at the militarization of the Grenadian people. The island could be used as a training ground for the spread of subversion in the region. Grenada was strategically located in the U.S. backyard.

Yet when the time came for action, intelligence staffs were caught badly off-balance. They had very few answers to the hundreds of questions that were asked. Despite the proclaimed importance to the United States of what was happening in Grenada, the CIA had no agent on the island. After Bishop's arrest, they began to appreciate the extent of their ignorance. On October 18, the CIA representative in Barbados listed seventeen separate queries on events in Grenada and handed them to staff of the Regional Security System and Barbados Defence Force for answering. If an agent had been on the ground or even if Grenada had been studied by intelligence analysts, these questions would not have been asked: "Who in the leadership of the PRG has remained loyal to Bishop? Who is the leader of the armed forces, Cornwall or Austin? What is the PRA's role in the situation? Was there a military parade on 17 October? Who are Coard's supporters in the cabinet?"

Perhaps the most potentially damaging deficiency concerned the U.S. students at the medical school. American citizens had been studying at the school for years, most of the staff were from the United States, and it had been a completely open organization, and yet on the late afternoon of October 22, the National Military Intelligence Center confirmed that the students all lived at True Blue campus, at the eastern end of the new Salines runway.

From the planning point of view, this was a tremendous error. A major part of the operation was supposedly to secure the students and ensure they could not be taken hostage. To do that required accurate knowledge of where they all were likely to be at H hour. True Blue accommodated only about a third of the students. More than 230 lived at the Grand Anse campus over the hills, 2½ kilometers away to the northwest, and many more were scattered in houses or apartments on the Lance aux Epines peninsula and elsewhere. Although the planners at both Atlantic and Special Forces commands learned about Grand Anse at the last moment, the troops deployed to rescue the students did not know until after their arrival at True Blue itself.

Hundreds of parents of students in the United States knew about Grand Anse. The telephone lines to the school in Grenada were in use up to, and during, the operation; Vice-Chancellor Bourne spoke to the chancellor in New York, U.S. diplomats actually visited Grand Anse on the Saturday and Sunday before Urgent Fury. The Barbados Defence Force plan, which was explained to McNeil and Crist on Sunday, showed Grand Anse as a phase 1 objective. This blunder could have been disastrous. But luck was to be an American ally during Urgent Fury.

Information was as plentiful in Barbados as it was scanty in the United States. Within the Barbados Defence Force was naval expertise on the beaches and seas surrounding the island. One officer had lived at Salines for eleven years. The Regional Security System intelligence officer had considerable knowledge of the PRG and PRA, and Barbados had infiltrated persons into Grenada on October 17 and carried out an island surveillance flight. All relevant information Barbados possessed, including an intelligence assessment of the strengths and deployment of the PRA, was passed to the U.S. embassy in Bridgetown. The defense attaché, Lieutenant Colonel Larry Reiman, dutifully sent everything he received to Washington; however, it did not appear to influence the planning. In fact there was no joint U.S.-Caribbean planning, and the role of the Caribbean contingents was not clear to either U.S. or Caribbean commanders. On October 25, when Caribbean troops started landing at Salines, at least one Ranger battalion commander knew nothing of their participation in the operation at all; for a brief moment, he thought they were the PRA.

‡ ‡ ‡

The military plan included in the NSDD, signed by the president on Sunday evening, was the sum total of four days' effort on the part of commanders and staffs of every branch of the armed services. That so much was achieved in so short a time was remarkable; that the assault went in a few hours late or that there was confusion is understandable. That the units were compelled to go in virtually blind, for lack of good information, was lamentable.

Atlantic Command, under McDonald, had the major planning responsibility. Nevertheless, it also had to accept any constraints imposed by the Pentagon. Atlantic had to accept the decision that it was not going to be a navy-marine corps operation but that all services and Special Forces had to have part of the action. Inevitably this led to a task force composed of units and staffs that did not know each other, had never trained together, often did not properly understand each other's procedures, and were forced to plan in isolation and ignorance of what others were doing.

There was a contingency plan gathering dust in the Pentagon, number 2360, which was supposed to provide for a Grenada intervention. This document specified that the overall command of such an operation would be given to the commander of U.S. Forces Caribbean at Key West, Florida, with the on-scene commander being the commander of XVIII Airborne Corps—in 1983, Lieutenant General Jack Mackmull. An air assault or airborne division from this corps, with one brigade on call, a carrier battle group, and a marine amphibious unit (MAU), were earmarked as the forces available. Likely objectives noted in this plan were Pearls and Salines airports, St. George's harbor, the supposed naval facility under development at Calivigny, and the radio transmitting station at Beausejour, north of St. George's. To the surprise of many, this plan was not activated; indeed, it was not even discussed at the initial main Atlantic planning conference on Saturday, October 22, although it had been one of Atlantic's assumptions in evacuation planning that the forces in this contingency plan would be available.

This meeting was the first joint conference that McDonald had been able to put together to consider Vessey's previous night's instructions to plan for a full-scale military option, as well as an evacuation. As it got under way at extremely short notice, the Special Situation Group in Washington was obtaining the president's telephone agreement to plan for military intervention.

As a high-level planning conference, it was not a great success. Many officers arrived late. Some, like the MAC representative, Brigadier Robert Patterson of the air force, did not make it at all. His absence hindered the airborne planning because it was his command that was to provide all the transport aircraft to get everybody (except the marines) to Grenada. Patterson was only told at midday on October 23 about his role; this, coupled with a flight delayed by bad weather, resulted in his arrival at Norfolk at 10:30 P.M. on October 23. Not surprisingly the army and Special Operations Forces planners with whom he needed to work had long since departed. Similarly there was no senior Marine Corps participant as the amphibious force was at sea; the Special Operations Forces representative was only a lieutenant colonel, while the army mustered a lieutenant colonel and three junior officers. The navy dominated proceedings.

Logistical problems were never considered at all. The JCS had deliberately not mentioned the operation to the head of their logistics, Vice-Admiral William Cowhill. Even the Atlantic's senior logistics planner, Rear Admiral Neil Ferraro, was told only 22 hours before H hour and consequently had no time to achieve anything. This exclusion was made in the name of security. Ferraro was later to say, "This was a no plan situation. To open it up would have dragged it all out, and brought in a whole cast of characters." By this Ferraro meant the Joint Defense Agency, yet another bureaucratic organization, born in 1979 to plan and coordinate the movement of rapid deployment forces. It was completely excluded from Urgent Fury on the grounds that it could not guarantee security. In the words of Colonel Russell Davis, its public affairs officer, "It did not have the capability to handle close-hold information." (This deficiency has now been remedied.)

The staff officers assembling that morning were mostly strangers to each other; some wore civilian clothes, which did not help in identifying who was who or who did what. Perhaps the most serious handicap, aside from the conspicuous lack of good intelligence on all aspects of the operation, was that nobody had a map. To plan a military operation without reference to a map is a sure way of ensuring participants are confused and unclear about their objectives.

Lieutenant Colonel Frank Akers was the operations staff officer at the headquarters of the 82d Airborne Division, based at Fort Bragg, North Carolina. He arrived at about 9:00 A.M., accompanied by three other officers to represent the army. He found the atmosphere strained, with most of the planners already looking haggard from lack of sleep. Akers himself had had little either. The previous evening he had been at a cocktail party when he was asked to come to another room by his opposite number at XVIII Airborne Corps. There he learned that the 82d was to participate in the planning of Urgent Fury. Akers was told he would be briefed early the next day and that he should attend the Norfolk meeting. At 11:00 P.M. he was informed that Atlantic Command wanted to talk to him on the telephone. The conversation was difficult; the naval staff officer at Norfolk was unfamiliar with airborne procedures and the line insecure. Akers called again on a secure phone at midnight. He was surprised to hear that the 82d was to gain military control in Grenada so that a new government could be established. Atlantic gave him some vague figures as estimates of likely PRA and Cuban strengths. He then told them that the 82d's readiness brigade could be alerted and passed on details of aircraft loading calculations. There was then little opportunity for rest before his early flight north.

Akers was able to salvage something useful from the hubbub at Norfolk. He went into a huddle with the JSOC representative, Lieutenant Colonel Richard Pack, and from him learned that the Special Forces were to go in first, followed by the 82d, and that both battalions of Rangers were involved under the JSOC. He was told that H hour was 2:00 A.M., October 25. They were unable to discuss air movement with the MAC because they could not find any officer from that command, but they agreed that the Rangers should fly in the MC-130E Combat Talon and C-130 Hercules transport aircraft, while the 82d used the larger C-141 Starlifters.

McDonald had been debating whether the navy and the marines, with the Special Forces, would be sufficient for the task. Because so little was known about the opposition and to ensure the ground forces did not become overextended, he decided that the 82d was required. During the morning Vessey called from Washington on a secure line. He deplored the lack of intelligence, telling McDonald that they would try to get a CIA agent on the island as a matter of urgency and, they hoped, more information would result from aerial reconnaissance flights. He passed on the president's verbal go-ahead to the planning of the military option, he agreed the 82d should be deployed, and he repeatedly stressed the need for operational security. All communications should be verbal, with no hard-copy messages. He underlined the need for speed and surprise. A rapid turnover by the Special Forces to conventional units and the Caribbean contingents was fundamental to all planning. Special Forces troops should not be seen. When the world woke up on October 25, all such units should be winging their way home.

Initially all participating units were to be alerted for an exercise, not an operation, to help prevent leaks. Normally the readiness brigade from 82d required eighteen hours to get moving, but the JCS chairman thought that too long, so Akers agreed to cut the time on the pretext of preparing for a training exercise.

When the 82d officers left Norfolk later that day, October 22, they were far from clear what was expected of their division. What were their objectives? When would they land on Grenada? How would their arrival phase in with the Rangers? What exactly was their role in the operation? How were they to cooperate with the marines? Where were the enemy, and what was their strength or likely intentions? Akers was unable to give satisfactory answers to these and other questions fired at him by his commander, Major General Edward Trobaugh, on his return to Fort Bragg.

Trobaugh, 51 years old, was an enthusiastic officer with an inclination to preface his remarks by shouting "Airborne." His previous ten years had been spent as a brigadier general commanding a brigade in the 25th Infantry Division, as executive assistant to the commander in chief, U.S. Pacific Command in Hawaii, as the assistant divisional commander of the 9th Infantry Division, as assistant commandant of the Infantry School at Fort Benning, and then as chief of the Military Assistance and Advisory Group in Spain. Just four months before, he had been given command of the renowned 82d Airborne. It was the pinnacle of his career. After hearing what Akers could tell him, he immediately initiated planning for his division to capture Grenada, allocating two brigades, each of two battalions, for the task. His concept envisaged seizing Pearls and Salines airfields, together with other objectives. Exactly what the Special Forces, the navy, or the marines were doing was far from clear to Trobaugh at this stage, but this did not dampen his enthusiasm. He was later to be surprised and disappointed when the final plan gave him only a supporting role.

Early on October 23, the ever-busy Akers went across to Mackmull's headquarters, also at Bragg, to brief him. Mackmull was concerned that plan 2360 was not being used. If it had, he would have expected his corps to provide the bulk of the troops and to command the ground operations himself. He appreciated at once that for an operation of this size and complexity, the 82d did not have the backup logistical support needed within the division. Therefore, on his own initiative, he ordered his headquarters to support Trobaugh. It was also worrying that there was no army officer of general rank at the headquarters of JTF 120. It was, at that level, still an entirely naval affair. On the *Guam* the operational headquarters would not have high-level army representation. Similarly the plan, as explained by Akers, did not seem to envisage a ground force commander on the island once the intervention got under way.

The lack of an army general was remedied that evening. Major General Norman Schwarzkopf was, to his great astonishment, pulled out from his command of the 24th Mechanized Infantry Division at Fort Stewart, Georgia, and told he was deputy to Metcalf and his adviser on army operations. His involvement, advice, or influence during the planning was unavoidably negligible. His total staff on the *Guam* were two majors, neither an expert in interservice fire support techniques. Like logistical problems, joint fire support details had been conspicuous by their absence from high-level discussions due to the short planning time frame and the insistence on keeping only the minimum of key people informed until the last moment.

Mackmull understood the need for coordinated planning with the Special Operations Forces. He had been intimately involved with them when he commanded the JFK Center and had personally supervised the development of Delta Force under Colonel Charlie Beckwith. Later that day he went over to visit the JSOC, together with Trobaugh. H hour was less than thirty-six hours away. That same night SEALs were destined to enter Grenada covertly, yet the army and Special Operations Forces commanders were only just meeting to discuss the operation. Effective cooperation was to prove virtually impossible to achieve below the rank of general.

‡   ‡   ‡

Like Atlantic Command, the JSOC at Fort Bragg had been alerted to their involvement in Urgent Fury by Vessey on Friday, October 21. Major General Richard Scholtes was the first commander of this new grouping of Special Operations Forces. For this operation he was to command a mixed bag of units, grouped together as Task Force 123 (TF 123). This task force was to have Ranger battalions, navy SEAL team detachments, an air force combat control team, and the army's Delta Force. The problem was that due to interservice rivalry, Scholtes had to find a mission for everybody.

From the little information available, it appeared to the Special Operations Forces planners that a number of potential targets were suitable for the specialized units. First, they needed to secure an air-field. However, there were two: Pearls in the northeast and Salines in the southwest. This was convenient because Ranger battalions special-ized in airfield seizure, so the 1st/75th could take Salines while the 2d/75th went for Pearls. Nothing much was known about the defenses at either, but Rangers were trained to land or drop on runways. Scholtes was aware that the safety of U.S. citizens at the medical school was of paramount importance. Therefore the securing of the campus, at the eastern end of Salines runway, would be given to the 1st/75th.

At this early stage it was not quite clear why Pearls Airport, which was too short for the larger military transport aircraft, needed to be taken. However, it provided a convenient objective for the 2d/75th, who might otherwise be left behind.

Because intelligence on the defenses around Salines was so sketchy and because the air force liked to have radio navigational beacons on the ground, plus a combat control team to control the airspace, it was agreed that a combined navy SEAL and airforce combat control team should be infiltrated into the Salines area before October 25. They were scheduled to go in on the night of October 23–24.

The safety of the governor-general had also been emphasized. He would represent constitutional authority on the island once it was all over; he would put together a new democratic government, so the Special Operations Forces planners earmarked another SEAL team to rescue him from his residence.

Then there was the radio station. This would need to be taken at the outset, not only to stop RMC broadcasts but to facilitate the United States telling Grenadians what had happened or what to do. A further SEAL team was tasked to capture the large, new, Soviet-supplied transmitting station at Beausejour.

So what was left for Delta? Well, there were the PRA headquarters in Fort Rupert, the PRA base at Calivigny, and the prison on Richmond Hill, full of political detainees. All merited consideration. Fort Rupert could be expected to be well defended, and on available naval charts and tourist maps, it was shown perched atop a high hill on the western edge of St. George's, with no good approach—possible but difficult. The camp at Calivigny was rumored to be heavily defended and could contain a large garrison, perhaps too much for a small Delta Force. That left the prison, fairly isolated, away from nearby civilian houses. Nothing was known about who was imprisoned there or if it was defended, but a surprise attack by helicopter-borne Delta troops at night should secure it quickly. In case the Special Forces teams were numerically too weak, a company of Rangers could go in with them.

The responsibility for delivering all these units to their widely scattered targets would be divided between the air force and the army. MAC's 1st Special Operations Wing, under Colonel Hugh Hunter, would take the Rangers and provide air-to-ground fire support, while elements of the army's 158th, 160th, and 101st Aviation Battalions would fly in the majority of the SEAL teams and Delta. This helicopter force was Task Force 160 (TF 160), nicknamed the Night Stalkers, under command of Colonel Terence Henry, and based at Fort Campbell, Kentucky. TF 160 was, and is, the unit specifically trained to carry Delta units on their covert operations.

This was the plan that Scholtes and his staff put together on October 22.

The marines of 22d MAU had been at sea since October 18, when they had sailed for the Mediterranean to take part in an amphibious exercise in Spain, before continuing to Lebanon to relieve the 24th MAU as the U.S. element in the multinational force. On the night of October 20, McDonald had diverted the group nearer to Grenada, to take station 500 miles to the northeast of the island. Captain Carl Erie was given no reason for the diversion but told that unless instructed otherwise, he could resume course for the Mediterranean at midnight on October 23.

Erie commanded the navy's Amphibious Squadron Four, including the amphibious assault ship USS *Guam,* the amphibious transport dock USS *Trenton,* the dock-landing ship USS *Fort Snelling,* and the tank-landing ships USS *Manitowac* and USS *Barnstable County.* Embarked were the 22d MAU under Colonel James Faulkner, composed of the marine battalion landing team 2d/8th (2d/8th BLT) commanded by Lieutenant Colonel Ray Smith; Marine Medium Helicopter Squadron 261 (HMM-261) under Lieutenant Colonel Granville Amos; and the MAU Service Support Group 22 (MSSG22) under Major Albert Shively. This force was designated TF 124 for Urgent Fury.

On October 21 Erie, Faulkner, and the other officers speculated on what they might have to do in Grenada. The consensus was to assist in the evacuation of U.S. citizens. As with the other services, planning was again handicapped by lack of information. As yet they had no specific mission, no idea as to the number or location of the civilians who might have to be evacuated, and no maps of Grenada. A nautical chart of the island, based on a 1936 British chart, was all that was available. However, two officers had some local knowledge. Commander Richard Butler, the senior staff officer of the amphibious squadron, had sailed a yacht around Grenadian waters six years previously, and Smith had recently studied a hypothetical landing in Grenada at staff college.

The next afternoon, October 22, Faulkner, Smith, Amos, and Major Ernest Van Huss, the MAU operations officer, met on the *Guam* to go through their plan. With nothing further to go on over the last thirty-six hours, the marine officers felt that the likelihood of their being required to land in Grenada was remote. Nevertheless, they produced their version of how best to secure and evacuate civilians, although they still had no idea as to numbers or even which civilians should be taken out. Assuming a hostile environment and the need to secure an evacuation site, it was agreed that Salines airfield must be seized. This would be the evacuation site. One company from 2d/8th BLT would take the airfield in a heliborne assault, while a second company made an amphibious landing over Grand Anse beach south of St. George's. Tanks and trucks would follow this company, and units would turn left to take up blocking positions to cut off Salines from the rest of the island. A third company was the reserve, with the possible task of taking Pearls airport if another evacuation site was proved necessary.

During that day the MAU were ordered to send a CH-53D, Sea Stallion, helicopter from HMM-261 to Antigua to pick up five persons who were to join the task force for the operation. It was thought that these would be State Department officials.

At 10:00 P.M. Erie received a message directing his force to turn toward Grenada and another one giving him the first indication of what opposition to expect. This, however, was in very general terms, with no tactical intelligence, or details of locations. The PRA was thought to be 1,200 strong, supported by 2,000–5,000 militia with 300 or 400 armed police. There were antiaircraft guns of the Soviet 12.7-mm and 37-mm type, manned by well-trained crews. The Cuban presence was accurately assessed as 30 to 50 military advisers, plus 600 construction workers.

At about the same time Metcalf signaled advising that it was the army that would conduct an airborne assault on Grenada. On the marines' role, if any, nothing. For another twenty-four hours, TF 124 remained in suspense, with no knowledge of what was to happen until at 10:00 P.M. on October 23, Sunday night, when the helicopter returned from Antigua. It carried not State Department representatives but liaison officers from Atlantic Command with new orders for the marines.

‡   ‡   ‡

Although perhaps not apparent to the subordinate commanders at the time, on Saturday Urgent Fury had the makings of a fiasco. The 82d Airborne, the Rangers under JSOC, and the marines at sea were all simultaneously planning to take the same objectives: Salines and Pearls airfields. These two locations, especially Salines, were seen as the major objectives of all the ground forces being deployed. This situation continued into the next day. Akers and Pack had got together on their own initiative; Mackmull and Trobaugh had visited Scholtes, but apart from that everybody was planning to do his own thing in isolation.

The intelligence picture improved little. On October 21 the best assessment available for planning stated that the PRA could muster 1,200–1,500 men and the militia 2,000–5,000. It was thought some six to twelve APCs and four to six ZU-23 AA guns were on the island, with some possibly deployed at Salines. Opinions differed on the amount of resistance to be expected. Atlantic felt that there would be scattered opposition at most, while the Defense Intelligence Agency and Barbados Defence Force thought there would be a stronger defense, particularly around Salines. Intelligence analysts predicted that the PRAF had minimum combat capability against a well-equipped force. The Cuban threat was rated as low; they were unlikely to offer much resistance.

But none of this was tactical intelligence concerning the objectives that the U.S. forces were to capture. Aerial photographs showed the layout of Camp Calivigny clearly but indicated no particular defenses. And it was not until after the Rangers were actually in flight to their target that it was finally confirmed that Salines runway was heavily obstructed. The impression given to the units going in at H hour was that it would all be over quickly and that little fighting was likely.

It was at 9:00 P.M. on October 21 that an employee of the National Security Agency went to the Defense Intelligence Agency in Washington. She brought with her some photographs taken during a visit to her brother at the medical school in Grenada. They clearly showed the campus at Grand Anse. And yes, lots of students lived there, as well as at True Blue. Three days before the invasion, this critical piece of information was available, but it never reached the combat troops or their staffs. Throughout the next few days, everybody continued to plan on the basis of securing the one campus. What happened? The details are not clear, but the Defense Intelligence Agency did prepare two copies of an intelligence brief that showed both Grand Anse and True Blue and sent them to JSOC and to McDonald's staff when he visited Washington on October 23 to brief Vessey on his final plan.

McDonald's staff officer (intelligence) learned from CIA sources and the National Photographic Interpretation Center on October 24 that both campuses existed. He informed the JSOC at about 6:00 P.M. that evening, but by then it was too late to affect the operations. Perhaps it was not passed down deliberately. Perhaps it was felt that this information would require fundamental last-minute changes, which would lead to confusion. Possibly to ignore it and hope for the best was the only practical option. If that was the thinking behind this omission, it was dangerous and risky; but on this occasion it turned out to be justified—another example of good fortune smiling on the U.S. forces.[1]

‡ ‡ ‡

At 11:00 A.M. on October 23, McDonald went to the JCS to seek approval for his plan. He got it but with some modifications. The JCS felt that the Calivigny camp must be a D-day objective and that the north of the island could be comfortably left to the marines. This freed the 2d/75th Rangers from taking Pearls, and they were tasked with attacking Calivigny instead. The same day JTF 120 was activated, and four E-3A AWACs plus eight F-15 Eagles flew to Roosevelt Roads in Puerto Rico. From then on two F-15s were on 24-hour strip alert to intercept and deter any flights from Cuba to Grenada.

Later in the day, Atlantic issued its own Operation Order for Urgent Fury. (A detailed Order of Battle for Urgent Fury appears in appendix C, and its deployment is shown on map 5.) In summary, the overall concept of the final plan was to seize the island by surprise during the early hours of Tuesday, October 25. H hour was to be 2:00 A.M. That is the time the first troops actually landed. By dawn, or very soon after, all objectives were to have been taken, including the securing of Sir Paul Scoon and the U.S. medical students. The first phase was to be carried out by JTF 123 (the Special Operations Forces and Rangers) and TF 124 (the marines of 22d MAU). The island was divided more or less in half, with JTF 123 responsible for the south and TF 124 the north. The D-day boundary ran from Beausejour Bay in the west to St. Andrew's Bay in the east, following the twisting main road across the island for most of the way. The commander in the south was Scholtes in a command and control aircraft; in the north, Erie and Faulkner on the *Guam*. The Rangers were to secure Salines airfield, True Blue, and Calivigny, while SEALs and Delta took their special targets in or near St. George's. The marines were tasked with Pearls.

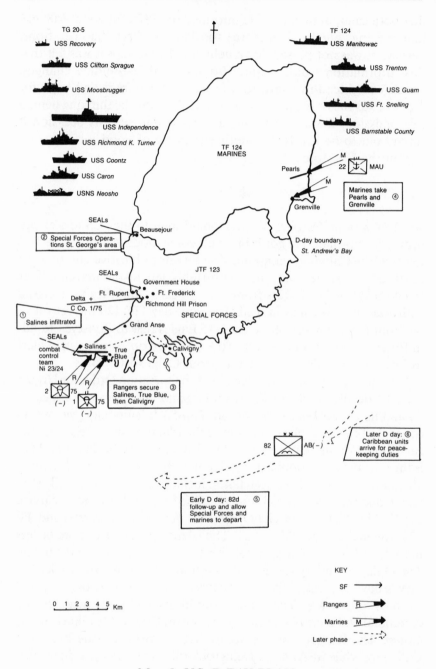

TG 20-5

USS *Recovery*

USS *Clifton Sprague*

USS *Moosbrugger*

USS *Independence*

USS *Richmond K. Turner*

USS *Coontz*

USS *Caron*

USNS *Neosho*

TF 124

USS *Manitowac*

USS *Trenton*

USS *Guam*

USS *Ft. Snelling*

USS *Barnstable County*

TF 124
MARINES

Pearls

M
22 ⚓ MAU
M

Marines take
Pearls and   ④
Grenville

Grenville

SEALs

② Special Forces Opera-
tions St. George's area

Beausejour

D-day boundary
St. Andrew's Bay

JTF 123

SEALs

Government House

Ft. Rupert   Ft. Frederick

Delta +

Richmond Hill Prison

C Co. 1/75

SPECIAL FORCES

① Salines infiltrated

Grand Anse

SEALs

combat
control
team
Ni 23/24

Salines

True
Blue

Calivigny

R

R

2 [✉] 75   1 [✉] 75
(–)   (–)

Rangers secure   ③
Salines, True Blue,
then Calivigny

82 [✕✕] AB(–)

Later D day: ⑥
Caribbean units
arrive for peace-
keeping duties

Early D day: 82d   ⑤
follow-up and allow
Special Forces and
marines to depart

KEY

SF ⟶

Rangers [R] ⟹

Marines [M] ⟹

Later phase ⇢

0 1 2 3 4 5 Km

Map 5. U.S. D-DAY PLAN

Phase 2 was the arrival early on D day (initially at H + 4 hours, around 6:00 A.M.) of the leading elements of TF 121 (82d Airborne) as the reserve force. They were scheduled to take over from the Special Operations Forces in the south, allowing them to fly out immediately from Salines. Later it was anticipated the marines would withdraw as well, leaving the 82d in a law and order role. This phase should have been completed on D day, or certainly by D + 1. With the arrival of the headquarters of TF 121, Trobaugh was to assume command in the south.

The last phase saw the 82d thinning out and handing over peacekeeping duties to the various Caribbean military and police contingents. This was to happen as soon as practical.

Task Group 20.5 was the naval battle group centered on the carrier USS *Independence,* with six accompanying warships and a fleet oiler. Under the command of Rear Admiral Richard Berry, it was tasked with providing surface and air support in the vicinity of the island. Embarked on the carrier was carrier air wing no. 6 with over eighty aircraft—Marine Corps A-6 Intruders and air force A-7 Corsairs.

Finally there was TF 126 under Brigadier General Meyer, based at Roosevelt Roads, Puerto Rico. Its eight F-15s of 33 Tactical Fighter Wing from Elgin Air Force Base, Florida, and four AWACs from Tinker Air Force Base, Oklahoma, were to prevent Cuban interference in Urgent Fury and carry out aerial reconnaissance over the island.

The distances from the United States to Grenada were huge, creating transportation and logistic difficulties (map 6). The C-130s needed refueling en route by KC-10 tanker aircraft, and a forward administrative base much nearer the island was considered vital. The Barbados government obliged by providing the U.S. forces with unrestricted use of their international airfield and allowing them to take over the old terminal buildings adjoining the new ones. Barbados was only 120 miles northeast of Grenada, so this was an ideal situation. In the days that followed, this airport took on the appearance of a military air base with hundreds of landings and takeoffs as planes staged and refueled.

Such was the plan that the president sanctioned when he signed the NSDD on the Sunday evening. The Rangers, marines, and 82d all had to make fundamental last-minute changes to their plans during October 23 and 24. Early on October 25 some 800 marines from 2d/8th BLT were to land in the vicinity of Pearls-Grenville, 600 Rangers would

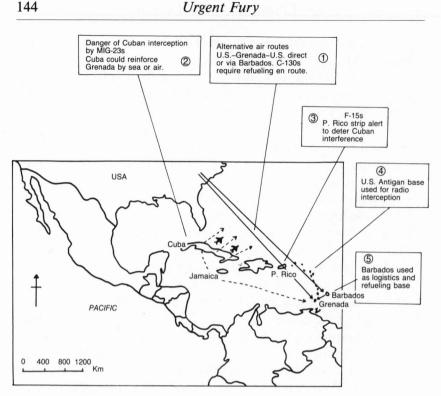

Map 6. U.S. STRATEGIC PLAN

land or drop at Salines (both Ranger battalions were only 50 percent of their normal strength), and about 60 Special Operations Forces troops, reinforced by 50 or 60 Rangers from 1st/75th, would tackle the targets in or around St. George's. The key to success was surprise. The planners were relying on the tight security preceding the operations, the ability of the SEALs and combat control teams going in on October 23–24, remaining undetected until H hour, landings taking place simultaneously during darkness, and the general expectation that opposition would be light.

8

The Other Side
of the Hill

Convey to Austin and Layne . . . that sending reinforcements is
impossible and unthinkable.
> — Fidel Castro to the Cuban embassy in Grenada,
> October 22

W ITHIN the PRA, officers and noncommissioned officers were
given heavy responsibility at an early age and junior rank. Majors or higher were automatically on the staff; captains usually worked
at a headquarters as well, while lieutenants or 2d lieutenants commanded troops at company level or above. Platoon commanders were
invariably warrant officers or senior noncommissioned officers. During Urgent Fury, a 23-year-old 2d lieutenant commanded the largest
PRA unit opposing the invasion on October 25. He was Raeburn
Nelson, the same officer who had commanded the third APC that
attacked Fort Rupert on October 19.

Nelson is a tall, good-looking man, with a ready smile. His short
four years in the army saw him undergo training from squad to
battalion level in Grenada, Cuba, and the Soviet Union—typical of
all the officer cadre of the PRA. Crash courses were designed to produce officers capable of assuming duties undertaken by much older,
and more senior, men in developed armies. The PRA was new. It was
to play a key role in Bishop's Grenada. There was a dearth of local
military experience, coupled with a limited pool of potential officers,
since political reliability was of equal importance to a desire for an
army career. Grenada had no military tradition or expertise apart from

Gairy's ill-disciplined Green Beasts, so it is hardly surprising that by late 1983, the number of regular PRA officers did not exceed thirty. With so few available, with so much to be done to create an army from nothing, with new equipment and weapons arriving by the ton, with the pressure to produce a nation in arms with the people's militia, it was inevitable that almost insurmountable problems arose. Despite this, and even allowing for Cuban assistance, the small nucleus of reliable officers, of whom Nelson was one, performed remarkably well when the test of combat came. It was the PRA, not Cubans, who launched the three distinct counterattacks: one against the Rangers and two against the SEALs. One was a complete success, and another almost succeeded, forcing Metcalf to change his entire plan of operations on the afternoon of D day.

Nelson's mother had five daughters but only the one son. (Nelson, however, counts ten or twelve; he is uncertain of the exact number of outside brothers, that is, children having the same father.) He attended the Government Combined School in St. George's until 1976. With his father's frequent absences and death in 1971 when Nelson was 11, it was his mother who brought him up, a not-untypical Grenadian family situation. At 14 he joined in the Bloody Monday disturbances against Gairy at the Careenage, taking boyish pleasure in throwing soft drink bottles at the police. He was horrified later when a policeman fired his .303 rifle through the door of the Seamen's Union building, killlling Rupert Bishop. Getting a decent job, even with a school-leaving certificate, was difficult in the late 1970s. Nelson drifted from the mosquito eradication program, to clearing the ground in the cemetery, to working as a groundsman at Queen's Park. Then came Bishop's coup and the recruitment drive for the army. Nelson, who had been in the Grenada Cadet Corps at school, joined up on April 3, 1979, although until then he had not been involved in politics. His cadet experience was put to use immediately. Although only a private, he was expected to drill fellow recruits at the old RFG station, then in use as a PRA base.

During his first six months in uniform, Nelson served on personal security duties for both Bishop and Coard; underwent an infantry weapons course at Hope Vale and on the range at Calivigny, under Guyanese instructors; and was trained by Cubans at Grand Etang, before being made an antitank squad commander. In October 1979 he went to Cuba. For a year he was taught a wide variety of military subjects, including advanced infantry training, armaments, military engineering, and topography. During this time he learned to speak passable Spanish. On his return home in late 1980, he was promoted to officer cadet and posted as second in command of Camp Calivigny. There he was also chief of armaments, with responsibility for all weapons and ammunition in the camp.

Nelson was an enthusiastic soldier, but that was not enough to ensure advancement, so in 1981 he became an applicant member of the party. In January 1982, during Armed Forces Week, the commander in chief, Bishop, presented him with his two single 2d lieutenant's stars. Later that year he became a candidate party member. He was selected in September as the group leader for a number of Grenadians going to Moscow for military studies. There, throughout five months of a grueling Soviet winter, he learned, through Soviet interpreters, the intricacies of mechanized warfare. He studied the techniques and tactics of armored, APC-borne infantry up to battalion level. He participated in exercises that spread mechanized units over seemingly endless snow-covered plains, and he watched as tanks and APCs advanced, attacked, or defended areas far larger than his own home island. Nelson describes the experience as "very good; interesting"; but the relevance of it all in the hills and heat of tiny Grenada was highly questionable.

Back at home, the PRA high command was anxious to form an elite motorized unit with infantry mounted in the eight BTR-60 PB armored personnel carriers that the Soviets had supplied. This new unit, called the Motorized Company, was to be based at Fort Frederick, and young Nelson was given the command.

Under Bishop as commander in chief, with Austin as the minister responsible and commander of the PRAF, was a complex hierarchy controlling the PRA, PRM, security service, prisons, police, fire services, and cadets. With Austin, in the Ministry of Defense and Interior at Butler House, were his two deputies, Layne and James. They were both political appointees holding the rank of lieutenant colonel. Layne, a former teacher, was deputy defense secretary, overseeing the military affairs of the ministry; James was the deputy for the interior and head of the security service and cadets. Both had achieved high rank early as they were founding members of the NJM. Both were loyal OREL supporters of Coard.

Within the PRAF all senior officers held military ranks, even if their branch was not actually part of the army. This explained why

St. Bernard, as commissioner of police, and Keith Roberts, in charge of counterintelligence and personal security, were majors. Similarly Justin Roberts was the superintendent of Richmond Hill Prison as a lieutenant, and St. Paul, chief of the prime minister's personal security, was a 2d lieutenant.

The staff of the PRA was a mixture of those using the army for political power and advancement such as Layne (who as time went on appeared to have his eyes on Austin's position), plus Cornwall, and Stroude, and the professional soldiers. Cornwall was not a career soldier, having spent much of his time in Havana as Grenada's ambassador, complaining bitterly of being bypassed in all important matters—and not paying his bills. Stroude was promoted major to increase his status as the political commissar of the army. The soldiers in this group were Majors Einstein Louison and Gahagan. The former was chief of staff until Bishop's arrest, and the latter was the operations officer.

Following the Cuban system, an officer who was the head of a department or camp was given the title of chief. Gahagan was chief of operations, Stroude chief of the political department and Prime chief of artillery, Warrant Officer Shane Ross chief of counterintelligence (within the PRA), Redhead chief of combat preparations, Fraser chief of logistics, while Mayers, until his death on October 19, was the acting chief at Calivigny. The substantive holder was Lieutenant Ruben Francis, who was away on a long course in Cuba.

‡   ‡   ‡

By the end of Bishop's four years, Defense and Interior was the most powerful ministry in the PRG. The objective was to have a nation under arms to defend Grenada from supposed imperialist attack or subversion. Bishop particularly favored the militia, frequently stressing its importance or urging the masses to join. Hand in hand with militia development went the creation and expansion of the PRA. The July 1982 blueprint, which required large-scale Soviet assistance to implement, called for a development plan spread over the three years 1983–1985. Soviet help to complete the establishment and training of the permanent infantry battalion, and five reserve (militia) battalions, was seen as the first phase. Three additional regular and nine more militia battalions were envisaged. To support these enormous increases were requests for vast quantities of arms, ammunitions, vehicles, fuel, uniforms, and repair facilities. To train Grenadians to use and maintain the hardware would require an influx of Soviet military specialists, plus a large-scale expansion of overseas training for PRA personnel.

To administer the militarization program, an extensive system of command and control had been set up throughout the island. (Appendix B sets out the PRAF structure and map 7 its deployment.) With the headquarters at Butler House and army headquarters at Fort Rupert, the country was divided into four military regions, each with its own headquarters and regular military staff, which included at least one Cuban adviser. A glance at map 7 will help in understanding the organization and in identifying the locations of all the main military headquarters or bases in Grenada at the time of Urgent Fury. The regions' task was primarily to administer, mobilize, and train militia units. Region 1, with its headquarters at Fort Frederick, and its chief, Lieutenant Colonel Layne, was the most important. It covered the two southern parishes of the island, St. George's and St. David. This was the most populated area, and the region was supposed to provide two PRM battalions, one from each parish, together with an AA battery. Reporting centers were the police headquarters at Melville Street in St. George's and St. David's village.

Region 2 was the large, sprawling central and eastern parish of St. Andrew. Its headquarters at Mount Horne overlooked Pearls Airport, for which it had particular defense responsibilities. It was the location of one PRM battalion plus an AA platoon of two 12.7-mm. guns.

Region 3 comprised the three northern and western parishes of St. Patrick, St. Mark, and St. John. Its headquarters was at Camp Villa just east of Sauteurs. This region also was the home of a PRM battalion.

Region 4, the smallest but still theoretically supposed to mobilize a militia battalion, was the northern island of Carriacou. The chief of this region was the infamous Abdullah, until he was summoned back for more urgent duties on October 13.

In an emergency, each militia battalion was supposed to activate one rapid mobilization company immediately, to be deployed within its region as the commander in chief saw fit. The remainder of each PRM unit would be used to protect designated key points in their areas. The PRA organization was not tied to the regions as such.

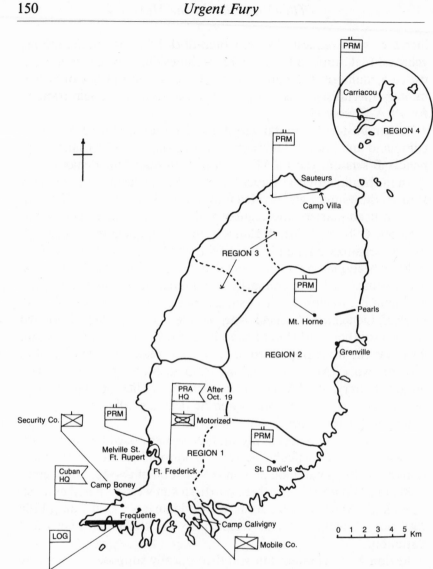

Map 7. PRM MILITARY REGIONS, HEADQUARTERS, BASES,
AND REPORTING CENTERS

Regular units or subunits were based all over the island as their duties
dictated. They were controlled from Fort Rupert, until October 19.
On paper, by 1983, the PRA should have been composed of a permanent battalion at Camp Calivigny, an AA battery in St. George's

(Fort Rupert), and a security company based on Camp Boney on the Quarantine Point peninsula. However, there were large shortfalls in manpower, few units had their proper establishment, and much reliance was placed on the militia's filling gaps on mobilization.

In addition to being the PRA's training facility, with an assault course and a firing range to the west, Calivigny was the home of the permanent battalion. The battalion's establishment showed a motorized company, a mobile company, a rapid mobilization company, antiaircraft, antitank, and mortar batteries, plus an exploration platoon. By late 1983 the motorized and mobile companies were at full strength, with the former under Nelson at Fort Frederick and the latter under Mayers at Calivigny. The exploration platoon, which consisted of the two Soviet BRDM-2 armored cars under 2d Lieutenant Michael Bridgeman, was normally deployed at Mount Weldale on security duties near the official residences of the PRG leaders. The AA, antitank, and mortar units relied for half their men on the PRM; the rapid mobilization infantry company was an entirely militia unit.

Prime, as chief of artillery, was responsible for the supervision and training of all AA, antitank, and mortar units. The AA battery was primarily tasked with the defense of key points in and around St. George's, such as Butler House, Fort Rupert, and Fort Frederick. It was equipped with both Soviet ZU 23-mm twin-barreled guns and some old Cuban 12.7-mm four-barreled heavy machine guns. Not much progress had been made with the mortar company; only three 82-mm mortars were actually in use with the mobile company, while the other three were at Frequente for the militia. The 75-mm recoilless rifle-type of antitank guns were mostly still greased up in storage.

Redhead's duties as chief of combat preparedness included ensuring proper training programs were carried out and responsibility for the Security Company. This unit was charged with around-the-clock protection of ministers' homes or offices and security at public meetings and rallies but not the provision of bodyguards, who came from the security service. It was a regular full-strength company of well over 100 men, with its headquarters at Camp Boney but with detachments on permanent duty at Butler House, Fort Rupert, Mount Weldale, and Parade where Bishop had private houses.

The marine side of the PRAF had not received much attention, and at the time of the intervention the Coast Guard consisted of four small patrol boats, based in the Careenage. The Soviets had promised four modern boats, to be delivered during the period 1983–1986, with two more coming from North Korea. A new deep-water harbour complex was to be built with Soviet assistance at Grenville, on the east coast. This was to facilitate transporting Grenadian agricultural exports to the Soviet Union but, like the airport, the harbor could, and undoubtedly would, have accommodated warships, including submarines.

Urgent Fury put an end to Bishop's plans to develop an airline, which in normal times would have been put to civilian commercial use but whose aircraft could be converted quickly to military purposes. It was on May 24, 1983, shortly after his return from Moscow, that Bishop had a lengthy meeting with the Soviet ambassador on the massive aid proposals for the next few years. In addition to the uniforms, trucks, patrol boats, and 3,260 tons of food, the ambassador gave detailed advice on the type of aircraft to be supplied. First there was the AN-26 transport plane for the Grenadian leadership. It would have a comfortable executive interior with "sofa and car space," although Sazhenev did not recommend the car-carrying configuration. This aircraft would fly regularly between Cuba and Grenada in Grenadian colors but with a Cuban crew and fifteen Soviet technicians servicing it in Havana. On October 25, the U.S. Marines captured an AN-26 on the tarmac at Pearls, together with its Cuban crew, but this was not the Grenadian VIP plane. Also taken was an AN-2 Colt rigged for parachute training.

This was not all. No fewer than five more aircraft, fitted out for commercial use to avoid a political outcry, each capable of carrying thirty-nine paratroopers plus 6 tons of cargo, were destined for Grenada, via Cuba. Again Cuban pilots were envisaged until Grenadians could be trained. The Central Committee had agreed to select four suitable candidates for this training at their April 18 meeting.

‡   ‡   ‡

Bishop and the Defense Ministry's plans for the PRAF were staggering. If all had gone well and the Soviets, Czechs, and North Koreans had fulfilled their agreements, by 1986 the PRAF would have had 4 regular infantry battalions, over 60 APCs, 108 ZU-23 AA guns, 50 GRAD P launchers, 160 military vehicles, 7 aircraft, 6 new patrol vessels, a workshop repair facility, a large new training base, a school for training Grenadian commanding officers and specialists, together with thousands of tons of equipment, stores, and ammunition. The militia would have grown to no fewer than 14 battalions. The consequential influx of Soviet advisers and technicians would have dwarfed the puny Cuban military presence. Grenada would have been completely dependent on Soviet finance, Soviet spares, and Soviet training. The goal was a Grenadian military base in the Caribbean, controlled by Moscow, if necessary through Havana. Bishop knew full well where he was leading his country, although many other Grenadians did not. When writing to the Soviet minister of defense, Marshal Dimitri Ustinov, in February 1982, the prime minister said, "And our Party and Armed Forces look forward with the greatest expectations to our comrades receiving training with the Glorious Red Army, in the land of the Immortal Lenin and the Great October Revolution which opened a new world to mankind."

Fortunately, for both Grenadians and the U.S. forces when they landed, most of all this militarization was a PRG pipe dream. Reality was quite different. The grandiose expansion plans for the period 1983–1986 had not yet started, and what was in place fell far short of intentions.

The orgy of self-criticism within the Central Committee during July, August, and September revealed a realization by the PRG leadership that all was far from well in the PRAF. In his statement to full party members on September 25, Austin protested that for over a year his duties with the construction program had forced him to neglect the army and its problems. He expressed grave concern, emphasizing how critical the military was in a revolutionary situation. The minutes record Austin stating, "The lessons of Poland showed that when the revolution was in danger and there was chaos in the Party and Society it was only the Armed Forces that were able to rescue the situation." They were prophetic words.

Austin's leadership had come under attack during the Central Committee meeting ten days before. Chris De Riggs had been the first to propose that he be replaced as commander of the PRAF by Layne, with Cornwall taking over as chief of political and academic work within the army. James, quick to support this suggestion, did not mince his words: "We all agree that the Army is in a state of rut and demoralisation, along with a serious ideological drift. The Army needs at this time Leninist leadership in that of Comrade Layne, and the political and academic work of Comrade Cornwall."

Both James and Layne had planned this bid for the army leadership and were testing the feeling of the meeting. As George Louison was later to stress, "James and Layne wielded the real power in the army. Austin never held the extent of their power. Layne was the Politburo person in the army. James was in charge of the Interior, police, intelligence. They wanted to wield military power rather than wanting to build an army of the highest professional standards. Their militarism was a militarism bent on political power."

Tan Bartholomew reiterated the "problems in the camps." He specifically pointed the finger at PRG leadership failings saying, "Ministers are buying new cars when soldiers cannot get food to eat. . . . The masses have lost confidence in the Army's capability to defend the revolution." He supported the appointment of Layne and Cornwall before switching his attention to the Ministry of the Interior. James's excessive overseas travel came under attack. Bartholomew recommended that "Comrade James, as leader, should not be allowed to travel because of the need to sit on top of the work."

Austin survived these criticisms—just. Ventour, Bain, Whiteman, and George Louison felt he should remain, largely because of his long experience with the military and his personal popularity with the soldiers. Strachan clinched it with a compromise: Austin to stay but Layne and Cornwall to serve under him full time on army affairs.

The Central Committee had every reason to be worried. The PRAF had serious defects, the most ominous being the low morale of many of the soldiers. Their material needs of pay, food, and accommodation had been badly neglected due to the poor economic situation. The monthly salary of U.S.$100 for a private did not stretch far. Although they were supposed to be rationed in camp, Sergeant Gabriel recalled being forced to serve rice and sugared water as a main meal. The PRA was encouraged to grow its own food on plots near the bases, but this had not worked satisfactorily. There were continuing difficulties with power failures, breakdowns of water supply or plumbing, and a general lack of maintenance in their barracks. In some cases troops had to live in tents for prolonged periods. The PRA was better off than the police, and although there had been no serious breach of discipline, the men were complaining. A large number were saying they would not renew their five-year contracts when they expired in 1984. Some had left already and slipped away to Trinidad. Some units were understrength, recruiting was a problem, and, as Austin had pointed out, the revolution depended on the army. Whiteman was undoubtedly on the right track when he said, "We have to find a moderate increase of salary for the soldiers, and a food aid package at the end of every month. . . . No amount of political work can move them without material aids."

Coard cleverly took advantage of Bishop's absence from the country in early October to use his position as deputy to approve a 15 percent pay raise, better leave, and an end-of-the-month food package to help ensure army allegiance in his confrontation with the prime minister—not that the troops actually saw any of these benefits as Urgent Fury intervened.

Within the PRM the situation was worse. "The militia is nonexistent," said Ventour at the mid-September Central Committee meeting. He was hardly exaggerating. A major effort was made to motivate the militia by convincing everybody of the seriousness of the threat. A new scheme was to be implemented to form a workplace militia: volunteers who would receive training at work and take over security duties at workplaces or defend them in an emergency.

In March 1983 there was an island-wide mobilization exercise for the PRM, in readiness for Reagan's long-awaited attack. It had revealed numerous shortcomings: poor turnout, lack of sufficient transport, inadequate leadership from PRM officers, a low standard of training, and little enthusiasm. It convinced the PRG that they had a long way to go before the militia could perform in combat. The centralization of so many of the militia's weapons in the stores at Frequente was not conducive to either training or rapid deployment, particularly as insufficient transport could be found to move them.

The culmination of the exercise was at Salines where a number of expatriates had houses, including Dr. Robert Jordan, an American tutor at the medical school. Although not permitted to get too close, he was able to witness a lot of firing, with troops and vehicles dashing up and down the runway. PRG top brass watching from Calliste hill included Bishop, Austin, and a group of senior Cuban officers. Much firing took place out to sea, including from a ZU-23 AA gun, with a PRA crew and Cuban instructors. A plywood silhouette of a helicopter was erected south of the runway, with the gun 200 meters away on the north side. The crew fired some twenty-five rounds, after which the Cubans fetched it back in a truck. There was much excitement and fury, with the target thrown to the ground, when the Cubans discovered it had been missed completely. The gunners did slightly better against parachute flares, hitting some of them. Dr. Jordan could not help but sympathize with any fishing or sailing boats, or indeed aircraft, that might have been in the area because no warnings had been announced.

Bishop took the chair at a Worker's Committee meeting on the evening of March 31, 1983. He was given a dismal picture. With workplace militia, a total of seventy-six workplaces had been visited, but only nineteen wanted training to start. Committee leaders reported the mood of no fewer than twenty-five workplaces as low, commenting that many did not see a need for a militia or believed that the propaganda of an American threat was exaggerated. Although some places wanted to "defend the revolution," many others suggested prayer as being a better way. Under the heading of "comments" the report submitted shows "pray"; "let the army deal with defense"; "no invasion"; "pardon line"; and "very strong religious feeling. Pray and wait." Bishop was not reassured.

The dropout rate from the militia had been steadily growing over the last two years. People became disinterested because they did not believe a serious threat existed; the training was badly organized, dull, and required attendance in their own free time, usually over weekends. The report criticized the instructors, who were often apathetic, boring, and disorganized. Mention was made of "too much fooling by younger members"; "make the training more interesting"; "weapon training to be conducted during working hours"; "more war games to keep the interest"; "more range work"; and "show movies of training of mercenaries in Miami."

As far back as April 1982, the Cubans and PRG had been aware of the PRAF's shortcomings. A high-level meeting had taken place in Havana, with the Cuban delegation headed by General Arnaldo Ochoa, vice-minister of the Ministry of the Revolutionary Armed Forces. All the Grenadian military hierarchy were present, including Bishop, Austin, James, Layne, and Einstein Louison, plus Coard and Strachan. Far-reaching decisions had been agreed: Cuban construction workers in Grenada were to be armed, Cuban officers were to train the militia, high-frequency radio links between Grenada and Cuba were to be established, an accelerated training program for PRA officers was needed in Cuba, and an extra company of Cuban troops should be sent to Grenada. All except the last had been implemented by late October 1983.

Discussions had not resolved such matters as the provision of ZU-23 AA guns to the Cuban construction workers, the use of Salines by Cubans in an emergency, more Cuban workers to build headquarters and barracks in regions 2 and 3, the need for more communications equipment, or the creation of a rapid deployment force to deal with any surprise attack.

The conference concluded with General Ochoa's highlighting what he felt were the Grenadians' military weaknesses. In his view the Americans would eventually invade; therefore some financial cutbacks in other areas might be necessary to boost defense. He did not consider, rightly, the unwieldy BTR-60 APC suitable for the island's terrain; the PRA was unstable, lacked training, and was not ready for combat. Command lacked continuity, with personnel being shifted too often; the PRA's structure and composition was wrong; and Grenadian defense plans did not reflect a proper combat organization or take account of the difficult, mountainous terrain. Ochoa ended with a recommendation that had the support of everyone: more political indoctrination for the soldiers.

‡   ‡   ‡

Eighteen months later, on October 19, 1983, the situation within the PRAF was worse. The RMC had to deal with the prospect of imminent attack by a vastly superior force; the Grenadian units were poorly equipped, partially trained, and understrength, while their morale was decidedly shaky. Some regular units relied heavily on the PRM to fill deficiencies in their establishment, but the militia was a broken reed. With Bishop's execution, the men and women who made it up were almost totally alienated from the RMC. Why should they fight to protect people who had just murdered their leader? Despite hysterical appeals for them to mobilize to defend the homeland, only a tiny fraction responded. With a paper strength of some 3,000, fewer than 250 reported for duty. Had the invasion come before Bishop's death, it would have been a different story, with thousands clamoring for arms. When the execution squad opened fire that afternoon, they killed the people's will to resist, just as surely as they killed their prime minister.

The sheer size of the probable invasion made almost any defense planning futile. The RMC realized they would have to confront not only large numbers of attacking troops capable of amphibious landings, helicopter assault, or parachute drop but massive fire support. Naval gunfire, ground artillery, tanks, helicopter gunships, and unlimited ground attack aircraft could be deployed against them. In response the PRA could muster no combat aircraft or ships, no helicopters, no radar detection system; they had only a handful of cumbersome APCs and a few antiquated AA guns without radar-assisted fire control. The ZU-23s were twin barreled automatic guns, with an effective antiaircraft ceiling of 2,500 meters (8,200 feet). Because they lacked radar, they were difficult to operate at night, in bad weather, or if the target was above cloud. Searchlights, of which the PRA had several, were needed to illuminate the target in darkness. Unless well dug in, the seated gunner was uncomfortably exposed to small arms fire and needed strong nerves to keep firing when under attack. The 12.7-mm was the 4-barreled heavy machine gun, gas operated, with a range of up to 1,500 meters. It had been in service for fifty years, and those held by the PRA were reconditioned, not new, weapons.

When faced with these daunting defense problems, the RMC quickly appreciated they could never win on their own. The best solution would be to prevent invasion by diplomatic means. If it could be delayed for a few days or, better, a week, it might just be long enough to let the world know what the United States was contemplating, with a consequential buildup of international pressure to stop it. The RMC pursued this option with vigor, sending telexes and telegrams to the United States and United Kingdom protesting any invasion as uncalled for and unnecessary. No foreign nationals were endangered, and anybody wishing to leave could do so.

There was another option, dreaded by the United States: hostage taking. Given the hopeless military situation, surely the only way they might halt the attackers in their tracks was to seize hostages. They could have done so easily at any time before D day and for two days after. The RMC did not. They did not even so threaten. Why? Primarily because, rightly or wrongly, they felt hostage taking would precipitate the invasion they so desperately wished to avoid. They were at great pains to try to reassure everybody that students, indeed all foreigners, were safe. What they did not understand was that the United States could never know in the light of their recent actions whether the RMC was speaking the truth.

However genuine the RMC's reassurances may have been before the invasion, they were desperate men, and once under attack, with their own lives at stake, their sole remaining option was to bargain hostages' lives for a U.S. withdrawal or their personal security. They made no attempt to do this. According to Grenadians I questioned, including Nelson, who was a member of the RMC, hostage taking was never, to their knowledge, considered or discussed. Perhaps they left it too late. With hindsight, it does, however, lend credence to their insistence all along that U.S. citizens were never in danger.

If diplomacy failed, the only allies the RMC could turn to were the Cubans. More than 40 military advisers and over 650 armed construction workers were in Grenada. With these reinforcements and with more flown in, with the prospect of the United States being involved in prolonged combat against Cuba, perhaps intervention could be avoided. Havana was deeply committed to the Grenadian revolution; it would not wish to see Grenada fall to imperialist attack, so an appeal for help could hardly go unheeded. Ideological solidarity should be sufficient to persuade Castro to forget the recent bloodshed. It was not.

From October 20 on, Cuban ambassador Rizo got little sleep. He was the intermediary between Austin and Castro, receiving, passing on, and explaining a host of messages as the RMC requested reinforcements and Cuba declined to provide them. The council not only wanted troops flown in but also for all Cubans in Grenada to fight under PRA command. This was asking too much.

Castro's position was difficult. Bishop had been his friend; Cuba had been committed for over four years to building the revolution in Grenada and had invested substantial sums in aid to the country. There were nearly 800 Cuban nationals on the island, with the prospect of U.S. military intervention mounting hourly. Coard and the RMC had perpetrated an appalling blunder in killing Bishop. It was not just senseless murder, but it had handed to the Americans, on a silver platter, a perfect pretext to invade and destroy all that had been achieved. It had the makings of a setback from which it might never be possible to recover. But how should Cuba help? Would the United States permit Cuba to fly in troops unmolested? Unlikely. How could Cuba cope with a direct military confrontation with the United States? Castro understood the impossibility of winning and of asking Cubans to die for a regime that had just executed their prime minister. Nevertheless, a complete withdrawal would be dishonorable. Even the RMC were fellow communists.

Castro appreciated that the only way to salvage something was to prevent invasion by diplomatic means. At 9:00 P.M. on Saturday, October 22, the U.S. Interests Section of the Swiss embassy in Havana received the following message:

> That the US side is aware of the developments in Grenada; that it is also aware of our position on these developments and of our determination of not interfering in the internal affairs of that country. That we are aware of their concern about the numerous US residents there. That we are also concerned about the hundreds of Cuban cooperation personnel working there in different fields, and about the news that US naval forces are approaching Grenada.
>
> That according to the reports we have, no US or foreign nationals, nor our personnel has had any problems. It is convenient to keep in touch on this matter, so as to solve favorably any difficulty that may arise or action that may be taken relating to the security of these individuals, without violence or intervention in the country.

In the United States, planning for the military option was under way, and Castro's plea to avoid intervention was not replied to until almost three days later. Some three hours after U.S. troops had landed, Cuba was told, via the U.S. Interests Section, that American forces had acceded to an OECS request for assistance: "The Government of the United States agrees to the Cuban proposal of October 22 to maintain contact concerning the safety of the personnel of each side. . . . U.S. Armed Forces presently in Grenada have been instructed to be in contact with the Cuban ambassador in Grenada to ensure that every consideration is given to the safety of Cuban personnel on the Island." Reality was different; Rangers and Cubans were fighting for control of Salines.

It had also been on Saturday that Castro disabused the RMC that Cuba would fly in troops to fight alongside the PRA. While agreeing that defenses should be strengthened, Castro made his decision crystal clear:

> If the US intervenes, we must vigorously defend ourselves as if we were in Cuba, in our camp sites, in our workplaces close by, but only if we are directly attacked. I repeat: only if we are directly attacked. We

would thus be defending ourselves, not the Government or its deeds. If the Yankees land on the runway section near the University or on its surroundings to evacuate their citizens, fully refrain from interfering. . . . Convey to Austin and Layne the following oral reply to their proposals: "That our force, essentially made up of civilian cooperation workers, is too small to be considered as a significant military factor vis-a-vis a large scale US invasion. That sending reinforcements is impossible and unthinkable. That the political situation created inside the country due to the people's estrangement on account of the death of Bishop and other leaders, isolation from the outside world, etc. considerably weakens the country's defense capabilities, a logical consequence derived from the serious errors made by Grenadian revolutionaries. . . . That they have to find a way to reach a reconciliation with the people, perhaps one way would be to clarify the death of Bishop . . . and seek out those responsible."

This plain speaking was not to the liking of the RMC, but it did not prevent them from responding immediately with renewed demands for reinforcements. On Sunday Castro sent another signal:

The Grenadian revolutionaries should try to win over the people for the defense of the country. . . . Cuba cannot send reinforcements, not only because it is materially impossible in the face of the overwhelming US air and naval superiority in the area, but also because politically, if this were to be merely a struggle among Caribbeans, it should not do so in order not to justify US intervention. . . . If Grenada is invaded by the US, the Cuban personnel will defend their positions in their camps and working areas with all their energy and courage. . . . It is impossible to assign them any other mission.

Again the RMC refused to accept. This time they wanted Cuban construction workers subordinate to the PRA high command and to sign a formal agreement on the responsibilities of Cuban and Grenadian troops in the defense of the island. On Monday, Castro, by now thoroughly infuriated, spelled it out:

Cuban personnel will defend their positions, that is, the runway up to the Hardy Bay filling and the area between Point Salines and Morne Rouge. . . . It would be better if that area [True Blue campus] were free of military personnel so that it would not be regarded as a battle ground which could justify armed actions by imperialism under the pretext of evacuating its citizens.

In fact this last message, due to be delivered at 8:00 A.M. on Tuesday, never reached the RMC. Nevertheless, there was no doubt in the minds of the council leadership that they were on their own militarily. The only concession made by Havana was to send a Colonel Tortolo, with a handful of assistants, to take charge of any Cuban resistance that became necessary and to ensure the RMC understood Cuba's stand. Tortolo arrived some seventeen hours before the Rangers and marines.

‡   ‡   ‡

By Sunday the RMC was certain they would have to fight. With U.S. warships in the area, with OECS soldiers moving to Barbados, with a clear invasion warning from Guyana, a full mobilization of the country was started. Diplomatic appeals had gone unanswered; no reinforcements would be forthcoming from Havana; the Cuban military presence in the island was tiny, and moreover, they, and the construction workers, had been given a restricted defensive role only in their camp areas. On top of this, the combat effectiveness and morale of the PRA was questionable. As mobilization appeals were largely ignored, there came the realization that they would be fighting with only a fraction of the militia. There would be no nationwide resistance. With 450–475 regulars and fewer than 250 militia, together with 635 Cuban construction workers and 43 military specialists at Salines, the RMC prepared to take on the military giant of the Western world.

The RMC planners in Fort Frederick first assessed the threat, trying to guess where and how the attack was most likely to come (map 8). They anticipated amphibious assault and heliborne landings, supported by gunships and ground attack aircraft. They assumed that Salines Airport would be an early target, possibly Pearls as well, and were certain that St. George's would be a main objective. There was agreement that amphibious landings were likely in St. George's harbor, across Grand Anse beach, and possibly at Grand Bay south of Salines. Any, or all, could be combined with helicopter attack plus air and naval gunfire support. Dawn and dusk were considered the most dangerous times. The high command was concerned at the vulnerability of its headquarters, exposed on the ridge so close to St. George's; the logistics chief, 2d Lieutenant Fraser, felt the massive armament and supply depot at Frequente was highly vulnerable to early ground attack and from the air.

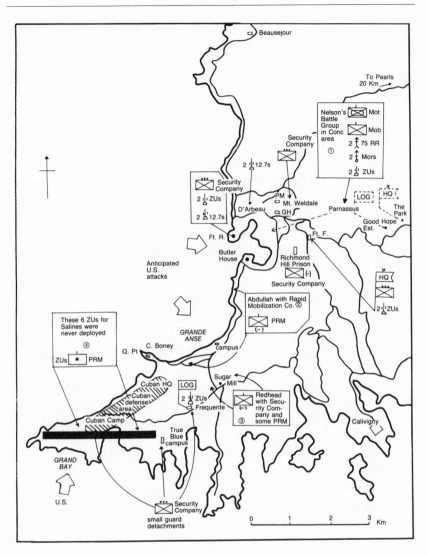

Map 8. THE RMC'S DEFENSIVE PLAN

They correctly deduced that the main area of operations would be in the southwest and St. George's. In fact, they predicted the U.S. attacks with considerable accuracy. At one time the U.S. Army, marines, and Special Forces were all contemplating taking Salines, with the marines going ashore at Grand Anse as well. In the final

U.S. plan, St. George's, Salines, and Pearls were the main H-hour objectives; Grand Anse came on the second afternoon. The RMC appreciated it was an ideal beach, but they did not realize the U.S. attacking units had no inkling that over 200 medical students lived there.

Three things soon became apparent. First, lack of sufficient manpower was going to necessitate the defenses being concentrated in the southwest. The rest of the island, including Pearls, would have to be virtually ignored. Second, AA defenses would play a critical part in the battle. Third, the logistics base at Frequente should be moved to a less exposed location before the invasion, and similarly the PRA headquarters should have an alternative position. What they could not know was that the United States thought army headquarters was still at Fort Rupert and that the significance of Frequente was unknown. In the event Fraser had been given an impossible task; transport was hopelessly inadequate for the huge quantities of stores to be shifted. A start was made, however, and some reserve stocks were deposited at Good Hope Estate in the hills, 4 kilometers east of St. George's. The Park, on the slopes of Mt. Pleasant 1,000 meters east of Good Hope, was selected as the fallback command post. It was never used.

Discounting headquarters and administrative staff, the RMC based the overall defense plan on having four infantry companies of over 100 strong (three PRA and one PRM), two AA batteries of six ZU-23s each (one PRA and one PRM), plus two more ZUs attached to the company at Calivigny, and three platoons of two 12.7-mm AA guns each (PRM). Although there were eighteen ZU-23s and more 12.7s on the island, there were insufficient trained crews to man them.

Second Lieutenant Nelson was given the largest and most important command. In effect, he had the only unit resembling an infantry battle group, composed of regular PRA troops from his own motorized company, with the mobile company from Calivigny, which had lost its commander (Mayers) on October 19. The motorized company had three infantry platoons—two mounted in the BTR-60 APCs and one in Gaz trucks. Nelson traveled in an APC, giving a total of seven in the company (the eighth had broken down at Frequente). There was also a small antitank squad of two 75-mm recoilless rifles. In total, there were about 110 men. The mobile company also had three platoons of infantry, commanded by sergeants and mounted in Gaz trucks, together with an 82-mm mortar platoon of three mortars under a warrant officer and an AA platoon with two ZU-23s under a sergeant. The mobile company had slightly over 100 men. This battle group was the main strike force of the PRA, with six infantry platoons, all mobile, plus mortar and AA fire support under command. Nelson's task was to defend St. George's. On Sunday evening, as the SEALs flew toward Salines, Nelson was settling his unit into a concentration area at Mt. Parnassus 2 kilometers east of the town, having moved out of Fort Frederick and Calivigny that afternoon.

The third regular PRA company was the security company under Redhead. The platoons of this company, which was normally well over 100 strong, were scattered around on static guard duties. Detachments of 20 or fewer were tasked with the close defense of Fort Rupert, Fort Frederick, Mount Weldale, Richmond Hill Prison, Frequente, and even a few gate guards on the campuses at True Blue and Grand Anse. A squad was responsible for routine security at Salines Airport. Redhead was given some fifty militia men as they trickled in, and with this mixed force, he was ordered to block the main road approaches to St. George's from the south. In particular he was to hold the area of the key road junction at Ruth Howard, near the Sugar Mill.

By Monday it was obvious that few of the militia were going to fight. The two battalions in region 1 could hardly muster 120 between them. Of these, 50 or so went to Redhead, while the balance constituted the so-called rapid mobilization company. Abdullah was given this unit with instructions to defend Grand Anse from Ross Point in the north to Quarantine Point in the south. He had little or no transport and only rifles and light machine guns.

Salines was to be left to the Cubans. They were to follow their government's instructions to defend their work areas, although the RMC's original plan envisaged the PRM ZU-23 battery deploying in this area as well. This would have given six guns around this key point, but as luck would have it, none was available because the militia crews failed to report for duty.

The AA defense of St. George's was in the hands of the regular ZU battery—less one platoon of two guns deployed to protect the logistics base at Frequente. There were two guns at Fort Rupert and two at Fort Frederick. These were augmented by four 12.7-mm guns and two at D'Arbeau above the quarry east of Queen's Park. These

12.7s had militia crews, and the ones at D'Arbeau were dug in, tasked with protecting the nearby power station plus the Mount Weldale area. According to Nelson these guns were professionally handled on October 25.

Finally the plan envisaged Pearls being defended by the militia from region 2, including two 12.7-mm guns positioned atop the conical hill immediately north of the runway. Their instructions were to destroy the control tower if the United States appeared about to occupy the airport. A delaying action only was envisaged in the north.

At Fort Frederick, the RMC leadership was busy moving from their tent into the dank, wet tunnels beneath the fort. There they would be uncomfortable but immune to aerial attack—and out of radio communications with their units.

9

October 25

Special Operations
in St. George's

A lot of things went wrong in Grenada because the Special Forces'
plan was overlaid by the conventional forces' plan.

— General Edward Meyer,
former U.S. Army chief of staff

N OT long after dark on the night of October 23–24, twelve navy
SEALs and four air force combat control team members were
standing up inside the noisy, dimly lit, interiors of two C-130 Hercules aircraft. They were about 30 kilometers off the southwest tip
of Grenada, ready to make what is probably the most difficult and
dangerous of parachute jumps: into water at night. The aircraft came
in low and level at about 600 feet, the pilots searching for the reassuring
lights of the USS *Clifton Sprague* and its safety boat. The invasion
of Grenada was about to start some thirty-six hours before the main
assault.

The planners at Norfolk and Washington were concerned that there
should be no problems on D day in ensuring the aircraft carrying
the Rangers got to Salines on time. Although the MC-130E Combat
Talons, with their sophisticated navigational aids, would be leading
the others, it was felt necessary to position radio guidance beacons
covertly near the runway. This, combined with an up-to-the-minute
local weather report, should make it doubly certain nothing went
wrong with navigation. The air force was adamant that this was a task

for their combat control team personnel, who were also trained and equipped to effect terminal guidance, or control the air traffic flow, from the ground. Additionally, not a lot was known about the runway—whether it was effectively blocked or what defenses were nearby.

The navy thought that because the combat control team would be dropped into the sea near a warship and continue by small boat that the SEALs must be involved. A joint SEAL–combat control team group was formed for what was an extremely tricky mission. Knowing nothing about the enemy at their objective, the team would need to make a lengthy sea approach in the dark, navigate to the Salines area, select a suitable landing spot, and get ashore undetected—assuming the parachute drop itself was successful. Then they would move to the vicinity of the runway. After positioning the beacons, the entire party must remain concealed until after the Rangers landed twenty-four hours later. This meant finding a good hiding spot, unlikely to be discovered by patrols during the daylight hours of October 24. All this had to be achieved before dawn. For this reason, their departure from the United States had been early on the afternoon of October 23. Such an operation required a high level of skill—and, with sixteen men plus equipment to conceal for so lengthy a period, not a little luck.

The sixteen men were divided equally into two groups, each allocated a 23-foot Boston Whaler boat, to be deployed by the *Clifton Sprague* at the drop zone. The boats' crews would signal by lights to the jumpers in the water and take the boats back to the ship after the SEALs and combat control team had gone ashore. The alternative method of using a submarine for the approach to the island had been considered but was rejected because the SEALs at Roosevelt Roads in Puerto Rico, where the submarine was based, had not yet been trained in the special techniques required for the men to leave or enter a submarine at sea.

The weather that evening was far from ideal for this type of mission; a 25-knot wind was whipping up the waves. Had it not been an operational drop, it would almost certainly have been cancelled. The aim was to jump upwind of the whalers and the safety boat, which would themselves be positioned upwind of the *Clifton Sprague*. The men were heavily laden with equipment, radios, and personal weapons strapped to their sides. Each wore an uninflated life vest over his equipment and stood in single file with his static line hooked up, waiting tensely for the jump.

In this type of jump, the parachute harness release buckle must be hit at exactly the right moment. In darkness it is far from easy for the jumper to judge when he is only a few feet above the water—the time to hit the buckle. If it is done too early, the jumper may plunge down from a considerable height; if left too late, he enters the water with his chute still attached, with the possibility of entanglement or being dragged through the water by the wind. If either error is made, the likelihood of drowning increases.

Although the *Clifton Sprague* had been sighted when the team leaped into the blackness, the ship was not as close as it should have been when the signal was given. Part of the problem was that the air crews were inexperienced; they had never practiced this type of operation under these circumstances. They were not well versed in the techniques, and one aircraft dropped well wide of the ship. Those in the whalers had considerable difficulty locating the jumpers in the water. At the end of a lengthy operation, Machinist Mate 1st Class Kenneth Butcher, Quartermaster 1st Class Kevin Lundberg, Hull Technician 1st Class Stephen Morris, and Senior Chief Engineman Robert Schanberger were missing. A 25 percent loss at the outset was a tragic blow. The remainder, in one whaler, started toward the island.

As they neared the coastline, trying to pick a suitable-looking beach, preferably Canoe, Black, Cato, or Grand Bays, on the extreme end of the southwest peninsula, they spotted a Grenadian patrol boat. To avoid discovery, they cut the engine, to drift silently until the danger had passed. Unfortunately the choppy sea swamped the boat and engine, which could not be restarted. After many fruitless attempts and with the amount of darkness left to complete their tasks dwindling fast, they limped back out to sea and were picked up by the destroyer.

This was a major disappointment to Scholtes. He considered this failure to put the landing team into Salines sufficient justification for postponing the entire operation for twenty-four hours, and he urged Metcalf to make D day October 26. There was consternation in both Norfolk and Washington, but a day's delay was asking too much. The State Department spoke out strongly against it; others were worried about the increased likelihood of security leaks; but Scholtes argued fiercely that the Special Operations Forces must get to Salines. A compromise was agreed: a reconstituted SEALs–combat control team would try again the next night—October 24–25.

This proved to be a decision with far-reaching adverse consequences. Because the group needed many hours of darkness to do their job, it would be impossible if H hour remained at 2:00 A.M. Atlantic Command, and the JCS, agreed to let it slip first to 4:00 A.M. and then an hour later. The conventional planners seemed to have no inkling what this would mean for those Special Operations Forces who needed darkness on D day to carry out their missions. Navigational aids were deemed more important than the achievement of surprise. While it would have made the MC-130 crews more comfortable with their direction finding, the inboard navigational systems were perfectly capable of locating Salines without ground radio beacons. Given the planners' lack of information about the enemy, this flagrant disregard for the foremost of military principles was a professional blunder that came within an ace of wrecking the entire operation.

On Monday another detachment of SEALs successfully parachuted in by the destroyer to link up with the remainder of the first group. That night they tried again. Regrettably the same fate awaited them: swamped boat, failure to reach the shore, and a return to the ship. It was a depressing start to Urgent Fury.

It has been asked why if on both occasions the SEALs and combat control team were able to make it back to the *Clifton Sprague* they could not get ashore and complete their mission. Only the participants can answer this for certain, but it is likely that they had too little darkness left and did not want to risk discovery, which would have compromised the whole operation. They were not in a position to know it was already compromised.

As a highly covert mission, it was flawed in its conception, with both navy and air force insisting on participating. This resulted in far too large a group for a task that relied on stealth and remaining undetected by day in a small area dominated by the enemy. Team members had not trained together, and the air crews were not experienced enough in special operations. The lack of suitable training by the SEALs at Puerto Rico compelled the adoption of a somewhat risky method of insertion, which was certainly more vulnerable to poor weather conditions.

The result of these two failures was four deaths and the inevitability of a daylight D-day assault.

‡   ‡   ‡

The U.S. Special Operations Forces community is a tightly knit world of its own within the general military bureaucracy. After dwindling to almost nothing after Vietnam, by 1983 it had grown to almost 13,000 personnel, and its annual budget had climbed past the billion-dollar mark. The army had the Green Berets, two Ranger battalions, three psychological warfare battalions, a civil affairs battalion, and their own rotary wing air transport provided by TF 160. All these operated under the 1st Special Operations Command (1st SOCOM) located at Fort Bragg. Then there were the men of Delta Force, the army's own antiterrorist unit, and the even more secret Intelligence Support Activity (ISA), known as "The Activity."

The ISA was established as a direct result of the continuous failure of the CIA to provide the sort of human intelligence required by the military for covert operations. It was so secret that for many months the CIA, the Pentagon, and even the White House were unaware of its existence. Its cover was blown in 1982 when it was mentioned in testimony to a congressional committee concerned with rescue plans for Americans still believed alive in Laos. It was controlled by the NSC staff, in particular Lieutenant Colonel "Ollie" North, and often recruited former CIA or Special Forces personnel who operated in civilian clothes, sometimes with their own weapons, in officially deniable intelligence-gathering activities around the world.[1] ISA personnel were often mercenary types, speaking foreign languages, a good example of which was the twenty-man group sent to Italy to assist the Italian police hunt down the kidnappers of Brigadier General James Dozier. They frequently penetrated Nicaragua and El Salvador, seeking information of value to the contra rebels. On occasion they were carried on their clandestine missions by helicopters flown by crews from TF 160.

The revelation of the Activity's existence caused a furor that resulted in the opponents of Special Forces, both inside and outside the army, demanding its disbandment. Counterarguments—that without such a force useful intelligence would dry up—won the day, so in 1983 President Reagan authorized its existence, placing it for administrative purposes under the Defense Intelligence Agency. This official recognition, however, was not sufficient to prevent a formal investigation into the affairs of the ISA, Delta, with which the ISA is frequently confused, and SEAL Team 6.

The investigations revealed a can of worms. Corruption was widespread, particularly the fiddling of expense accounts and misspending of public funds. Members of these units spent flamboyantly on high living at luxury hotels when on training missions. Within Delta there was evidence of over $200,000 of double billings on expenses during the period 1981–1983. Members of the unit had some of their missions paid for by the State Department, but the men still claimed from the army for their lodging. Disciplinary proceedings were instituted against dozens of Delta personnel. The commander, Colonel Sherman Williford, was later promoted and replaced by Colonel William Garrison, whose orders were to restore confidence in the force.

The principal culprit in the ISA was Lieutenant Colonel Dale Duncan, who was charged with diverting huge sums of secret funds into his own pocket. A court-martial sentenced him to seven years' imprisonment, against which he appealed, in 1986, with trials pending against two other officers. Examples of ISA extravagance cited by the investigators were the purchase of a hot air balloon, a Rolls-Royce car, and the rental of a luxury yacht to keep up appearances.

SEAL Team 6 did not escape untarnished. It was revealed that they had bought a number of high-performance Mercedes-Benz sedans, claiming the automobiles were inconspicuous.

The second largest Special Operations Force organization belongs to the navy. SEAL Team 6 is the navy's antiterrorist unit, about 175 strong, with a base at Dam Neck, Virginia but more often under training at Fort Bragg alongside Delta. Like Delta this unit comes directly under the JSOC, which bypasses the conventional chain of command, reporting directly to the JCS and NSC in Washington, D.C. This highly trained unit has particular responsiblity for combating maritime terrorism or hostage taking at sea.

The bulk of the navy's Special Operations Forces are divided between Naval Special Warfare Group One (NSWGI) in Coronado, California, and NSWG2 at Little Creek, Virginia. It was this group that provided the SEAL detachments for Urgent Fury, apart from Team 6. Within these groups are naval special warfare units, special boat squadrons, swimmer delivery vehicle (two-man miniature submarine) teams, and light attack helicopter squadrons. The personnel are lightly armed, highly skilled individuals, whose specialty is underwater demolition and covert beach landing reconnaissance.

The air force's Special Operations Forces are primarily tasked with providing fixed-wing transport and air-to-ground fire support, although they also operate a squadron of the new MH53-J Pave Low III helicopters for quick, clandestine insertions and extractions of small subunits. These forces are grouped together under the 1st Special Operations Wing at the Air Force Systems Command base at Hurlburt Field in Florida. Here are found most of the MC-130Es in the 8th Special Operations Squadron and the AC-130Hs (Spectres) in 16th Special Operations Squadron. 1st Special Operations Wing is part of the 2d Air Division, which in turn is subordinate to the 23d Air Force at Scott Air Force Base in Illinois. The specialty of the air crews is low-level night flying over long distances to ensure penetration of enemy territory without radar detection.

The marines in 1983 did not have any Special Forces, but, intense interservice rivalry being what it is, this situation could not last. It demanded its own antiterrorist capability. In 1987 the corps got its way; the Atlantic Fleet's Marine Security Force Battalion was established at Norfolk and another at Mace Island in California later that year. In addition to supplying security detachments ashore, each battalion provides fleet antiterrorist security teams of about 250 men for use at short notice anywhere. Colonel Clarence Hill was the first commanding officer.

By the end of 1983, as Urgent Fury approached, the Special Operations Forces community was in turmoil. Not only were they under investigation for criminal malpractices, but they had not been able to prove their operational worth. Their only attempt in Iran had been badly bungled. They could not point to any success in a major terrorist incident, such as achieved by the British, or German special units or by the Israelis, whose Entebbe raid will undoubtedly remain the outstanding success story of the rescue of hostages in seemingly impossible circumstances. This was not all. Over the previous year or so, over half the Special Operations Force units had failed to achieve good enough "readiness ratings." Many had been rated C-3, meaning marginally ready (C-1 is "fully ready," C-2 "substantially ready," and C-4 "not ready").

Urgent Fury came at exactly the right moment for all the Special Operations Forces: it gave them a not-to-be-missed opportunity to prove themselves and establish that they could do the sort of job for which they had been created. Unfortunately, for a variety of reasons, including a number of circumstances outside their control, Grenada did not give them the triumph they sought.

‡   ‡   ‡

The JSOC was a hive of activity from October 21 on. Major General Richard Scholtes, recently promoted, was responsible for overseeing the planning of TF 123, as the combined force was called. The Ranger battalions, Delta, SEAL Team 6, and the necessary helicopters from TF 160 were under his command.

Like the other staffs, the officers at the JSOC had meager information on likely targets. They would have to select their objectives, make a guess at the opposition, and hope that darkness and secrecy would give them tactical surprise at the moment the helicopters arrived overhead. Flying low, in dark-painted, specially equipped, quiet aircraft, they had every reason to believe they could come in fast out of the blackness and overwhelm any sleepy opposition within a few minutes. Two o'clock in the morning of October 25 was the agreed H hour.

Special Operations Forces are very lightly armed, often carrying only small arms—no heavy machine guns, no mortars, and usually no rocket launchers. Either they go in quickly, do their job, and get out before they encounter serious opposition, or they must be reinforced speedily by more heavily armed conventional forces. In Grenada the planners opted for the latter: go in and remain until other units linked up with them early on D day. When this happened, they would withdraw, preparatory to leaving the island at the first opportunity.

With the safety of U.S. citizens supposedly being of paramount importance, the True Blue campus was an obvious objective. But for reasons that are obscure, this task was given to the Rangers, almost as an adjunct to their airfield clearance duties. The plan was to seize the Radio Free Grenada transmitting station, 6 kilometers by road north of St. George's; Government House, to secure the person of Sir Paul Scoon; and Richmond Hill Prison, to release political detainees.

Two of the three targets selected for Team 6 and Delta were of questionable value militarily. The successful seizure of the radio station and the prison would have no real significance to the overall objectives of the intervention. Both could easily have been ignored and allowed to fall into U.S. hands when the operation was over. To control the transmitting station at Beausejour might be helpful in preventing PRA broadcasts or in facilitating U.S. broadcasting later, but there was no operational urgency in its capture. There was something else the planners did know about this new, Soviet-supplied installation: even if it was seized or destroyed, its loss would not prevent Radio Free Grenada from continuing to broadcast from the studios behind

Grand Anse beach. This is what actually happened. The powerful transmitter at Beausejour was installed not so much to improve local broadcasting as to ensure the beaming of PRG propaganda around the region. With Beausejour out of action, the studios continued to use their old transmitter and, later, their mobile broadcasting vehicle, until midmorning on October 25.

The prison was of even less importance than the radio station. Nobody had any idea of who was inside. It could be assumed that a number of prominent anti-Bishop Grenadians had been detained, but to employ the army's top antiterrorist unit to secure their early release, in preference to American nationals, must remain one of the most extraordinary decisions of Urgent Fury.

SEAL Team 6 was also given the task of capturing the St. George's power station, although it was not a top-priority target. This was what is known as an on-order objective: the unit is briefed to secure it but after completing its primary mission, and then only on receipt of further instructions. In the circumstances of launching a full-scale invasion, the importance of a power station is zero. If the attackers win, the power station will be theirs for the asking; if they lose, it will be the least of their worries.

There was a lot more sense in securing the governor-general. To lose their one link with constitutional legality through death or seizure as a hostage would be a major political setback. For one thing, the letter requesting the intervention, lying in Brigadier General Lewis's briefcase, would never be signed.

The composite force that was hurriedly assembled for the operation was something of a hodgepodge. There was Delta, SEAL Team 6, C Company 1st/75th Rangers, and (probably) some ISA operatives, all to be delivered to their targets by TF 160. With the Rangers providing additional firepower support, SEAL Team 6 was tasked with the Beausejour transmitting station and Government House, while Delta went for Richmond Hill Prison. Each separate attack would go in simultaneously at 2:00 A.M.

The Monday decision to make H hour 5:00 A.M. completely wrecked the Special Forces' chances of achieving surprise. Their missions could succeed only if there was minimal opposition. True, they would still try to get in just before daylight, but they were cutting it inexcusably fine, with no margin for delay whatsoever. This was asking for the impossible, as most of those involved knew.

A tight timetable of how to get men and machines over the island on schedule had to be put together. There was no way the UH-60 Black Hawks or the two MH-6 Little Birds could cover the distance, so they would have to be packed up inside some C-5A Galaxies and assembled much nearer to Grenada. The airport at Barbados provided the answer. The Galaxies could deliver both the men and aircraft to Barbados, with the last stage of the operation starting from there. Conveniently, Barbados was only forty-five minutes' flying time from their objectives.

This prepositioning would be done on Monday and during that night. The two MH-6s were flown to Barbados early on Monday and assembled in Aero Services' light aircraft hangar opposite the main terminal before flying off to Union Island that afternoon.[2] The C-5As were based at Dover Air Force Base in Delaware, the nine Black Hawks with their crews from TF 160 were at Fort Campbell, Kentucky, and the Special Operations Forces troops were at Bragg but could be picked up from nearby Pope Air Force Base. That was the movement plan. Three Galaxies would fly to Fort Campbell, TF 160 crews would load their Black Hawks, three to each aircraft, and then board themselves for the flight to Bragg. There they would meet up with the Special Operations Forces, and the whole force would fly to Barbados on Monday night. Army teams would reassemble the Black Hawks, and the troops would board in time to leave Barbados while it was still dark, at around 4:00 A.M.

All nine helicopters would depart together, but once over Grenada, two carrying SEALs would head for Beausejour; another two, with more SEALs, would go for Government House. The remaining five with Delta and the Rangers would head for the prison.

At exactly the same time, both Ranger battalions would land or drop at Salines in the south, and the marines would take Pearls in the north.

‡   ‡   ‡

Captain Keith Lucas loved flying. He was extremely proud of his role as pilot of a UH-60 Black Hawk in TF 160. A German and Spanish speaker, who had given up law school for a military scholarship, Lucas had qualified as a helicopter pilot after a year at Fort Rucker, Alabama. His first posting had been to the 101st Airborne Division at

Fort Campbell. There he had heard about the secret 158th Aviation Battalion, where priority was given to getting airborne and staying there as long as possible and as often as possible. Lucas successfully volunteered for a year's duty with the 158th. It was an elite unit, elements of which combined with those of the 160th Aviation Battalion to form the "Night Stalkers," or Task Force 160. Its job was to get Special Forces, particularly Delta or ISA, personnel into or out of secret operations. This entailed continuous training at night, flying at treetop level over long distances.

As Lucas was well aware, 1983 had not been a good year for TF 160. By October no fewer than five major mishaps within the unit had killed sixteen crew members, almost half the entire army's total of thirty-four deaths. As recently as August 1983 one of the unit's helicopters had gone down off the coast of Panama killing two of the crew, with Lucas's company commander, Major Larry Sloan, being the only survivor. Officially the helicopter was on a training mission, but this was thought to be a cover story to conceal a covert mission into Nicaragua. That such missions ever took place has been denied. Nevertheless, the father of Warrant Officer Donald Alvey, who died when his Chinook helicopter crashed off the Virginia coast in March 1983, is reported as saying, "Don flew a bunch of missions into Nicaragua. He'd go somewhere and pick up a group of people in a clearing in the jungle—armed troops speaking Spanish—and take them to another clearing in the jungle."

The strain on crews was intense as both they and their machines were pushed to the limit. When on such "training," uniforms were not worn, and it was common knowledge that if a crew did not return, their deaths would be attributed to a training accident. Relatives would be so informed. Stringent security was enforced within the unit as to all training or operational matters; even if the existence of TF 160 could not be denied, its tasks certainly were.

Lucas's Black Hawk, like the other eight that were to fly the Special Operations Forces into Grenada, was a state-of-the-art machine. It had been specifically designed from Vietnam combat experience to go where the fighting was hot and survive. Intended to lift a squad of eleven fully equipped troops, it could be used to insert subunits into the battlefield or to effect medical evacuation rescues. In this capacity, it could carry four stretchers. It was also capable of carrying heavy loads slung underneath, such as two 105-mm howitzers, with the crews onboard, something no other aircraft of comparable size could achieve. Because it was required to withstand direct hits from heavy small arms fire and cope with severe impacts, the Black Hawk was well protected. The cockpit area was armored, self-sealing fuel tanks were installed, backups were provided for all systems, and the main rotor blades were built around a hollow titanium spar, giving the ability to absorb a hit from a projectile up to 23-mm caliber. The main gearbox could continue to function for thirty minutes with the loss of all its oil. The Black Hawk was constructed to take an impact of up to 42 feet per second. Because of the requirement to avoid detection or, if located, to survive, its designers provided low noise, low radar cross-section, low engine exhaust signature, and an infrared suppressor. Dual flight controls, twin engines, and triple electrical and hydraulic systems made the Black Hawk a unique aircraft.

Lucas, the captain of his aircraft, sat in the right-hand pilot seat with his copilot, Chief Warrant Officer 2 Paul Price, beside him. For Urgent Fury the Black Hawks had crews of four or five. The balance of Lucas's crew consisted of Warrant Officer 1 Jon Ecker, as an additional copilot-navigator, and two crew chiefs. The senior was Sergeant Gary Minerve, who was supported by Specialist 4 Loren Richards. In action the task of these two would be to man the pintle-mounted M-60 machine guns, firing out of the two front doors. Black Hawks are not attack helicopters and therefore have no heavy armaments. Firing M-60s from a fast-moving aircraft at fleeting ground targets makes a noise but little else. To hit the enemy would be most unusual. Reliance is placed on other supporting aircraft or fire to dampen down the defenders' enthusiasm as the Black Hawks charge in.

The commanding officer of TF 160, Colonel Henry, alerted his unit for an exercise on Sunday. There was no briefing; no maps were issued and no destination given. Lucas and the others merely knew that they would load their helicopters onto C-5As and accompany them on an exercise. At Fort Campbell none of the crew had any inkling that this was not just another of the many test deployments to keep the unit on its toes. When they departed on Monday, many never bothered to take their flak jackets—an omission that was to be regretted.

For this exercise, A Company provided four helicopters under Captain Frank Whitehead, B Company two, under Major Michael Dickerson, and C Company (158th Aviation Battalion/TF 160) three, commanded by Major Sloan.

Monday at Fort Campbell was hectic and confusing. The three Galaxies arrived from Dover early in the morning, but there was much loading, unloading, and reloading before they left for Pope Air Force Base. At Pope the SEALs, Delta, and C Company 1st/75th were waiting to join them; in all, about 100 men climbed aboard the huge lumbering giants for the longest leg of the journey, to Barbados. Also boarding at Pope was Brigadier Patterson, still desperately trying to catch up with what was going on and not a little exhausted from lack of sleep. It was only 24 hours since he had learned of his role, flown from McGuire Air Force Base to Norfolk, too late for McDonald's main conference, and then down to Pope in time to get a lift on the Galaxies going south.

Patterson traveled on the same aircraft as the army colonel commanding the Special Forces. So far there had been no opportunity for any proper briefings or for the crews and Special Forces to get together to coordinate their individual missions. Little was known except that it was now obviously not an exercise and that Grenada was the destination. Patterson was surprised that the Special Operations Forces colonel appeared concerned about the time, insisting that the flight was late. Patterson, who was the flight commander, disagreed, telling him that there was plenty of time; in fact, the aircraft were throttled back because he did not want to arrive too early. After some argument it was realized that Patterson was unaware of the new H hour and the overriding urgency of getting to their objectives by 5:00 A.M.

At Grantley Adams Airport, Lucas and his TF 160 comrades were not reassured by events. The first Galaxy had touched down at 2:48 A.M., followed by the other two at approximately twenty-minute intervals. When all three were on the ground it was nearly 3:30 A.M., and they should all be leaving for Grenada within forty-five minutes at the latest, if they had any hope of getting there by 5. Nine Black Hawks had to be off-loaded, assembled, armed, the crews briefed, and the Special Operations Forces taken onboard. To do all this in forty-five minutes was asking the impossible, even with no hitches. There were hitches.

Delays mounted as the army personnel struggled to get the helicopters ready to fly. Then it was discovered that the M-60 ammunition that had been loaded was unbelted, so this had to be replaced. Four o'clock came and went, then 4:30, then 5:00, and still all the aircraft were on the ground, each the scene of frantic activity. While the helicopters were being readied, the Special Forces' commanders, and Captain Barno from the Rangers, organized their teams. Lucas and the TF 160 crews could finally link up with the troops they had to take in and be briefed on their missions.

The four A Company Black Hawks were destined to take SEAL Team 6, two aircraft going to Beausejour and two to Government House. B Company's and C Company's aircraft were taking the Delta-Ranger force to Richmond Hill Prison. It was obvious to Lucas and the others that next to nothing was known about what to expect or details of the terrain near their targets. The available maps were virtually useless. Lucas was in C Company and therefore attacking the prison. His brief made no mention of any likely obstacles or serious enemy interference; in fact, he was told that all that was required was to set the troops down on some grass fields near the prison. The impression given was one of, "We don't know much about the objectives, but don't worry; we will surprise them, and anyway it should be a walkover." The listeners could only hope this was correct. They were going to arrive in daylight, trusting that opposition would be negligible, and that, if necessary, the Spectres over the island could provide supporting fire, as TF 160 had none of its own.

At 5:30 A.M. the Barbados prime minister, Adams, arrived just in time to see the nine aircraft taking off. He was able to take a photograph of them all silhouetted against the dawn sky as they rose up above the old terminal buildings, before turning southwest toward Grenada. It was an impressive, and exciting moment for the watchers below.[3]

During their short flight, Lucas and his crew were quickly disillusioned as to the chance of arriving unexpectedly. They tuned into the frequency of Radio Free Grenada, the destination of the first SEAL detachment, and were shocked to hear a broadcast that the invasion had started. Indeed it had. The marines were ashore at Pearls, and the Rangers were dropping at Salines. Minerve and Richards loaded and test fired the M-60s, one of which jammed. No sooner had it been cleared than they were approaching the northeastern part of the island. It was well after 6:00 A.M., and the sun was up; they were going to reach their objectives seventy-five minutes late. Below them, as they neared the coast, the sailors and marines onboard the *Guam* and accompanying ships looked up in some astonishment as the Black Hawks roared overhead.

‡   ‡   ‡

The high command of the RMC at Fort Frederick was quick to organize two local counterattacks early on the morning of October 25. One was a complete success, and the second caused considerable alarm on the *Guam,* eventually resulting in a radical change of the U.S. plan for the whole operation.

At around 8:00 A.M. Lieutenant Prime was placed in command of an attack to retake the Beausejour transmitting station, which had fallen earlier that morning. Prime was told to find Nelson in St. George's, obtain an APC and troops, and commandeer some vehicles for the move north. Nelson reluctantly released one BTR-60, a platoon of around twenty men from the mobile company, with one 82-mm mortar and its crew. A jeep, a van, and a minibus completed the transport of Prime's force, which drove north along the coast road at about 9:00 A.M. As they came to the crest of the Happy Hill ridgeline, they halted by the Health Centre, with the station only 500 meters away to the northeast, on the flat ground on the left of the road, just the other side (north) of the Beausejour river bridge.

Prime spoke to the people nearby, who confirmed the U.S. presence in and around the transmitter building, before making his plan. First, the mortar was positioned on the ridge, close to a nearby school, to provide overhead fire support. The remainder would advance down the road, with the fifteen soldiers in the civilian vehicles debusing before the bridge to deploy on the left of the road. They were to approach the perimeter fence on foot to try to surround the building. The APC, with Prime himself, would continue over the bridge before opening fire with the heavy turret-mounted machine gun.

The pilots of the two Black Hawks had had little difficulty finding their objective, which was a few hundred meters from the beach, clearly identifiable by the high mast alongside the building. The SEALs leaped from the aircraft to dash for the building, quickly overpowering the four or five guards, whom they tied up inside. By 6:30 A.M. the station was theirs. Their instructions were to hold it, not blow it up, until relieved later that day. The commander decided to be aggressive, so he positioned a number of his men in concealed ambush positions beside the main road. The first victim was a solitary PRA soldier driving a light van. He was captured and joined his comrades inside the building.

Next was a truck full of PRM heading south for St. George's. They were caught in a heavy cross fire, which killed five, wounded others, and scattered the remainder in complete disorder. Not long after 9:30 there was a shout of warning: an APC and other vehicles were approaching (map 9). As the APC crossed the bridge, firing started.

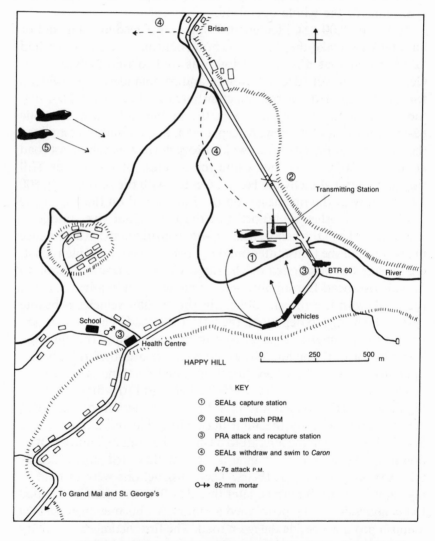

Map 9. CAPTURE BY AND THEN WITHDRAWAL OF SEALS
FROM BEAUSEJOUR TRANSMITTING STATION

The PRA infantry went to ground and opened up with their PKM machine gun. The APC began raking the area of the building with its turret gun. The walls had not been made to withstand heavy-caliber bullets so offered no protection to the SEALs, or the captured PRA, crouched inside. The defenders had no answer to the APC or the mortar; they carried no rocket launcher, and many of the men were armed only with short-range submachine guns and pistols. Worse, there were no Spectre gunships overhead. Had the SEALs had this support, they would have made short work of the APC, but all the gunships were heavily engaged over Salines. None of the AC-130s had been specifically earmarked to assist the Special Forces that morning, and it was only after they got into serious difficulties around St. George's that AC-130 support was made available—two or three hours after the first assault. Casualties began to occur, including some among the prisoners. After about an hour, with the enemy closing in, the APC immune from attack, the SEALs decided they could hold no longer, so they abandoned the building to retreat toward the beach. They spent the rest of the day in hiding, but after dark they had another clash with PRA before they jumped into the sea for a long swim out to the *Caron*.[4]

When it was realized that the transmitting station was not only still intact but had been recaptured, air attacks were initiated from the *Independence* throughout the afternoon and evening. The mast defied every effort to topple it. Even the *Caron*, which put in some target practice that night, firing twenty or thirty rounds from 5-inch guns, hit nothing of significance.

Prime and his men withdrew that evening as news of the landings at Grand Mal filtered through, to don civilian clothes and go into hiding.

‡   ‡   ‡

The noise of the aircraft overhead, plus the banging of the AA guns, had aroused Sir Paul Scoon, his wife, and staff very early. Clearly Grenada was under attack, so the governor-general was persuaded to retreat to the cellar under the main building, where he stayed until the arrival of SEAL Team 6.

The remaining seven Black Hawks came in low over St. George's at about 6:15 A.M. They had a hot reception. Reality was far removed from what they had been led to expect. Four AA guns at Fort Rupert, one or two at D'Arbeau, two more at Fort Frederick, together with some of Nelson's APCs en route to the town, and any PRA soldier who could fire his weapon opened up. The two helicopters destined for Government House circled frantically trying to identify the building. It proved far from easy on the initial attempt, and it was some minutes before the circle near the front gates to the grounds was spotted, enabling the pilots to be certain of their objective. As they flew down, hovering to locate a suitable landing zone, the fire they received from the ground became intense, forcing both to abort their mission and fly back out to sea. The aircraft had been hit, and several occupants were wounded. They reached the *Guam,* where the wounded were offloaded while the crews readied themselves for a second try.

This time both made it (map 10). One came down in the front garden, hovering some 15 feet from the ground while eleven SEALs slid down a rope. The other did the same on the tennis courts at the rear of the house, where another eleven descended, under fire from the area of Coard's house nearby. Both Black Hawks lifted off immediately.

The SEALs met no resistance from the policemen on duty, whom they rounded up and searched. The young officer in command was taken to the governor-general and, after satisfying himself, with the aid of a photograph, that it was indeed Sir Paul Scoon, proceeded to explain that he had come to ensure his safety. There was no plan to leave immediately by helicopter. The intention was to await the arrival of ground forces later in the day. In the meantime the governor-general and his staff were put in the main dining room, little realizing it would be another twenty-four hours before they could leave it.

The U.S. troops were positioned inside and outside the buildings. Layne was not long in reacting. The counterattack came from across the tennis courts from the area of the Mount Weldale security unit and at the eastern entrance, where an APC strove to force its way through the gates. Like their comrades at Beausejour, the SEALs were almost defenseless against armored vehicles, but their radios were working, so they were able to summon air support. At around 10:15 a Spectre was able to pump streams of 20-mm and 40-mm shells into the wooded area north of the house and to damage the APC. The AC-130 then had to fly back to Puerto Rico and Barbados in a fruitless search for more ammunition.

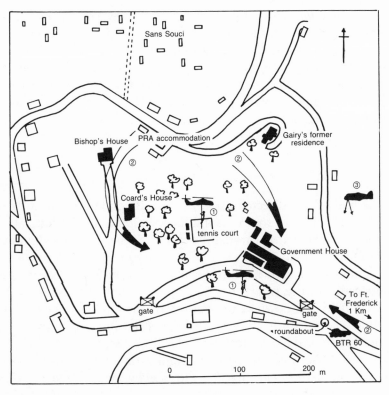

KEY

① SEALs descend from Black Hawks on second attempt

② PRA counterattacks

③ Subsequent AC-130 support

Map 10. ATTEMPT BY SEALS TO RESCUE
GOVERNOR-GENERAL

By midday the SEALs were still trapped, and enemy units were pressing to recapture the building. There was a lot of firing, most of it inaccurate, which stripped the leaves off the trees in the garden and smashed many windows but failed to wound the defenders. Metcalf continued to use the Spectres to keep the attackers at bay, but this situation could not be permitted to continue indefinitely. Although radio and, for a while, telephone contact was possible between the SEALs and the forces at Salines, the impression at Scholtes's headquarters, and on the *Guam,* was that the position at Government House was desperate. The information indicated that the defenders were running out of ammunition and, with casualties mounting, would not be able to hold on throughout the night. On the basis of this intelligence and the critical need to secure Sir Paul, Admiral Metcalf decided to make a radical change of plan. But despite all the shooting, the siege of Government House was to end the following morning without a single injury to either the SEALs or civilians.

‡ ‡ ‡

If the hail of fire directed up at the five Black Hawks heading for the prison came as a shock, so did the location of the building itself. It bore no resemblance to what the crews and Special Forces had been led to expect (map 11).

Captain Lucas and his crew searched in vain for the open space supposedly nearby, where they could put down their passengers. The nearest field was down at the bottom of the hill at the edge of the harbor. The prison itself was perched on the spine of a high ridge, with what looked like almost vertical sides covered with dense jungle and scrub. The walls of the compound were 20 or more feet high, topped with barbed wire, together with watchtowers at strategic points. It looked as impregnable as Alcatraz. There was no possible landing zone nearby. The only way would be hover above ground to allow the troops to slide down ropes. But with the aircraft stationary and the men on the ropes and inside perfect targets, this would be suicidal. Even if they got to the ground, climbing the slopes and the walls in daylight with a fully alerted enemy was a hopeless task.

Worse, nobody had told them that the ridge on which the prison was built was dominated by a higher ridge 300 meters across the deep valley to the east. Sitting on this ridge, 150 feet higher than the prison, was Fort Frederick with its garrison and AA guns.

It was the fire from Fort Frederick that was particularly galling for Lucas and the other Black Hawks. As they came low into the valley, searching for any conceivable way to get down near their objective, they presented targets that were well nigh impossible to miss, with the firers in some cases level with or even above the helicopters. At the critical moment, when everything had gone wrong, there was no

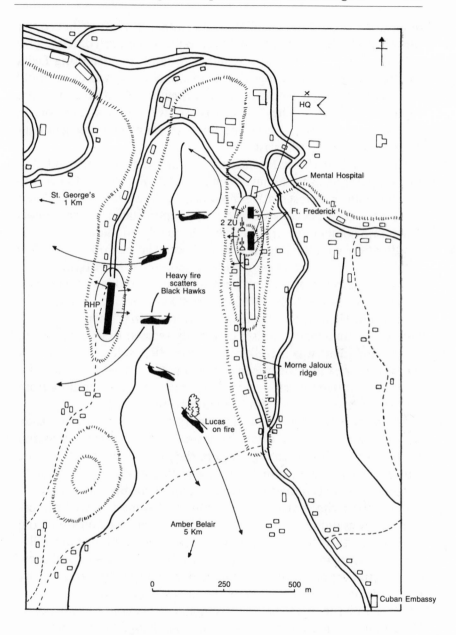

St. George's
1 Km

Mental Hospital

Ft. Frederick

2 ZU

Heavy fire
scatters
Black Hawks

RHP

Morne Jaloux
ridge

HQ

Lucas
on fire

Amber Belair
5 Km

0   250   500
                        m

Cuban Embassy

**Map 11. DELTA FORCE AND RANGERS REPULSED
FROM RICHMOND HILL PRISON**

suppressive fire support available from other aircraft or helicopter gunships. The Black Hawks had been sent in unescorted, relying on a docile, sleepy enemy and the ability to land the assaulting Delta and Ranger personnel alongside the prison. Nothing was as it should have been. What meager information they had been given was the opposite of reality. They were seventy-five minutes late for an unrealistic H hour, and now the Spectres were fully engaged over Salines and unable to assist.

The aircraft on the *Independence,* in particular the 15th and 57th attack squadrons, should have been available. But there had been no army or Ranger representatives present when the pilots received their briefing for D day. In consequence, as one report stated, the navy pilots "went into combat the first day with absolutely no knowledge of, or coordination with, the Ranger and the Special Forces' operation. Due to this reason all aircraft were initially prohibited from flying south of the northern sector without permission until midday of day one."

Grenadian photographer Wayne Carter was watching incredulously from below. He heard the helicopters approaching. Then "suddenly there was a tremendous noise; everybody seemed to be firing from everywhere." This was literally true. Every PRA soldier or gun crew at Fort Frederick and the prison opened up. Combined with the noise of the aircraft themselves, plus the M-60 machine guns shooting from the helicopter doors, the din was indescribable.

If it seemed frightening to those on the ground, for those inside the Black Hawks it was infinitely worse. With the aircraft banking, turning, and twisting, first going up, then down, the troops in the seats at the rear were strapped into a nightmare situation. Although the aircraft had been made to withstand hard crashes and the crew's cabin and the vital parts of the aircraft had some armored protection, the sides did not, and neither did the canvas seats on which the passengers sat. As they were thrown around, they could see the bullet holes appearing in the fuselage. Then men began to get hit, both crew and troops. Legs and arms were smashed, blood spattered everywhere, men screamed. The panic inside the aircraft was real.

On the first run in toward the prison, Lucas's aircraft quickly began to take hits. While Lucas concentrated on flying, on watching the leader, to see if a landing was possible, Minerve and Richards sprayed the ground with machine-gun fire. With the helicopter being thrown around so violently, any aiming was impossible, but the shooting gave them something to do. Within a few moments, Lucas was struck in the right arm, and Richards's leg was smashed. Then they pulled away from the death trap, to regroup over the sea. Amazingly, all five were still flying despite being hit repeatedly. The machines were standing up to the hammering better than the men were.

Within a few minutes, they were ordered in again. At around 6:30, they made a second attempt, with the same predictable results. Lucas, still flying despite his wound, was in the fourth position when his aircraft was struck again. This time five rounds smashed through the windscreen above the armored shield, hitting Lucas in the chest and head and killing him instantly. Copilot Price, whose head was grazed, took over the controls as the aircraft began to belch black smoke. In the rear was pandemonium.

Price flew south, fighting to keep the aircraft airborne and to escape from the vicinity of the prison and the town, where defenses were heaviest. The other aircraft scattered to get away, except for one, which stayed alongside Price as he struggled to maintain height. Whether he could have reached a ship at sea is highly improbable; he had lost fuel, and the helicopter was on fire. With wounded men onboard, to land or crash in the water was to be avoided at all costs. It was better to land somewhere near Salines, where friendly forces should be found.

As the two Black Hawks passed almost over the PRA base at Frequente, Price's aircraft was hit again. Now the controls locked, so he could not steer a straight course. They lost height rapidly. It seemed possible they were going into the sea, but they crashed just on top of Amber Belair Hill. The impact was stunning. The aircraft broke in half, with the main rotor blades tipping forward over the cliff to fall into the water and rocks below.

Joe Gaylord, filming the Rangers's drop at Salines from his small hotel 750 meters away on Lance aux Epines, caught the moment. Within a few seconds, the fuel ignited, and the wreckage blazed fiercely. One person who saw the film said, "It didn't look the sort of crash anybody would walk away from." Incredibly, some did. Price and Ecker were able to scramble out to assist in pulling Richards and Minerve, who had been wounded in the side, free, before the fire engulfed the aircraft. Of the men at the back, at least three were dead, the others injured or wounded. The crash had thrown some clear but had trapped two when part of the fuselage rolled over. There was no way that Lucas's body could be freed at that time—6:40.

It was to be some three and a half hours before the casualties were taken off to the *Guam*. The reason for this unacceptable delay remains obscure, but it was apparently deliberately held back. Part of the explanation lies in the fact that the army Black Hawk pilots had not been trained to land on seaborne helicopter platforms, and instances occurred of their being denied permission to try, particularly at night. One of Admiral McDonald's official recommendations afterward was that army aircrews should receive such training and that "waiver of qualification should be considered in life-saving situations." An even more bureaucratic reason caused delays in some flight missions in Grenada: lack of funds in the right budget. McDonald later commented, "The need to fly missions without delays for funding considerations, with the anticipation that funding reconciliation will follow was paramount to success." In other words, the navy did not have the cash to pay for fueling army helicopters. They did so in the end, but with hesitation and delay. McDonald recommended that "transportation expenditures be referred to the Secretary of Defense level for equitable distribution throughout the Services."

Whether it was lack of training or lack of funds or some other reason, it prolonged the agony of the injured lying in the dirt on Amber Belair, and it may possibly have resulted in unnecessary deaths. Medical evacuation flights during Urgent Fury seemed far less prompt than veterans of Vietnam remembered.

The escorting Black Hawk hovered briefly over the burning wreck, looking at the rotor blades in the water, before flying off. Over the next three hours, helicopters came and went, with the injured still on the ground. From one of the Black Hawks, nine men, probably Delta and Ranger personnel, slid down a rope to secure the area and assist survivors. PRA troops who had seen the crash approached from Frequente and Ruth Howard to the north but were driven off by a Spectre, although not without a short firefight. By 8:30 A.M. the wounded were being carried down the steep hillside to the tiny, rocky beach below the crash site. Eventually, not long after 10:00 A.M., a navy rescue helicopter arrived to take everybody out.

The Special Operations Forces attacks in or around St. George's had ended in failure and, in one instance, disaster.[5] The courage of the crews and the troops they carried was outstanding, but the plan they attempted to implement was hopelessly flawed. To this day, the casualties at Beausejour and Richmond Hill Prison have never been admitted, apart from Captain Lucas's death.[6] It is reliably reported that three other noncrew members died in the crash. The only crewman to escape unscathed was Ecker, while many, if not all, the passengers of this aircraft were wounded over the prison or injured in the crash. A conservative estimate of the total wounded for these two operations is twenty to thirty.

10

October 25

The Drop
at Point Salines

We thought the U.S. troops were going to evacuate the students and withdraw, but, after they landed they began attacking our positions and taking prisoners.

— Lieutenant Colonel Orlando Matamoros Lopez, Cuban officer responsible for the defense of their military mission headquarters north of Salines

MAJOR Einstein Louison lying in his cell in Richmond Hill Prison; Barbara and George Reeves, a retired British couple in their house at Lance aux Epines; Michael "Heads" Mason, and Allan "Squeeze" Mitchell, both living in the little village of Calliste, all had something in common. In the early hours of the morning of October 25, they heard an aircraft droning around and around overhead. Estimates of the time vary from 3:00 A.M. to 4:30 A.M., but all are emphatic that there were planes about long before the main parachute drop at Salines. None knew that it was Major Michael Couvillon of the U.S. Air Force piloting a reconnaissance AC-130 Spectre gunship or that onboard was the pathfinder group of the Rangers about to launch the long-awaited invasion of Grenada. The plane flew high, but the five people who heard it were only a fraction of the scores of others who wondered in the darkness if the noise above finally signaled the start. Louison heard some AA fire but could see nothing. "Squeeze," however, came out of his small house up on

Calliste hill overlooking the runway. He peered up into the sky, waiting and watching. Then suddenly he saw something falling—parachutes, over the eastern part of Salines. He shouted and pointed; others nearby saw them. He heard some firing but not much. He had the distinct impression they were dummies to draw fire.

‡   ‡   ‡

The afternoon of Friday, October 21, was routine as far as Lieutenant Colonel Ralph Hagler was concerned—that is until his phone rang at two o'clock. Hagler was the commanding officer of the 2d/75th Rangers, based at Fort Lewis, Washington. He was a highly experienced soldier and, like most other officers of his age, a Vietnam veteran. The caller instructed him to report at once to Fort Bragg in North Carolina, to the headquarters of the JSOC. No details could be given. Hagler flew off next morning on his long journey, arriving at around 7:00 P.M. He found Lieutenant Colonel Wesley Taylor from the 1st/75th already there. Both officers reported to Scholtes, who told them they were going to invade Grenada. Taylor was to land or drop at Point Salines in the south, to secure the runway, protect the U.S. medical students at the True Blue campus, then clear any obstacles and prepare to defend the airfield. Hagler was going north. His battalion was to seize and hold Pearls Airport and link up with the marines of the 22d MAU who would be coming ashore nearby. Hagler had the option of landing or dropping on his objective, depending on the tactical situation or whether the strip was effectively blocked. So much for the good news.

The bad news was that there was no hard intelligence on the enemy locations, strength, or intentions. The maps available were hopelessly inadequate. Both Taylor and Hagler had to make do with black-and-white photocopies of the out-of-date British 1:50,000 tourist map. Time was tight; H hour was to be 2:00 A.M. on October 25. Worst, they were to lead battalions reduced to 50 percent or less of their normal strength, due, in part, to the limited number of air force crews trained for night operations with the MC-130 and C-130 transport aircraft. Taylor was also told that he would lose C Company, under Captain Barno, because Scholtes needed a Ranger company to support the special operations. Both officers left the headquarters to plan.

Rangers are highly trained light infantry. Normally they do not expect to fight with anything heavier than 60-mm mortars or have transport larger than gun jeeps and 250-cc motorcycles. They are a vital element of the army's Special Operations Forces, capable of performing a wide variety of covert operations, including the securing of airfields at night using night vision devices. All Rangers, with their coveted black berets, are parachute trained. Some are also experienced free-fallers or can steer their chutes over many miles after jumping at high altitudes. A Ranger battalion has a headquarters and a headquarters company for command, control, and basic logistics, together with three rifle companies. Each company, lettered A, B, and C, consists of three rifle platoons plus a weapons platoon, which carries the two 60-mm mortars and the light, hand-held, antitank launchers. Depending on the circumstances, a number of men in the companies will man the gun jeeps mounting M-60 machine guns. Like other special operations forces, they are equipped and trained for quick operations. They go in, complete their task, and move out or at least link up with heavier supporting units. They do not have the capability or firepower for prolonged operations against stiff opposition, unsupported.

Hagler's battalion was alerted for an exercise deployment at 9:00 A.M. on October 22, and, while their commanding officer was still flying to Fort Bragg, the men spent the day getting ready. The 2d/75th flew out from the adjoining McChord Air Force Base to Hunter Army Airfield near Fort Stewart, arriving by 2:00 P.M. on October 23, Sunday. Thus far nobody suspected it was anything more than a test exercise, but rumors were rife on deplaning in Georgia. They had arrived at the sprawling military complex of Fort Stewart, the home of their sister battalion, the 1st/75th Rangers, which at 5:00 A.M. had also been alerted for the exercise.

The instructions that they must fight with such depleted units came as a shock to both commanding officers. Taylor, although minus C Company, was able to keep the other two with virtually their normal structure, plus a few reinforcements. Both A Company, under Captain John Abizaid, and B Company, under Captain Clyde Newman, had about 150 men each. Two tactical battalion headquarters were formed from another 50 men, giving the 1st/75th a fighting strength of 350. Hagler had to make do with fewer, so he was compelled to tell his company commanders, Captains Francis Kearney of A Company,

Thomas Sittnik of B Company, and Mark Hanna of C Company, to select their best men only. This resulted in companies varying from 50 to 80. Like Taylor, he had two tactical headquarters. It was their fervent hope that Salines and the medical students were not heavily defended.

Hagler's next shock came late on the afternoon of October 23. Just as he had completed his plan to take Pearls, he received a change of mission. Now he was to follow Taylor into Salines, assist in securing the airfield, and then attack Camp Calivigny, the supposedly well-protected main base camp of the PRA. Again the critical problem was lack of information and the fact that Calivigny was some 12 kilometers from the airfield. His battalion of under 250 was to march to the new objective, in darkness, with no proper maps, across unfamiliar terrain, and against an enemy whose dispositions and strength were unknown. The 2d/75th would need to be in position to assault at dawn, which, with a 2:00 A.M. drop, was asking a lot. Hagler and his staff worked feverishly to put the new plan together. Like the seizure of Pearls, the Calivigny objective had to be secured as early on D day as possible. Even if there was no opposition at all on the approach march, the operation looked highly optimistic, but Hagler produced his final orders later that night.

On Monday, while their men zeroed weapons, the two officers were forced to alter their calculations drastically. The original timings were all changed. The 2:00 A.M. H hour was put back to 4:00 A.M., then to 5:00 A.M., just fifteen minutes before first light, because the SEALs needed time for their second attempt to infiltrate into Salines. What had started out as a night operation now had every likelihood of taking place in broad daylight. Virtually all hope of tactical surprise had disappeared, certainly for the 2d/75th. They now had to drop or land in daylight, march in daylight, and attack Calivigny in daylight.

What was particularly frustrating was the absence of intelligence on the defenses, if any, at the objectives. Where were the enemy positions? Did they have AA guns deployed? What sort of obstacles blocked the runway? Was the medical school guarded? They hoped the SEALs and combat control team would provide some of the answers, but even if they did, the Rangers would be airborne, and last-minute adjustments must be made in flight. Little did they realize that their frustrations were just beginning.

To carry the Rangers and give air-to-ground fire support was the responsibility of the air force's 1st Special Operations Wing, under Colonel Hunter. The 1st/75th was allocated five C-130 transports and two MC-130Es to lead the way. These aircraft came from the 8th Special Operations Squadron. The MC-130Es are basically C-130s with precision navigation and terrain-hugging equipment. They are designed for deep-penetration, low-altitude night operations—exactly the sort of aircraft to ensure the Rangers got to the right place on time in the dark. The ordinary C-130s could follow behind these two. The 2d/75th would get five C-130s for their lift. That left fire support and reconnaissance, which were supplied by three, and later four, of the 16th Special Operations Squadron's AC-130 Spectre gunships. This squadron, at Hurlburt Field in Florida, is the only active-duty unit flying Spectres in the air force; they are remarkable aircraft. Their sophisticated computers, detection devices, and surveillance equipment permit pinpoint shooting at targets hidden by darkness or cloud.

With five officers and nine enlisted men, the Spectre combines reconnaissance and strike capabilities. It is armed with two 20-mm vulcan cannons firing 2,500 rounds a minute; a pair of six-barreled 7.62-mm Gatling machine guns, each capable of up to 6,000 rounds a minute; a 40-mm gun; and, thrusting out of the left side parachute door, the "beeg" gun, a 105-mm M-102 cannon capable of firing eight 40-pound shells every minute. They became a familiar feature in Grenada, circling around and around, tilted slightly to their left, emitting long, tearing noises as a stream of shells left the guns. They proved ideal weapons, providing a heavy volume of precision fire at ground targets. However, Grenada, like Vietnam, did not possess an air force or even radar-controlled AA defenses. The Spectre is very vulnerable in a hostile air environment.

Abizaid's A Company would lead, with pathfinders well in advance of the remainder of the company, whose primary task was runway clearance. All in the pathfinder group were military free-fall parachutists and would use this technique in dropping over Salines at about 3:30 A.M. They would fly to Grenada in a reconnaissance AC-130 about ninety minutes ahead of the company. Their task would be to report on the situation on the ground to the incoming aircraft, identify, and mark with lights if possible, the landing zone or drop zone, and in this instance carefully probe the surroundings of True

Blue. Avoiding the enemy was essential. It was a highly covert part of the operation but well within the Rangers' capability.

The main body of A Company would travel in the two MC-130s to clear the strip for the bulk of the battalion coming in thirty minutes later. There was no margin for error if Abizaid was to complete his task in darkness. Thirty minutes is not long, and serious enemy interference would throw the whole plan out of gear.

The next five C-130s would hold Taylor and the rest of the 1st/75th. In the third aircraft would be Taylor himself and the flight commander, Major General William Mall, the senior MAC representative on the operation. Also with Taylor was his tactical headquarters, plus a platoon from B Company. In the fifth C-130 was the executive officer, Major John Nix, with the alternative command post.

Their mission was to seize the airfield east of Hardy Bay and, of equal importance, secure the safety of the U.S. citizens at the True Blue medical facility. Although the Rangers were capable of landing or dropping, the feeling was, when they boarded, that they would be landing. The loading had been done mainly on that assumption because neither battalion had been led to expect much opposition. Intelligence on the state of the runway was uncertain, but it was thought that given an element of luck, landing would be feasible. If so, the plan envisaged pulling up as near to True Blue as possible and roaring out of the aircraft with the gun jeeps to storm the campus.

Surprise was unlikely. A Company would have been on the ground for half an hour, and it would be daylight.

Following immediately behind Taylor was Hagler with the 2d/75th. He was to land and secure the runway west of Hardy Bay, reorganize quickly, and march on Calivigny. Both battalions would have the benefit of the three Spectres on call, and the whole operation in the south of the island would be controlled by Scholtes in his EC-130 command and control aircraft. When the runway was secure, he intended to set up his command post at Salines. With luck, all should be over by midday. Then the Rangers would hand over to the incoming 82d Airborne units and go home.

‡ ‡ ‡

Few plans survive the first shot in their entirety, and the Rangers' was no exception (maps 12 and 13). In their case, though, changes

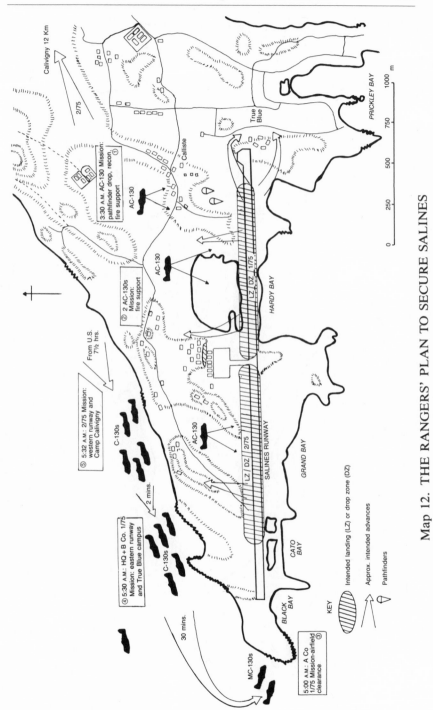

Map 12. THE RANGERS' PLAN TO SECURE SALINES

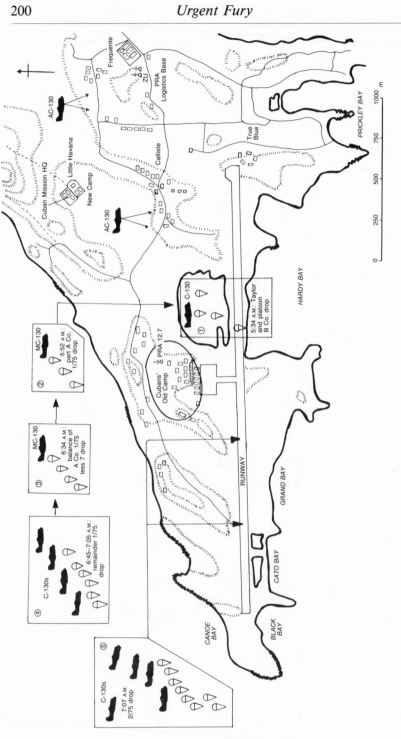

Map 13. THE RANGERS' DROP IN REALITY

started long before any shots were fired. Four hours prior to their departure from Florida, Atlantic Command ordered one of the three supporting AC-130s to leave an hour earlier, at 6:30 P.M., on October 24 to give more time for reconnaissance over Grenada and to ensure Abizaid's pathfinders had adequate time on the ground. At 7:30 P.M., the remaining two took off, well in advance of the troop lift. Within a short time, one developed an engine fire and was forced to return. It was replaced quickly, but instead of three aircraft arriving together, their arrival would be staggered. This turned out to be advantageous, for it enabled continuous gunship support over Salines for a much longer period than the planners had envisaged necessary.

At Hunter air base on the evening of October 24, both Ranger units were making their last-minute preparations for invasion, while in Grenada Austin was trying to make his second telex appeal to Prime Minister Thatcher to stop it. At 7:15 that night, the 1st/75th was assembled near the runway listening to the commanding officer's final briefing when the noise of engines drowned his words as seven aircraft taxied across. Taylor was annoyed to learn from the flight commander, Mall, that he was expected to board at once instead of two hours later. A hurried consultation revealed that the Rangers' flight schedules were not the same as those being used by the 1st Special Operations Wing. There was a frantic rush to load. By dint of hard work, and not a little cursing, the first MC-130 was rolling down the strip at 9:30, only twenty-five minutes late. This loss of time was easily made up during the flight. Nevertheless, there was an annoying oversight affecting Taylor's aircraft. All had arrived at Hunter without hatch antennas attached, and in the scramble to get away early, there was no time to rectify this omission. In flight, the only way Taylor could communicate with his men would be through the aircrew's radios.

Inside each darkened plane, the scene was almost identical. While the senior officers huddled up front near the radios, studying maps or photographs and discussing events, the Rangers were squashed shoulder to shoulder down each side. It was a long flight, and after a while some managed to overcome the tension and sleep, either slumped in the front of jeeps or lolling half-upright in their seats. In the cargo bays in the center were the gun jeeps, packed with stores and reserve ammunition, motorcycles, medical supplies, and, in at least two instances, an AH-6 or MH-6 Little Bird helicopter.

These Hughes 500 helicopters, painted black, with no identifying insignia, could be carried by a C-130 without dismantling, the rotor blades held by a safety restrainer. The Little Bird is a multimission combat helicopter with a crew of two but with space for four fully equipped troops. It can perform offensive operations with a variety of armament kits. Two TOW missiles, which are guided to the target by wire, can be carried on either side of the fuselage. Also 2.75-inch rockets, a minigun, and a .30-caliber Hughes chain gun can be fitted. This helicopter is specifically designed for night operations, being equipped with infrared night-flying devices. It has armor protection, self-sealing fuel tanks, and infrared suppressors to reduce vulnerability to heat-seeking missiles. Although numerous witnesses saw these helicopters in Grenada and they are visible on film and photographs, their presence on the island has always been officially denied. Those on the island were fitted with the M-56 mine-dispensing system, something of an overkill.

Within half an hour, Taylor heard that the runway was definitely blocked. Somewhat belatedly, aerial photographs had revealed the obstructions that had been put in place several days earlier. There was no news of other defenses. Taylor was concerned now as to whether A Company could land, and if so, clear enough runway for the remainder of the battalion in thirty minutes. It could prove impossible, especially if the enemy were waiting. Perhaps the SEALs would supply further information before H hour.

At 11:20 P.M. it was reported that enemy had been seen near True Blue, but there were no details. Then half an hour into Tuesday, Taylor got the news that the SEALs had failed again. He struggled with his dilemma for another hour before deciding that Abizaid and his men must jump. The risks in attempting to land were too great for the airfield clearance company. The Rangers inside the two leading MC-130s began to rig for a drop.

Two hours later, at 3:30 A.M., Couvillon arrived over the island. Although flying high, the aircraft was heard on the ground and attracted some AA fire from the guns at Frequente. The pathfinder team leaped into space over Salines, falling like stones through the darkness until their altimeters showed 2,000 feet; then they pulled their cords. "Squeeze" Mitchell and others saw them draw a few shots from PRA positions. Regrettably something went wrong—either with the chutes or the altimeters of two of the free-fallers, and they plummeted into the ground. That made six accidental parachute deaths before the operation had properly started.[1]

Details of this bad news were unknown to Taylor, but Couvillon confirmed heavy vehicles blocking the runway. The likelihood of Abizaid's clearing the strip in time for the battalion to land was now remote. At 4 o'clock Taylor decided that everybody must jump, except for jeep crews and some administrative personnel. With only an hour to H hour, the real confusion was about to start. Taylor had passed his order up to the signaler to send over the crew's radio, and he was given the thumbs-up sign, which he assumed meant message passed. This was not the case with the fifth, sixth, and seventh aircraft, where Taylor's instructions had not been understood.

In the fifth aircraft, Nix had anticipated his commanding officer's decision to jump, and the Rangers had rigged themselves accordingly. However, shortly after, the loadmaster firmly announced they would be landing. With much swearing, the troops derigged; they removed their H-harness, rucksacks, main and reserve chutes, and life vests, stuffing them into kit bags and stowing them in the forward part of the plane to facilitate the speedy off-loading of the jeeps and equipment in the center. Not long after completing this, the loadmaster reappeared and yelled, "Only thirty minutes fuel left. Rangers are fighting. Jump in twenty minutes."

To be told to jump instead of land is not good news, especially having spent so much time and effort derigging a short while before. Now there was no time to rig everything for a drop. Chaos reigned as everybody struggled to get their gear, unpack nonessentials, and load up with ammunition taken from jeeps. Mounds of discarded kits choked the aisles as the men fought to put the main chute on their backs and the reserve on their chests (although on this occasion Hagler decided not to wear the reserve; at 500 feet they have no time to open if the main one fails). Then the rucksack must be hooked up under the reserve and personal weapon strapped to the left side. This takes time under normal conditions. Inside an aircraft only minutes away from an operational jump, it causes pandemonium. There is no space to move around, and proper checking by jumpmasters is impossible, so reliance must be placed on buddy rigging, whereby nearby comrades check each other. Such was the scene inside the fifth aircraft—and in the sixth and seventh too.

Unbeknownst, as yet, to Taylor, he had his first four C-130s prepared to jump, but the last three still expecting to land and about to be thrown into total confusion when the correct order finally got through. At this crucial moment, fifteen minutes before H hour, the pilot of the leading MC-130 reported that his navigational equipment was malfunctioning; he could not guarantee the drop zone in the dark. Worse, they were passing through a rain squall, so he considered a lead change with the other MC-130 unsafe. The pilot pulled away to the south and radioed Scholtes with the problem.

Scholtes responded that H hour was postponed yet again to 5:30 and that the leading two aircraft with A Company should veer off and abort their first run in. For Taylor this was almost too much, and he angrily complained about first being told to leave two hours early and now his being required to jump ahead of his clearance unit. He attempted to put together a last-minute plan in which his third aircraft would lead. The seven planes would try to reform into two serials, or groups, with one minute between each. Then to cap it all, Taylor discovered that numbers six, seven, and eight had derigged. They were told to orbit until they could get ready to jump.

The original simple plan was in shreds. As Taylor's C-130, flown by Lieutenant Colonel James Hobson, made its final approach to Salines at 150 knots and 500 feet, it was 5:31 A.M. and almost daylight on a windy (20 knots), partially cloudy day. As if that was not bad enough, a PRA searchlight at the western end of the runway locked onto the plane as it flew in. The operation had the makings of an unmitigated disaster: the enemy had been alerted; surprise was lost; some 600 men were about to be dropped piecemeal onto a bare runway within a few meters of enemy positions. A parachute drop should be over in a matter of moments; there was no knowing how long this one would take now. Taylor, through no fault of his, was about to lead his men into a jump that was a textbook example of how never to do a combat drop.

‡   ‡   ‡

At midday on October 24, an AN-26 aircraft from Cubana Airlines touched down at Pearls Airport. Austin headed the RMC welcoming party. A flurry of saluting announced the arrival of Castro's delegation to Grenada. The leader of the mission, Colonel Pedro Tortolo Comas,

38, was no stranger to the island; he had been head of the military mission until May 1983. A graduate of the Soviet Frunze Military Academy and Voroshilov Staff College, Tortolo held the key post of chief of staff of the Army of the Centre. He had been selected for this particularly tricky mission because of his recent knowledge of Grenada and the PRG and PRA leadership. He was accompanied by a small staff, the most senior of whom was Carlos Andres Diaz Larranaga who, at 41, was the Caribbean section chief in the America Department of the Central Committee of the party.

Tortolo's mission was tricky because Cuba had no intention of attempting to reinforce the island militarily, despite the desperate appeals from the RMC. Coard and Austin had wanted troops, and wanted them quickly. Instead they received Colonel Tortolo. He was later to say, "I went to convey the ideas of our Party, of Fidel, and the Ministry of the FAR [Revolutionary Armed Forces] regarding the organization of our defense in the event of an attack." He was referring to the Cuban defense of their work areas and personnel, not the overall defense of the island. In fact, as the intervention was only a few hours away, Tortolo had little time to achieve any significant military preparations even if that had been his main task. As it was, he and Diaz reemphasized that Cuban personnel, including military advisers, would defend themselves if attacked but nothing more. The Cuban military would not deploy with the PRA units they had been training but would be confined to the airfield construction site at Salines and the Cuban mission headquarters, at what was known locally as Little Havana, about 1,200 meters northeast of the terminal buildings. Later that afternoon he went to the Cuban embassy on Morne Jaloux ridge, before going down to Salines to supervise preparations. Both he and Diaz were to remain at Little Havana for the duration of the fighting. Diaz was to die there.

It was at Salines and Little Havana, and only there, that Americans and Cubans were to clash. The rest of Grenada was left entirely to the PRA. Even for the limited defense of the Cuban work areas and living quarters, Tortolo's problems were numerous. First, the bulk of the personnel available were construction workers, not professional soldiers. The average age of these 635 men was 38, and a substantial number were over 50. Although virtually all had received basic military training in Cuba at some time, many were unfit and overweight. They knew how to handle small arms, which were kept in racks concealed behind bed sheets, at the end of their barrack rooms. They had access to mortars, machine guns, and recoilless rifles, but the AA guns were in the hands of the PRA. They were not organized as a military unit until the last moment, when the military advisers joined them to group them into ad hoc subunits.

The Cuban military in Grenada were a mixed bunch, totaling forty-three, all ranks. On October 25, no fewer than four of these were colonels and nine lieutenant colonels. Out of a total of thirty-four officers, only six were designated as the infantry training team, the remainder being specialists in signals, stores, logistics, finance, or translators. One officer was a woman.

Another difficulty was that the Cubans' mission headquarters, and directly opposite it, the "new" camp, which together constituted Little Havana, had not been sited for defense. These buildings, with their sophisticated communications links to their embassy and overseas, were sitting in the center of a bowl, dominated on all sides except the southwest by hills and ridges within 200 meters. To defend the place required the holding of these hills. The "old" camp, the sprawl of huts just north of the partially built terminal, was at least on high ground. From these low hills, only fifty to sixty feet high, the majority of the runway was visible. From positions up there, it would be easy to make life untenable on the strip itself. Dug-in machine guns and mortars were all that was needed, and the Cubans had these weapons.

Nevertheless, Tortolo was restricted by his explicit orders, plus the lack of time. At both camps, trenches were dug, men were allocated their positions, telephone lines were laid, and two makeshift medical posts were set up. The runway was blocked by metal stakes joined by wire, trucks, construction equipment, yellow tankers, and drums. These obstructions were being put in place as early as October 20, as reported by the Barbados Defence Force reconnaissance flight on that day. Food, fuel, and water were stored in case they were cut off. Each worker had an AK rifle with about 100 rounds, and teams were detailed to man the mortars and recoilless rifles. But they were to fight only if attacked. Castro's orders on this point were made clear to everyone. If the Americans attacked or fired on their positions, only then should they resist. Castro also made it plain that Cuban personnel were not to interfere with actions to evacuate U.S. citizens from the medical school. From the military point of view, this completely pulled the rug from under Tortolo, but it was the political decision of the Cuban commander in chief himself, and Tortolo had been sent to ensure it was carried out. He was also to ensure that if fighting did start, Cuban military honor was not sullied by poor performance.

In keeping with this policy of noninvolvement the families of many Cubans were packing just in case. The *Vietnam Heroica,* the Cuban ship in St. George's harbor, which provided a backup overseas radio link to Havana, was designated as a place of refuge for Cuban women and children.

Of the PRA there was little to be seen at Salines on the evening of October 24. As usual, only the small airport security detachment was present near the Great House. Over at the eastern end of the runway, at the medical school campus, all was quiet. The occupants were not under guard as such, no defensive positions had been prepared, and the RMC appeared to have taken Castro's advice to avoid all military activities in the area with the exception of a few gate guards. Austin, in his desperation not to precipitate an invasion, was particularly solicitous of the students' welfare up to the last moment. He had telephoned Dr. Bourne on the morning of October 24 asking if classes had resumed, and Stroude had visited the campus that day to speak to the students, being taken around by the bursar. Austin ended his phone call by saying, "I want to thank you for all you have done, and I am not going to forget it."

Invasion had been expected nightly from October 23. Since Sunday evening, Radio Free Grenada had broadcast frenzied warnings and appeals for the militia to report for duty. Grenadians, the announcer said, "are prepared to fight to the last man and woman to defend our homeland," adding, rather lamely, "though it is equally prepared to hold discussions . . . in order to find a peaceful solution." The Sunday broadcast had ended, "An invasion of our country is expected tonight." If the SEALs had succeeded, they would have been technically correct. As it was they were thirty hours out.

Lieutenant Colonel Orlando Matamoros Lopez, a 43-year-old veteran from the ranks of the Cuban rebel army of 1958, was responsible for the defense of the Cuban mission. He was awakened at dawn by the roar of aircraft and the banging of AA guns. Grabbing his pistol and rifle, he ran, with others, to his assigned position. The Cubans were located up on the hills surrounding the mission and the old and new camps. Everybody could see the Rangers jumping. Clearly the invasion had started. But were the Americans actually going to attack? Matamoros later explained, "We thought the U.S. troops were going to evacuate the students and withdraw but, after they landed, they began attacking our positions and taking prisoners." He continued, "Some planes were shooting at the logistics base of the Armed Forces of Grenada [Frequente], and its anti-aircraft guns were shooting back. Then we saw the parachute troops landing on the runway and the military hardware brought ashore. This operation lasted for quite a while."

‡   ‡   ‡

Matamoros was correct. From the moment Taylor jumped at 5:34 until the drop was completed, including the 2d/75th and seven stragglers from A Company 1st/75th who had not made it on an earlier pass, over an hour and a half was to elapse.

Hobson ignored the searchlight, leveled off, and flew straight down the runway from west to east. Standing tense inside the C-130 waiting for the green light was Taylor, his headquarters group, with the platoon from B Company. Both battalions had agreed to reduce the drop height to well below normal to 500 feet to give the jumpers only twelve to fifteen seconds in the air, with minimum exposure to enemy fire. Also they were dropping onto a long, narrow drop zone, with water along the south side and, in the Hardy Bay area, on both sides within a few meters of the tarmac. This meant they could not afford a long descent, with the possibility of drifting too far. The idea was to get down quickly and not become scattered in the process. Hagler's men jumped without reserve chutes, while Taylor's wore theirs.

All the Rangers were staggering under enormous loads as they stumbled down the cluttered aisles toward the rear doors on each side of the aircraft. Later 1st Lieutenant Raymond Thomas, 2d/75th, said:

> Most people jumped with excessive loads. . . . I jumped with an M-60 machine gun, my rifle and my .45. I also had about 1000 rounds of 7.62 ammunition and some frags. It was probably the heaviest rucksack I'd ever carried. A guy right in front of me thought he had a hernia. He didn't think he'd be able to get out. They would have just climbed over him.

They were to jump out rapidly, although few could manage more than a stumble, from both doors simultaneously—the shotgun method. This way four men would be in the air every second. Both battalions were using the T-10 chute, not the usual MC1-1B, although some jumpers did not realize this until the canopy cracked open above them. The MC1-1B has two toggle ropes, which facilitate steering the chute to a greater extent than is possible with the T-10. It was felt that the chances of midair entanglements were less with the stable, less steerable T-10.

Taylor's aircraft drew fire from the fully alerted Frequente guns. The PRA detachment at Salines had positioned an old 12.7-mm four-barreled, heavy AA machine gun on the ridge north of the terminal. This opened fire as well, sending streams of tracer rounds into the sky. All of Taylor's men were out before Hobson, in a piece of superb flying, dove south almost over the roofs of True Blue and slowly pulled up less than 100 feet from the sea.

The next two aircraft came in shortly after Taylor, but the pilots did not like the amount of fire they were drawing, so both aborted their drop. Almost any PRA soldier who could fire his weapon was now doing so. The fireworks looked fairly impressive but little damage was being done, although several planes were holed, mainly in the tail area, indicating inexperienced firers not aiming correctly. This setback meant that Taylor and his forty-odd men were strewn along the bare runway on their own. It was time for some suppressive fire from the Spectres.

At this moment, two were overhead. One, flown by Major Clement Twiford, took on the PRA 12.7-mm gun just northwest of the runway together with the ZUs at Frequente, while Couvillon concentrated on close support of the few Rangers on the ground. Although their fire was effective, and at Frequente succeeded in seriously wounding 2d Lieutenant Fraser, the chief logistics officer of the PRA, the aircraft, firing in support of Taylor, had problems. At the crucial moment, the 40-mm cannon refused to track, and one of the 20-mm guns could not be fired because it would not feed or eject shells. On top of this, the 105-mm gun had to be fired manually, with the lanyard, rather than automatically. Nevertheless, these difficulties did not stop the firing, which was aimed primarily at suspected positions in the houses north of the runway. It was not long before Couvillon, who had been airborne the longest, had to leave to refuel in Barbados.

His task was taken over by Lieutenant Colonel David Simms, and it was he who was later able to disperse some enemy approaching Lucas's downed UH-60 at Amber Belair.

At 5:52, almost twenty minutes after Taylor's drop, one of A Company's MC-130s came in. All but seven of the men jumped before the plane cleared the drop zone and swung south out to sea.

There was now a very long wait for the next drop. In the sky above and around Grenada circled no fewer than nine C-130s and one MC-130, apart from Scholtes's EC-130 and the Spectres, all waiting to get into position to approach the drop zone. Inside, many of the conditions were chaotic, with equipment littered everywhere as troops struggled to get ready. Fuel was tight as they had to keep enough to reach Barbados, forty-five minutes' flying time away. At last, at 6:34, exactly an hour after Taylor jumped, he got the rest of A Company on the ground. There were now about 120 men grouped south of the runway. But the operation still dragged on, and it was not until 7:05 A.M. that Taylor had his whole force with him.

Then it was Hagler's turn with the 2d/75th. It would have been too confusing to let him jump before Taylor, so his five planes were compelled to circle, praying that the fuel would last.

Not long after 7:00 A.M., Hagler was able to lead his aircraft in a tight group, one behind the other. He was the first man to jump, with the rest of the battalion out within less than thirty seconds. By 7:10, all the Rangers who jumped were safely down, all except for Specialist 4 Harold Hagen of the 2d/75th, who broke a leg. Considering the circumstances, it was nothing short of miraculous. There had almost been a fatal accident when Specialist William Fedak's static line became entangled as he jumped, dragging him against the tail of the aircraft. He was hauled back in by Technical Sergeant James Tisley, shaken but uninjured.

The Rangers had initially been given the mission of securing two airfields, Salines and Pearls, by night, either by landing or dropping. It was all to be over quickly. Hagler at Pearls would link up with the marines, while Taylor was relieved by 82d Airborne units. It was a simple plan, well within the capability of both battalions. Unfortunately, neither of the two commanding officers was left with a straightforward mission for long.

Because there was so little intelligence about Grenada, particularly on enemy strengths, locations, or intentions, Scholtes considered it vital to try to get the SEALs in again on Monday night. This meant delaying the Rangers H hour to fifteen minutes before first light. It gave them absolutely no margin for delay at all. In fact it was tantamount to telling both battalions to take their objectives by day, which made it impossible for either of them to achieve surprise.

Less than thirty-six hours before the operation, Hagler was switched from Pearls to the south, to follow Taylor into Salines. His primary new task was Camp Calivigny, which was thought to be heavily defended. He was not to be allowed to take this by surprise, by a coup de main, or in Ranger style by landing or dropping nearby. The 2d/75th was expected to march the 12 kilometers like an ordinary infantry battalion. Hagler was to advance in daylight, through unknown enemy-occupied terrain, to attack an objective about which little was known with a battalion at under half-strength. This was not a task for a Ranger unit, and the chances of its being accomplished on D day were zero unless everything went according to plan, there were no unforeseen delays, and the opposition did nothing.

Given the new 5:00 A.M. H hour, Taylor's planning problems were acute. He still tried to do in half an hour of darkness what was originally to be done in three and a half. This proved an impossibility. Things began to go wrong early. First, since his aircraft had no hatch antennas, total confusion reigned inside the planes as they approached the drop zone, which led to a drop that should have been over in five minutes taking ninety. Then there was the rushed loading at Hunter because the air force and army had different flight schedules, which was largely the reason nobody had time to fix the antennas.

During the flight, Taylor continued to receive bad news over which he had no control. The runway was reported blocked. The SEALs had failed, so no new information was forthcoming, and there would be no navigational guidance beacons at Salines. On nearing Grenada, they hit a rain squall, and the leading MC-130 had a navigation equipment failure, so the drop was delayed by another half-hour. Just as Taylor tried to sort this out, he learned that three aircraft were still expecting to land. More delay. Finally, after he personally was on the ground with his headquarters, on his own, the next two planes aborted because the pilots considered the fire too heavy. By contrast the 2d/75th were down, eventually, as a unit in a few seconds.

The Rangers lacked basic information on which to plan effectively; they were compelled to accept unrealistic timings for H hour, which prevented surprise; and in the case of Hagler's battalion, they were given an objective well beyond their capacity unless resistance was nonexistent. The plan they were forced to adopt took no account of the inevitable difficulties that occur in every military operation. It is a fact that things always go wrong, as they certainly did on this occasion. Any plan must have a degree of flexibility, a margin for error and the unexpected, and above all should try to achieve surprise and not assume a docile enemy.

The Rangers should have received a very bloody nose at Salines on October 25, but they did not. Not a single man was killed by enemy action during the drop. Two men died in parachute accidents, and one broke a leg. The reason: Castro's order to the Cubans, whose positions dominated the runway, not to fire unless attacked. It was pure good fortune.

Right: Captain Keith Lucas (then a lieutenant) in his Black Hawk. Note the Night Stalker badges on his helmet. (*Photo courtesy of Stan Lucas.*)

Below: The eastern half of Pearls Airport, taken from the PRM AA gunners' position on top of a hill beside the runway. (*Photo courtesy of Lieutenant Commander Peter Tomlin.*)

Above: Maurice Bishop, flanked by Sir Paul Scoon (left on dais), takes the salute at a militia march at a Heroes' Day parade in St. Patrick's. (*Photo courtesy of the* Nation *newspaper, Barbados.*)

Below: Marines escort newly captured PRA prisoners to temporary compounds for interrogation at Queen's Park. (*Photo courtesy of Sergeant C. Grey, USMC.*)

Above: The PRA attacks Fort Rupert on October 19 in an attempt to kill Bishop. Note the smoke from burning vehicles obscuring the operations room building, and the narrowness of the approach road, which the three APCs block completely. A ZU-23 AA gun is visible under covers on the left. (*Photo courtesy of the* Nation *newspaper, Barbados.*)

Below: A BTR 60 APC outside Bishop's house on the morning of October 19. Note the crowd with placards pushing past to rescue Bishop from house arrest. (*Photo courtesy of the* Nation *newspaper, Barbados.*)

USS *Guam* with its complement of marine helicopters on the flight deck (*Photo courtesy of 22d MAU.*)

Bishop's excavated grave at Calivigny. (*Photo courtesy of the* Nation *newspaper, Barbados.*)

A view of St. George's from Fort Rupert, looking northeast. Mount Weldale is the tree-covered hill in the center, with Government House on the right of the slope, and Bishop's (the white house) in the trees on the left. (*Photo courtesy of Mary Gundy.*)

A captured photograph showing the PRA practicing night firing with a 12.7-mm AA gun. (*Photo courtesy of 22d MAU.*)

A PRA warehouse at Frequente stacked with ammunition. (*Photo courtesy of the Department of Defense.*)

Vice Admiral Joseph Metcalf III, commander of Task Force 120. He had his headquarters on the USS *Guam* as the on-scene commander of Urgent Fury. (*Photo courtesy of the U.S. Navy.*)

Brigadier General Lewis, Major Hartland, and Barbados Defence Force soldiers await their flight to Grenada. (*Photo courtesy of Willie Alleyne Associates, Barbados.*)

Major General Crist, USMC, Brigadier General Lewis, Prime Minister Adams, and Colonel Barnes discuss plans at the airport in Barbados on D day. (*Photo courtesy of Willie Alleyne Associates, Barbados.*)

Cuban prisoners at Point Salines old camp. (*Photo courtesy of the author.*)

U.S. medical students awaiting a flight home from Point Salines. (*Photo courtesy of Willie Alleyne Associates, Barbados.*)

Richmond Hill Prison: the objective of Delta Force, C Company
1st/75th Rangers, and Task Force 160, taken from the area of Fort
Frederick. Behind is St. George's Harbor, and the white building on
the left is Butler House, Bishop's PRG headquarters. (*Photo courtesy
of the* Nation *newspaper, Barbados.*)

Captain Giguere's Cobra a moment before crashing into St. George's Harbor at about 1:00 P.M. October 25. At the top right is Major DeMars's CH-46 escaping after rescuing Captain Howard from Tanteen field, under covering fire from Giguere. (*Photo courtesy of AP.*)

Fort Frederick, from the valley between it and Richmond Hill Prison. It was the PRA headquarters during the fighting, and it was the heavy fire from here that drove off the Delta Force assault on the prison early on D day. (*Photo courtesy of Mary Gundy*.)

The entrance to the tunnel at Fort Frederick used as the PRA command post during Urgent Fury. It proved impervious to air attack. (*Photo courtesy of the author*.)

11

October 25

The Struggle
For Point Salines

Keep sending battalions until I tell you to stop.
> — Major General Trobaugh, commander
> of 82d Airborne Division at 3:20 P.M. at
> Point Salines in a radio conversation
> with his headquarters

A T 5:34 A.M. Taylor and forty-two men were on the ground, in a most unenviable position. Strategic surprise had been lost on the Sunday; tactical surprise had been impossible ever since H hour slipped to 5:00 A.M.; now yet another principle of war had been flouted: concentration. Urgent Fury was ultimately to involve 20,000 servicemen in one way or another, but at dawn on that Tuesday, in the critical southwest corner of the island, the point of the spear was a battalion headquarters and one infantry platoon. The platoon was from B Company, which was not supposed to have dropped until after A Company had cleared the airfield.

Taylor and his group were totally exposed to view and fire from the low hills 200 meters away north of the runway. There was no cover whatsoever. The ground to the south of the strip was grass covered, with a few folds here and there, which the Rangers used to provide meager protection. Had the PRA been properly dug in around the terminal and on the ridges south of Calliste, rather than the Cubans who were uncertain what to do, Taylor and his men might not have survived. They were perfect close-range targets for machine guns and mortars. But the Cubans had their orders, and the few PRA in the vicinity were concentrating on firing at aircraft rather than troops on the ground, and the Rangers were mostly in dead ground as far as the PRA were concerned.

All this was unknown to Taylor. He was well aware of his vulnerability and the need for fire support onto any likely enemy positions. He was later to say, "After landing the biggest concern was finding cover and setting up communications to direct suppressive fire from AC-130 Spectres circling the airport." This was the primary task of Major James Roper, Taylor's air liaison officer. Roper quickly established contact with Twiford's and Couvillon's aircraft, which began pouring shells into the vicinity of Frequente and potential positions north of the strip.

Taylor was greatly relieved to discover that his group was not under effective fire. There, in front of him, was the runway covered with obstructions, the removal of which was one of his battalion's tasks. Abizaid's A Company was still airborne, but the platoon from B Company was at hand. These men were ordered onto the runway to start clearance. There were trucks, bulldozers, tankers, drums, and stakes driven into the ground with wire between them. Some vehicles had keys in them; some were hot-wired. A Cuban bulldozer was used to flatten stakes and push aside drums. Miraculously, for fifteen minutes, this platoon continued clearance work virtually uninterrupted. Taylor made no attempt at this stage to move to secure the True Blue campus. He saw as his priority getting clearance started and awaiting the remainder of his two companies before tackling the unknown defenses of the medical school. The original planning had never envisaged a quick dash to secure the students on foot, but rather that it should be secured after, or simultaneously with, airfield clearance. Little opposition was anticipated when the Rangers had boarded their aircraft; there was thought to be a good chance they could land, and gun jeeps would drive to the campus. With the element of surprise gone hours before, Taylor needed to assemble his command before anything else.

Twenty minutes after landing, Taylor saw one of A Company's MC-130's coming in low, with Rangers leaping from the rear doors. This aircraft was an attractive target, and machine-gun, small arms, and AA fire was directed against it. The shooting had no effect on the aircraft and caused no casualties, but Taylor called a halt to clearance operations, moving his headquarters from some rocks south of Hardy Bay to a tiny peninsula east of the bay. There he had to wait another forty minutes for the remainder of A Company. Half an hour after that, he had his battalion on the ground, without a single casualty.

It was 7:30, however, before Abizaid was able to coordinate the actions of his platoons (map 14). He appreciated that the enemy on the hills just north of the runway dominated everything and his first task must be to secure this ground. Also he must get to the True Blue campus. He ordered the 1st and 3d platoons to attack across the runway, using M-60 machine guns and 60-mm rocket launchers for supporting fire. Number 2 platoon was to approach True Blue along the beach south of the runway. The two assault platoons crossed the tarmac without loss, firing and advancing toward the village of Calliste. As they moved toward a school, a Spanish-speaking Ranger yelled out to the enemy to surrender. The response was increased firing, which killed the only Ranger to die in the fighting to secure the runway. Private Mark Okamura Yamane was hit in the neck while operating his M-60. Squad leader Sergeant Manous Boles from 1st platoon led the attack toward the school, gallantly driving a captured bulldozer. His men, crouched behind it, succeeded in reaching the top of the hill, where they found an abandoned 12.7-mm AA gun.

Inside the True Blue campus, at 7:30, most students had been awake for several hours, roused by the noise of aircraft overhead. Later, when shooting started, many, like Christine Gigliuto, dived under their beds. Some hid in bathtubs, and others peered out to see what was happening. Twenty-two-year-old Harold Harvey stated, "Then I saw the paratroopers jumping. It was really thrilling to see, kind of like an old John Wayne movie, but I knew people were going to get killed." Stephen Renae, watching as well, saw "planes diving and strafing at ground targets we couldn't see. The worst thing was not knowing where the planes were from." A few minutes after 7:30, American voices were heard yelling to those inside to identify themselves and telling students to lie on the floor. There was some firing between advancing Rangers and the PRA guard detail at the main gate. To the students, it was very noisy, very confusing, and very frightening, with a number of bullets from the cross fire smashing windows and penetrating the buildings. Within fifteen minutes, the campus was secured, the PRA detachment retreating north into the hills. No students had been harmed, no hostages taken, and no casualties inflicted on the Rangers. The troops and students were jubilant. But it came as a shock to the troops to discover that the students they had found were fewer than half the total number. Grand Anse had never featured in the Rangers' plans. Although the battle for the hills north of the runway raged for several hours more, from then on True Blue's participation was confined to acting as an aid post.

On the runway, the 150 men of Newman's B Company had been tasked with pushing northwest in the direction of the control tower and the hills beyond the terminal. They received heavy fire from the Cubans in and around their old camp, but the Rangers' advance soon had them on the run. One Cuban was killed and twenty-two surrendered to B Company as they moved steadily northward. By 9:55 Newman's men had reached the fuel storage tanks on high ground 600 meters northeast of the terminal. From this scrub-covered vantage point, they could look down into the Cuban mission headquarters at Little Havana. Cubans, clearly visible inside the compound and on the high ground nearby, started to set up two mortars, but the Rangers opened up with a captured 12.7-mm, which scattered the crews.

By 10:00 A.M., B Company was firm on the fuel tank hill, while A Company held the Calliste high ground 500 meters across the valley to the southeast. Neither company contemplated further advance, and the action of 1st/75th was initially confined to consolidating their positions and sniper fire. From the area of a small building just west of the Cubans' compound, however, 90-mm recoilless rifle fire was proving effective against A Company. They pulled back from their exposed positions, leaving observation posts on the ridge, while gunship assistance was summoned.

Metcalf had directed that the four AH-1T Cobras of HMM-261 squadron with 22d MAU fly south to support the army in the Salines area. The marine pilots had difficulty making any radio contact with the air force AC-130s or ground units; the radio frequencies given to the marines were incorrect. However, after a fruitless flight by the first pair of Cobras, marine captain Gary Watson, wingman to marine captain Douglas Diehl, picked up an army frequency. Diehl and Watson flew south, making contact with the 1st/75th's forward air controller. Neither pilot could make sense of the target identification message because the Rangers and marines were using different maps. With considerable ingenuity, however, the forward air controller used a reflecting mirror to pinpoint the house that concealed the recoilless

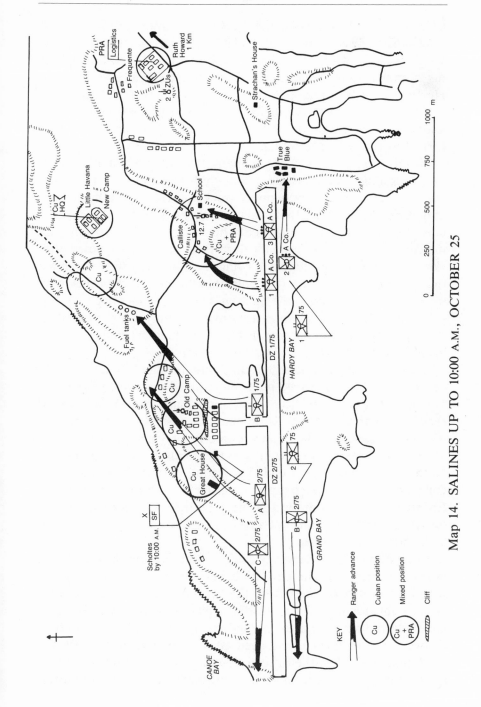

Map 14. SALINES UP TO 10:00 A.M., OCTOBER 25

rifle. Still slightly uncertain, the two Cobras came in. Suddenly both pilots heard the controller yell, "That's it! That's it! It's right under you!" Watson swung left, while behind him Diehl fired bursts from his 20-mm cannon. Watson circled round to come in a second time. He fired a TOW straight through a window, which destroyed the building. Three Cubans ran for a nearby truck, so Watson fired another TOW, hitting the vehicle, which exploded. Both Cobras returned to the *Guam* to refuel.

Shortly after 10:00 A.M., B Company 1st/75th was horrified to see two Ranger motorcyclists heading straight for the Cuban mission from the terminal area. They were on the track in the valley totally exposed and obviously oblivious to the fact that they were riding directly into enemy positions. They came under heavy fire. Both fell from their machines wounded and lay in the dust. Because of their exposed position, B Company was unable to bring them in. They were to remain there, protected by sniper fire, until midafternoon, when they were evacuated during a lull in the fighting due to surrender negotiations.

The 2d/75th had had an easier time. Not only did the battalion drop quickly as a unit, but they met little resistance when they assisted in clearing the area west of Hardy Bay. Kearney's A Company moved into the partially completed terminal buildings and up into the old camp. Here they discovered many abandoned weapons, including a 12.7-mm AA gun, recoilless rifles, and small arms, in and around the Cuban barracks. Sittnik's B Company pushed along the narrow piece of land south of the runway toward Point Salines, while Hanna's C Company cleared the low hills to the north down to Canoe Bay. Nothing of interest was found. The battalion escorted and guarded Cuban prisoners, although the plan was for it to advance on Calivigny. Enemy resistance had proved far stronger than was anticipated, and the impossibility of getting to Calivigny that day was obvious to Hagler and, indeed, to Scholtes.

By 10:00 A.M. both Ranger battalions were firm on their positions north of the runway. The 1st/75th held the area east of the terminal, with B Company on the left on the fuel tank hill and A Company on the right around Calliste, including a platoon at True Blue. Hagler's men held the terminal area, the old camp, and the high ground to the west. Salines airfield had been taken. It was secure enough for the Rangers' C-130s, the Special Forces' aircraft, all of which had refueled in Barbados, to land. Within four hours of the first drop, nine of the twelve Ranger transports had landed and off-loaded. Scholtes arrived to set up his headquarters in the small buildings a few meters west of the terminal, destined later to be the airport fire station. Nearby was the assembly area for the Black Hawks and Little Birds of TF 160.

At 10:45 Hagler was incredulous to see what he thought were PRA soldiers disembarking from a C-130. He had not been told to expect Caribbean reinforcements.

‡ ‡ ‡

During the planning process, there had been confusion over the arrival time in Grenada of the 82d Airborne's leading elements. Akers certainly understood they should be on the ground by H plus 4 hours, that is, about 9:30 A.M. However, for some reason, this was changed by Atlantic Command to a departure from Pope (Fort Bragg) at H plus 4 giving, with a five-hour flight, an arrival of H plus 9. This was much too late for a rapid takeover from the Special Forces, even if this had been possible. Similarly it meant the Caribbean units would arrive before, rather than after, the 82d.

None of the contingents in the Caribbean Peacekeeping Force knew what to expect on arrival or, more important, what their mission was, except for rather vague peacekeeping duties. They went prepared to fight, but they were not under command of the Americans. The U.S. troops were not briefed on their participation. The U.S. high command had not included them in their planning and had told them nothing about the D-day objectives of the U.S. forces. As McDonald was to admit in his official report to the JCS chairman three months later, "During preliminary and final planning, the control of the CPF [Caribbean Peacekeeping Force] was not coordinated with CJTF 120 [Metcalf] creating early confusion on the planning for inserting the CPF." Brigadier General Rudyard Lewis, who was double hatted as the chief of staff of the Barbados Defence Force and regional security coordinator, was to have been the Caribbean representative with Metcalf on the *Guam*. Colonel Ken Barnes of the Jamaica Defence Force would command the Caribbean Peacekeeping Force on the ground.

Even this arrangement went wrong. Lewis, who was anticipating a helicopter ride out to the *Guam* at 11:00 P.M. on Monday, was telephoned at 5:00 P.M. by Ambassador Bish to say Metcalf and the aircraft were waiting for him at the Barbados airport. But he was in the midst of final preparations and could not leave then. The helicopter never returned, so Lewis went in the next day on the first available C-130. In his own words, "We went in completely blind." Nobody had even bothered to tell him the code name of the operation—Urgent Fury.

Arriving midmorning were 300 West Indian troops and paramilitary police. Jamaica provided an infantry company, Barbados a strongly reinforced platoon of some 50 men, Antigua and Barbuda a squad, and Dominica, St. Lucia, and St. Kitts detachments of armed police special service units. A group from St. Vincent arrived the following day, plus a larger contingent of Barbadian policemen. All Caribbean personnel wore blue armbands to distinguish them from the PRA.

With fighting still going on north of Salines, Lewis was left to his own devices. The arrival of the Caribbean Peacekeeping Force had been unexpected, there was no ground headquarters to report to, and there was no joint tactical plan with any prescribed role for his troops, so Lewis established his headquarters in the Great House on a hill 100 meters west of the terminal. It had been used as offices by the Cuban engineers building the airfield and was full of briefcases, papers, personal effects, and cash. All these were locked in one room while the peacekeeping force units deployed in the old camp and the hills close by. Lewis agreed, in discussion with Major General George Crist of the marines, who accompanied the peacekeeping force as senior liaison officer, and Scholtes, that he should relieve the 2d/75th of responsibility for prisoners.

By nightfall some 250 captives, including ten to twelve PRA, had been rounded up and the Cuban barracks ransacked. The accommodation in old camp was ankle deep in litter.

Tomlin, who earlier in the afternoon had had twenty-seven Cubans, with three recoilless rifles, emerge from some nearby bushes to surrender to him, was put to work with a senior police officer, Collis Barrow, organizing the accommodations for the prisoners. Cuban doctors, nurses, and cooks were identified; food was provided; and several buildings were taken over for shelter. There were a number of wounded prisoners, but the nearby former Cuban dressing station had little in the way of medical supplies. Tomlin sent for the Jamaican Defence Force medical officer, who when he arrived had a brief look around and departed. No assistance was forthcoming from that source.

At around 7:00 P.M. the Caribbean Peacekeeping Force was able to provide valuable assistance to the SEALs, trapped in Government House. There was radio contact between the SEALs inside and Scholtes's staff at Salines; indeed the telephone system throughout the island was still functioning. Lewis had spoken to Sir Paul personally that afternoon. The SEALs kept indicating that PRA counterattacks were coming from the prime minister's house and across a tennis court. Spectre fire support was required. The problem was that nobody had maps showing a tennis court. Major Hartland of the Barbados Defence Force was summoned to Scholtes's headquarters. With his detailed local knowledge, he was easily able to explain the layout of Government House grounds, pinpoint the tennis court, and enable the gunships to shoot with impressive accuracy. The PRA fell back.

‡ ‡ ‡

At 2:05 P.M. the first C-141 Starlifter bringing 82d Airborne troops touched down at Salines. Out stepped Major General Trobaugh, accompanied by his forward headquarters staff and A Company 2d/325th.

The previous thirty-six hours had been frustrating for Trobaugh. His mission had been changed to one of mopping up or law-and-order duties. Like other commanders, his information on Grenada was sketchy; he was supposed to take over from the Special Forces and Rangers early on D day, but his delayed departure had made that impossible. Then he had an annoying argument with the MAC staff over the twelve Starlifters assigned to carry his units. They all arrived rigged to land at Salines, whereas Trobaugh wanted the parachute option. Eventually he got his way, and the aircraft were rigged for a drop. Also worrying was his position in the command setup. He was TF 121 commander, but the plan involved two other task forces operating on the ground in Grenada: JTF 123 under Scholtes, plus TF 124 under Erie, with the marines ashore in the north. There was no ground force commander as such, and Trobaugh rightly foresaw coordination problems. These difficulties were exacerbated by poor to nonexistent direct radio communications between 82d Airborne, the marines, and Metcalf on the *Guam*. Eventually a special army communications team had to be set up on the *Guam* to try to resolve this situation.

The divisional plan had envisaged deployment to Grenada in two phases: an assault echelon and a follow-on echelon. The assault units consisted of the divisional forward command post, the forward command post of 2d Brigade under Colonel Stephen Silvasy with two infantry battalions, two field artillery batteries, an engineer platoon, a military police platoon, and four Stinger teams from 3d/4th Air Defense Artillery Regiment (ADA). This grouping was usually referred to as a "combat slice." The battalions were the 2d/325th under Lieutenant Colonel Jack Hamilton and the 3d/325th under Lieutenant Colonel John Raines. The affiliated artillery batteries were B Battery for 2d/325th and C Battery for the 3d/325th, both from 1st/320th Field Artillery. Each had six 105-mm howitzers, which, due to scarcity of airlift capacity, were deployed separately in four three-gun troops.

The follow-on echelon was Colonel Steven Scott's forward command post from 3d Brigade, with Lieutenant Colonel George Crocker's 1st/505th and Lieutenant Colonel Hugh Shaw's 1st/508th. With them went A and B Batteries of the 1st/319th Field Artillery, each with only three guns.

These units were to deploy light, that is, without vehicles, manpacking all their equipment. As long-range radios were vehicle-mounted, this effectively curtailed communications. As the executive officer of 2d/505th put it, "No vehicles meant no radios." His battalion was to commandeer at least thirty civilian vehicles after arrival in Grenada to increase mobility. As with the Rangers, this also meant the troops were frequently grossly overloaded. The infantrymen in Grenada moved slowly, suffered from heat exhaustion, were unable to climb hills quickly, and tended to confine themselves to roads or tracks. None felt the weight of their equipment more than the radio operators and Stinger teams. A Stinger crew member carried about 110 pounds, which made it impossible for them to keep up with their units off the tracks. Although there was no air threat, no fewer than twenty-seven Stinger teams deployed to Grenada by the end of October. They had no vehicles, so had they actually fired, resupply would have been a major problem.

When Trobaugh had taken off at 10:07 A.M., it was uncertain whether he would jump or land. He was not in the picture as to what was happening at Salines, so during the flight, he tried to listen in on Scholtes's radio net. But communications were difficult, and he learned little. However, after two and a half hours it was confirmed that Salines had been secured. Not that that necessarily meant it was safe to land the Starlifters on the unfinished runway, the western end of which was still only surfaced with gravel and oil. To check this out was the task of Brigadier General Robert Patterson, the vice-commander of the 21st Air Force, MAC, from McGuire Air Force Base. Patterson, a highly decorated officer with almost 300 combat flying hours, landed from Barbados in a C-130 at 11:30 A.M. He gave the go-ahead for daylight landings, but with no airfield lights, night landings for any aircraft larger than the C-130 were too risky.

Shortly before Trobaugh's aircraft touched down, Newman with B Company 1st/75th decided that something must be done to rescue the two wounded Ranger scouts. Collecting some Cuban prisoners and a Spanish-speaking Ranger, Newman, holding a bullhorn, slowly advanced toward Little Havana with the Cuban construction workers in front. He called out to the Cubans to surrender, whereupon two came forward with their weapons above their heads. Sergeant Clayton advanced to the compound where he found about 150 Cubans apparently willing to give up. He also discovered two dead and twenty-three wounded. Clayton continued to negotiate and shortly before 3:00 P.M. was able to escort out the wounded plus about seventy prisoners. The remaining eighty had decided to fight on. At the compound, he was able to destroy several heavy weapons, including mortars and recoilless rifles. This initiative from B Company was a serious blow to the Cubans' ability to resist.

At that time Trobaugh was unaware of this success. After disembarking, he had expressed his surprise at finding Taylor with his command post still only 20 meters from the runway, jumped on a Cuban dump truck, and was driven to meet Scholtes at his headquarters west of the terminal. The picture painted was far from rosy.

The original plan called for the Rangers and Special Operations Forces to leave Grenada on October 25, but Trobaugh was rapidly disabused of any such possibility. Salines had been secured, the students at True Blue were safe, and the marines had Pearls. These were the pluses. The debit side was longer. Resistance had been heavier than expected, the Cubans and PRA were still fighting, there was another campus at Grand Anse full of students waiting to be rescued, and there was no way the two under-strength Ranger battalions could secure Camp Calivigny as planned. The worst news concerned the rough handling given to the Special Operations Forces in operations around St. George's. Trobaugh learned of the failed attack on Richmond Hill Prison, the successful PRA counterattack at Beausejour, and the fact that the SEALs had not secured the governor-general but rather that they, and he, were under siege. He felt fully justified in sending his colorful signal for reinforcements: "Keep sending battalions until I tell you to stop." His request was relayed upward to Washington, where a worried Weinberger eventually agreed to it. Within another three days, no fewer than six battalions of the 82d were in Grenada.

‡ ‡ ‡

Sergeant Randy Cline was in A Company of the 1st/75th Rangers. He came from Belle Union in Indiana and had been a policeman and deputy sheriff before joining the army. Like many others in his battalion, Cline had been alerted at his home by a telephone call early on the morning of October 23 but did not think it was anything other than an exercise and joked with his wife about seeing her later in the day. He never returned. He flew to Grenada with his battalion, but unlike the majority of A Company, he did not parachute onto Salines runway.

Cline was in command of a gun jeep, jeep team 5, so he was not part of the frantic scramble to rerig for a drop as the C-130 circled around and above the island. He and his jeep crew of four Rangers were required to remain with their vehicle until the aircraft landed. After most of the company had jumped in broad daylight, Cline's aircraft headed at once to Barbados for fuel. Several hours later, he flew back, landed safely, and drove off the aircraft to report to Abizaid, his company commander. He was given a mission: to take his jeep to secure a road junction about 200 meters north of the True Blue campus, just forward of his company's position. With him went Privates Timothy Domick, Marlin Maynard, Mark Rademacher, and Russell Robinson. If you drive along the track north of the runway in an easterly direction, it is easy to miss True Blue. The campus is hidden in a dip in the ground, southeast of the end of the runway. At the time Cline tried to find the right crossroads there were numerous new tracks, which bore little relation to those marked on any map. Cline's jeep drove past True Blue along a dusty dirt road heading northeast toward Ruth Howard. He passed the spot where Lieutenant Brizan had been shot four and a half years before, continuing for some 2 kilometers before he was certain they were in the wrong place. By that time he was well into the area held by the PRA company under Redhead.

The PRA had set up a small ambush about 800 meters northwest of True Blue alongside the road up which Cline had just driven. The soldiers were concealed in the bushes, with one or two shallow trenches, and had seen the jeep go past. When Cline turned around, they were waiting for him. They opened heavy fire on the fast-moving vehicle from very close range. Cline and his men responded with the M-60 and their rifles, but they had been caught by surprise, and the jeep was wrecked. The uneven fight did not last long. Although at least one PRA soldier was shot dead in his trench, Cline, Maynard, Rademacher, and Robinson were killed. Domick, although wounded, was able to make his way on foot back to his unit. Cline, his three crewmen, and Yamane were the only Rangers killed by enemy action in Grenada.

It was along the same road, in midafternoon, that the PRA launched their third counterattack—a brave, but hopeless, attempt to retake the eastern end of the runway. At about 3:30 P.M. an observation post in A Company spotted three BTR-60s approaching fast. They accelerated down the track, quite close together, came through 2d platoon's position, and opened fire in the direction of the runway with their turret machine guns. The Rangers reacted at once, firing any weapon that was to hand, including rifles, light antitank weapons, and recoilless rifles. The leading APC screeched to a halt and reversed sharply, straight into the second one. After two misses, the vehicles were hit by rockets and disabled. The crews bailed out through the roof hatches, leaving two dead. The third one turned around, retreating rapidly in the direction it had come, helped on its way by a rocket into its rear. It was able to continue until it was spotted by Simms in his AC-130 overhead. He destroyed it.

A totally unsupported attack by about twenty-four men had no hope of success at that time. It was too weak and too late. Had it been launched in the early morning during the hour and a half it took the Rangers to drop, with a stronger force such as the whole of Nelson's battle group, it might have had a different ending. As Sergeant James Bradford, 1st/75th said, it was a "valiant, heroic, but stupid move."

The finale for the day for the Rangers involved A-7 aircraft from the carrier *Independence* and, again, A Company 1st/75th. The PRG mobilization minister, Strachan, had commandeered a delightful house perched atop a prominent hill 1,000 meters east of the end of the runway. Its location had provided the two or three PRA guards with a spectacular view of the day's events below them. Late in the afternoon, they had seen some Rangers come within range and opened fire, effectively pinning the U.S. troops and wounding one or more.

They were Abizaid's men, and he wanted to call up an AC-130, but none was available, so the A-7s were summoned instead. They intended to use their MK-20 bombs to destroy the house. After three separate passes had produced dud bombs and with the target uncomfortably close to his forward positions, Abizaid wanted to stop. However, the pilots were rebriefed, the Rangers put out marker panels to make sure they were not hit by mistake, and Abizaid reluctantly agreed to another try. This time the bombs hit and exploded, Strachan's house collapsed, and the wounded Rangers could be evacuated.

‡   ‡   ‡

Since Colonel Tortolo's arrival the previous day, not a great deal had been achieved by the Cuban construction workers, or military advisers, in their work areas. Tortolo and his civilian counterpart, Carlos Diaz, had established themselves at the military mission. The workers were divided into makeshift units under army officers and assigned heavier weapons, such as recoilless rifles and mortars. There were two distinct areas to be defended. The first was the old camp on the hills immediately behind and to the west of the terminal. This area housed the bulk of the men working at Salines in a cluster of fifteen to twenty wooden barrack rooms. Nearby were a number of expatriates' private houses. Excellent views and fields of fire over the terminal and the central portion of the runway were obtainable. Here the majority of the Cubans were given their defensive positions. There was no extensive digging, although some shallow shell scraps were dug outside buildings on the rim of the ridges. Recoilless rifles were located on the long ridge behind the terminal at the rear of the position, pointing southeast toward Hardy Bay. A mortar base plate position was set up immediately north of the barracks complex. A command post–observation post linked by field telephone lines forward and to the rear, was positioned on the highest point of the ridge.

Medical arrangements were makeshift. An aid post was located on the hill behind the old camp, but the doctor normally assigned to the construction workers was in Cuba. Drugs were in short supply; after Bishop's death, the situation on the island prevented resupply. This was the position when fighting started. Dr. Gustovo Martinez, a Cuban doctor, explained, "We did as much as we could with the little we had. . . . We didn't even have any alcohol, and we had to use rum to disinfect the wounds and give injections. There was no possibility of operating on any of the wounded."

The second Cuban position was at Little Havana, where Matamoros coordinated the preparations. Down in the valley was the military mission headquarters with its communications center, offices, and accommodation for senior military personnel. Fifty meters away across the road was the new camp, under construction to relieve the pressure on the facilities at the old camp. Here also was a large parking lot. To defend this area necessitated the occupation of the hills that overlooked it.[1] Matamoros himself said, "Our buildings were in a hollow, so the defense was organized on the hills around the Military Mission and the new and old camps." This meant deploying some men up onto the Calliste ridge, although the village was some 1,000 meters from Little Havana. The workers were told their positions, told that an invasion might come at any time, and told to defend themselves if attacked. They did not move out to their battle locations on the night of October 24–25. Once the landings started, they left their camps to deploy.

The duty officer at Little Havana on October 25 was Major Luis Acosta, a 42-year-old transportation specialist from Havana. It was his task to supervise Tortolo's communications during the fighting. He was assisted by the only Cuban female military officer, Lieutenant Garcia Salina, who normally worked as a translator. Radio links were established to the defenders on the nearby hills, forward to old camp, and to the embassy. Garcia has described how "we got into contact with the embassy right away. Through it we received direct orientations from our Party, Government, and Commander in Chief. . . . We passed on decisions and orders from headquarters to the various chiefs and battle areas."

One of the few Cuban infantry officers in Grenada was 1st Lieutenant Silva Rodriguez. The roar of aircraft had awakened Silva before dawn. He collected his group of workers, each with an AK rifle and

100 rounds of ammunition, and moved quickly to his defensive position on the hills behind the terminal. Silva and his men watched the Rangers dropping, observing some moving along the shore line toward True Blue campus. He then became heavily involved in the fighting against U.S. forces as they advanced toward his position. He was hit on the right hand, his back, and on the right arm but evaded capture until the next day.

Although the PRA security detail at Salines set up a 12.7-mm gun just to the north of the old camp and got it into action against the C-130s as they flew above the runway, the great majority of the Cubans obeyed their orders not to fire unless attacked. The 12.7 itself drew fire from the Spectres overhead, but it was not until the Rangers had dropped, collected themselves, and started firing that the battle was joined by the construction workers. Fifty-four-year-old worker Leonel Cairo, who was seriously wounded, had been told to observe and report the U.S. troop movements. He recalled, "I saw the parachute troops landing. They grouped on the beach and then slowly began to engage in reconnaissance. The Yankee planes landed on the runway. I kept watching their movements. A few minutes later we were attacked. I had a rifle and shot back."

As was to be expected with poorly trained personnel with marginal motivation, resistance was seldom prolonged. Some fought hard, but most gave up or withdrew when their ammunition ran out or they were wounded. They had no answer to the AC-130 gunships. While in numbers they were approximately equal to the Rangers, they were not professional soldiers. Nevertheless, they had, on the whole, performed better than expected in the circumstances. Had they opened up from properly prepared positions as the Rangers were landing, the outcome of the struggle for Salines would have been seriously in doubt. Nevertheless, their defense of Salines was stronger than anticipated; it set back the U.S. invasion timetable, causing the task force commanders to revise upward their estimates of enemy strength. Their resistance slowed the whole schedule of the intervention; after D day the Americans became more uncertain, more cautious, slow to move out of the Salines area.

By early afternoon Nelson's battle group was seriously depleted. Instead of using this force as a complete unit, the RMC high command had used it as a reserve from which to take ad hoc subunits to reinforce other operations. At about 3:00 P.M. Layne came on the radio ordering Nelson to release his only remaining APC platoon for a counterattack at Salines. Under its platoon chief, Warrant Officer McEwen, it was decided to approach the objective by a circuitous route east of St. George's, thinking they would be less likely to be spotted from the air. McEwen had no idea of where the U.S. forces were or what exactly he was to attack. He knew he was on his own, with no likelihood of support. He had twenty-four men in three APCs. He moved off via Tempe, down the Morne Jaloux ridge road, past the Sugar Factory, to Ruth Howard and the Sugar Mill. Here he encountered elements of the security company under Redhead, who had been involved in the fighting during the morning in the Calliste area. After McEwen's departure, Nelson realized the futility of such an isolated, weak attack and set off in his jeep to catch McEwen in an attempt to stop him. He was too late. He met briefly with Redhead near the Sugar Mill, followed the APCs down the dusty road toward Salines for a short distance, and then gave up. McEwen roared on until he met A Company 1st/75th.

‡ ‡ ‡

By late afternoon Trobaugh had three infantry battalions at Salines. Both 1st/75th and 2d/75th were to come under his command, allowing Scholtes to extract his Special Operations Forces and go home once the debacle in Government House had been resolved, and he had Hamilton's 2d/325th. The remainder of this battalion had arrived before nightfall, but Raines's 3d/325th had been diverted to Barbados because attempts to improvise sufficient runway lighting failed. At Grantley Adams Airport, 3d/325th transferred to C-130s and, together with three 105-mm guns, arrived in Grenada at 2:46 A.M. on October 26.

Metcalf had decided that the Ranger battalions should switch to CTF 121 (Trobaugh) at 7 P.M., but although Trobaugh knew, Hagler was not told until three and a half hours later, while Taylor knew nothing about it until 6:30 the next morning. At a crucial time when planning and coordination for continuing operations should have been in progress, nothing was happening. Command and control fell victim to confusion. Trobaugh was aware that some marines had landed on the coast north of St. George's at 7:00 P.M., but he was not the ground force commander, and his communications with the marines were at best intermittent. Equally frustrating was the fact that although he could see the USS *Guam* on the horizon, more often than not he was unable to speak to Metcalf. The army command post and the admiral commanding were in direct line of sight, only a few miles apart, yet radio contact was impossible, except occasionally via satellite. Trobaugh confined himself to assessing his own situation.

Intelligence reports on the enemy were nonexistent. Some 250 prisoners, mainly Cubans, were being guarded by the Caribbean Peacekeeping Force. Hamilton's men had taken over from A and B Companies, 1st/75th, and the CIA had finally arrived on the island, complete with two air-conditioned vans, which were parked near his command post at the eastern end of the terminal buildings. In contacting the Rangers, he discovered for the first time that both battalions were at 50 percent of normal strength. This, coupled with the fact that he was uncertain when the 3d/325th would arrive and the unexpectedly stiff opposition, reinforced his earlier belief that he needed a lot more men. He had no way of knowing how many Cubans were on the island, and he didn't know the strength of the PRA, but he did know that all the Special Force missions on D day had failed and that Sir Paul Scoon's safety was still in doubt. Calivigny was still a long way away, and a lot of U.S. citizens were penned up at Grand Anse awaiting rescue.

It was some relief when Raines arrived with his battalion, plus a troop of howitzers, in the early morning. With a brigade of two battalions, Trobaugh gave orders to Colonel Silvasy. Hamilton, with 2d/325th, was to move through the Ranger positions to push north as far as Morne Rouge and Frequente, while Raines with 3d/325th was to clear the True Blue peninsula. An advance of 1,500 meters was contemplated, with the 2d/325th having to deal with the remaining Cubans at Little Havana. It might be possible to reach the Lime and Grand Anse campus.

The Rangers were well content with their day (map 15). Despite the chaos on the aircraft, despite the drawn-out daylight jump in front of enemy positions, they had got away with it. They had secured the airfield and True Blue at the cost of seven dead, including the two pathfinders, and some six wounded. Although there had been a lot of Cuban shooting, the enemy had, with a few exceptions, retreated or surrendered when under close attack. But if the Rangers thought they were going home on Day 1, as the plan envisaged, they were to be disappointed.

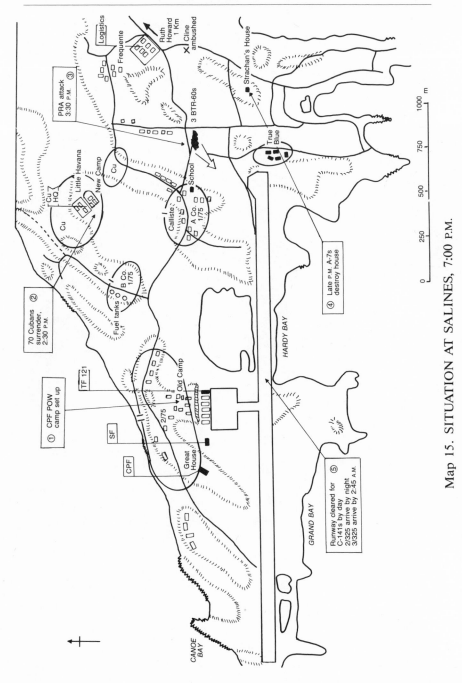

Map 15. SITUATION AT SALINES, 7:00 P.M.

12

October 25

Pearls Airport and the North

Keep feeding me, keep feeding me.
> — PRM gunner to her loader on a
> 12.7-mm AA gun at Pearls Airport

T HE final version of the intervention plan envisaged the most powerful element of the sledgehammer taking a swipe at the nut in the north of the island. It missed, hitting thin air, through no fault of the marines who made the dawn landings. Intelligence on what was happening in that part of Grenada was nonexistent, so there was no way of knowing that the RMC had abandoned the defenses to the local militia battalion, which, like the others, had largely failed to put in an appearance. There was only a handful of them in the vicinity of the airport. Nevertheless, the marines' assault was preceded by the only entirely successful D-day Special Operations Forces mission, undertaken by the SEAL Team 4 detachment traveling with the task force. Of the six attempted insertions by Special Forces, this was the only one that completed its mission as planned. Later in the day, it was to be the marines that were used to rescue the D-day plan from disaster, when they were rushed south to advance on Government House early on October 26, to relieve beleaguered SEALs and the governor-general.

Initially the Atlantic planners had considered using only the navy and marines of TF 124 for Urgent Fury. They were readily available, at sea, capable of putting troops ashore by helicopter and over the beaches. They were a self-contained, hard-hitting force of just under 2,000 marines. The amphibious assault ship USS *Guam* was the ideal ship from which to control such an operation, with its sophisticated communications and medical facilities. The marines had been anticipating making landings on the southwest peninsula until the arrival of Metcalf's signal at 10:00 P.M. on October 22, telling them the army would conduct an airborne attack on the island.

This must have been a frustrating time for 22d MAU, and its commander, Colonel James Faulkner, for if there was fighting to be done, they were the obvious choice to take the brunt of it, or so they thought. There were just over 800 marines in the infantry battalion of 2d/8th BLT. They carried formidable firepower, having recently been restructured into a new organization, with fewer marines but more heavy weapons. A total of 134 grenade launchers were carried, together with 32 Dragon antitank guided missiles, eight 50-caliber heavy machine guns, plus eight 81-mm mortars. To increase mobility, the battalion had no fewer than fifty-two jeeps under its direct control, with call on some twenty-four more from other units.

The marine battalion had three rifle companies, lettered E, F, and G, a weapons company, and the usual headquarters and supply company for control and logistics. Each rifle company had three rifle platoons of thirty-six men and a weapons platoon with its three 60-mm light mortars and machine guns—over 150 men. For Urgent Fury, Lieutenant Colonel Ray Smith commanded 2d/8th BLT with his Alpha command group, while his executive officer, Major Joseph Streitz, remained with the Bravo group ready to take over should Smith become a casualty. Captain Henry Donigan commanded E Company, Captain Michael Dick had F, and Captain Robert Dobson G. Weapons company was under Captain Chris Gunther.

Smith had a lot more apart from the battalion. There was H Battery 3d/10th Artillery under Captain Bradley Gates with eight 155-mm towed howitzers, with a range of 22,000 meters. These guns positioned just south of Pearls could have hit Salines. Armored support was available from the five M-60 tanks of 3d Platoon, A Company, 2d Tank Battalion, while fourteen amphibious assault vehicles (LVTP-7s) of 4th Platoon of A Company, 2d Assault Amphibian Battalion were available to land the marines through the surf. Finally 2d/8th BLT had its own reconnaissance and engineer platoons, plus a TOW section.

The helicopter lift capability was provided by the marine medium helicopter squadron 261 (HMM 261) under Lieutenant Colonel Granville

"Granny" Amos. This squadron normally consisted of twelve CH-46E Sea Knights, with a troop lifting capacity of twenty-five combat-ready men each, or approximately two rifle companies. However, it had been reinforced for its Lebanon duties to include four CH-53D Sea Stallions for heavy resupply loads or carrying a slung howitzer, four AH-IT Cobra gunships for fire support, and two UH-1N Hueys for command or liaison duties. Amos's command also included several logistical, maintenance, and support detachments.

To sustain these two combat units was the task of the composite Marine Service Support Group number 22 (MSSG 22). Its commanding officer was Major Albert Shively. Here were to be found a mixture of detachments concerned with keeping the BLT and HMM in action. Landing support, maintenance, medical, dental, supply, engineer, motor transport, explosive ordnance disposal, and military police were all represented.

The USS *Guam*, which eventually also carried Metcalf with his staff, had onboard the commander of TF 124 (Erie), Faulkner with his MAU headquarters, E and F Companies 2d/8th BLT, and HMM 261. Both rifle companies could be airlifted if need be by the CH-46s. Sailing on the USS *Trenton* was Smith with his headquarters, plus the weapons company of 2d/8th BLT and the headquarters and shore party of MSSG 22. USS *Fort Snelling* carried the tanks, the reconnaissance platoon, TOW section, navy SEAL detachment, and underwater demolition team. G Company, earmarked for possible beach landings, was onboard the USS *Manitowac* with the LVTP-7s, while its sister ship, the USS *Barnstable County*, carried the howitzer battery and engineers. It was a formidable force with substantial mobility and great versatility, able to act independently over a considerable period.

‡   ‡   ‡

The arrival onboard the *Guam* of the liaison officers from Atlantic Command at 10:00 P.M. on October 23, carrying a draft operation order for Urgent Fury, caused somewhat of a stir. Smith and Amos were summoned to the briefing, arriving late. However, they quickly learned they had barely thirty hours in which to plan their new mission: to seize Pearls airfield and Grenville town and neutralize any opposition in the area. They had the north. The south, including St. George's, belonged to the army, while the carrier battle group centered on the *Independence* would provide support as required.

Around midnight, both officers sat down to decide exactly how to achieve their objectives.

Like the army, they wanted to arrive in Grenada while it was still dark. A daylight landing by sea or air made no tactical sense. However, they had been told that no landings could be made before 4:00 A.M. on October 25, which did not give them any leeway. Both officers agreed that H hour for heliborne troops and L hour for troops landing over the beach should be simultaneous, at 4:00 A.M. The marines were carefully briefed on the rules of engagement. Heavy weapons could not be used indiscriminately but only if essential to accomplish the mission. The object was to liberate, not attack, Grenadians. There were to be no search-and-destroy operations.

Intelligence was still vague. Officers were lucky to get naval charts of the island, without grids. Commander Butler warned that heavy surf and high winds along the east coast could make an amphibious landing impossible. Before a beach landing could be confirmed, a detailed reconnaissance was essential. The SEAL detachment from Team 4 had this mission. Meanwhile 22d MAU's plan envisaged a heliborne landing by a rifle company each at Pearls and Grenville, with the remaining company following up with a surface landing.

On October 24 the bad news was the time change of H hour to 5:00 A.M. The most they could expect was half an hour of rapidly evaporating darkness. At about 10:00 P.M. two Seafox boats, each with a small group of SEALs plus a crew of three from special boat unit 20, left the security of the *Fort Snelling* for a 15-kilometer ride in rough seas. The Seafox has a high speed, low profile, and its own .50-caliber machine gun and 40-mm grenade launcher. These craft succeeded in reaching the beach area east of Pearls around midnight, after a most uncomfortable journey. There followed several hours of careful probing of the airport perimeter and close examination of the beaches, reef, and surf conditions along that section of the coast. Some Grenadian militia were seen and heard around the terminal buildings but nothing to indicate strong defenses. At 4:00 A.M. they sent the message, "Walking Track Shoes," by radio. This meant tracked amphibians would find a landing extremely hazardous, and other landing craft would find it impossible. Butler's forecast was correct; Erie cancelled the proposed amphibious follow-up. The initial assault would be entirely heliborne; the LVTP-7s would be used only if daylight revealed a better beach.

Smith and Amos got little sleep that night as they revised their plan yet again. They had several problems, not least of which was the weather. Normally up to four CH-46s could take off from the *Guam*'s flight deck more or less simultaneously, but conditions were not normal. It would be dark, there were high winds with frequent rain squalls, the *Guam* had to be headed into the wind for takeoff, and radio silence was imposed. All this meant that embarking the marines and lift-off would be a slow process. Helicopters would take off singly, which meant a subsequent rendezvous would be difficult, time-consuming, and fuel expensive. There was no possibility of a simultaneous assault by the two companies. Therefore Grenville would have to wait because Pearls was considered the more important objective. If H hour for Pearls was 5:00 A.M., that for Grenville would be in full daylight with no possibility of surprise.

Although only 10 miles from land and the CH-46s had a range of over 100 miles, prolonged waiting by the leading helicopters at an airborne rendezvous would consume excessive fuel. Amos could not guarantee putting the assault company down together without some aircraft having to return to refuel. It required careful calculations of time and distance—plus luck. As it turned out, the leading company landed without its commander, Donigan, whose helicopter was refueling at the time. Like their army comrades in the south, the marines' planning had been hasty and hindered by factors outside their control.

Poring over naval charts and aerial photographs, Smith and Amos endeavored to select suitable landing zones near their objectives. Originally the idea was to come down on the runway itself, but Amos did not like it. A 275-foot hill covered with scrub was located just north of the runway, dominating it completely. Amos feared this could be occupied by AA guns or other troops, so he persuaded the MAU headquarters to switch the landing zone south. He selected what appeared to be a disused racecourse some 700 meters south of the airport. It was code-named LZ Buzzard and seemed from the photographs to be covered with low bushes. This would be the spot for E Company to land under Donigan; from there they would move to secure the airport. The landing zone site chosen for F Company under Dick, who was to follow the leading company but seize Grenville, was also an apparently disused racecourse farther south some 800 meters northeast of the town.

Amos was in command of the landing operation. He was responsible for delivering the assaulting marines to their landing zones on time. Once on the ground, Smith would take over. It was decided that the helicopters would be divided into four divisions of transports, each with three CH-46s, plus one CH-53D for the jeeps and heavy weapons, and one division of four escorting Cobra gunships. Two Cobras would be airborne at one time. This meant that only two platoons of marines could be carried as a maximum by each transport division—not a lot when information on the defenses was so scarce. What appeared to be ample time had been allowed, with the first takeoff scheduled for 3:00 A.M., giving two hours to H hour. But even this was not enough because the slow, single aircraft launching coupled with the poor weather delayed the first helicopter. It did not leave *Guam*'s flight deck until 3:15 A.M. In consequence E Company elements arrived at LZ Buzzard at 5:20 A.M., just as it was getting light.

The marines had a sleepless night. Briefings and the preparation of equipment occupied much of their time. Some snatched a few minutes' rest; others watched John Wayne in the film *Sands of Iwo Jima*, thought to be an appropriate movie for the occasion. Reveille sounded at 1:00 A.M. for everyone. A hurried meal was eaten and live ammunition drawn. Then the marines settled nervously down to await their flight into the unknown. On deck HMM-261's maintenance officer, Major Melvin DeMars, was supervising the flight deck crews and maintenance teams in preparing the Sea Knights. Among the pilots, only a sprinkling had combat experience; the crew chiefs had none. DeMars made sure that senior noncommissioned officers with Vietnam service were spread out among the aircraft to act as a steadying influence. Visibility was low, and although all the helicopters carried night vision goggles, not all the pilots had been trained in their use. Once they were airborne, all radio contact between aircraft or the ship was forbidden. It was far from an easy flight.

By the time the first helicopters crossed the coastline, the rain had stopped, and there was sufficient light for the pilots coming in low to make out some terrain features. They first noticed that the landing zone, far from resembling a racecourse, had palm trees and tall bushes growing all over it. This was highly disconcerting, although as yet they had not been fired on. Amos, who accompanied the leading flight, searched the ground for an alternative. The trees seemed sparser in the northwest corner, so he went in, followed by the others, for a successful touchdown. The only mishap occurred during attempts to unload the Sea Stallion. Two TOW jeeps became jammed together in the cargo bay, defying all efforts to free them. Marines struggled unsuccessfully for thirty minutes to disentangle them before tipping one jeep out of the rear door. The cost was one marine with a broken leg, another with a broken arm, and one wrecked TOW launcher.

It was not until the next flight of helicopters approached the landing zone, when visibility had improved, that the militia gunners on top of the hill, north of the runway that had worried Amos, opened up. The total opposition around Pearls did not amount to more than a weak platoon, mostly dressed in T-shirts and jeans, with only a handful in uniforms. One of the gunners on the hill was a woman, who in the excitement of seeing the helicopters coming in from the sea was heard to shout, "Keep feeding me," to her loader on a 12.7-mm gun. Her aim was poor, so the erratic bursts from the two 12.7-mm guns caused no damage. They did, however, attract the attention of the Cobras, which fired 20-mm cannon and 2.75-inch rockets at the site. It was the end of the militia's efforts to take on the helicopters (map 16).

Meanwhile on the ground, Donigan detailed a platoon to protect the landing zone while he advanced with the remaining two toward the airfield, preceded by the Cobras overhead. As the marines neared the terminal, several short bursts of automatic fire were directed at them. Fire was returned, and the marines saw a group of Grenadians fleeing toward the western end of the runway. Nobody was hit on either side. By 7:30 A.M. Pearls was secure, with the unexpected capture of two Cuban aircraft and their twelve crew members—the first prisoners of the intervention.

Smith by now had taken charge on the ground. He told Donigan to seize the hill from which the AA guns had fired, as it appeared to be still occupied. The marines, heavily encumbered with backpacks, weapons, and flak jackets, slowly labored up the steep slope, expecting heavy firing at any moment. There was none. As they neared the top, the PRM detachment dropped their weapons to flee down the rear slope. Some winded marines tried to follow, but they had no chance of catching the Grenadians. The two 12.7-mm guns, small arms, with a stock of ammunition were secured.

Antitank weapons were deployed, while Donigan was instructed to regroup his company preparatory to advancing west along the axis

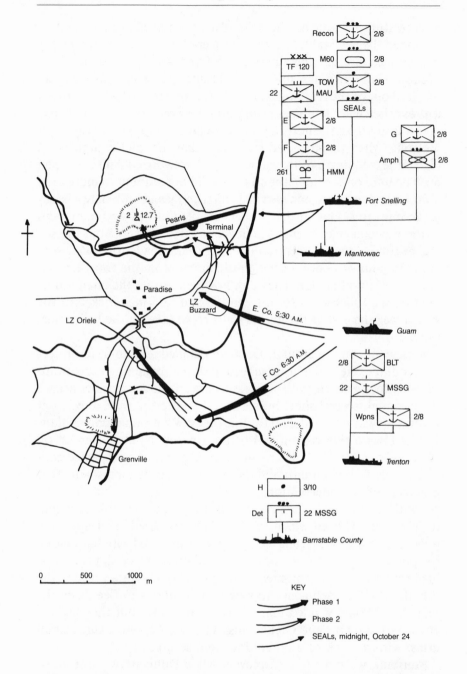

Map 16.   22d MAU'S OPERATIONS AT PEARLS, OCTOBER 25

of the road. His platoons were scattered, so it was not until midmorning that he was ready to move out. At that moment the PRM fired their mortar from a baseplate position in the hills immediately west of the runway. Their targets were the terminal area, where three rounds landed, and LZ Buzzard, which received five. A round then misfired in the tube, and rather than risk dealing with this, the militiamen abandoned the mortar. There were no casualties.

It was not until 6:30 A.M. that F Company approached their landing zone. Daylight revealed the same problem as had faced E Company: palm trees. Amos, who was still airborne, spotted a playing field free of obstructions, just east of the road running north from Grenville to the village of Paradise. Eminently suitable for helicopters, it was, however, surrounded by a high wall, so if the enemy occupied the wall, life on the field would be short for deplaning troops. But there was nothing else; Amos made the decision to use it, hoping that the feeble opposition at LZ Buzzard, and the people in Grenville who appeared to be waving in welcome, were favorable signs. They were. Nobody fired on F Company as they landed on LZ Oriele or when they advanced cautiously into the town. In fact, the citizens of Grenville had been waving in welcome, and they busied themselves identifying militia personnel, and arms caches, even lending their vehicles to carry the captured weapons. Dick spent the morning setting up roadblocks and conducting searches around the town.

After the difficult days of planning, with the constant changes, the poor intelligence, the miserable weather, which compelled a piecemeal insertion almost one helicopter at a time, the marines had deserved their share of luck. Opposition was negligible, so by midmorning they had secured both objectives at a cost of two accidental injuries. At the airport, they were to erect a sign above the terminal entrance that read Marine Corps Air Base Douglas, in honor of a former comrade, Sergeant Major Douglas, who was killed in Lebanon. It is now in the corps museum.

‡   ‡   ‡

By noon Metcalf was none too happy with progress. Resistance to the army in the south had been unexpectedly prolonged, the Cubans were still fighting, and it looked as though there could be more enemy units uncommitted. Intelligence staffs were guessing, raising opposition strengths, which at the time, judging by the results of the first six hours they were justified in doing. As Metcalf knew, the SEALs had been chased away from the Beausejour transmitting station; Delta, with C Company 1st/75th, had been badly mauled in their attempt to take the prison; the PRA could grab U.S. hostages at any time at the Grand Anse campus; and the Rangers were no nearer to taking Calivigny. In the south there were only two weak Ranger battalions with 300 Caribbean soldiers and policemen. The 82d Airborne could not start arriving until late afternoon.

As if all this was not enough, there was the crucial problem of the governor-general, trapped inside his house with a handful of SEALs. Of all the Special Forces operations, this was the most critical politically. The restoration of constitutional authority depended on securing Sir Paul Scoon. If he were killed or taken hostage, there would be a lot of explaining to do. Metcalf could ensure air-to-ground fire support from the Spectres or possibly the Cobras, but what was needed were strong reinforcements actually on the ground at Government House. The only solution was to use the marines, still fresh and unbloodied in the north. Somehow they must get into St. George's to sort out the mess at Mount Weldale, and it must be on October 25.

While thought was being given as how best to move the marines, Metcalf ordered their four Cobra gunships south to help the army. The Cobras, in pairs, took it in turn to be airborne over the island. When Metcalf's instructions reached them, Captain John "Pat" Giguere with copilot Lieutenant Jeffrey Scharver, and Captain Timothy Howard with Captain Jeb Seagle were on station. The *Guam*'s helicopter direction center told them to fly south and contact the air force Spectre for a mission. Despite trying repeatedly, neither could get any radio response from the Spectre or an army unit. They returned to refuel. The next pair—Diehl and Watson—found the frequency and assisted the Rangers against the Cubans.

When Giguere and Howard took off again around 12:45 P.M., it was the start of an hour of heroic action that ended in both helicopters' being shot down, with the loss of three out of four gallant officers. Initially they were tasked with strafing the RMC's headquarters at Fort Frederick, which had caused such havoc among TF 160's Black Hawks earlier that morning. Now, however, there were only two helicopters, Cobras, which lacked the advanced armored protection of the UH-60s. Both pilots had been briefed to avoid destroying civilian houses nearby if possible, which meant attacking on a fixed course for a risky length of time. If they fired TOW, they must hover. Likelihood of civilian casualties was the reason given later for not using naval gunfire or aircraft from the *Independence*. The former is notoriously indiscriminate, but fixed-wing aircraft were called up to attack solitary snipers in houses on several occasions. Indeed Fort Frederick and the adjacent mental hospital were hit later that afternoon by A-7s after the loss of the marines' aircraft.

Heavy firing greeted both Cobras as they circled in preparation for their run-ins. They were within range of almost every type of weapon in the St. George's area, as well as those at the fort. Again and again they attacked until, on his fifth run, Howard's aircraft was hit by AA fire, one round piercing both engines, while others shattered Howard's right arm and leg and knocked out his copilot, Seagle. Howard described it:

> We were only about 1200 feet, which was another thing in our favor. I couldn't use the pedals, so I set the stick where I thought it would level the helicopter and propped my left foot around it. As I pulled it towards me, the bird hit hard. I was sure the crash would kill us. It hit so hard the canopy removal systems must have activated because all the windows blew out. Even though the helicopter bounced very hard off the deck, it didn't flip over.

It was an incredible piece of flying that brought the Cobra down on a sports field near the harbor in St. George's known as Tanteen. The helicopter started to burn furiously, and Howard was unable to get out. Fortunately Seagle recovered consciousness and hauled him away from the wreckage. Lying on the grass a few meters from the Cobra, both men came under inaccurate small arms fire from the direction of the hills around the town. Howard gave Seagle his pistol, telling him to find assistance.

Within minutes PRA soldiers were approaching the edge of the field. At that moment the Cobra finally exploded in a ball of flame, causing the rockets still onboard to "cook off." The resultant lethal fireworks display discouraged any closer move. Miraculously Howard had retained his radio. His plea for help was received by Giguere, who roared over the field firing 2.75-inch rockets at PRA soldiers, who had again started to advance. This attack drove them off. Meanwhile,

Giguere had summoned a CH-46 to attempt a medical evacuation. It was piloted by Major DeMars with Lieutenant Lawrence King, Gunnery Sergeant Kelley Neidigh as door gunner, and Corporal Simon Gore as crew chief. This rescue was highly hazardous. Giguere had to lead the CH-46 in over the town with both aircraft exposed to the AA guns at Fort Rupert and the 12.7-mm at D'Arbeau. Giguere had to try to provide cover while DeMars touched down, picked up Howard, and got away again. He had to do this on his own. DeMars appreciated the risks:

> He was going to provide cover for me as I went in, as I set down, and provide escort back out. . . . That was a very difficult thing for him to do, to have to cover an aircraft going into a landing zone with only one aircraft because, as he would come in to make his runs on target and turn back off, he would have no one to cover him. So he was going to expose himself to some pretty serious triple-A fire in order to cover me into the zone.

Both helicopters came in, with Giguere rocketing the AA sites while DeMars landed near Howard. More small arms fire hit the CH-46, slightly damaging the stabilizing equipment. Neidigh must have thought he was back in Vietnam as he grabbed his M-16 rifle, leaped down, and sprinted across to Howard under fire. He half-dragged, half-carried Howard to the aircraft, where he was assisted by Gore to haul him onboard. But where was Seagle? DeMars hesitated to leave without him, but he was nowhere to be seen. They waited a few moments, not knowing he had been shot and killed, until DeMars realized any further delay might cost the grievously wounded Howard his life. The CH-46 successfully ran the gauntlet of the St. George's AA guns, thanks to Giguere's fearlessly continuing to distract their aim. Howard's life, but not his right forearm, was saved in the hospital aboard the *Guam*.

Giguere's and Scharver's luck ran out at 1:40 P.M. as they flew away from the town over the harbor. Their Cobra was struck by AA fire. One moment it was flying normally. The next it plunged like a stone into the water—a tragic loss of two outstandingly courageous officers.

This crowded hour of intense combat was the only such occasion for the marines during Urgent Fury. It was to earn no fewer than five Silver Stars for the main participants. Giguere and Scharver received theirs posthumously, while DeMars, Howard, and Neidigh lived to wear their bronze star medal, with its tiny silver star set in the center.[1]

The marines had lost half of their Cobras. The same lesson that TF 160 had learned earlier had been drummed home again in the afternoon: unsupported helicopters over St. George's invited disaster. Later the same afternoon, A-7 Corsairs from the *Independence* attacked Fort Frederick, strafing the area repeatedly with rockets, cannon, and bombs. The RMC leadership cowered in their tunnel, immune to all efforts to destroy them. Not so the mental hospital patients next door. The hospital adjoined the fort, sharing the same entrance, and was flying a Grenadian flag. No maps marked it for what it was—indeed it was shown on most as Fort Matthew—so it was hardly surprising that it suffered severely from these air attacks. It was badly damaged, with some seventeen patients killed and many more injured. Uninjured patients wandered the streets for several days. It took a week before the rubble of the "Crazy House," as Grenadians called it, was finally removed from all the bodies.

‡ ‡ ‡

How best to move the marines quickly, and where to put them? Those were the urgent questions confronting Metcalf. The obvious answer as to method was by helicopter. There were enough CH-46s to lift two companies, and two companies were ashore near suitable landing zones. But it was not as simple as that. Pearls Airport could not be abandoned. Neither could G Company come ashore to relieve E Company because an amphibious landing on that part of the coast was still too risky. One LVTP-7, with a handpicked crew, had already tried and, although successful, confirmed the dangers. In fact it was intended that G Company be helilifted off the *Manitowac* into Pearls. Grenville, however, was friendly. F Company could be sent immediately, while G Company was dispatched by sea to land over a suitable beach on the sheltered west coast.

But where to land? The helicopters could put down on any reasonably flat ground in St. George's; marines could rappel down ropes from hovering aircraft if necessary. But could crews and troops be exposed again to the sort of reception meted out to the Special Operations Forces and the Cobras? The answer was definitely no; any landing must be well away from known enemy AA positions. The planners on the *Guam* picked Grand Mal Bay, 1,500 meters north of the town center, so it could be reached quickly on foot if necessary. It was ideal for amphibians, but a landing zone for the lumbering, ungainly Sea Knights would be problematic.

Without the knowledge of its commanding officer, who was at Pearls and not in radio contact with the *Guam*, 2d/8th BLT was scattered on a new mission. The *Manitowac* was ordered to take G Company with the thirteen remaining amphibians around the north of the island; the *Guam*, together with the *Fort Snelling* carrying the tanks and TOWs, and the *Barnstable County* with the howitzer battery, went south, also making for the west coast. The *Trenton* was to remain off the northeast of the island. Ashore E Company would remain guarding Pearls, while F Company was earmarked for a heliborne insertion at Grand Mal. H hour was to be 4:30 P.M. for both the sea and air landings; the aim was to press on into St. George's to relieve the SEALs at Government House that evening. Metcalf was concerned that the coming darkness would enable the PRA to intensify their attacks or possibly infiltrate into the building to overwhelm the defenders. The operation envisaged the tanks and howitzers going ashore after the rifle companies so that, apart from E Company, all of TF 124 would be operating in the south, in or around St. George's. Reports, later proved to be erroneous, had been received that the SEALs had suffered heavy casualties and were low on ammunition. It was a major change of plan necessitated by the failure to secure the town early on, and it would later require an alteration of boundaries, with the marines-TF121 boundary to run from Ross Point in the west to Requin Bay in the east.

For Lieutenant Colonel Smith, the changes put in motion around 1:00 P.M. heralded the start of what must surely have been his most frustrating time in the marines (map 17). His command had been sent into battle without him, and it was to be nine hours before he finally caught up with his leading companies at Grand Mal. G Company, followed later by F Company, were on their own, without contact with battalion headquarters during the potentially critical period following their insertion close to St. George's. Luck was to smile on them again. By that time the PRA reserve under Nelson had been frittered away, and there were no Cuban battalions deploying north of the town, as intelligence rumors on the *Guam* had indicated. The

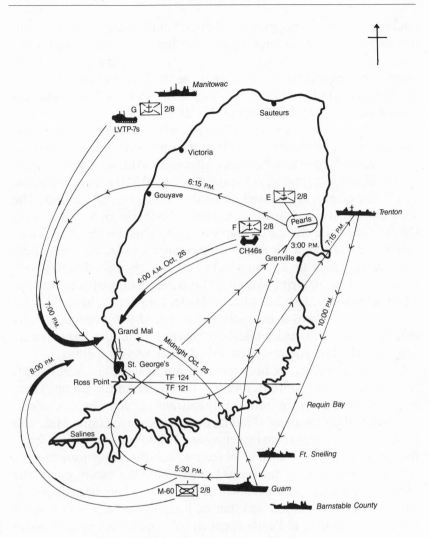

Map 17.   CHANGE OF PLAN AT 1:00 P.M., OCTOBER 25,
22d MAU'S MOVEMENTS

landings were to be unopposed, although Smith and his company commanders had no way of knowing that. To them, they were being thrown piecemeal into a battle without proper orders, communications, or an on-scene headquarters to relate to, as the BLT's Bravo command group was committed to Pearls, while Smith flew backward and forward desperately trying to rejoin his unit.

For Smith it all started about 3:00 P.M. while he was still controlling operations at Pearls and Grenville and anticipating the remainder of his command's coming ashore that afternoon. Although he had heard the possibility of a landing at Gouyave or Grand Mal mentioned before he left the *Guam*, he received no further signals on the subject. The reason was that the radio link was giving trouble, even over the water. On the *Guam* the change of plan was going ahead without Smith or his executive officer, while a frantic reconnaissance platoon commander was standing high up on the weather deck of the *Fort Snelling* with a hand-held radio, trying to contact his commanding officer. Around 3:00 P.M. he succeeded. The platoon leader told Smith that an assault on the west coast was to be made; in fact the *Manitowac* had already left, steaming northward, while the others (except for the *Trenton*) were going south. The young officer asked what was happening.

Smith's comments are not recorded, but, leaving his executive officer in charge, he boarded a resupply helicopter for the *Guam*. There he had a quick briefing from the operations officer. The new operation involved G Company's landing over the beach at Grand Mal, with F Company's joining them by helicopter. H hour was only some forty-five minutes away; the final objective was the governor-general's residence; and nothing much was known about the enemy, except the rumors of a Cuban battalion north of the town had not been dispelled. Smith's only consolation was that he had grabbed a proper map of the island, captured at Pearls Airport, so he had some idea of where he was going—not that this was much use while he was separated from his companies.

Smith's first reaction was to rush to the flag plot compartment (operations room) to explain forcefully that 4:30 landings were an impossibility. If H hour was not postponed, G Company would land on its own without any possibility of coordinating F Company in time. It was agreed to delay H hour to 6:30 P.M. This message reached the *Manitowac* after it had lowered its ramps, launched its safety boats, and G Company was ready in its amphibious assault vehicles.

Smith now needed to return to Pearls, rejoin his command group, tell his executive officer what was happening, get F Company organized for its heliborne assault, and then fly to the *Manitowac* before H hour. It was then nearly five o'clock; there was sufficient time. His temper was not improved when it took him thirty minutes to find a helicopter to take him to Pearls—or so he thought. The problem was that the helicopter direction center had instructed the pilot to fly to Salines, not Pearls. By the time Smith, now thoroughly enraged, discovered this error, more precious time had been wasted. He finally touched down at Pearls just twenty minutes before the scheduled Grand Mal H hour. It would take at least that time to reach the *Manitowac*—if they could find it in the dark.

Dashing around, Smith collected his command group, rushed back to the same helicopter, ordering the pilot to find the *Manitowac* or, if that was impossible, the *Guam*. They took off in darkness. Then the unfortunate pilot was unable to make radio contact with anybody except the *Trenton*, which had remained to the northeast of the island. Around and around they flew, frantically peering into the black night, using up fuel and finding nothing. After an hour, with fuel low, there was nothing for it but to land on the *Trenton*. More delay followed while Smith tried to get a flight to the *Guam*. By this time he was, as he described it, "so frustrated I could barely see." It was then about 11:00 P.M. He was back on the *Guam* where he had started six hours earlier; it was eight hours since he had first received confirmation of the Grand Mal operation, and it was to be another hour before he finally got there.

‡ ‡ ‡

Luckily for G Company, there was no Cuban battalion awaiting north of St. George's. Nelson had reported to Fort Frederick personally at around 6:00 P.M. for fresh instructions. Layne told him to regroup and establish a blocking position on the high ground near the village of Fontenoy just south of, and overlooking, Grand Mal. The selection of this area showed uncanny tactical sense. But these were orders Nelson could not carry out because all that remained of his battle group was the antitank platoon. So instead of moving north, Nelson contented himself with positioning one of his guns at Green Bridge at the mouth of the St. John's River at the southwest corner of Queen's Park and the other at the small bridge 350 meters to the east. Thus the ideal blocking position on the northern slopes of D'Arbeau Hill remained unoccupied.

Nelson too had had his frustrations. On Sunday, when he had moved into his concentration area in the hills east of St. George's, he was given his mission to defend the town by the operations officer, Gahagan. This was soon changed. Now Redhead would assume responsibility for St. George's while his units became the RMC's central reserve. By Monday, however, Nelson was again ordered into the town. His units knew their locations and radio communications within his command were good, so the move started well. However, it was daylight and No. 1 platoon came under fire on the road from helicopters engaged in the Richmond Hill Prison attack. No casualties were inflicted so the units arrived in St. George's and deployed to defend against an attack from the harbor. Nelson, who had lost one APC to mechanical failure in the concentration area, now rode in a jeep and established his headquarters at the school near the cathedral on the southwestern slope of Hospital Hill. He had a superb view over the town in all directions.

Next Gahagan arrived with new orders. The marines' landings at Pearls were worrying the high command. By then it was realized that an all-out attack on the town was unlikely, so Nelson was to take his force to block any advance from the northeast in the area of Mt. Gay and where the road is dominated by hills around Beaulieu. While trying to organize this, Prime arrived telling him to detach troops and an APC to assist with the counterattack at Government House. At the same time, around 9:00 A.M., Prime instructed him to release another APC, some infantry, and his mortars for Prime's counterattack on the Americans at Beausejour. Thus by midmorning, Nelson had had almost half his command taken from him. Meanwhile, the three remaining APCs busied themselves firing up at opportunity targets in the sky above the town. The afternoon saw the removal of the last APC platoon for the counterattack at Salines. By the time Dobson and his company started landing at Grand Mal, there was nobody available to oppose them.

This was probably just as well from the marines' point of view, as G Company and the five tanks that started coming ashore just after 7:00 P.M. had to wait another nine hours before F Company began arriving by helicopter. This lengthy delay was due to a combination of adverse factors. First, proper command and control by Smith had been impossible due to his being unable to rejoin his command, together with the persistently bad radio communications between units. Then there was the necessity of having to ferry F Company from Pearls across the island with helicopters from the *Guam*, which was now off the west coast, making the journey longer, with more frequent refueling required. It was also a pitch-black night, with the landing zone at Grand Mal actually on the narrow beach so that only two helicopters could land at a time. It had been decidedly quicker and simpler by sea.

Not that G Company had been spared its share of frustration. The day had started for Dobson with his company's sitting in the amphibian assault craft at 3:45 A.M. ready to land at 4:30. Hourly postponements came for landings at 5:30, 6:30, 7:30, followed by cancellation.

Shortly after midday, Dobson was told the amphibians would go in empty while his marines were helilifted ashore. At 1:30 P.M., with the company waiting on the flight deck, Dobson was called to the bridge to be informed that he was now to land on the northwest coast, possibly in the Victoria area. There was no mention of Grand Mal. With the *Manitowac* now sailing around the north of the island, Dobson's men hurriedly reembarked in the amphibians. They passed Victoria, with no orders to land. The next signal the ship received indicated Gouyave was the likely objective. Another false alarm. By now it was getting dark, and his men had had more than enough of sitting cramped inside the amphibians for one day. At 5:50, Dobson summoned his platoon commanders, explaining that because he had received no orders from battalion headquarters it now seemed unlikely that a landing would be made that day, so they should leave all their equipment on the vehicles while the marines got some sleep.

Inevitably, no sooner had he given these intructions than he was summoned back to the bridge, this time to land at Grand Mal at 6:30 P.M. The landing zone was code-named Fuel (the narrow, restricted strip of land between the shore and the hills had a small fuel tank farm at the northern end). Still not knowing what he was expected to do, still out of touch with his commanding officer, Dobson got his men back aboard the amphibians, and G Company was launched on time. The thirteen tracked LVTP-7s made for the beach in single file in pitch blackness. The first one crawled ashore at 7:01 P.M.

Later the utility landing craft began bringing in the tanks, jeeps with .50-caliber machine guns, and TOWs. It was getting decidedly crowded at LZ Fuel.

Dobson secured his position by posting a platoon to the north and south of the landing zone across the road, dispatched a reconnaissance patrol to the south, while consolidating his position and awaiting further orders. It was not until 11:00 P.M. that a helicopter was heard overhead. There was no sign of the enemy so red lights were put out to indicate a landing zone and a UH-1 carrying the MAU air liaison officer, Major William Sublette arrived. Sublette told Dobson that there was apparently a strong enemy force between them and St. George's, but he could expect F Company to reinforce them by helicopter after midnight. Dobson asked Sublette to make contact with Smith on his return for further instructions.

Sublette's return virtually coincided with Smith's arrival on the *Guam* so he immediately offered to guide Smith back to LZ Fuel. The Huey, followed by Smith in a CH-46, touched down around midnight. The Sea Knight was too large for the landing zone, so its rear wheels were in the water when Smith with his Alpha group disembarked. After the long hours of exasperating delay, Smith's humor had returned. As he waded ashore, he reflected that it was a novel experience: "A heliborne ship-to-shore movement where you still had to wade through the surf."[2]

‡ ‡ ‡

Neither Vessey, McDonald, nor Metcalf was happy at midnight on October 25 (map 18). Although they did not appreciate it, they had had a lucky day. A lot had gone very wrong, but they had secured Salines and Pearls, they had suffered negligible casualties, and now the marines were poised to rescue the governor-general early the next day.

If those were the credits, the debit list was depressingly long. Nothing had gone according to plan. The operation was far from over as had been hoped; there were reports of many more Cubans deployed in the St. George's area; and resistance had been tougher than expected. The major setback had been the costly failure of all but one of the Special Operations Forces' missions. At the end of the day, Sir Paul Scoon was still lying on his dining room floor amid shattered glass and flying bullets, where he had remained for the best part

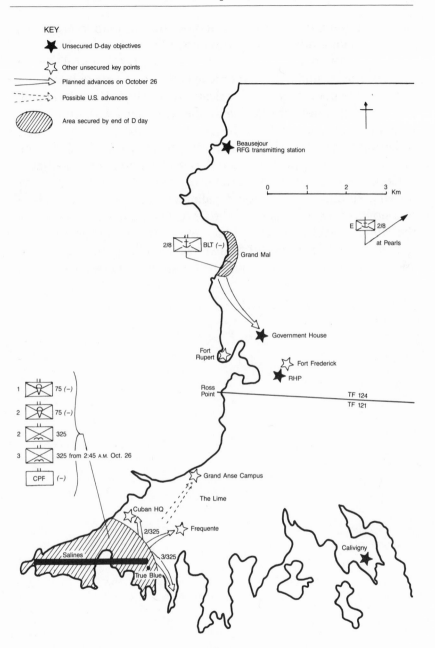

KEY

★ Unsecured D-day objectives

☆ Other unsecured key points

→ Planned advances on October 26

⇢ Possible U.S. advances

⬭ Area secured by end of D day

Beausejour
RFG transmitting station

0   1   2   3 Km

E ⊠ 2/8
at Pearls

2/8 ⊠ BLT (−)
Grand Mal

Government House

Fort
Rupert   ☆

☆ Fort Frederick

★ RHP

Ross
Point

TF 124
TF 121

1 ⊠ 75 (−)

2 ⊠ 75 (−)

2 ⊠ 325

3 ⊠ 325 from 2:45 A.M. Oct. 26

CPF (−)

☆ Grand Anse Campus

The Lime

Cuban HQ

2/325

☆ Frequente

Salines

3/325

True Blue

Calivigny ★

Map 18.   SITUATION AT MIDNIGHT, OCTOBER 25, AND
PLANNED ADVANCES FOR OCTOBER 26

of sixteen hours so far. Even the noon change of plan to rescue him by that evening had proved an impossibility.

The U.S. forces had been plagued from the start by unrealistic timings, piecemeal landings, overburdened infantry, command snarl-ups, unbelievably poor radio communications, and lack of tactical intelligence—all aggravated by having to operate on land with naval charts or tourist maps. A regrettable belief, of which the planners had been rudely disabused, was that unsupported helicopters could fly around St. George's or charge blindly into the attack without inviting disaster.

Good fortune had saved the Rangers from paying the price for taking an hour and a half to drop at Salines. Good fortune had dictated that no hostages be taken, that the RMC had no intention of seizing the students still at Grand Anse, and that among the countless weapons supplied to the PRA, there were no hand-held surface-to-air missiles. At the end of D day, the situation could easily have been much worse.

13

October 26

St. George's and the South

We packed those helicopters with about sixty students each.
— Captain Mark Hanna, commander,
C Company 2d/75th Rangers

S IR Paul Scoon, Lady Scoon, and nine staff members had spent an anxious night, without sleep or food, on the dining room floor of Government House. It was obvious to Sir Paul and his companions that things had not gone according to plan. The young officer in charge of the SEAL Team 6 detachment had anticipated being relieved during D day, so the prospect of a night trapped inside the building was worrisome. There was the strong possibility of a night attack, and although there were no casualties so far, ammunition expenditure had been high. The officer had informed Sir Paul that bringing in a helicopter to lift him out was too dangerous; the only alternative was to wait for the morning. Morning brought the marines of Captain Dobson's G Company.

In the early hours of October 26, before the arrival of F Company, Smith had started his move on St. George's. He was a mere 2 kilometers north of the town, but there was only one road south; it hugged the shoreline and was completely dominated by steep slopes to the east. In some places there was only the width of the road itself between the sea and the hillside. D'Arbeau Hill in particular was a perfect spot from which to block an approach from the north. One or more simple obstructions on the road at its narrowest points, covered by fire from the high ground, could cause confusion and delay. Smith, who still thought there might be a strong Cuban force between himself and his objective, had no option but to advance in single file along the road. With the reconnaissance platoon on foot in front, followed by two platoons in amphibians, backed up by the five M-60 tanks, Dobson's G Company snaked its way slowly through the darkness toward St. George's. Back at the landing zone, a rearguard platoon awaited the arrival of F Company.

Nelson's men at Queen's Park and Green Bridge heard them coming. The unmistakable screaming and rattling of tank tracks and gears was too much for them. They faded away after firing a few shots, allowing G Company to occupy Queen's Park without difficulty. The park was to become the marines' base for the next few days. Here Smith established his command post.

Smith had originally instructed Dobson to try to secure the high hill immediately south of Gretna Green, called Hospital Hill or Old Fort Hill, which completely dominates the town.[1] But because opposition was so slight, G Company was told to push on up to Government House. Dobson dismounted his men and advanced cautiously up the steep incline toward Mount Weldale, on top of which were Bishop's, Coard's, and the governor-general's houses. Of the PRA who had kept the SEALs bottled up for over twenty-four hours, there was little sign; a squad was detailed to occupy Bishop's house, and the remainder moved through the trees and bushes to the grounds of Government House itself. By 7:30 A.M. they had linked up with the SEALs and were astonished to discover that there were no casualties at all.

After a while it was decided that it was still too risky to try to bring in a helicopter to lift out Sir Paul and his wife from the tennis courts so he and his entourage had to make their way on foot, under close escort, to Queen's Park. Around midday he was taken by helicopter out to the *Guam,* but later that afternoon he was returned to Point Salines, where he was accommodated in a nearby house. At around 4:00 P.M. Brigadier General Lewis showed Sir Paul the backdated letter requesting military intervention. Sir Paul signed. He was scheduled to broadcast that evening to Grenada on a temporary transmitter that the U.S. forces had set up, so he went through the draft speech with his wife. Lewis spoke that night on a satellite radio-telephone to Buckingham Palace to inform the palace that the governor-general was safe.

Meanwhile Smith, with F Company, had arrived at Queen's Park. He gave G Company its next mission: Fort Frederick.

Since the heavy air attacks the previous afternoon, the RMC command post had lost touch with what was happening. Layne and Gahagan made some attempts to issue orders, but without proper radio communications, this was virtually impossible. Commanders like Nelson had to report personally for instructions, or messengers had to find them. The PRA's will to resist had dwindled fast on the first day, with many soldiers concealing their weapons, throwing away their uniforms, and going into hiding. The marine night landings at Grand Mal had been a shock, especially the arrival of tanks. By late October 25 or very early the next day, Austin and his senior staff agreed that the situation was hopeless. Word was to be passed around to cease resisting, don civilian clothes, and avoid arrest. These instructions were received by some, others abandoned their positions anyway, while a few pockets continued the fight. For men like Austin, Layne, James, Stroude, Cornwall, and Strachan, there was no possibility of escaping detection unless they could flee overseas. While it was still dark, early on October 26, Austin and the other RMC leaders split up into groups and slipped out of their dark tunnel in civilian clothes, leaving Fort Frederick to its fate.

Dobson approached the fort carefully from the northwest, through dense scrub and trees that covered the sides of the ridge. Grenadians whom he had questioned indicated a company of the PRA could still be in occupation. He detached several men with machine guns to cover his final approach from some high ground about 300 meters north of the fort. As the marines neared the walls, they observed parties of men climbing down the far side, apparently abandoning the position. G Company was able to walk in unopposed. In the tunnel they discovered the RMC's deserted command post complete with classified documents, together with maps of the island's defenses. Strewn around were little heaps of crumpled uniforms, whose owners had fled. A large haul of weapons and ammunition was captured, including three new 82-mm mortars.

‡　‡　‡

Despite the ban on all reporters' getting into Grenada, which was rigorously applied until October 27, a group of seven journalists, including four Americans, had slipped in on D day. They chartered a light aircraft in Barbados on October 24 (Monday) to fly to Union Island, a beautiful yachtsman's haven belonging to St. Vincent, only 25 miles north of Grenada. From there they sailed to Carriacou, where they hired another small boat for the trip to St. George's. Early on Tuesday morning, with the battle raging in the sky, they audaciously sailed into the harbor at about the same time as the Cuban vessel the *Vietnam Heroica* was moving out.

Once ashore they were quickly detained by PRA patrols. It was, however, a fairly friendly detention, and with the continuous strafing attacks by gunships and A-7s, which inevitably provoked heavy AA fire, the journalists were content to remain under cover until after dark. By then the knowledge that the telex office and telephone exchange were only 200 meters away was too much for them. They were in a unique position—the only journalists witnessing the intervention from the center of St. George's but unable to tell anybody. Corporal Alister George was the PRA noncommissioned officer who had been given, or assumed, responsibility for them. Eventually, after several appeals that it was vital that the rest of the world know what was happening, George agreed to try to find the keys to the telex office. After several unsuccessful attempts, he allowed two of the group down to the offices to try to get in without the keys. After kicking down a wall, they reached the telex machines, only to find them out of order; so was the telephone exchange next door.

Corporal George was a confident young man—confident in the ability of the PRA to defeat the Yankees and confident that the RMC would fight to the last. He explained, "[Austin] is very much in command. All the Revolutionary Council are in battle." He insisted (correctly) that although Salines Airport had fallen, the U.S. forces had not advanced beyond a crossroads a mile from the runway.

Later that first evening, George agreed the journalists could go to the St. James Hotel, just a few meters below Fort Rupert. George aroused the owner with the announcement that "guests of the revolution in need of a room" had arrived. When the journalists thanked him for his help, George responded, "That is what the revolution is about, assisting people."

After a noisy night, with gunfire from the air and the ground crashing out almost continuously, the journalists wended their way north through the streets of the town. They observed that looters had been around in the darkness; two bank entrances were smashed and a number of stores ransacked. As they approached Queen's Park, they met the marines. Ever anxious to improve their knowledge of the situation, a marine platoon commander asked the age-old army question, "Can you please tell us what the fuck is going on?" Then a little hesitantly, perhaps wondering if something had happened during the night that nobody had told him about: "Is the Grenadian army on our side or theirs?"

The journalists met up with Smith at his command post to ask for assistance with communications to get their stories out. While they were waiting for a helicopter ride to the *Guam,* another marine officer approached his commanding officer with a black marine. The officer explained that this man was originally from Trinidad so might be of help "with the native language." Smith's response was not recorded.

After a couple of hours, three of the party flew to the *Guam,* only to be told that the ship's communications were far too busy with military traffic. What they were not told was that Metcalf had expressly forbidden facilities to the media.

‡   ‡   ‡

The 82d Airborne, which eventually had six infantry battalions in Grenada, suffered two deaths by enemy action. Both men were from the same battalion, Hamilton's 2d/325th, and both were from B Company. One was the company commander, Captain Michael Ritz, shot at night during a reconnaissance in front of the Cuban positions. The other was a squad leader, Staff Sergeant Gary Epps, who was killed on the morning of October 26 when a recoilless rifle he was attempting to unload exploded. Ten months later, Major General Trobaugh, accompanied by Colonel Silvasy, the brigade commander, was the reviewing officer at a dedication ceremony at Fort Bragg when the plaque naming the Ritz-Epps Sports Complex was unveiled. As it turned out, B Company's attack to secure the Cuban headquarters at Little Havana early that day was the only combat action the division was required to undertake.

At dawn that morning, Trobaugh's intention was to use the 2d/325th and 3d/325th to expand the tiny foothold that had been seized by the Rangers in the southwest corner of the island. The two Ranger battalions would be a quick reaction reserve force, with the three

105-mm guns that had arrived being available for support from Salines. The artillery gun position was initially south of the runway, but with all the potential targets north of the strip, this was highly dangerous to the scores of aircraft using it. This error was rectified; the guns were deployed north of the runway in the open ground immediately east of the terminal buildings.

Disappointingly, no further reinforcements had arrived as hoped. As early as 2:30 A.M. on October 26, Secretary of Defense Weinberger had approved two more battalions, followed later by another two, but none reached Grenada that day, although Colonel Steven Scott's 3d Brigade with 1st/505th, and 1st/508th took off from Pope at 10:07 A.M. Apart from brigade headquarters and a small element of Crocker's 1st/505th, none reached Grenada until October 27.

The delay was caused by the intense air traffic control problems over Salines. Radio communications were poor; many C-141 Starlifter crews were not trained to land on unlit runways; and strenuous efforts to improvise lights had been unsuccessful. Brigadier General Patterson, with a staff of five, had set up headquarters in Barbados, but the sheer number of flights compounded the other difficulties, preventing his being able to control the flow. The result was that aircraft were often "stacked up to the ionosphere," as one commander described it, circling over the island, waiting for the runway to clear. There were no unloading ramps, so getting planes turned around was a slow, laborious, process, often taking up to an hour for a single plane. Such was the fate of Scott's battalions on October 26.

Patterson's task was impossible. At the other end, in the United States, the Military Airlift Command was sending aircraft south as fast as possible. It was not uncommon for a five-hour flight to Grenada to end with six hours circling the island, until near-empty fuel tanks compelled a landing in Barbados or Puerto Rico. Waiting for a Salines touchdown was long and frustrating. It would also have been highly vulnerable had the opposition possessed sophisticated AA defenses.

Control of the air flow was supposed to be through Military Airlift Command channels, but many units tried to circumvent the system and arrange flights direct. In the United States walk-on government officials would appear demanding passage, and then, after arrival in Grenada, expected unscheduled assistance with food, transport, and accommodation.

All of these problems were unknown to Ritz as he contemplated his mission, due to start at daylight. His company had been detailed by Hamilton to assault the Cuban compound from its present location on the fuel tank hill to the west, while A Company gave fire support from the Calliste hills in the east. C Company would be in reserve. After taking Little Havana, B Company was to push up onto the Morne Rouge high ground and, possibly, on order, reach the Grand Anse campus.

Ritz decided to take out a platoon leaders' reconnaissance patrol at 4:30 A.M., while it was still dark, to explore the approach to the enemy position along the ridgeline that overlooked it from the west. This ridge was only 250 meters from the Cubans in the valley, and there was every likelihood that more were occupying the ridge itself. The patrol consisted of the company commander, 2d Lieutenant Stephen Seager, and Sergeant Terry Guinn. They moved cautiously forward through the long grass and dense scrub that covered the ridge. In the blackness, it was difficult not to make noise as their boots crunched on twigs or scraped bushes. They were a considerable distance from their own lines, descending a saddle northwest of the compound, when they bumped the Cubans. Bursts of close-range machine-gun and rifle fire hit them. Ritz was killed at once, Guinn collapsed badly wounded, and Seager flung himself down unscathed and starting crawling and firing to distract attention from his fallen comrades. By 5:30, however, Seager's platoon had advanced sufficiently to drive the Cubans down into the compound so that Guinn could be rescued.

It was a depressing start for B Company to have lost their commander and a platoon leader so early. The situation looked difficult for a while after the advance began as the company came under intense small arms fire from enemy positions that were hard to pinpoint in the grass and bushes. A number of men in the leading platoons were wounded, so no attempt was made to assault the Cuban compound until it had received a severe pounding by A Company's machine guns and mortars, plus the guns at Salines, together with gunfire from ships at sea. Numerous strafing runs by A-7 Corsairs were called in to hit the unmistakable cluster of buildings in the valley, still flying a large Cuban flag, which served as a convenient identification marker for the pilots.

This bombardment soon produced results. Inside the buildings, casualties mounted as Tortolo and Matamoros struggled to continue the defense. They were crouched behind a low wall that surrounded the parking lot of the military mission, along with Diaz, the senior Cuban civilian official. Made of flimsy concrete blocks, the wall offered no protection from bullets or bombs. Their position was becoming untenable. Matamoros later described it:

> When the sun came up, they concentrated their fire, throwing mortars, planes, cannon, and machine guns against us. I was wounded by the fourth mortar shell. Tortolo wanted to see what the matter was with me. I shouted that I'd been hit in the waist but was OK. He asked if I could crawl over to where he was, and I said no, but that we couldn't hold that position, and that we should leave it [the compound] and go to the hill behind the offices to be protected from a direct hit.

Not long afterward, a bursting grenade or mortar bomb killed Diaz and another man nearby. Matamoros again urged Tortolo to leave the area of the buildings for the comparative safety of the hillside behind, and under cover of billowing smoke, the Cuban commander did so, joined shortly afterward by another group of survivors.

Inside the buildings, the situation was critical. Later, the 26-year-old translator, Lieutenant Garcia, who was assisting with communications, told how at the height of the battle they received a message from Castro urging them to continue the fight and not to surrender. She was soon tending wounded, resorting to tearing down curtains to use as bandages.

By now, most of the defenders favored surrender; to continue invited pointless slaughter. Tortolo, however, decided to make a break for it with a small group, including Garcia. Although he had been hit in the right leg, he managed to make his way painfully up the steep slopes of the Morne Rouge hillside. Garcia recalled, "We walked along the crest of the hills, avoiding all paths so as not to be seen, and stopping every so often to rest. We went on that way until we got to a place where we could see the northern and southern coasts of Point Salines and the valley where the airport was." They were then a stone's throw from sanctuary, the Soviet embassy.

Meanwhile at the compound, Cubans were signaling they wished to surrender before emerging from the battered buildings. A number started up the hill in the direction taken by Tortolo's party; Hamilton ordered nearby machine guns to fire in front of rather than at them. Three escaped, while the others in the compound ducked back into the buildings at the sound of the shooting. It was all over. A platoon advanced down the slope to accept the surrender of eighty-six Cubans.

Sixteen dead were discovered in the ruins or nearby. Although the Americans could not know it, it was the end of Cuban resistance to the invasion.

During the afternoon, the 2d/325th inched forward on foot. B Company hauled themselves and their heavy packs to the top of Morne Rouge, while C Company moved eastward as far as the now-deserted supply base at Frequente. Here they found a huge cache of weapons and ammunition in the warehouses, which the PRA logistics chief, Fraser, had been unable to move.

Back at Salines, the 82d was in the process of taking over the area, including the prisoners from the Caribbean Peacekeeping Force. At around midday witnesses were amused to watch an 82d Airborne colonel administering a tremendous dressing down to a humble master sergeant wearing his paratrooper's red beret. The sergeant had arrived, feeling very pleased with himself, in a jeep with three prisoners in civilian clothes tied up in the back. He thought he had done well when he pulled his captives out of their expensive Mercedes car and bundled them protesting vehemently, into the jeep. The colonel disagreed. The prisoners were Russians—the number two in charge at their embassy, an intelligence officer with a mouth full of steel teeth, and their driver. Diplomatic immunity secured their immediate release, while the colonel berated the unfortunate sergeant for his initiative and for wearing his beret, not his steel helmet. Those watching were uncertain which "crime" the colonel considered the more serious.

‡　‡　‡

The safety of U.S. students had been the principal pretext for the intervention. As such, it was repeatedly emphasized to the public that the situation in Grenada endangered their lives; therefore U.S. forces were fully justified in going in to secure them. Seen from the U.S. viewpoint at the time, it was a compelling argument, which convinced many Americans. In fact U.S. citizens were in no danger until the operation was launched. The assault on the island could easily have precipitated the taking of hostages by desperate men driven to desperate means to save their own lives. But rescuing students was really a smokescreen to conceal the real motive: the seizing of an unprecedented opportunity to rid the Caribbean of an expanding communist threat and at the same time permit the military to regain credibility in a situation in which they could not lose.

If Urgent Fury had had as its main objective the securing of U.S. students, then the event revealed serious errors of judgment, if not outright bungling, on the part of the planners. The rescuing of hostages, even potential hostages, requires, above all else, long and detailed planning based on accurate information. The operation will fail if surprise is not complete. In Grenada both of these ingredients were totally lacking. Up to the last moment, U.S. planners, and the troops carrying out the operation, had no knowledge of the existence, let alone the whereabouts, of over half the students. The information about the campus at Grand Anse reached the planners too late, and they made no attempt to inform the units on the ground. Not surprisingly the unit commanders could make no proper tactical plans. The Rangers at Salines had no specific plan to capture True Blue; in fact, it was of seemingly no greater importance than airfield clearance, the main task of the company dropping first. The successful securing of the True Blue students was almost entirely fortuitous; the RMC had no intention of harming them anyway.

With the Grand Anse campus operation, it was a similar story: from the time the commanders on the island knew of its existence early on October 25, U.S. troops took thirty-three hours to get there. The campus was only 2½ kilometers away from Salines. Had the U.S. planners truly believed the students' lives were at risk, such a delay was incomprehensible. Even when the rescue mission was launched late on the afternoon of October 26, it took the form of a daylight helicopter charge following a massive bombardment of likely enemy positions around the campus. It succeeded superbly. All of the students were evacuated without any injuries. In fact, the PRA had no intention of harming them, and luckily nobody had been hit by any of the numerous American bullets that penetrated the buildings from the direction of the beach.

This time there was much more information available on the exact location of the students, the buildings, and PRA positions. Not only were telephone and radio links established with the campus, but the planners were able to discuss the situation with students and staff at True Blue. The military made extensive use of a ham radio operator, Mark Barettella, inside Grand Anse. The Pentagon planners authorized the civilian Federal Communications Commission to assemble a group of six ham radio operators in the United States to monitor Barettella's messages on a specially authorized frequency. This group acted as a relay station for State Department and army queries on what was happening in the campus. One of these operators was Dr. Fred Jacobs, whose daughter, Stefanie, was trapped in the same dormitory as Barettella. The main problem that developed was the number of unauthorized hams who used the same frequency to try to contact Barettella for information for journalists, who had been barred from the island.

Lieutenant Colonel Hagler, who knew about the existence of the Grand Anse campus by 10:30 A.M. on October 25, had discussed the problem with Trobaugh shortly after his arrival that same afternoon. The telephone system was still working, albeit erratically, throughout Tuesday, and contact was established by this means between True Blue and Grand Anse. Radio communications between Trobaugh and the *Guam* were still unreliable—they were severed every time the *Guam* changed course—but Barettella could speak to the ship satisfactorily. This luck, together with the telephone, was a tremendous help; not only was it possible to get estimates of PRA strengths or positions and to know that soldiers were not in the dormitory buildings, but also the students could be given careful instructions as to what to do, where to go, and how they would be rescued.

Just after 10:00 A.M. October 26, Barettella confirmed to Metcalf that a number of PRA troops were in the vicinity of the campus, although not in the school buildings. A Ranger patrol the previous night had spotted four guards nearby. These troops were Abdullah's men, and their defensive efforts seemed to be concentrated across the road south of the campus and on either side. There were no obvious positions on the beach looking seaward. Metcalf instructed Trobaugh to secure the campus by nightfall.

It was to be another Ranger task. Hagler's 2d/75th, which had so far had an easier time than Taylor's battalion, was selected. He was initially instructed to plan on moving on foot, to the left (west) of Hamilton's men, seize the campus, and then get the students into trucks and escort them back to Salines. This idea was relayed to Grand Anse, and most of the students believed they would be got out on the morning of October 26.

It was not to be. Schwarzkopf, on the *Guam*, thought it should be a heliborne operation with the marines' aircraft, because the 82d helicopters had not yet arrived, carrying in the Rangers and lifting out the students. Metcalf agreed to the change. Perhaps understandably, the marines were not too keen on the idea to start with. They had lost two of their four Cobras, the enemy were fully alerted, it would be daylight, and the beach selected as the landing zone was narrow, with palms growing down onto the sand. However, Metcalf directed the MAU commander to make HMM261 available to support the Rangers. Amos flew to Salines to confer with his friend, and a classmate from the Virginia Military Institute, Hagler. They sat down on concrete blocks at the unfinished terminal to put the operation together.

Hagler had good intelligence on the situation at the campus through speaking by telephone to students and discussing details with True Blue staff. From what he was told, a sea approach onto the beach appeared to be the best plan. But there were at least 200 students, probably more, to be brought out, as well as taking in the Ranger battalion and extracting them again. All the marine helicopters would be required, together with careful coordination of flights and timings. It was agreed that command and control would best be exercised from the air, in a marine UH-1, with Amos, Hagler, and an army officer as fire support coordinator on board.

The problem was to devise a plan that hit the enemy hard, got the Rangers in quickly to cordon the school buildings, ensured collection and escort of the students to waiting helicopters to evacuate them, then extracted the Rangers (map 19). Hagler proposed to use his three companies, each reduced to about fifty men. The initial assault would be by A Company under Captain Kearney, arriving on the beach in front of the campus in three CH-46s. Following immediately behind would be Captain Sittnik's B Company in three more Sea Knights. The task of both the leading companies would be to cordon the campus to prevent any direct ground interference with the evacuation. Next C Company, commanded by Captain Hanna, also in three CH-46s, would arrive to locate the students and pack them onto the four CH-53 Sea Stallions, which would be the last helicopters to land. As each division of three aircraft landed, the Rangers were to leap out and run to their positions, while their helicopters took off immediately to allow the next division in. The whole sequence would be repeated in reverse order to extract the troops as soon as the students were safely airborne.

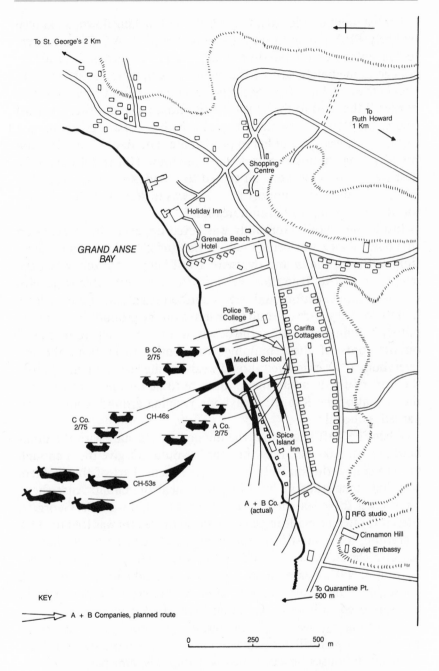

To St. George's 2 Km

To
Ruth Howard
1 Km

Shopping
Centre

Holiday Inn

Grenada Beach
Hotel

*GRAND ANSE
BAY*

Police Trg.
College

Carifta
Cottages

B Co.
2/75

Medical School

C Co.
2/75

CH-46s

A Co.
2/75

Spice
Island
Inn

CH-53s

A + B Co.
(actual)

RFG studio

Cinnamon Hill

Soviet Embassy

To Quarantine Pt.
500 m

KEY

A + B Companies, planned route

0   250   500
                     m

Map 19. MARINES AND THE 2d/75th AT GRAND ANSE

For ten minutes prior to the first CH-46's touching down, all known or likely PRA positions were to be bombarded. A-7 Corsairs were to concentrate on the buildings marked on maps as a police training college immediately east of the campus. A Spectre gunship was to fire on the long line of cottages known as the Carifta Cottages, which bordered the road to the south. In addition, naval gunfire, army artillery, the Rangers' mortars, together with the marines' remaining two Cobras, were scheduled to participate. The Radio Free Grenada broadcasting studios alongside the Cinnamon Hill Hotel were to be destroyed, although they had ceased to broadcast the previous day. The preparatory fire support program was to start at 3:00 P.M., with the Rangers going in ten minutes later.

Inside the school, everybody was keyed up, expecting evacuation that day. Full use was being made of Barettella's unique communications with the *Guam* and overseas. Until later in the day when the telephone link to True Blue was lost, the staff were able to receive details of U.S. intentions and instructions on exactly what the students had to do. They had to group themselves on the ground floor of dormitory buildings away from the beach; white sheets were to be placed on the roofs of these buildings to identify them from the air. Everybody to be evacuated should wear a white armband, and before the start of the bombardment, all were to lie on the floor to await the arrival of the Rangers. Anybody running around would be regarded as hostile.

When the staff heard that the mission would start with the bombardment at 3:00 P.M., they thought it would not give them enough time to collect the students and prepare them. Part of the problem was that some students lived in houses near the Grand Anse shopping center some 800 meters east of the school, toward St. George's. Attempts must be made to get them in, so the *Guam* was told to delay everything for at least forty-five minutes. Metcalf accepted that the Rangers should now take off at 4:00 P.M., with the bombardment starting at 4:05. Some 36 students were brought in from outlying houses, making a total of over 230 awaiting evacuation. A CH-53 was supposed to have a maximum load of 55 persons.

Unfortunately, even this operation was not going to rescue everybody. It was still not realized that some 200 more students were scattered in houses between the two campuses, and particularly on the Lance aux Epines peninsula 2 or 3 kilometers south of Grand Anse.

Most of these would be left behind until October 28 or 29, while 21, including Dr. Lennon from the school, who lived even farther away at Westerhall, were missed completely and never left Grenada at all. If the RMC and PRA had any intention of taking hostages, nothing the U.S. forces did, or could have done at this stage, would have prevented it. Further evidence that hostage taking was never contemplated was the experience of John Doyle of Lindenhurst, New Jersey, who shared a house with four roommates well away from both campuses. On the morning of October 26, they heard the banging of rifle butts on the kitchen door so they fled to the bathroom. Doyle, however, felt it might be safer to confront the intruders, so he returned to the kitchen to face a heavily armed group of PRA soldiers. The troops established a base in the house, using a radio set to communicate. After three hours, the five students were released unharmed. Doyle later described how "I asked them to please lock up when they left." When he eventually returned, the house was empty, locked, but with a stack of AK-47s left behind.

Two staff members elected not to be evacuated: Dr. Robert Jordan and an assistant. When he heard about the impending airstrike at 4:00 P.M., Jordan decided to stay to protect valuable equipment and prepare for the next course. He was joined by the woman and a dog. Jordan had seen some fifteen or twenty PRA in the vicinity of the school that day, preparing positions near the Holiday Inn, 600 meters up the beach toward the town, and at the Carifta Cottages. They had also positioned a 12.7-mm AA gun in the buildings north of the campus.

When the bombardment started, Jordan and his companion dived under their desks. The window blew out; the noise was indescribable. The two of them, with the dog, went into the nearby laboratory. They decided the safest place would be the huge walk-in freezer used to store cadavers, so in they went to join two mutilated corpses. The noise continued for about ten minutes, but they waited before emerging. They had missed the evacuation completely. They saw a few PRA running away, but otherwise the place was deserted. Jordan was worried that the PRA soldiers might return to loot the premises so he devised a most ingenious scheme to deter intruders. There were twenty or more corpses in black plastic bags on tables in the laboratory, so they went around undoing the bags to expose the gruesome contents and propped up several corpses at the windows. They proved an effective deterrent; nobody entered the buildings that night. Both of them searched the school afterward for wounded, but found no blood, no bodies, nothing, except numerous bullet holes in the walls facing the beach.

That night Dr. Jordan and his friend were disturbed by a duel between a 12.7-mm AA gun, in position near the kitchen of the Spice Island Inn just south of the campus, and a Spectre gunship and retreated back inside the freezer. The AA gun would fire and move, fire and move, while the Spectre circled around, returning the fire with long, tearing bursts. The aircraft tried unsuccessfully for most of the night to knock out the gun, until around 3:00 A.M., after a prolonged and intensive pattern of firing, there was no response from the ground. In the morning Jordan found only piles of empty cases and torn-up ground.

It was not only American citizens that were taken out by the Rangers and marines from Grand Anse. A young British couple had their honeymoon rudely cut short by the intervention. Ernest and Angela Chiu were holidaying at the Spice Island Hotel, staying in a beach bungalow, when the battle started early on Tuesday morning. Mrs. Chiu said, "I thought we were going to be killed. I never heard a more frightening noise. It was as if thousands of troops were firing all round us." The couple spent much of the time in their bathtub. During a lull on the morning of October 26, they came out onto the beach to look around. Through binoculars, Mrs. Chiu looked toward St. George's: "We could see Fort Rupert above the capital, and it was full of holes. The office of the former Prime Minister Maurice Bishop [Butler House], had also been gutted by fire. There was no roof left, just the walls were standing."

When the Grand Anse assault got under way, the Chius jumped back into the bathtub. After the firing ceased, they heard a yell, "This is the U.S. Army peacekeeping force. Run and run fast." Mr. Chiu later described how "we ran to the beach and I remember looking up and seeing the soldier with his face all covered with black paint and covered in sand. I was so scared my mouth felt as if it had turned to concrete." The honeymooners were rushed about 200 meters down the sand to a waiting CH-53, bundled aboard, flown to Salines, and then in a C-130 to Barbados. An unforgettable start to their marriage.

‡ ‡ ‡

That afternoon incoming and outgoing flights of transport aircraft were interrupted as no fewer than nineteen helicopters warmed up at Salines, waiting for the 150 Rangers to board. The air throbbed with the roar of engines and the whirring of rotor blades as 4:00 P.M. approached. They had about a 6 kilometer flight, including a wide sweep northward out to sea, before a dangerous descent onto a narrow strip of sand. The beauty and tranquility of one of the loveliest bays in the Caribbean was about to be shattered.

The first aircraft away contained Amos and Hagler, with the fire support coordinator. Theirs was a difficult task: to control the whole operation and deal with the unexpected. They were followed by three CH-46s, then three more, then the last three. By some mishap, the lift-off was confused: the leading flight of three had only one of A Company's helicopters and two from B Company, which meant that the second flight had two from A and one from B—an annoying muddle that would have to be sorted out on the ground.

Five minutes after takeoff, the softening-up process began with Corsairs screaming in low from the sea, an AC-130 wheeling around overhead, and guns and mortars thumping out their shells. As the first helicopters neared the shoreline, the escorting Cobras added their missiles and cannon fire. Supporting fire continued until twenty seconds before touchdown.

The plan had envisaged A Company, in the first three aircraft, forming a cordon south of the campus while B Company, coming in next, took the northern sector. Plans rarely work out. In addition to the mix-up with the composition of the flights, the first three CH-46s, coming in in echelon one behind the other, missed the designated landing zone on the beach in front of the school. Instead they put down 500 meters southwest of the campus, almost opposite the radio station. The following three did better but were still not in the correct location. There was a delay as the Rangers sorted themselves out before doubling to their proper positions to form a perimeter.

Although there was sporadic small arms fire at the helicopters as they came in, the only serious damage was caused by an overhanging palm tree. One of the CH-46s could not avoid its rotor blades' hitting the tree, causing the pilot to shut down and abandon the aircraft half in the surf. One of the Rangers inside described the desperate scramble to get out as water poured in through the half-open rear ramp:

"As soon as we hit the shore we headed down the beach. We ran about 500 meters 'til we linked up with the rest of the guys, and joined the perimeter. Scared the shit out of me!"

When the last of the eight CH-46s cleared the beach, Amos called in the CH-53s. As they were landing, Hanna's C Company ran to collect the students who, obeying instructions, had remained hidden in the buildings with mattresses propped up at windows as protection against flying glass. Within moments, the students and staff were scrambling onboard, Hanna having to push 60 or more passengers into each aircraft; 233 were flown out from the landing zone without any injuries. It had all gone very smoothly so far, with the only military casualty being a Ranger slightly wounded by mortar fire. The students flew from Salines to Barbados and then on a C-141 to Charleston, South Carolina, for an emotional, tumultuous homecoming.

While the evacuation was under way, Lance Corporal Martin Dellert, the crew chief of the downed helicopter, had run out to examine the damage. Finding nothing serious, he dashed back to the pilot to say, "I think we can fly it." Pilot, copilot, gunner, and crew chief clambered back onboard and started up. Shuddering and vibrating violently, the Sea Knight staggered back to Salines.

With all the civilians away, a yellow smoke grenade was thrown on the beach as a signal to the CH-46s circling over the sea that it was time to return for the Rangers. During the extraction, another CH-46 fell victim to a palm tree. This aircraft was in the second group of three lifting off. Part of the tree crashed through the rotor blades, completely destroying the system. This mishap did not delay the extraction, and the entire operation was over in twenty-six minutes, a remarkable achievement considering the potential hazards. Not long after leaving the beach, however, Hanna realized he had eleven men missing. In the rush to load, they had been left behind.

These men had moved up the beach as a flank guard so had been unaware, until too late, that they had missed the extraction. Hanna tried repeatedly to get a helicopter to rescue them, but he was unsuccessful. Over the radio, the squad was told to try to make their way out on foot, via Quarantine Point, to the area of the 82d Airborne troops in the southwest. They did not have any of the 82d's radio call signs of frequencies, and despite a lot of fiddling with their set were unable to make contact.

By now it was almost dark, and the prospect of trying to approach the 82d's positions through the scrub would be inviting disaster, so they opted for a different method of escape. Lying on the beach half out of the water was the chewed-up remains of the CH-46. For some reason, it had been deliberately shot to pieces by aircraft after it had crashed. Nevertheless, rummaging through the wreckage revealed three rubber boats. They inflated the boats, and, using helmets and rifle butts as paddles, moved slowly seaward. But it soon became apparent that two of the boats were full of holes and unusable, so everything and everybody, except for two men who had to swim alongside, were piled into the third boat. For hours, they battled with the tide and current, making poor headway until they were spotted by a helicopter, which dropped flares to guide in a rescue launch. It was 11:00 P.M. before they finally reached the destroyer *Caron*.

‡ ‡ ‡

In terms of missions accomplished, October 26 had been a successful day (map 20). The Cubans had surrendered at Little Havana, the governor-general had finally been rescued, the PRA logistics base had fallen, and over 230 civilians had been evacuated from Grand Anse—all at a cost of two men killed. In the north, E Company 2d/8th BLT had spent the day collecting arms caches around Pearls, and in the extreme south, Raines's 3d/325th had uneventfully occupied the True Blue peninsula. No further infantry battalions had arrived, and that night TF-121's front line stretched from Morne Rouge in the west, southeastward through Frequente, to the True Blue peninsula. In St. George's the marines were firm at Queen's Park and had made some inroads into the outskirts of the town. Fort Frederick had been captured, and there was little evidence of serious resistance, most Grenadians appearing to be delighted with the intervention. The RMC leadership had fled, and most of the PRA had thrown away their uniforms to mingle with the civilian population.

The fact that battle was all but over was not, seemingly, evident to the U.S. commanders, who still thought in terms of more Cubans to overcome and the urgent need for reinforcements. Nobody seemed able to read the battle so far or put together a reasonable intelligence assessment of what was happening on the other side of the hill. The negligible number of combat casualties, the hundreds of POWs, the

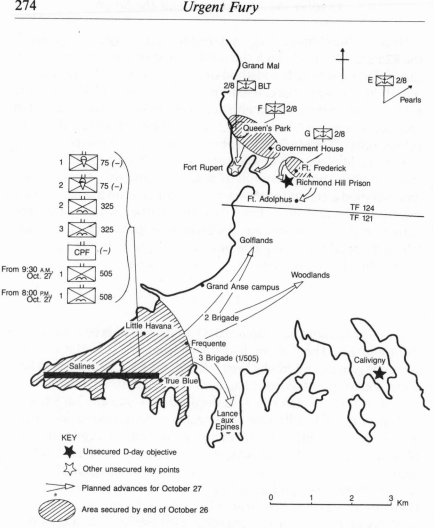

Map 20. SITUATION AT MIDNIGHT, OCTOBER 26, AND
PLANNED ADVANCES FOR OCTOBER 27

welcoming cooperation of so many Grenadians, the capture of the
RMC headquarters at Fort Frederick, and the ease with which U.S.
citizens had been freed, without the complications of hostages or injuries, does not seem to have meant anything to the U.S. high command. The unmistakable signs that it was all over bar the shouting
were either unnoticed or ignored. TF 121 seemed preoccupied with

the need to secure every inch of ground before making any substantial advance.

Trobaugh's orders for October 27 reflect the innate slowness of his operations. He did not think he could get to Calivigny until October 28, though during the early morning hours of the twenty-seventh his Combat Aviation Battalion, which had arrived in Barbados in C-5A Galaxies on the twenty-sixth, began flying into Grenada. By dawn on Thursday, many of the Black Hawks had arrived. It was at this time also that the three medical evacuation Black Hawks of the 57th Medical Detachment of XVIII Corps flew in, one being sent to Pearls, the other two staying at Salines. The main problem was fuel. It was discovered that the 10,000 gallon fuel bladder at Salines was empty, so many of the aircraft had to be used to ferry small 500-gallon bladders to and from the *Guam*.

Trobaugh's orders were that 2d Brigade, with the 2d/325th and 3d/325th, push forward to the Golflands and Woodlands Estate area, about a kilometer south of St. George's. Scott's 3d Brigade consisted of only a few elements of the 1st/505th, but as they were reinforced during the next day, they were to search and secure the Lance aux Epines peninsula. A cautious crawl of 2 kilometers was all that seemed possible for October 27 in the south.

14

October 27

St. George's and the South

We didn't find anything worth shooting at.
— 1st Lieutenant Raymond Thomas, 2d/75th Rangers,
after the assault on Camp Calivigny

S HORTLY after first light on Thursday, October 27, long columns of infantry from the 82d slowly uncoiled themselves from their overnight locations. Without their vehicles and weighed down with excessive loads, they showed little or no inclination to leave the roads or tracks. As the temperature rose, the troops, sweating profusely, were somewhat apprehensive as to what the day would bring. On the left, Hamilton's 2d/325th led the way down from the Morne Rouge high ground, onto the coastal flat land behind Grand Anse beach. The main distraction for them was the exploding ammunition in the Radio Free Grenada studio building. Since late the previous afternoon when shells and rockets had set it alight, periodic explosions shook the rubble. The more nervous of Hamilton's men threw themselves flat each time ammunition "cooked off." By 9:20 A.M. the 2d/325th entered the burned-out remains of the old police training college at Grand Anse. There was no opposition.

To the south, over on the other side of Morne Rouge ridge, Raines's 3d/325th began to move forward slowly, ever so slowly, down the road from Frequente, past the drive-in movie toward Ruth Howard, the Sugar Mill, and eventually the Woodlands Estate area. The scout platoon was in the lead, and it was a very long time before the last troops in the battalion snake were able to move out. There was a lot of stopping and starting, much bunching up, as the long line wended its way forward. Resistance was limited to occasional sniper fire—nothing serious. The 3d/325th was advancing along the boundary between the 2d Brigade, and 3d Brigade on the right.

Lieutenant Colonel George Crocker's 1st/505th had a late start. His was the only infantry battalion of Colonel Scott's 3d Brigade in Grenada that morning, and even then all the companies were not assembled until after 9:30. Their task was to secure the high ground overlooking Grand Anse Estate before exploring the Lance aux Epines peninsula. When they were ready to advance, the only opposition was the heat and the hills.

This was a relatively quiet start to the day. The afternoon was to be a disaster.

‡   ‡   ‡

Back in Washington, Vessey was far from happy with the progress. Like the other senior commanders, he still believed there could be serious fighting ahead. From the initial overconfidence and the assumption that there would be minimal resistance, thus permitting a one-day operation, commanders quickly announced the opposite: there were Cubans behind every bush. Vessey confined himself to saying, "We got a lot more resistance than we expected," but Admiral McDonald told the press on October 28 that there were at least 1,100 Cubans on Grenada, "all well trained professional soldiers," who had "been impersonating construction workers." These sorts of remarks were later revealed to be nonsensical, but at the time the defeat of the Special Forces at the very start had to have some explanation (as did the slow advance of one of the U.S. Army's elite formations) other than faulty intelligence, poor planning, or lack of drive. On October 27, a good example of how commanders clung to the belief that Cubans still abounded and that there was tough combat to come was the assault on Camp Calivigny. It worried Vessey that this camp had been a D-day objective of the 2d/75th Rangers, yet forty-eight hours later, no U.S. forces were even approaching it. The JCS signaled at midday that Calivigny must be taken by nightfall. It had become an embarrassment, reflecting on the competence of TF 121. Twenty mintues later, Metcalf ordered Trobaugh to attack.

Calivigny camp had been built by the Cubans on a deserted, scrub-covered peninsula, marked on most maps as Egmont. Apart from accommodation buildings, its facilities included a rifle range in the valley to the west, plus an assault course just alongside the 2 meter high southern perimeter fence. This was the PRA's training depot and the peacetime home of the so-called permanent battalion, which in late 1983 had effectively one company at the camp. To U.S. observers, however, it had taken on a much more sinister significance. Intelligence sources claimed it was the center of the Cuban military efforts on the island, that secret naval construction work was planned in the nearby bay, that it was the central training base for the spread of military subversion in the region, the president had named it in statements on the militarization of Grenada, and it was much photographed from the air. The site had been selected for its remoteness. It was well away from prying eyes; nobody could approach it by land except via a long, rough track from the village of Calivigny. The whole peninsula was strictly off-limits to unauthorized visitors. The small plateau on which it was sited was some 125 to 150 feet above the sea, with very steep, sheer cliffs to the south. Virtually the only sea approach was into the little cove to the west, which gave access to the rifle range valley. It was not a popular place with the PRA soldiers, who found it excessively hot and a long way from the bright lights of St. George's.

It is puzzling why the JCS considered it so essential to assault Calivigny after the Rangers had been unable to get there on D day. By this time, it had no tactical or strategic importance. Calivigny was to the PRA what Fort Bragg is to the 82d Airborne—their normal peacetime home. In the event of an invasion of the United States, Fort Bragg as such is of no real significance; only the units that happen to be there are important. An attack on the United States, or even the threat of such an attack, is unlikely to see the 82d remaining in the barracks at Fort Bragg; they will be deployed where they are needed, not stay to defend the fort. So with Calivigny. As we now know, all the troops had moved out of the camp on October 23, as soon as invasion seemed imminent. With reflection, this should have been apparent to planners or their intelligence staffs, but seemingly it was not because a full-scale battalion attack was ordered.

Trobaugh detailed Hagler's battalion for the mission—it had been his originally anyway—reinforced by C Company of the 1st/75th now recovered from their Richmond Hill Prison setback and returned to their battalion. To these Rangers, the prospect of yet another difficult task caused a few misgivings initially. It seemed to some that the Rangers were doing all the fighting, that they had done their fair share, and they had, after all, been led to believe they would be pulled out at the end of the first day.

It looked like another hastily put together operation against a well-defended enemy position. At least, that is what the participants were told. Intelligence reports put the garrison at 600, including Cubans and Soviet advisers. Warrant Officer Thomas Speaks, a helicopter copilot, later stated, "We were briefed that there were 600 Cubans at this barracks, and that there would be six antiaircraft guns defending the place. We all thought it was a suicide mission." These comments were supported by 1st Lieutenant Raymond Thomas: "We were told there were 30 Russians and 400 Cubans at Edgemont, that it was almost a suicide mission."

Colonel Scott took overall tactical control of the mission at about 1:45 P.M. There was not a lot of time to plan and coordinate with an H hour set for 4:30 P.M. following half an hour's extensive bombardment. The plan was simple: to flatten the camp and then for the Rangers to charge in in the UH-60 Black Hawks of Lieutenant Colonel Robert Seigle's Combat Aviation Battalion. The helicopters for the actual assault would be provided by Major William Elder's B Company. The Rangers and crews had barely an hour to plan or carry out briefings—no time for reconnaissance by the junior commanders, so their planning was done from the available aerial photographs of the camp. The quality of the prints was high, the roofs of the buildings showing white, with dark shadows on their eastern and southern sides. Two large, white, rectangular patches near the southern perimeter were also thought to be buildings, although they did not cast any shadow. The suspected AA position in the scrub, on slightly rising ground on the eastern side of the camp, did not show up at all.

Hagler provided all three of his rifle companies, and he had the additional sixty or seventy men of C Company 1st/75th under command. They would attack in four company waves, or flights, each of four Black Hawks. The helicopters would orbit out to sea, then fly in in successive waves just above the water at 100 knots. Approaching the camp from the south, each group would have to climb rapidly, above the cliffs, before setting the troops down in the camp itself. The M-60 door gunners would provide close fire support.

A and C Companies, 2d/75th, were to land at the southern end of the compound with A Company on the left and C Company on the right (map 21). They would line up and sweep through the camp, while B Company landed to the southeast to assault the suspected AA position before rejoining the other companies in the north.

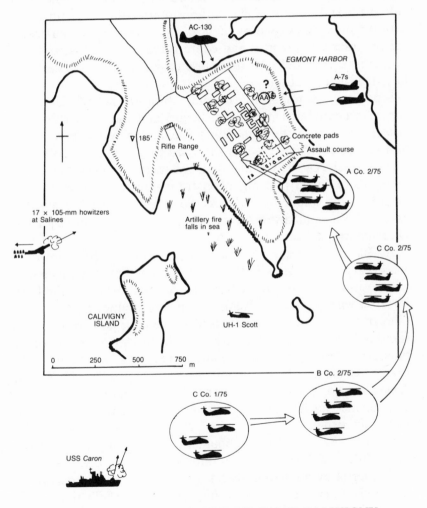

Map 21. RANGERS' ASSAULT ON CAMP CALIVIGNY

C Company 1st/75th would arrive last, as a reserve, to secure the southern perimeter area. If the preparatory bombardment was a success, there should be little left for the infantry to do.

The thirty minutes of supporting fire by aircraft, army artillery, and naval guns was to be the biggest bombardment of the entire operation, with no chance of causing civilian casualties. They could pound the place to pieces. Caron's two 5-inch guns were to join with the three batteries of M-102 105-mm howitzers 8,000 meters away at Salines, while from the air AC-130s and A-7s would combine to provide shells and bombs. Hagler's fire support officer was unfamiliar with the procedures used by the 82d's guns back at the airfield, so the program was planned and coordinated by Scott's fire support officer from 3 Brigade. The navy also provided a gunnery liaison officer for the operation.

Scott intended to control the attack from the air in a UH-1 helicopter, accompanied by Hagler, Seigle, and the gunnery officers. Before the start of the preparatory fire, he flew up to have a quick look at the objective. He was surprised to see little, or no activity. The so-called AA site was deserted, and there was no evidence of the hundreds of Cubans, or any other troops for that matter, prepared to defend the camp. Nevertheless, Scott saw no need to abort the assault or the bombardment; everything would continue as planned. He remained airborne to watch.

At 4:00 P.M. the seventeen guns from the three batteries of the 1st/319th and 1st/320th Field Artillery opened fire from Salines. The gun position was out on the bare ground east of the terminal, each howitzer with its crew of five or six gunners grouped around it, with piles of ammunition boxes stacked up behind, and rows of shells standing neatly on their bases ready to hand. A few flimsy concrete blocks had been placed near some of the guns as a token gesture toward protection. It was assumed there was now no danger from enemy fire. Fortunately this was an accurate assumption; a few bursts of machine-gun fire, or mortar rounds landing in the area, would have caused havoc.

Each howitzer was to fire about 30 shells, making a total of some 500 in all. At Salines, it was an impressive demonstration, watched with interest by numerous spectators. To Scott in his helicopter, at the receiving end it was not so impressive. The shells were missing the camp completely. Round after round plunged uselessly into the sea, as Scott fumed at his inability to do anything about it. His impotence was due to the absence of the fire support officer from 3 Brigade; he had been bumped from the helicopter at the outset and was therefore unable to contact the guns to make corrections. He was obliged to watch the entire bombardment, with the exception of a solitary shell that hit the target, fall harmlessly into the water. It was afterward discovered that the artillery had misplotted their own positions by 700 meters, had inaccurate coordinates for Calivigny, and had left their artillery aiming circles (compasses on tripods) behind at Fort Bragg.

Scott was not impressed with the navy's shooting either, although at least the naval lieutenant had managed to get aboard the aircraft and tried desperately to adjust the fall of shot. The results were disappointing, infuriating Scott even more. It was at about this stage that *Caron* ceased firing, on Metcalf's orders, because he considered there was a danger of the shells striking the aircraft in the vicinity, and he mistrusted the radio link between the destroyer and Scott. With H hour approaching, Calivigny was so far almost unscathed.

Scott put back the attack by fifteen minutes to permit the air force and marine pilots in to do the job. The Spectre hosed shells into the camp, while A-7s flew eight sorties, blasting the buildings and surrounding area with rockets and bombs. By the time they flew off to allow the assault to start, there was little left of Camp Calivigny.

The first group of four Black Hawks was led by Elder personally. They roared in over the waves and climbed sharply to the cliff top before suddenly appearing over the southern part of the peninsula. Immediately below them were the remains of the barracks, shattered, but with the perimeter fence more or less intact. The camp seemed closer to the edge of the cliff top than it was in reality, so the helicopters had to decelerate fast to pick their exact landing spot inside the fence. The flight came in quickly, one behind the other, with fifteen or so Rangers keyed up inside each aircraft, ready to leap from the open doors at the moment of touchdown.

Elder was the only pilot in the first flight to put down correctly and safely near the southern camp boundary. As he did so, the Rangers jumped, all exiting without mishap. The following two helicopters came in too fast and overshot the intended landing zone, coming in to land farther into the camp. The second touched down, and the Rangers had started to dismount when the third suffered some damage, spun forward, and smashed into the second.[1] The fourth Black Hawk saw the crash and veered hard right to avoid it, thereby landing badly in a ditch (probably part of the nearby assault course) and damaging its tail rotor. The pilot was unaware of the damage and attempted to lift off. The aircraft rose up sharply and then seemed to spin forward before crashing. Three Black Hawks were down in twenty seconds.

In human terms, the damage was far worse. The flying debris and the chaos of swirling rotor blades had killed three and badly injured four of the Rangers who had already dismounted from the helicopters. These were the only 2/75th Rangers to die in Grenada. Those still inside the second and third aircraft escaped. The dead were Sergeant Eric Slater and Specialists Sebastian Greiner and Joseph Lannon, all from A Company, all chopped to pieces by spinning rotor blades. One of the survivors lost his leg; another, who was trapped under the fuselage of the fourth aircraft, was to be paralyzed from the waist down. This was Staff Sergeant William Sears, whose grievous injuries included a broken back, two broken legs, numerous broken ribs, and collapsed lungs. It was at this moment that Sergeant Stephen Trujillo, a medic, was to earn his Silver Star. Without regard for his own safety, he dashed forward into the wreckage to treat and extricate the injured. His actions were instrumental in saving several lives. In an unusual gesture, he was later to receive his award from the president personally at a joint session of Congress.

A Company regrouped, while C Company landed safely, using the large concrete slabs on the edge of the compound that had been thought to be building roofs on the photographs. They were merely concrete foundations of some sort, which proved ideal as landing pads. The Rangers then advanced through the camp to clear the buildings. B Company landed correctly before moving through the scrub to the suspected AA position. Finally in came C Company, 1st/75th, to an infinitely more comfortable reception than had been awaiting them at Richmond Hill two days before.

After all that, they discovered no enemy—no bodies, no wounded—nothing except for a devastated barracks strewn with rubble. Mayers's headquarters offices were in ruins with nothing recognizable remaining, except in the foundations on the eastern side, the words "I love Fidel" were faintly visible, scratched into the concrete. In the weeks that followed, it was to become almost a military tourist attraction for U.S. forces on the island, with visitors making special helicopter trips to see what souvenirs they could salvage from the debris. It was subsequently used as the site on which to blow up unwanted captured ammunition or equipment. Even four years after, it was possible to find rusted Soviet or U.S. ammunition boxes, old AA gun magazines, and both LAW and 7.62 rounds, scattered in the grass.

If there had been a handful of PRA troops left, they fled at the start of the bombardment. As the exasperated platoon leader, Thomas put it, "We didn't find anything worth shooting at." That night the Rangers camped in the ruins.

‡ ‡ ‡

At 4:00 P.M. the leading troops of the scout platoon of Raines's 3d/325th were approaching the Ruth Howard/Sugar Mill road junction, having advanced 1 kilometer since early that morning. Suddenly they came under fire from a sniper located behind them and to their left, north of the road.

The shots actually passed over the jeep carrying the Air Naval Gunfire Liaison Company (ANGLICO) team back down the road. This group is a fire support team provided by the navy/marines to control naval gunfire, or aircraft, operating in support of ground forces. ANGLICO teams are usually under the command of a junior officer or a warrant officer, with several accompanying radio operators. These teams had been alerted for Urgent Fury too late to reach Fort Bragg in time to join the leading 82d battalions. When they arrived in Grenada, it was discovered that they could not do their job because they lacked the necessary radio codes, call signs, and frequencies to communicate with the supporting arms coordination center on the *Guam.* They tried to remedy this by flying out to collect the information direct from the ship, but still breakdowns plagued them.

On this occasion the chief warrant officer spotted the house from which the firing came, so he resolved to use his initiative to take it on as an opportunity target. But there was a problem—several in fact. The standard procedure was for the chief to obtain clearance from brigade headquarters before engaging a target, but because of another communications snarl-up, he did not have the radio instructions, or codes, for the 82d Airborne. Also he was not in contact at that time with the battalion he was supporting, the 3d/325th. To go physically and find the headquarters was an option, but it was rejected because of the time it would take, and it would mean leaving the jeep full of radios on the road. He did, however, discuss the problem with Captain William Stephen, who was the air liaison officer with Crocker's 1st/505th, which was at that time nearby, to the south of the Ruth Howard road. They agreed that the chief, who could clearly see the target with people at the window, was in a better position to control the shooting.

The chief tried to call in a Spectre gunship but was told none was available. He was convinced of the need to act, so he made contact with the flight leader of four A-7s that had been busy over Calivigny. Although the chief did not know that brigade headquarters had moved (nor did the infantry battalions), he was certain of Raines's position, and Crocker used smoke to indicate his. It did not seem to be a difficult mission. The target was a white house with a red roof, on the ridge north of a drive-in movie. He described it to the pilot, giving him a bearing of 270 degrees from the Sugar Mill.

The leading A-7 came in very low, under 200 feet, for no fewer than three passes. As the aircraft flew over the target, the chief called "mark on top," indicating that he had located the house. The pilot seemed happy and told his wing man that the flight was active but not to fire until he did.

The aircraft came in low and fast. To the consternation of the chief and Stephens, they did not seem to be on the correct bearing, and as they drew near, the pilot was heard to say over his radio that he could see people near the house. This did not fit with the actual target. The chief yelled to abort the mission a second or so before the leading aircraft opened up with his 20-mm cannon—too late to stop a stream of shells ripping into Silvasy's new command post.

The pilot had fired into a gray building west of the drive-in movie, causing chaos and seventeen casualties, three of them serious. The worst was Sergeant Sean Luketina, a radio operator from the 82d's signal battalion, who had both legs smashed. Medical evacuation to the *Guam* was delayed, supposedly by a rain squall. Luketina later died of gangrene in his legs at the Walter Reed Hospital in the United States.[2]

Meanwhile, the pilot had heard the cries to cease fire, so the whole flight pulled away. The chief, not realizing the damage that had been done, continued to radio more information on the target's location, but the pilot had had enough and refused to engage again. The aircraft returned to the *Independence*. But the ANGLICO chief did not give up easily. Next he called in a flight of A-6 Intruders, which flew several identifying runs over the house. This time it was to be Mk-20 bombs, not cannon fire. The first bomb missed the house, and the next one failed to explode. This was too much for Crocker, who yelled at Stephens to stop; he would deal with snipers without close air support.[3]

‡ ‡ ‡

Progress was better in St. George's. While three battalions of the 82d gingerly moved northeast, or east, toward the town and Lance aux Epines, two companies of marines had the task of securing the city, together with possible PRA positions along the Morne Jaloux ridge.

G Company's first job was to capture Richmond Hill Prison. October 27 was to be one long remembered by the prisoners, some of whom had been incarcerated for four years. Political detainees like Winston Whyte and Lloyd Noel, who had once been Bishop's attorney general, gained their freedom that day, as did George Louison, his brother Major Einstein Louison, Radix, and journalist Alister Hughes. Like many other PRAF, the guards at the prison had no stomach for continuing the fight beyond the Wednesday, and it was during that day, or early on October 27, that they discarded their uniforms and disappeared, leaving the prisoners locked inside. The prisoners had made a serious attempt to break out on Wednesday, but it was premature; there were still sufficient guards to quell it. One prisoner was shot dead in his cell. Before the marines arrived, most of the inmates had managed to free themselves without interference.

Just prior to Dobson's men moving out, they received some welcome news from Smith. The group of journalists who had met him at Queen's Park included Hugh O'Shaughnessy, from the *British Observer*, who had been to the prison and was able to confirm that it was undefended. Dobson sent a platoon immediately, securing the prison by 8:00 A.M.

G Company now began to advance along the road that followed the spine of Morne Jaloux ridge southward. They cautiously approached their next objective, Fort Adolphus. The troops could see it was occupied and was flying a flag that nobody recognized. It looked as though a major assault might be needed to secure it. Smith obtained permission to use air support, plus naval gunfire, to soften the defenses, and he also discussed the deployment of TOW missiles and heavy machine guns with Dobson. Nevertheless, they used none of these heavy weapons. Afterward Smith recalled, "I'm not sure what stopped us from doing it. The only thing that stopped us from going in and prepping it, is that we had been so successful without shooting that I recall consciously making a decision: It's working, let's keep doing it the way we're doing it." He then told Dobson, "Just scout it out. If you take any fire, back off and we'll blow the hell out of it." This is what G Company did. Fort Adolphus was revealed as the home of the Venezuelan embassy.

With the dominating hills and ridges behind the town cleared, F Company could now move in to clean up St. George's. It was a silent city; nobody was on the streets, no vehicles moved, and of the PRA there was no sign at all. Out to sea were the warships—some close inshore, others a blur on the horizon. The two bastions of Bishop's regime, Butler House and Fort Rupert, had been heavily pounded from the air during the previous two days. The once-impressive white walls of Butler House were smashed and the building gutted by fire. It was rumored that the fire was deliberate, like that at the former police headquarters in Melville Street, done to ensure the destruction of sensitive documents before the arrival of the U.S. forces. This was not in fact the case. Butler House proved a mine of classified documents, thousands of which were flown to the United States for analysis and later publication. Bishop's former headquarters remains in ruins to this day, a place to which visitors can climb to admire the magnificent view and reflect on its former fame.

When Dick's leading platoon entered Fort Rupert, it too was deserted by the living but sprawled on the top square, among the lumps of concrete and stone that littered the ground, was the body of a PRA soldier. The buildings were wrecked, but the wall at which Bishop was shot survived, as did the basketball post, both now pitted and scarred by American bullets as well as communist ones.

Smith was now overextended. E Company was still based at Pearls, while the other two were fully committed in the town itself or on the surrounding ridges. He decided to form a temporary rifle company out of his artillery battery. So H Battery came ashore, leaving its guns on the ship, to become infantrymen, based at Queen's Park, but with responsibility for patrolling the town and carrying out numerous searches for arms dumps or PRA personnel in hiding. This allowed F and G companies to continue south.

The marines were still plagued by communications difficulties. It was this lack of an effective radio link that delayed Smith's receipt of the new boundary line between his unit and the 82d. Metcalf, whose ear had been effectively captured by the 22d MAU's operations officer, Major Van Huss, was pleased with the way the marines were performing, so he wanted them to continue coming south.[4] To facilitate this, he moved the interforce boundary to run from Ross Point in the west to Requin Bay in the east. Smith did not learn of this until late on October 27, while the 82d's units remained unaware until the following day when the linkup was finally made. News of the change never got down below the brigade commanders. The marines in particular became more and more concerned about the whereabouts of friendly forces as they approached the 82d. Nobody wanted any "own goals." Although a linkup radio frequency had been designated, call signs had not been distributed, and joint fire control measures had not been established. As it transpired, the marines were wise to be cautious as the leading 82d troops thought they were in a free-fire zone.

The last task of the marines on Thursday was to "liberate" what they were told were 400 U.S., British, and Canadian citizens clamoring for evacuation from the Ross Point Inn. Back in the United States, President Reagan was due to address the nation on the situation in Grenada, so it was imperative that American nationals be safe. F Company was ordered to get to the inn fast. They arrived just after dark to discover some twenty foreigners, mostly Canadians, who although pleased to see the marines were happy enough to stay where they were.

‡ ‡ ‡

By nightfall Trobaugh had been reinforced by the second battalion of the 3d Brigade. This was Lieutenant Colonel Hugh Shaw's 1st/508th. Much to its annoyance, this battalion was destined to take no part in any operations. Its task was security at Salines, despite the fact that there were still two more battalions to arrive, both of which would be involved in mopping up over the next few days. On the ground little progress had been made, with a kilometer still separating the marines at Ross Point from the nearest 82d battalion (2d/325th) just to the north of Grand Anse. Raines's men had halted north of the Sugar Mill, while Crocker was on the high ground north of Lance aux Epines peninsula, which had not yet been secured. Apart from some random sniper fire, most of it against the 3d/325th in the center, there had been no enemy interference with progress, yet no battalion had moved much more than a kilometer that day.

The explanation is to be found in a number of factors. First, Trobaugh was not pushing, not driving his units forward, being seemingly content to expand his bridgehead gradually around Salines, seeing no reason to speed things up. True, his communications with the *Guam* were erratic, but he could have flown out to the ship in a few minutes if he was unsure of what to do. And, like the other commanders, Trobaugh could not bring himself to believe it was all over, indeed had been so for at least twenty-four hours. Reports and rumors of Cubans still warranted extreme caution. The lack of actual resistance, plus the cooperative friendliness of Grenadians, was not interpreted correctly.

But this was not quite all. Researchers from Walter Reed Army Institute of Research prepared a report, published in early 1987 in *Military Review*, on the overloading of the infantry in Grenada. The joint authors were Major James Dubik, a Ranger officer, and Major Terrence Fulterton, a psychologist at the Walter Reed Army Medical Center. Their report was based on interviews with personnel of seven of the nine battalions that participated in Urgent Fury, many taking place on the island shortly after combat. Not only were the majority of the infantry without their vehicles for most of the first few days, but they were not acclimatized to the heat. Most of the troops sweltered in rip-resistant polyester fabric uniforms, decidedly unsuitable for the tropics, while their quartermasters belatedly put in requisitions for thousands of the old Vietnam combat fatigues. The hills were steep, if not particularly high, and many soldiers were overburdened. As the report states, in one day twenty-nine soldiers in one battalion collapsed with heat exhaustion, another battalion's aid post treated forty-eight heat casualties, and a third used up their entire supply of intravenous solution on heat cases. The hills and the heat were as effective as enemy action in causing losses.

Regarding the actual weight carried and its effect, the report gives some revealing examples. One soldier recalled:

> We attacked to secure the airhead. We were like slow-moving turtles. My rucksack weighed 120 pounds. I would get up and rush for 10 yards, throw myself down and couldn't get up. I'd rest for 10 or 15 minutes, struggle to get up, go 10 more yards and collapse. After a few rushes, I was physically unable to move, and I'm in great shape. Finally after I got to the assembly area, I chucked my rucksack and was able to fight, but I was totally drained.

Another said, "I thought the rucksacks we were taking had too much in them. . . . It proved out when we got down there. . . . There were all those guys sitting on the side of the road with IV tubes in them. There's no way the guys could do it. We got most of those heat casualties walking up that one hill." Finally, after describing how his unit had to sit halfway up a hill waiting for the remainder to struggle up, one soldier added, "Even the commanding officer fell out of that one. He was dead tired; he also lost all of his radio-telephone operators."

The cause of this overloading was uncertainty. There was uncertainty back in the United States during preparations for the operation. Commanders had meager information on the enemy, the terrain, even on their own role and objectives. The result was that, with some exceptions, they overloaded their men—just in case. Perhaps the most damning comment of all made by the authors of the report was that during neither the planning nor the early part of the operation did the initial assault units know whether they would be reinforced. One Ranger commander remarked how surprised he had been to see the 82d start arriving. He had no idea it was participating at all.

The combination of all these factors kept progress to a crawl on October 26 and 27 in the extreme south.

Trobaugh's orders for October 28, given while still without radio contact with the marines only a kilometer away, saw Silvasy's brigade linking up with the 2d/8th BLT, while Scott's men cleared Lance aux Epines (map 22).

The fourth day should see the critical southwestern area of the island secured. But now it was being rumored that hundreds of Cubans and PRA had taken to the hills, with the prospect of a protracted campaign of jungle-type operations to get them out. This was viewed with dismay.

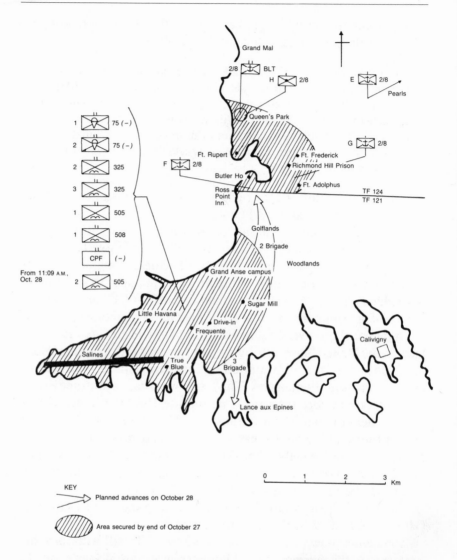

Map 22. SITUATION AT MIDNIGHT, OCTOBER 27, AND PLANNED ADVANCES FOR OCTOBER 28

15

Mopping Up

"Reagan number one!" Pause. "No, Eugenia Charles number one, Reagan number two."
— Grenadian woman in St. George's, October 28

AUSTIN, James, and Layne were determined to escape from Grenada. They left Fort Frederick together during darkness in the early hours of Wednesday. The news of the U.S. landings at Grand Mal, coming on top of an afternoon crouched in the tunnel under continuous heavy pounding from the air, had convinced them and the other PRA leaders at the fort that the end was not far off. A message was sent out to all units that they were to hide their weapons, discard their uniforms, and disappear. Although some troops either did not receive these instructions or ignored them, the great majority melted away on October 26, including officers like Nelson, who by that time had no units left. Changing into civilian clothes, Nelson went home to his small house perched precariously on the steep slope overlooking River Road and Queen's Park, where he awaited arrest.

But for the three military leaders of the RMC, it was not quite so easy. Although no longer in uniform, they could not just go home like the others. In all probability, arrest for them would mean death. But where to go, and how, posed daunting difficulties. Who could they rely on to hide them or help them? They all agreed there was only one possible refuge—Guyana. Perhaps there, President Forbes Burnham would give them sanctuary. After all, a Guyanese officer had assisted Austin when he attacked the Green Beasts camp; Guyana had supplied defense force training teams to the PRA; Austin had visited the country several times; it was only a few hundred miles to the southeast, and it was due to Burnham's telephone warning that they had received confirmation of impending invasion. Guyana was the only possibility. But how? It had to be by sea. This meant a boat, preferably an ocean-going yacht, of which there were scores in the island, because a yacht would not attract attention. Hundreds of such boats sail up and down the chain of islands that make up the Leewards and Windwards. The entire area is a yachtsman's paradise, particularly around Grenada and the Grenadines to the north. They felt that once aboard a suitable yacht, they had a chance, but to get it, they required money and somebody with access to a boat whom they could trust to take a bribe.

Austin and the other two managed to put together U.S. $7,000 in cash for the deal and armed themselves with Makarov pistols, an AK rifle, and several grenades. When they left Fort Frederick for the last time, they drove south, avoiding the obvious Morne Jaloux road, taking instead the twisting route through St. Paul's, Laborie, and Becke Moui, heading for the beautiful Westerhall Point peninsula where so many rich expatriates had their hideaway bungalows. They were looking for a personal friend of Austin, an East German named Gerhard Jonas. Jonas was an adviser on military or security matters to the PRG, who had been in Grenada for several years and had made a point of getting on well with Austin, cultivating his friendship in case favors were ever required. He had also made a point of mixing with the other expatriate community.

The time had come for Jonas to repay some of his debts. If anybody would be willing to get a yacht for the fugitives, it would be Jonas, who should also know of any suitable houses at Westerhall or nearby in which they could shelter. Jonas, although frightened, agreed to help and directed them to a small, empty bungalow with its own tiny jetty, facing Westerhall Bay halfway down the peninsula. They could hide there for a day or so until a boat could be arranged; the owner, Douglas Stone, was out of the country.

On the morning of October 27, back at the Caribbean Peacekeeping Force headquarters, Major Hartland and Lieutenant Commander Tomlin came to the conclusion that Austin and some of the other RMC or PRG leaders might try to escape by sea. Hartland, who knew the area and its inhabitants extremely well, guessed that anybody who needed a yacht in a hurry would try to get one from Spice Island Charters, whose small yachting marina was located on the beach at the northwest corner of Lance aux Epines. The two officers considered it was worth investigating, although the boatyard and the peninsula were both still well beyond the U.S. front line. They took their idea to Crist and Lewis, who agreed to a reconnaissance, and supplied a captured Gaz jeep with a U.S. soldier as an escort. So with Hartland, who was unarmed and had lost one eye in a grenade accident many years before, driving flat out, they roared out of the Salines area. They sped past the knocked-out APCs, past long lines of 82d troops on the roadside, with Tomlin clinging desperately to the sides of the jeep quite convinced they were going to crash or run over an American soldier, until they turned south toward Lance aux Epines. There was no activity at the marina, but the owner agreed that enquiries had been made to hire a yacht to go to Westerhall. She suggested they might find out more at Dod Gorman's house up the hill nearby.

On arrival there, they were greeted as liberators by some thirty or forty people gathered inside. The group included a number of U.S. students who lived on the peninsula. They were part of the third major grouping of students on the island, and like those at Grand Anse, their existence was unknown to the U.S. forces deployed to rescue them. Hartland and Tomlin had to explain that they hoped they would see their compatriots in due course.

In the house was John Kelly, the British representative in Grenada, with his wife. Kelly, a former trade union official who had got on well with the Bishop regime, gave the distinct impression he was none too happy with the arrival of the U.S. military. He had expended much effort establishing a good working relationship with the PRG and had even grown a Bishop-type beard (now hastily shaved off), so he followed the British attitude at the time in condemning the intervention. It was his wife, although Kelly himself must have known, who approached Hartland and Tomlin with exciting information.

She indicated a European man sitting in a corner who, she said, knew the whereabouts of Austin and two others staying in a house at Westerhall. When the officers approached, the man pretended he was drunk and could not speak good English, but Tomlin persevered until after some two hours it became clear that the man was Jonas. He had indeed been contacted by Austin. And yes, he was to secure a yacht to take them to Guyana. Austin, Layne, and James were at that moment waiting for him at Westerhall.

In the hope of saving his own skin, Jonas agreed to go to Salines and cooperate in a plan to capture Austin. Tomlin duly took him to Lewis, and together a scheme was agreed. The yacht would be hired and sailed around to Westerhall by Tomlin with Jonas, plus three or four U.S. soldiers concealed below. On arrival, Jonas would go ashore in a small boat to persuade Austin that all was well and that they could start their voyage to Guyana. Jonas was to get them to wrap up their weapons in plastic sheets against the water and put them at the bottom of the boat. He would row them toward the yacht, but about halfway he was to lose an oar and then jump overboard to retrieve it. This would be the signal for the soldiers and Tomlin to throw stun grenades and cover the fugitives, calling on them to surrender. If they declined, they were to be shot.

This plan was accepted by Lewis and Crist, but it had to have Trobaugh's agreement (map 23). In civilian clothes, Tomlin walked across to TF 121's command post in the terminal. After a long wait, he explained what had happened and how they intended to capture Austin. Trobaugh was initially unenthusiastic, declaring it could not be done. He had no Special Forces people; who did they propose to take? Trobaugh looked around the room saying, in effect, "Any of you guys want to go on this crazy scheme?" The first man to volunteer was Trobaugh's aide, Captain Robert Hoidahl, who claimed Special Forces training, and he mentioned others. Trobaugh gave the go-ahead. The U.S. team consisted of Hoidahl, a lieutenant, and two senior noncommissioned officers.

By 4:30 P.M. they were all, including Jonas, back at the marina, having been to Gorman's house again because he had radio contact with the *Guam*, and it was necessary to explain the presence and purpose of the yacht sailing out of Prickly Bay. The owner agreed to give them the yacht, and her boyfriend took them to it, insisting that there was plenty of fuel onboard.

At 5:00 P.M., just after the Rangers had landed at Calivigny, they set sail. There was a lot of wind with quite a heavy sea running. On deck in T-shirts were Tomlin at the helm, an extremely anxious-looking Jonas, and one soldier; the other three were out of sight below. The journey would be about 7 miles, around Prickly Point, south of Calivigny Island and Fort Jeudy Point, then north around Westerhall Point into the calmer water of Westerhall Bay.

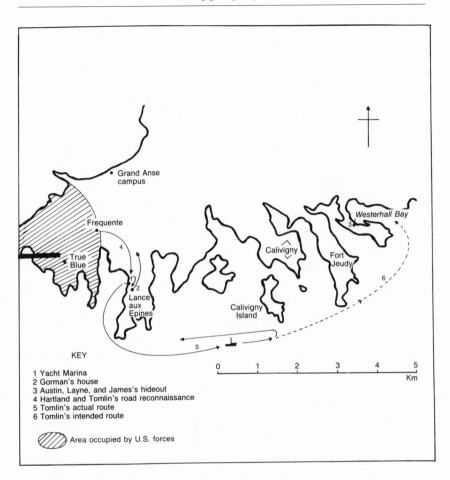

Map 23. LIEUTENANT COMMANDER TOMLIN'S PLANNED
CAPTURE OF GENERAL AUSTIN

Despite deteriorating sea conditions that brought a lot of spray,
they maintained 6 or 7 knots. Just before Calivigny Island, disaster
struck: the engine died; no fuel was left. The yacht started to swing
toward the rocks as Tomlin, the only sailor among them, yelled instructions to hoist the sails. Even with the sail up, the stiff easterly
wind prevented any further progress. Reluctantly Tomlin brought the
boat around to head back the way they had come. The weather
worsened, making handling the yacht difficult and exhausting. It was

well after dark when they finally limped back to the marina. They all spent the night at Gorman's house.

The following morning Tomlin was determined to try again, but Jonas was concerned to get back to Austin to reassure him that a boat was being arranged. Staff at the command post gave him a letter to get him through U.S. roadblocks, so he set off. When he returned, it was to confirm that Austin, Layne, and James were still there and suspected nothing. At this stage, it might have been a lot simpler to drive to the vicinity of the house, surround it on foot, and call for a surrender.

Tomlin had spent the morning collecting diesel fuel, going over to speak briefly with Metcalf who had come ashore to meet Trobaugh, and generally getting organized for a repeat performance that afternoon. But it was not to be. Trobaugh returned to his headquarters to announce the operation was off. It was too dangerous; it should be a Special Forces' mission, and he was withdrawing his men. Tomlin and Jonas were told to await the arrival of the Special Forces team. They did not arrive that day, although a German-speaking CIA interrogator did. He proceeded to take over Jonas.

A Special Forces group arrived on October 29, and Tomlin briefed them at the terminal. They required permission from their own JSOC headquarters. Without this, they claimed, they could do nothing because they could not afford to take any more casualties after Tuesday's disasters. When Tomlin returned later, it was to be told that their headquarters considered it too dangerous, too risky, so the operation was definitely off. The CIA removed Jonas. It was to be another twenty-four hours before Austin and his companions were captured, but not by the Special Forces, after sitting undisturbed in their house for five full days.

‡   ‡   ‡

On October 28 Admiral McDonald attended a Defense Department news conference in Washington. Officials were now saying 1,100 Cubans were fighting in Grenada, and the admiral announced that 638 of them were prisoners at Salines. So where were the remainder? McDonald replied: "I think they're going back into the hills. They're fighting a delaying action or they're taking us on to defend the military areas that they have been assigned to. As those places are being overrun—I would say with restraint of force—they are disappearing into the mountains."

Cuban captives had exaggerated their own numbers, inexperienced troops exaggerated the resistance they encountered, intelligence staffs just could not seem to read the battle, and the early failures, together with the subsequent snaillike advance in the south, combined to convince U.S. senior commanders that the opposition must be much larger and stronger than was initially anticipated. Reality was that serious opposition had ceased two days before.

Most of the mopping up had to be done in the north, where Donigan's E Company 2d/8th BLT had been left on their own since the early hours of October 26. After a day spent seizing arms caches pointed out to them by friendly locals, E Company was ordered to reconnoiter into the Mt. Horne area on October 27. Donigan assembled a mobile column, with a platoon in jeeps, and trucks or flatbeds contributed by Grenadians, together with two TOW jeeps and some Dragon antitank detachments. They filled up with fuel captured at Pearls before moving out, climbing steadily as the road approached the Mt. Horne agricultural station. Nobody impeded progress. At the station, they discovered the abandoned command post of the PRA's Military Region 2, complete with radios, maps, documents, and other military equipment.

They were now on the edge of the mountainous interior of the island. Towering above them was the massive Mt. St. Catherine feature, with a peak of 2,757 feet. It was jungle covered, with the higher ridges often hidden by cloud. The marines had no proper maps, but they could see it was wilderness country, ideal as a sanctuary for any determined PRA or Cubans. Grenadians at Mt. Horne urged them to investigate the precipitous, twisting track that led up to the cable and wireless station, perched 2,000 feet above sea level on a summit some 1,500 meters east of Mt. St. Catherine. Up there, they said, some PRA might be found.

Donigan agreed to give it a try, although his small force would be confined to the track, vulnerable to ambush every meter of the way. In the event, they struggled to the top with a few vehicles without incident. Just as they came up the final ridge, several PRA, carrying what was thought to be a mortar, were seen scurrying away. The marines opened fire through driving rain but did not appear to inflict any casualties. Nobody shot at them, but a search revealed some discarded mortar and antitank rounds.

The return was worse in the rain. The steep track became doubly treacherous. Eventually the inevitable happened: a TOW jeep, with its trailer, jackknifed and overturned. Both the driver and passenger were injured and needed a medical evacuation, which was impossible by helicopter in the poor visibility and difficult terrain. The two were put on makeshift stretchers on a flatbed truck for the remainder of the journey down the mountain. The schoolyard at the tiny village of Paraclete provided a usable landing zone, so the company's forward air controller called in a CH-46 to fly out the casualties. The rest returned to Pearls without further incident.

The next day, after another road reconnaissance had accidentally arrived on the outskirts of Sauteurs without encountering any enemy, Donigan sought permission to take the town. Before his request could be granted, the battalion command post received information of a possible large arms cache at Mirabeau hospital, about 1 kilometer southwest of Mt. Horne Estate. That afternoon Donigan set out again with a platoon-sized force, but the cave, pointed out to them by the local people as the arms cache, was empty. The marines, now on foot, decided to search the area of the hospital itself, which was on top of a ridge above them. Leaving a squad with the vehicles, Donigan led the remainder up the slope, well spread out and moving carefully. As they neared the crest, the dense vegetation gave way to a banana plantation, and a suspicious-looking civilian carrying coconuts was detained to prevent him from giving any alarm. As the leading marine reached the top, he halted, pointing silently with his rifle at three men standing by a Land Rover. Somebody shouted, "Freeze!" The three exchanged some hurried words and then ran. Marines opened fire, knocking over two men, but the third escaped through a house. Both casualties were wounded—one, who died later, badly. They were subsequently identified as Cubans.[1]

At about the same time, the squad with the vehicles was shot at from an unknown number of enemy. Fire was returned into the gathering darkness, but within a few minutes, all was quiet. There were no casualties. As Donigan, who had heard the firing, started to withdraw from the hospital area back toward the vehicles, his group received fire from the ridgeline. Heavy fire from rifles, machine guns, and a LAW rocket was directed at seven or eight men above them. The marines were unscathed again, but it is likely they inflicted some casualties on the enemy. Donigan then returned to the airfield.

On October 29, the 2d/8th BLT took several important prisoners. In the south in St. George's, the capture of Coard, his wife, and Strachan coincided with a visit of Metcalf, who came ashore that day to see the marines. Once more it was fellow Grenadians who tipped off the troops as to their hiding place, but this time it was the marine gunners of H Battery who secured them. Acting quickly on the information, Captain Bradley Gates's men surrounded the house on the outskirts of the town. Using a bullhorn, Sergeant Michael Thrussell yelled for them to come out. Nothing. Another shout. Still no response. Finally, "Come out or we will blow the place up." Reluctantly, slowly, with hands on his head, Strachan emerged into the sunlight, followed by Phyllis Coard with her two children, and finally the flabby figure of Coard himself. Down in the dirt, they were forced to lie while they were searched and secured with handcuffs. Thousands of dollars in cash were found on Phyllis, but what plans they had, if any, to escape the island remain a mystery.

Grenadians gathered to watch. Soon a crowd had assembled, jeering and taunting. "C for Coard, Cuba, and Communism"; "Give us Phyllis, we'll deal with Phyllis"; and at Queen's Park where the captives were taken to be flown out to the *Guam*, a man screamed for Coard: "We want to take him apart, piece by piece."

Meanwhile back at Pearls, an informant had indicated the house in Grenville where 2d Lieutenant George, the commander of region 2 and the nonexistent PRM battalion, was hiding. Lieutenant Rand Hammel's platoon had no difficulty in securing George, who was a mine of information on the PRM units that were supposed to be defending Sauteurs. Approval was given to take Sauteurs on the afternoon of October 29, but E Company did not leave Pearls until 3:30 A.M. the next day. One platoon remained at the airfield, while the rest of the company deployed for the attack. Donigan's plan envisaged dividing his force into three groups. The first would be the 81-mm mortar platoon, which was to take up a position off the road on the high ridge near Mt. Rose, about 3,000 meters south of the town. From there the mortars could support the attack if necessary and act as a radio relay station as communications were problematic in the hilly terrain. Another group, known as Team Mike, was tasked with securing the PRA Camp Villa, at the end of a 300-meter track east of Sauteurs. The rest of the company would clear the town itself. By 5:15 Team Mike radioed that they had taken Camp Villa with no opposition.

Donigan drove to the edge of the town, dismounted, and advanced into the deserted streets. Sauteurs awoke to American occupation.

Most citizens were cooperative, particularly when the marines started to give U.S. ration packs to hungry people. More PRM soldiers were identified, including another officer, Major Bartholomew, who surrendered quietly. Information led to further finds of weapons and ammunition. Donigan's medical corpsman was called to assist a Grenadian woman who was hemorrhaging badly after giving birth. A helicopter medical evacuation was needed urgently, but once again radio communications failed at a crucial moment. To get a helicopter from the *Guam* required the request to go from Sauteurs to Mt. Rose (the mortars), to Pearls, to the *Trenton*, and then to the *Guam*. The link between the *Trenton* and the *Guam* was not working. The unfortunate woman's condition worsened. In desperation Captain Thomas Davis, the forward air controller, put out a general call on the helicopter's frequency. Finally, at 8:45 P.M. a CH-46 arrived at the improvised landing zone lit by jeep headlights. The woman recovered, but it was a close call. It had taken nearly three hours to get her out.

While E Company was winning the hearts and minds of the population of Sauteurs, their comrades in G Company were moving on the two remaining unoccupied towns in the north, Gouyave and Victoria. Although the Caribbean Peacekeeping Force had moved into St. George's on October 28, with a platoon going to Pearls the next day to take over some security duties from the marines, Smith felt he could spare only one company for the drive up the west coast. Nevertheless, Dobson's men were well supported; at 3:30 P.M. on October 30, the column of armored amphibious vehicles, with the marines, wriggled its way northward from Queen's Park. Above them flew a command and control UH-1 to act as a radio relay link and two TOW helicopters for close support. Just offshore two utility landing craft carrying two tanks kept station, and naval aircraft and gunfire were on call if required. Nothing barred their progress, except just south of Gouyave, where the road passes between the sea and high cliffs, a ditch had been dug. Rather foolishly, those who made the ditch had left their bulldozer nearby, so the column was not delayed for long. A platoon was left in Gouyave while the rest of the company continued to Victoria, arriving unopposed at about 7:00 P.M.

The night of October 30–31 saw the 2d/8th BLT spread even more thinly than usual around the island. F Company was at St. George's with H-Battery and the battalion command post, while G Company had a platoon in Gouyave and the remainder in Victoria. E Company was at Sauteurs, except for one platoon still at Pearls. The marines occupied almost two-thirds of the coastline of Grenada. But they still had another mission before they could resume their interrupted journey to Lebanon: the northern island of Carriacou, Military Region 4, Abdullah's old stamping ground.

Again rumors abounded. PRA units, even North Korean soldiers, were possibly garrisoning the island; more were said to be escaping from the mainland to make a last stand. Metcalf ordered the marines to make a combined surface and air assault just before dawn on November 1, exactly a week since they had landed at Pearls.

The last day of October was spent in planning and preparation. All the scattered marine units had to be reembarked on their ships and briefed for the attack. This occupied the whole day, so it was not until nearly 8:00 P.M. that the ships could start sailing toward the island. The main village, Hillsborough, is located about halfway up the western coast of the 15-kilometer-long island. Three kilometers southwest of Hillsborough is the light aircraft strip at Lauriston Point; the PRA headquarters was at Belair Estate, 2 kilometers northeast of the village, on a hill.

The marines planned for F Company to make a heliborne landing on the airfield, while G Company came ashore over the beach at Tyrrel Bay. H hour for both companies was 5:30 A.M., with a SEAL team having gone ashore in the Lauriston Point area at 3:00 A.M. to check out any defenses. After the landings, F Company would advance into Hillsborough, while G Company made for the suspected PRA base at Belair Estate.

All went smoothly. The people of Carriacou were delighted to see the marines; it was even suggested to Smith that the U.S. flag be raised to announce that the island belonged to the United States. The nineteen PRA soldiers turned out in civilian clothes to surrender. Smith paroled them all, telling them to report back next morning. A football match was arranged, and the kids had a grand time climbing all over the helicopters. At 7:00 A.M. on November 2, elements of the 82d started arriving to relieve the marines and take into custody the PRA troops who had dutifully paraded as ordered.

By late afternoon 22d MAU was once again on its way to the Mediterranean.

‡ ‡ ‡

October 28 was a great day for the Rangers. Both battalions boarded C-141 aircraft at Salines to fly home. At Hunter Army Airfield on October 29, they touched down exactly a week after first being alerted for an exercise. They were tired but jubilant after three days of intense operations, during which they had been used for most of the risky or potentially dangerous tasks. It was the Rangers who had escorted the Special Operations Forces inside the bullet-riddled helicopters on D day, seized Salines, secured True Blue campus, assaulted Grand Anse, and finally attacked Camp Calivigny. That things had gone wrong— that vital tactical information was faulty, that communications were often impossible—was not the fault of the Rangers. They had led the way and performed their duty admirably. Like all of the other troops during the first few days, they had had their share of luck, particularly on D day when their prolonged daylight drop could have been a disaster but for Castro's explicit orders to his construction workers. Between the two battalions, they had carried out four battalion-sized operations with the loss of ten dead (five accidentally) and ten seriously injured (five accidentally). These figures exclude several who died and others who were wounded in the attempted attack on the prison. In military terms, the losses were extremely light. With hindsight, we know what was happening in the other camp, that the Cubans were not professional soldiers, and the PRA resistance had crumbled by the second day. But this was not apparent to the Rangers. To them the Calivigny assault had the makings of a suicide mission.

As they descended from the first C-141, to music from the band of the 24th Infantry Division and the welcoming smile of the army chief of staff, General John Wickham, the Rangers were proud men. Wickham pinned several combat infantry badges on Rangers, picked to represent the others in the battalions who had also qualified.

On the morning of October 28, the leading platoon of Hamilton's 2d/325th moved carefully along the coastal road from Grand Anse toward St. George's. The platoon commander was unaware of the locations of any of the marines in the town and did not have radio contact with them. Suddenly up ahead was a roadblock. After some hesitation and confusion, they realized that it was not the PRA but marines—F Company. They had reached the Ross Point Inn. The linkup between TF 121 and TF 124 had at last been achieved.

On Friday Trobaugh got the remainder of his infantry reinforcements. At around 11:00 A.M. Lieutenant Colonel Keith Nightengale's 2d/505th flew in, followed late that night by the 2d/508th under Lieutenant Colonel Ralph Newman. Trobaugh now had two brigades, each of three battalions, with which to consolidate the U.S. hold on Grenada. For another four days, there would also be the marines, but they never came under Trobaugh's command. By that evening little progress had been made on the ground in the southwest. Scott's headquarters was near the Sugar Mill, and Crocker's 1st/505th had occupied the Lance aux Epines peninsula, discovering, almost four days after the landings at Salines, over 200 more U.S. citizens still awaiting "rescue." Many of them had had a grandstand view of the Rangers' descent on Tuesday morning from their houses only 2,000 meters east of the runway.

Arrangements were made during that day to evacuate these students, and others, by Black Hawk helicopters to Salines and then back to the United States. All appeared happy to go; the only person showing some strain was the Libyan ambassador, who was dashing around among the students trying to ensure none of his own staff got aboard the helicopters to defect. In the end, the official count of persons evacuated was 662 U.S. citizens and 82 foreigners. Even then, 21 others were overlooked and never left the island.

During the day, a PRA informant told Raines that Bishop had been buried at Calivigny. A team was later guided to the spot and excavations carried out. There was not much left to put in the black plastic bags; Abdullah had done his gruesome task thoroughly. Charred bones, some tissue, clothing associated with Creft, and personal effects of the Bains and Maitland were sifted from the soil. Of Bishop nothing could be identified; indeed the investigators claimed that none of the remains was consistent with a man well over six feet tall. More mysterious still, no traces of heads or hands could be found, and there appeared to have been only five bodies in the pit, not nine.[2]

It was not until October 29, perhaps as a result of Trobaugh's visit to the *Guam* on that day, that the 82d exerted themselves sufficiently to probe beyond the confines of the southwestern toe of the island (map 24). Searches were made of the Mt. Hartman Estate and the Egmont (Calivigny) area, but it was left to the new arrivals, the 2d/508th, to make the major effort of the day. A reconnaissance in force took them as far east as the village of Crochu, only 1,500 meters

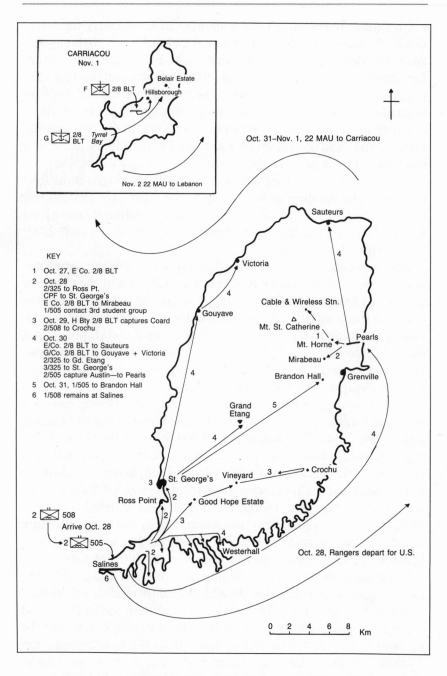

Map 24. MOPPING UP, OCTOBER 27–NOVEMBER 2

from the sea. There was confusion at the start because Newman was expecting to be accompanied by some of the marines' M-60 tanks, but quite why they were thought necessary on that tortuous road across the island over the hills is uncertain. Had they gone with the infantry, progress would have been reduced to a crawl, but they did not. Somebody came up with the idea, quite rightly, that the small bridges might not take their weight. Then the planned route would take the force over the boundary into the marines' area of responsibility, and there was some argument before this was accepted.

Mounted on loaned Grenadian trucks and U.S. vehicles, the column from 2d/508th made remarkable progress in comparison with the previous four days. First they uncovered the alternative supply dump that the PRA had tried to establish at Good Hope Estate (near Corbeau). Here were five trucks packed with ammunition, with another seven loads dumped on the ground. They continued eastward through village after village, meeting no resistance whatsoever; the people were delighted to wave them on or even to provide more vehicles if any with the force broke down. St. Pauls, Vineyard, Vincennes, Thebaide, Pomme Rose, and finally Crochu, 18 kilometers across the breadth of the island; it was the farthest single advance of the entire operation.

On Sunday, October 30, General Vessey and Admiral McDonald arrived in Grenada. Although outwardly cheerful and smiling as he drove around St. George's, Vessey was disappointed with Trobaugh and the 82d for the slowness of their operations. Three and a half days to advance 5 kilometers against a few snipers was not very impressive, even if they had lacked vehicles initially.[3] Vessey pushed Trobaugh to get moving. Grand Etang, up in the mountains, was said to be a PRA base with stockpiles of arms and equipment. If Cubans and Grenadians were making for the hills, why was Grand Etang still unsecured? Trobaugh sent Hamilton with the 2d/325th. It is a beautiful drive northeast from St. George's, the road snaking through tiny villages, with quaint names like Snug Corner, until after about 8 kilometers there is a stiff climb up onto the watershed, the pass over the mountains, by Grand Etang lake. It is halfway to Grenville. Like the 2d/508th farther south the day before, Hamilton's men were unopposed and found little except an abandoned APC and some suspicious tunnels. The battalion remained in the Grand Etang area for the night.

In the south the 82d was also on the move, this time to the Fort Jeudy peninsula and Westerhall Point. Jonas had been questioned by the CIA and revealed the location of Austin's hideout. He was required to play the role of Judas again, to lead in C Company 2d/505th. At around 3:30 P.M. after some confusion as to which house to surround, the paratroopers cordoned the area, and Jonas shouted to Austin to come out. Agitated voices were heard inside, and after a short pause, the RMC's leadership trio emerged, betrayed by an East German anxious to save his own skin. Instead of boarding a yacht for Guyana, Austin, Layne, and James went by truck and helicopter to the brig on the *Guam.*

October 31 saw the marines reembarking onto their ships in preparation for the Carriacou landings and subsequent departure from Grenada, leaving the island to the 82d and the Caribbean Peacekeeping Force. While the latter concentrated on policing and security duties in St. George's, the paratroopers continued to conduct searches or arrest PRA suspects for interrogation. On November 2, as the marines sailed for the Mediterranean, hostilities were declared over. The next day Metcalf's TF 120 was disestablished, and operational control of all U.S. forces in Grenada passed to Trobaugh, as commander, U.S. Forces Grenada.

‡   ‡   ‡

The sledgehammer had crushed the nut. At what cost? The Cubans had 24 killed in combat, another 59 wounded, and 602 unwounded prisoners were repatriated to Cuba over a period of four days, starting on November 4—this, from a total of 784 Cubans on the island at the start of Urgent Fury, 44 of them women. Of the dead, only two were professional soldiers: 49-year-old Captain Erico Grandales Nolasco, a transportation specialist, and 1st Lieutenant Oscar Nunez Gil, an infantry officer of 30.

The Grenadians suffered the most. Their military casualties have never been separated accurately from civilian ones. An estimated 67 died, including 17 in the bombing of the mental hospital and another boy accidentally shot by a U.S. serviceman with his pistol sometime later. The figure of 358 has been suggested as the total wounded or injured, but its accuracy has not been verified.

The Caribbean Peacekeeping Force suffered no losses or injuries.

Over the American casualties, controversy still reigns while the number of Special Operations Forces men killed or wounded remains a closely guarded secret. It was announced that 18 U.S. servicemen had been killed one way or another, but this was increased to 19 with the death of Luketina in hospital. The two Ranger pathfinders' deaths, when their parachutes failed to open, have never been officially acknowledged. Regrettably over half of these (ten) were the result of parachute accidents, helicopter crashes, or, in one case, dying from friendly fire. At first the official figure for wounded or injured was 115. Some months later, when this did not fit with the number of Purple Hearts awarded, it was upped to 152. A high proportion of these were accidental injuries rather than combat inflicted, and at least 16 were the result of the strafing of Silvasy's command post. The final higher count for the wounded includes 20 to 30 Special Operations Forces and C Company 1st/75th personnel.

The mopping-up phase of Urgent Fury involved prolonged searching of people and houses, followed in many instances by arrest and interrogation. Hundreds of suspects were rounded up, mainly on information provided by fellow Grenadians, and sent to an improvised detention center run by the 82d's military police at Salines. Nelson described how after his arrest at his home on November 13, he was sent to Salines and forced to crawl into a large wooden packing case through a small hatch. It was one of ten such boxes, each about 8 feet in length, height, and width, which were used to confine more important prisoners before questioning. There was nothing inside except for a piece of foam to lie on, and there Nelson remained for two days, except when he wished to go to the toilet. By November 15, the initial screening of prisoners was complete, so the center was closed. All the detainees who were likely to face charges were handed over to Caribbean Peacekeeping Force authorities at Richmond Hill Prison, by then reopened to receive PRG and PRA guests.

The searching revealed thousands of weapons and tons of ammunition, much of it stacked up in the warehouses at Frequente but some in dumps or caches of various sizes all over the island. Such finds were well publicized as evidence to prove to the world how militarized Grenada had become.

Had the planned deliveries for the period 1983–1986 ever been made, the stocks of weapons, which would have included GRAD P rocket launchers and over 50 APCs, would have been horrendous. As it was, the amount of arms secured by the United States was not nearly as alarming as the postintervention publicity made out. U.S. Army inventories made in November 1983 and two months later vary wildly. In November, 9,825 rifles of various types are listed; in January, the figure falls, inexplicably, to 4,068. With 82-mm mortars, the November record shows 10, while the later one jumps to 20. With ZU-23 AA guns, the number drops from 12 in November to 10 in January. Even taking the highest figures to be nearest the mark, the result is not overwhelmingly impressive: 10,000 rifles, many of them antiquated or reconditioned, a handful of medium mortars, and the equivalent of two batteries of long-outdated AA guns. The PRA and Cubans can hardly be described as well armed in comparison with the troops sent against them. As far as weapons are concerned, the president was correct when he said, "We got there just in time." Two years later, it would have been a different story. Similarly, huge stocks of documents were seized for analysis. Never before had a Western power been given such access to the secret workings of a communist state through its own papers. It was a rich haul, eventually made available to public scrutiny as the Grenada Papers.

The searching gave rise to numerous allegations of looting. There is no doubt that looting occurred, but how extensively or who was to blame has never been acknowledged. One of the first instances was in the Cuban workers' barrack rooms at the old camp. Each room was systematically ransacked for cash, valuables, and souvenirs. Bags and suitcases were ripped apart, drawers forced open, cupboards smashed. The debris of personal effects, clothes, and papers covered the floors in room after room; nothing was untouched. Who was responsible? The Rangers had been through the area early on the morning of October 25, but they were involved in combat and had no time for the thorough and deliberate looting that occurred. The next troops into the area were Caribbean units of the Jamaica Defence Force and others, but the culprits have never been officially established.

Shops, particularly in St. George's, suffered, but here the looters were Grenadians helping themselves to valuables or food during the chaos of the days following the start of the operation. There were several complaints by Grenadians that items such as watches or jewelry disappeared after U.S. troops had searched an area. But this is an old trick and one that a number of Grenadians were quick to learn. Two instances, however, are more specific and more serious.

First, Lady Scoon had all her jewelry stolen from Government House. It disappeared after she and Sir Paul had been rescued and taken to the *Guam*. In this instance, there was ample opportunity for civilians, marines, or Caribbean troops. When the theft was discovered, it was too late and too difficult to investigate. Then there was the statement of Specialist 4 Arthur Brogden, who described a soldier of the 82d finding two large diamonds in a house near the Cuban embassy, later valued in the United States at over $30,000. Specialist 4 Joseph Rizzi recalled, "As we moved out, I witnessed soldiers literally destroy houses, stealing all kinds of stuff, mostly from people who had retired from England and different parts of the world." He was referring to the many empty bungalows along the south coast, on peninsulas such as Westerhall.

These instances are only one side of the coin. Most troops were remarkably well behaved, and the hundreds of soldiers who, after stopping and searching a Grenadian, allowed him to go on his way with the phrase "Have a nice day" did a great deal for the military's public image. General Jack Farris, who took over as commander of the U.S. forces on the island from Trobaugh in early November, cites a revealing incident. He was approached by a Grenadian woman after church one day; she showed him a note that she wanted to frame in her house. According to the general it read: "Sorry we had to bust your door down. We walked your dog. We cleared up his mess in the kitchen. We used your stove to heat up our C-rations. Have a nice day. First Squad, Third Platoon, A Company, 505th Infantry." This sort of behavior was by far the more common, and those Grenadians who suffered damage and could substantiate it afterward as having been done by the U.S. forces were paid a generous compensation in cash.

Far more prevalent than looting, in its strict sense of theft of valuables, was hunting for military souvenirs, particularly weapons. From time immemorial, soldiers have sought to take home something from a battlefield to show their children or grandchildren in years to come; the Americans and Caribbean troops in Grenada were no exception. The favorites were Makarov pistols and AK-47 assault rifles. The Barbados Defence Force took back several; one of them polished and mounted for display, hangs in Brigadier General Lewis's office. Another, suitably inscribed, was presented to the prime minister, Tom Adams. But the Americans have a law against this sort of thing. Federal law and military regulations forbid the importation of automatic weapons, which is what AKs are. A lot of such weapons got back into the United States, but some soldiers were caught, court-martialed, and imprisoned. A captain was dismissed and sentenced to a year in jail; a staff sergeant was dismissed with nine months in prison; a sergeant was dismissed with two years' imprisonment; and at least two soldiers and two marines suffered similar fates. They were stiff sentences.

Despite these somewhat draconian examples, Vice-Admiral Metcalf was only cautioned when he and his staff were caught bringing weapons into the country. The incident was reported in the press as follows:

> According to officials at the U.S. Customs Service, 24 AK-47 assault rifles captured in Grenada were seized on November 3rd from Vice Admiral Joseph Metcalf and several senior aides at the Norfolk Naval Air Station in Virginia. Customs officials turned the arms over to the Naval Investigative Service. A Navy spokesman, Capt. Brent Baker, said Thursday that Metcalf had ''been cautioned regarding the capture and disposition of enemy weapons following a battle. . . .'' The Navy considers the matter closed.

Metcalf was later promoted to deputy chief of operations for surface warfare.

16

Reaction, Rewards, and Retribution

It was the first time ever I was glad to see Americans.
— A British schoolteacher on Grenada

THE scene shifts eastward by 6,000 miles to Angola, where 36,000 Cuban troops are the backbone of the Marxist MPLA in its endless bush war against the guerrilla armies of Jonas Savimbi. It is a war that Cuba is not winning and is a constant drain on its manpower and resources. It is highly unpopular with the troops sent there, a dangerous, exhausting, and frustrating campaign against an elusive and effective enemy. Many thousands of Cubans have been killed or crippled in Angola. Had Salines Airport ever been completed under Bishop, Cubana airliners moving troops to and from Africa would have refueled there.

In 1986 a mixed MPLA and Cuban convoy of trucks, armored vehicles, and infantry was probing into the wild, hilly, central interior of the country, seeking to corner some of Savimbi's forces. It moved along a track in an extended column cautiously, for this was part of the country over which the MPLA had lost control. It was advancing through terrain that provided countless ambush opportunities. On this occasion, the attack, when it came, was pressed home; the firing was heavy, catching the trucks and troops at a disadvantage. The MPLA and Cubans had to fight hard to extract themselves. There were a number of killed and wounded. One of the bodies, lying dead in the dust, belonged to a 41-year-old private soldier named Pedro Tortolo Comas.

Tortolo had returned home to Havana on November 5, by no means certain of his reception. He was too old a hand to be taken in by the communiqué on his actions that had been read over the radio to the Cuban people on the evening of November 1. The very fact that some official explanation of his performance was considered necessary was ominous. He had, after all, survived, had not been taken prisoner, and he had left his command post before the final surrender to seek sanctuary in the Soviet embassy. The public announcement stated:

Communique by the Government of Cuba concerning the situation of Colonel Pedro Tortolo, November 1, 1983.

Colonel Tortolo, who led the heroic resistance at the last line of defense of the Cuban construction workers and collaborators, is alive. Tortolo, with a handful of men on October 26, left the rubble of his command post in the main installation of the last Cuban position, which was totally destroyed, and broke through the U.S. encirclement until he reached a point where they made contact with members of the Cuban Embassy.

Our Embassy, considering that he had honorably fulfilled his duty to fight heroically against the overwhelmingly superior forces without surrendering to the enemy; that all organized resistance was already impossible; that it was equally impossible to move on towards the mountains to continue fighting as was his aim, since all roads were blocked; and because the precise instructions received were to fight in the areas of work and dormitories if they were attacked; and wishing to save the lives of these valuable fighters, they were ordered to proceed to the site of the representation of a friendly country, located near where they were. There, Tortolo sought and obtained diplomatic protection for them.

For various reasons, it was not considered convenient to disclose this information until now.

On the evening of his arrival, Tortolo was required to give an extensive press conference, which was televised throughout the country. Dozens of foreign media representatives were present, and Tortolo was subjected to a barrage of questions following his version of what had happened. After extolling the heroic behavior of the construction workers, he accounted for the retreat to the embassy:

Everyone was of the conviction there that no one would surrender and the entire collective fought in that spirit. Comrades died; there were those wounded; they took prisoners and forced us to disperse, breaking the U.S. encirclement when it was impossible to hold out any longer.

When we learned through the Soviet Ambassador that we would go with them, it was a painful moment. We talked with the group that was there, and the first thing that came to our minds were the comarades who would not be returning with us: we asked for a minute's silence and sang our national anthem. We all began to cry; we felt very deeply for those who had been much more valiant than ourselves, for those who gave their lives in defense of the honor and principles of the homeland and of the Revolution.

Despite these pronouncements, Castro was far from satisfied with the military's performance in Grenada once the fighting had started. Only 2 of the 43 army personnel had been killed and 7 wounded. The dead were a middle-aged transportation captain and a reservist 1st lieutenant; four of the wounded were lieutenant colonels, hit by the bombardment of the Little Havana mission headquarters. There had been too many early surrenders (250 by late afternoon of October 25); the military leadership had not been effective in stiffening the workers' resolve. The United States had not been made to pay a sufficiently high price for invasion and the collapse of the Grenadian revolution.

Tortolo, a highly trained senior officer, had not remained with his men to the last. Cuban military honor was in question; a commanding officer must take the responsibility. But any action, any disciplinary proceedings, must not be hurried. Time must elapse to allow some of the public heat to evaporate from the Grenada debacle. After some months, Colonel Tortolo, together with most of the other military officers, was court-martialed. Found guilty of dereliction of duty, Tortolo was reduced to the rank of private and posted to Angola. He never returned.

After hostilities ceased, there was a lot of wrangling among the U.S. authorities, the Cubans, and the International Red Cross concerning the repatriation of Cuban personnel and dead bodies. With American prompting, Sir Paul Scoon announced that all Cuban diplomatic staff must leave Grenada within twenty-four hours. Their embassy was surrounded by U.S. troops on the evening of November 1, with nobody permitted to enter or leave. At a meeting on the following morning between Rizo and Gillespie, who had been designated the U.S. ambassador on the island, the Cubans refused to leave until the repatriation of all their citizens had been completed—a not-unreasonable attitude. Their note stated that the only way the United States could get them out was with the use of force. They also sought information on the number of prisoners, wounded, and dead. Rizo wanted to visit the captives, together with the graves of those killed, for identification purposes. At this stage, the U.S. officials were unwilling or unable to answer the queries, and they permitted no visits.

One of the problems was that the Cubans killed in the fighting had been buried hastily in a makeshift grave with no proper registration or attempt at identification. Some bodies were put in plastic bags and some were not, and they shared the grave with a number of PRA dead. It was not until November 10 that exhumation began in the presence of the Red Cross and a Cuban official. The task was most unpleasant; more than two weeks had passed since they had died. The Cubans were not allowed to make identifications in Grenada. As the corpses were brought up, the Cuban representative protested that several bodies were in PRA olive green uniforms and therefore must be Grenadians because the Cubans had fought in civilian clothes. It made no difference; all thirty-seven were flown to Barbados the next day. Arrangements that had been made to carry out proper identification in Barbados fell through when the government there refused permission. A Cubana plane took them home the next day.

With the living, arrangements were easier. The first group allowed out under the supervision of the Red Cross were the sick and wounded. Fifty-seven of them, accompanied by ten Cuban medical staff who had been working on the island, flew out to Barbados on November 2. There they transferred to a Swiss plane, with Red Cross markings, for the final flight home. Only about 300 Cubans were at the José Marti airport at Havana—the public had been discouraged from attending—although the official welcome included Castro, in army fatigues, his brother, Raul, the General Staff band, and an eighty-four man ceremonial guard of honor, together with a fleet of ambulances.

Castro made no formal speech but greeted each person with a handshake or a touch and a few words. The first man off was in his forties, wearing soiled blue jeans rolled up over a wounded leg. The rest followed, some on stretchers, one old man in his sixties sitting in a wheelchair, while others walked. They looked tired, dazed, and dirty.

Some were shirtless; some had arms in slings. One was a woman with a limp. None had any personal luggage—only what they stood up in. They were all put on the ambulances and driven past the guard of honor to the hospital where their families were waiting.

Between November 4 and 8, the diplomats and the prisoners left Grenada. The band and guard of honor were kept busy receiving each planeload as it arrived in Cuba, Castro heading each official welcome. The first man to disembark was an agricultural worker, Luis Rosales Rivero, who came down the steps proudly holding up a small Cuban flag. He had managed to conceal it on his person despite several searches; now he presented it to Castro.

A decree announcing five days of national mourning was issued from the Palace of the Revolution on November 13. This was for the Cuban dead, who were to be given full military honors, including a lying in state of the coffins in Havana. Flags were at half-mast; all public entertainment was suspended. Before any ceremonies could begin, however, the Cubans had to be identified and separated from the Grenadians. To permit this, the flight bringing the thirty-seven bodies landed at the city of Holguin, not Havana. There thirteen Grenadians were identified, and General Raul Castro made a lengthy speech in their honor. They were provided with coffins, draped in the Grenadian flag, and placed under guard for the public to see before arrangements were made to return them to their own country.

The culminating ceremony for the twenty-four dead Cubans was held in Revolution Square, Havana, on November 14. The highlight was the address given by Castro, bareheaded and in uniform. It was a lengthy speech, with much vilification of U.S. imperialists—Reagan in particular. Castro dwelt on the murder of Bishop and Cuba's aversion to the RMC. He recalled: "Our relations with Austin's short-lived government, in which Coard was really in charge, were cold and tense, so that, at the time of the criminal Yankee aggression, there was no coordination whatsoever between the Grenadian Army and the Cuban construction workers." He regarded (correctly as it turned out) the Americans' public preoccupation with the safety of its students as a pretext for the attack. He claimed: "No U.S. citizen had been disturbed at all prior to the invasion, and if anything endangered them, it was the war unleashed by the United States." Castro was also uncomfortably near the truth when he declared: "Mr. Scoon clearly stated that he approved of the invasion but said that he had

not previously asked anyone to invade Grenada. A few days after landing, Mr. Scoon—lodged in the *Guam* helicopter carrier—signed a letter
officially requesting the intervention."

The Cuban president was clearly upset with the waste of all the
economic aid supplied to Grenada. Early in his speech he emphasized this point: "For instance, the value of our contribution to
Grenada in the form of materials, designs and labor in building the
new airport came to $60 million at international prices—over $500
per inhabitant. It is as if Cuba—with a population of almost 10
million—received a project worth $5 billion as a donation."

What he did not, could not, acknowledge publicly was the enormous setback the communist revolution in the Caribbean had suffered. Years of work had been undone; there might never be a full
recovery. Grenada under Bishop was destined to become a Marxist, military state, to be used as a springboard for subversion
throughout the region. Coard's ambition and stupidity had wrecked
all that.

‡   ‡   ‡

The reaction of world opinion had been predicted accurately. Nine
out of ten countries or international bodies raised their hands in
horror. No notice was taken of the reaction of all but a small minor-
ity of Grenadians. The people who had been invaded welcomed the
invaders, regarded them as liberators, even going so far as to want
U.S. troops to remain far longer than they did. This message, from
the people closest to events, was lost outside the Caribbean. Grenadians had been rescued from a life under ever-increasing "manners."
The island was to be a communist bastion, an ever more menacing
reminder to the rest of the region that their way of life was threatened. This is what it would have become. That it did not was because
President Reagan acted, albeit primarily for reasons of national
self-interest.

The U.N. Security Council was quick off the mark, with the
Nicaraguan envoy demanding an emergency session on October 25,
as soon as news of the invasion was received. The Jordanian president of the council summoned the meeting shortly after 11:00 P.M.
that night. The debate dragged on until October 28, with the result
a foregone conclusion. The draft resolution condemning the U.S.

action had been proposed by, not surprisingly, Guyana, with the support of Nicaragua and Zimbabwe. It developed into a political slanging match. The Cuban delegation described the U.S. justifications for intervention as "squalid little footnotes they used to cover up their disgusting acts." Ali Treiki for Libya proclaimed that the United States had celebrated U.N. Day by invading Grenada. "Where will it stop?" he demanded. It stopped on October 28 when Jeane Kirkpatrick, U.S. ambassador, vetoed the resolution. Eleven members supported the condemnation of Urgent Fury; an acutely embarrassed Britain, Togo, and Zaire abstained.

On November 2 the U.N. General Assembly went over the same ground again. This time nobody could use a veto, so the final resolution that "deeply deplores the military intervention, and calls for an immediate end to armed intervention and the withdrawal of foreign troops" was passed by 108 in favor, 27 abstentions, and 9 against. Interestingly the participating countries had the support of El Salvador and Israel. Like so many similar U.N. resolutions, it had no effect on the situation whatsoever.

Two days later, in Grenada, it was mainly diplomats, not troops, who were withdrawing from the island. They were being expelled on the orders of Sir Paul Scoon, the expulsion being organized by the U.S. military. The Soviet embassy had become the sanctuary for fifty-three Cubans (they actually outnumbered the Soviets by four), fifteen North Koreans, six East Germans (not including Gerhard Jonas), and three Bulgarians. All left on the same plane after eight hours of delays.

It had been an exhausting night for all concerned, starting at 6:00 P.M. the previous evening with the arrival of five buses at the former Flying Dutchman Hotel. Baggage was heaped on trucks, while the diplomats and families were ferried to the airport to be put through a rigid security procedure. The only man to escape the screening was the Soviet ambassador. Paratroopers frisked each one carefully as they came forward, hands on heads. Photographs were taken of each individual and documents closely scrutinized. It was a laborious process that was interrupted at 2:00 A.M. when those examing the baggage discovered two boxes containing arms. No fewer than thirty-eight AK-47s, each with a round in the chamber, were revealed. Then another crate with 300 magazines, together with pistols, hidden under some typewriters, came to the light. Gillespie called over journalists and photographers to show them the find. It delayed, but did not prevent, the departure, which included Tortolo, for Havana via Mérida on Mexico's Yucatán peninsula. There Castro headed the familiar reception party, coming forward with hugs for the Cubans and hand-shakes for the others while the band played martial music.

The forty Cubans still at their Morne Jaloux embassy were not mov-ing yet. As Rizo's Chicago-born wife, Gail, explained, "We feel that no Cuban diplomatic staff should leave until all Cubans can leave Grenada." She had, however, accompanied her husband to Salines to see off those Cubans leaving with the Soviets, who were mostly construction workers who had found it easier to seek safety in the nearby Soviet embassy rather than try to reach their own.

Twelve hours after the expulsion of the diplomats, a fourteen-man congressional delegation from the United States arrived on a three-day fact-finding mission. Although many Americans were shocked when they got the news that their troops had invaded Grenada, most were prepared to give the president the benefit of any doubts, par-ticularly when the safety of U.S. students was emphasized as being the overriding reason for the operation. Among the congressmen were a number of skeptics, prepared to oppose the president if they felt his actions unjustified. Within the three days, the great majority were convinced that Reagan had been correct—that U.S. citizens had been endangered and, moreover, that some U.S. troops should stay as long as necessary to ensure the setting up of a democratic government.

Congressman Thomas Foley (D–Washington) stated afterward that "a very large majority of the delegation feels that the President acted correctly to protect American lives." Robert Michel (R–Illinois) declared, "There was a threat to our citizens." Bill Alexander (D–Arkansas) was moved by an old Grenadian woman who had clasped his hand in hers before saying, "Thank you for saving my life." Michael Barnes (D–Maryland) admitted, "I have reluctantly concluded that U.S. military action was justified in this very unique instance." It was Ronald Dellums (D–California) who remained unconvinced to the end. Perhaps less swayed by the strong emotions evinced by Grena-dians, perhaps more experienced in the motives of government, perhaps persuaded by his meeting with officials at the medical school, Dellums's opinion was that "the American students were not the primary objective of this mission. . . . If this mission was dedicated to the safety of the students, why didn't they go after them [Grand

Anse and elsewhere] the first day?'' The U.S. authorities were not prepared to answer his question—at least not fully.

At the White House on November 7, while congressmen were still on the island, the president was hosting hundreds of the students to a grand welcome-home party. Defense Secretary Weinberger and General Vessey were present to listen to the Marine Corps band playing marches and the president's speech. The students mingled on the South Lawn with military personnel who had participated. They waved small U.S. flags, appearing genuinely exuberant with their rescue. The president drew applause when he said, ''It is very easy for some smug know-it-all in a plush protected quarter to say that you were in no danger. I have wondered how many of them would have changed places with you.''

The U.S. administration has sometimes been accused of trying to ensure success with a difficult problem by throwing dollars at it. Similarly, within the armed services, particularly the army, an operation can be regarded as a success only if the military throws sufficient medals around afterward. To the outsider, it often appears that the bigger the muddle, the more the medals. In Grenada, there were some outstanding examples of courageous performance of duty, especially evident among helicopter crews in TF 160 and the marines, who had to face intense fire over St. George's on the first day. Four of them lost their lives, and a number were badly wounded.

Within a few weeks of Urgent Fury, the army had issued some 8,500 medals (later rising to 9,802), excluding the Armed Forces Expeditionary Medal, which automatically went to anybody who participated in some capacity from October 23 through to November 21, 1983—nineteen days after hostilities had been declared over. This was the first time since 1975 that the issue of this medal had been approved. The number given out certainly exceeded 14,000 and was probably nearer to 20,000. The army deployed two understrength Ranger and six paratroop battalions on the island. The Rangers acknowledge five deaths from hostile fire, with several more in C Company 1st/75th who died inside the helicopters over Richmond Hill Prison; the 82d had one. Only two companies of the 82d (2d/325th) became involved with any serious combat, and that was on the second day at Little Havana. Despite this, the army issued 812 Bronze Stars (59 with the *V* denoting valor): ''For heroic or meritorious achievement of service, not involving aerial flight, in connection with operations against an opposing armed force." The Army Commendation Medal had 5,079 recipients (99 with the *V* for valor), given for meritorious achievement of service, which in this instance seemed to be little more than going to Grenada when ordered to do so. Some 2,946 Army Achievement Medals were handed out for meritorious service in any capacity in a noncombat area. It is not uncommon to see servicemen who never saw combat in Grenada wearing three medal ribbons for their contribution.

Equally extraordinary was the issue of 3,100 combat infantry badges to members of the 82d Airborne, while the 1st and 2d/75th Rangers collected a mere 430 between them. The only airborne unit to see anything remotely resembling infantry combat was the 2d/325th at Little Havana on the morning of the second day. Their ponderous performance during Urgent Fury was well rewarded.

Similarly, to units that were on the island or in the designated area nearby (which included Barbados) during the five weeks' qualifying period, a Battle Streamer was awarded. The Streamer, with the words "GRENADA 1983" on it, is attached to the unit's flag. In January 1984 no fewer than sixty-four separate units were listed as eligible for this streamer. The military police did particularly well, with the 17th MP Brigade, 503d MP Battalion, 65th MP Company, 108th MP Company, 118th MP Company, and the 21st MP Company all qualifying.

Even the navy, normally less lavish with awards, could not refrain from giving a navy unit commendation to TF 124. The secretary of the navy signed the citation, which read, in part:

> For conspicuous gallantry and intrepid action against a heavily armed rebel force threatening the personal safety of American citizens and the established Government of Grenada [perhaps meaning Bishop and the PRG]. . . . Through calculated forethought and incisive action by the officers and men of Task Force 124 . . . the lives of hundreds of American civilians were saved, rebel forces were subdued, and the Government of Grenada restored.[1]

The air force was not to be outdone. Although only one airman received a Purple Heart, 3,076 other awards were made, excluding the Armed Forces Expeditionary Medal. These included 272 Bronze Stars, 841 Air Medals, 1,649 Air Force Commendation Medals, and 311 Air Force Achievement Medals, all given for varying degrees of "outstanding achievement or meritorious service"—as distinct from carrying out normal duties.

The total medal count for Urgent Fury was between 30,000 and 35,000.

The military had lost none of its Vietnam generosity with medals, where millions of awards were made, cheapening their value in the eyes of everybody, and resulting in ridicule of the system.[2]

‡   ‡   ‡

Grenada was in a mess after Urgent Fury. Its economy had collapsed, tourists had been frightened away, people were hungry, roads had disintegrated, agriculture was no longer functioning, buildings had been smashed or burned out by the U.S. forces. Thousands were out of work, there was no government, and the task of restructuring society was fraught with problems of security, compounded by the hundreds of former PRG or PRA sympathizers still at large.

Sir Paul Scoon set up an interim government of prominent Grenadians whose task was to get an administration functioning and organize a general election as soon as practical. This took over a year; the elections were held in December 1984. The United States was generous with financial assistance, not only to make good or compensate for war damage but for other development projects. These included Salines Airport, which was officially opened by Sir Paul on October 28, 1984, although work continued on access roads and other facilities for some time afterward.

Other countries, including Britain, also assisted. As the U.S. forces gradually withdrew over the coming months, law and order was first handed over to the Caribbean Peacekeeping Force and then to the Grenada Police Force. Unless there was security, nothing could be achieved. The confidence of Grenadians and, above all, of potential investors and businessmen had to be built up. A massive witch-hunt was to be avoided. Hard-core PRG and PRA personnel were arrested, and held for interrogation; some were released, while others were charged and detained for trial.

Britain took a particular interest in the creation of a new police force. The problem was that a large force was needed quickly, and although the top police commanders could be brought in for a time from overseas, the great bulk of the force must be Grenadian. It proved impossible to start completely afresh. If a tight screening of applicants, or indeed of officers still in the force, had been rigidly applied, there would only have been a handful available. The most difficult task was in selecting or retaining officers. Could those who had served under Bishop be relied upon? Many of them had to be; there was nobody else. Officers who had received training in Cuba, held high rank under the revolution, tipped off the NJM when Gairy left the country in 1979, previously had had stolen property at their home, been on the committee of the political department of the PRG—all had to be accepted. Reminders of the revolutionary days were commonplace. It was some time before police recruits could be prevented from marching around swinging their arms across their bodies and lifting their legs in the goose step.

There was much talk of creating a Caribbean defense force, a multinational organization that would have been 1,800 strong, responsible for security in all areas outside the competence of the police. Prime Minister Adams was a keen advocate, appreciating that such a force would mean no national armies were necessary and that its multinational composition would have effectively prevented it from turning on any government in a military coup. Discussions broke down over costs. Instead each police force in the smaller islands formed a paramilitary special service unit. The United States provided substantial equipment and training teams to create them, but for the years following the intervention, these units have been plagued by poor leadership, the wrong type of training, lack of motivation, and misuse of personnel. Like most other compromises in the security field, they offer minimal deterrence to terrorism, subversion, or coups. In some islands they are regarded with suspicion by the authorities, so elaborate precautions are taken to ensure that personnel cannot get to their arms quickly.

It took some months before Grenadians could be induced to take an interest in politics again. They had had enough of politicians. Many wanted the U.S. forces to stay on; a period of recuperation was necessary, and where were the new political leaders to come from? The United States did not want the results of the intervention upset by the ballot box. It was critical for the right kind of person, the right kind of party, to win the election. No more dictatorships of the left or right were to be allowed. Of great concern to the Americans was the arrival back in Grenada of Uncle Gairy.

Gairy resurrected his old GULP, which he repainted in the U.S. colors. The Salines Airport should have been named "Ronald Reagan International Airport," he said and at the top of his party's manifesto was stated, "America Must Stay." It made for interesting reading. Among calls for better roads and health were others for permanent U.S. and British military bases, the reintroduction of "the beautiful sport of horse-racing," an Easter water festival ("seven days of bonanza for all businesses"), the eradication of scruffy dress among teachers, and exemption of church ministers from customs examination.

In mid-1984 there was every likelihood that Gairy would win. GULP's rivals were three small, new parties, plus Bishop loyalists like Radix, George and Einstein Louison, and Gahagan, who had formed the Maurice Bishop Patriotic Movement (MBPM). A confidential meeting was held between the new parties where other Caribbean leaders, principally Tom Adams, banged a few heads together to produce a workable coalition, called the New National party (NNP). Its leader was Herbert Blaize, a somewhat frail old contemporary, and archrival, of Gairy. He could be expected to follow a middle-of-the-road course, with a good chance of winning support among the voters. The NNP did not lack for cash; the United States was determined to ensure Blaize's victory at the polls.

The MBPM stood little chance. Perhaps 10–15 percent of the younger Grenadians, those who had held authority under Bishop who now had nothing, would vote to put Radix and his followers back in. A few, like gardener Daniel Takoo, still preferred the times under Bishop. He even went so far as to recall, "The Cubans worked hard and did good work." Others, like Michelle Gibbs, a black American Marxist, who had been seen to applaud when she saw Captain Giguere's helicopter fall into the harbor, also mourned Bishop's demise, but their numbers were small.[3] Radix held a few rallies, often furtively at night, in remote corners of the island. On one occasion he is reported to have proclaimed about the NNP, "They are so low they could pass beneath a razor blade." A little later on the same occasion, Sir Paul was described as "Scoon de Tycoon, OBB. An Obedient Black Boy for the Yankees. Paul Scoon is a coon!" Gairy did not escape Radix's wit either, when he described how "on that beautiful day in 1979, this nation got rid of Mr. UFO, KCMG, ABCDEFG."

At the December 1984 polls, the MBPM got no seats, trailing far behind the other two parties. The winner was Mr. Blaize. He is still there, as is Sir Paul Scoon, who has been privileged to reside at Government House under Gairy, Bishop, Austin, the interim government, and now Blaize. His record as a survivor, not only under harsh dictatorial regimes but also under fire, must be unrivaled.

‡　‡　‡

By mid-November Richmond Hill Prison was back in business, under new management, to receive into custody Grenada's former government and military leaders. Unable to escape from the island, unwilling to take to the hills, and with hundreds of people eager to denounce them, there was no way that PRG and PRA officers could avoid arrest. It was only a matter of time. Nelson, who was detained on November 13, was one of the last to be pulled in.

The prison was always filthy and disgracefully run under Bishop. Now it was in an even worse condition. The staff lacked proper uniforms, cooked their meals on open fires, and slept in dirty, broken-down bunks. Their facilities were barely an improvement on those of the detainees. With the arrival of Lionel Maloney, all this quickly changed. Maloney, a senior Barbadian prison officer in his early sixties, volunteered for the job knowing full well the enormous difficulties. He was, and is, a tough disciplinarian—just what the prison needed. When he arrived, the warders were scared of the prisoners, still saluting their former bosses, such as Austin or Layne, and calling them respectfully by their old military ranks. The inmates behaved as they liked, cursing and insulting the staff. Prison regulations were ignored.

Maloney changed all this, turning chaos into order and by doing so restoring the morale of his staff. As he recalls, "When I first came here, this prison sounded like a fish market every day. Today you can hear a pin drop in any corner." Not only was discipline strictly enforced through absolute compliance with the prison's regulations, but living conditions were dramatically improved. Maloney had little money from official sources, but he said he did "a lot of begging." Paint, new stoves, bunks, and innumerable other items were acquired. The end result was startling. I remember how impressed I was with the general air of efficiency, smartness, and cleanliness when Maloney showed me the prison in 1986. Prison officers called their charges to attention and saluted the commissioner before reporting to him. In the maximum security wing, where those under sentence of death were confined under twenty-four-hour surveillance, the atmosphere was the same. Coard, Austin, Strachan, and the others climbed to their feet when the accompanying officer banged on the door and shouted, "Stand up—Commissioner."

Maloney had his detractors among those who, like the PRG detainees, had grown accustomed to putting people under "manners" themselves rather than receiving discipline. Visiting defense lawyers and relatives of the accused tried again and again to get the commissioner removed. They did not succeed; Maloney followed the letter of the law. Detainees got exactly what they were entitled to under the regulations; they were firmly and fairly applied. Coard and his followers had been quite happy with the regulations when they held authority, but with the boot on the other foot they squealed loudly.

For some months after Urgent Fury, until more staff were recruited and trained, the security of the prison was the responsibility of the Caribbean Peacekeeping Force, with the Jamaican force providing a platoon for guard duties, although Maloney retained overall charge. Nelson remembers, after he had threatened the Jamaican platoon commander, he was given fifteen days on No. 2 Diet: a regime of bread at 10:00 A.M., dry vegetables at midday, and bread with butter at 4:00 P.M., with a bucket of drinking water in the cell. No. 1 Diet was bread twice a day plus water. At one stage, Nelson had two weeks of that. After a four-day hunger strike and with the assistance of lawyers, there was some improvement in the regulations. Once the regulations changed, Maloney immediately complied. They were his bible.

Former Central Committee members did not take kindly to suffering under their own system. They were quick to allege torture, inhuman conditions, and being beaten to sign confessions. At 10:00 P.M. on February 20, 1984, Strachan was being escorted back to his cell after questioning when he shouted out to the others that he had been beaten and forced to sign a statement. This caused an uproar, with shouting, foul language, and much banging on doors. Austin claimed he was not afraid to die but vowed retribution against the "torturers." Coard too proclaimed he was not frightened of death but was only concerned that he take a couple of people with him when he went.

The allegations of mistreatment were directed at the team of Barbadian Criminal Investigation Department investigators who were assembling the evidence against the accused, under Inspector Jasper Watson.

The job was a testing one, which police from other islands had declined or had been found incompetent to perform. For month after month, these officers had to sift the evidence, conduct interviews, and investigate the charges of murder under circumstances of hostility, fear, threats, and abuse. At the end of the day, Watson and his assistants were fully exonerated by an official inquiry into the torture allegations.

Phyllis Coard was confined in the female compound, not far from the old goat pen whose use she and her husband had seen no reason to prevent. In April 1984 she managed to smuggle out a letter to a prominent British left-wing activist, Dame Judith Hart, a member of Parliament, who was at that time the president of the United Kingdom Committee for Violations of Human Rights in Grenada. She wrote of the island at the mercy of foreign troops; people cowed and threatened; the impossibility of obtaining a fair trial; of torture, including herself being beaten for six hours; harassment of defense lawyers; lack of funds to pay for their attorneys; and intimidation of defense witnesses.

On August 27, 1984, Phyllis Coard decided to try a hunger strike to bring about a redress of her grievances. She refused all meals, contenting herself with sipping water. During the next two months, her weight dropped from 168 pounds (for a woman of 5 feet, 4 inches, she was decidedly plump) to 133 pounds, and she complained of weakness, headaches, night blindness, fainting, nausea, muscle cramps, insomnia, and pains in various parts of her body. Once she collapsed in court. Nevertheless, after some eight weeks of self-inflicted suffering, she retained sufficient strength to make a futile attempt to break out of the prison to attend court. She was convinced that the authorities would not let her appear in court because of her condition. When two officers entered her cell to give her medication, she threw water in the face of one officer, dashed out, and climbed up on top of the gate to the women's compound. The alarm was sounded, and a large gathering of senior staff, including the commisioner, arrived. She threw herself to the ground and had to be carried back to her cell.

A special medical report on Phyllis Coard was compiled for the chief justice of Grenada at the time, Archibald Nedd. The three doctors concluded that her symptoms were consistent with lack of food; there was no evidence of organic disease; a return to normal feeding would restore her to reasonable health; otherwise the hunger strike would ultimately lead to coma and death. Phyllis started to eat again.

During October, while Phyllis was still starving herself, a far more serious threat of a breakout from the prison came to the light. It was nothing short of a plan for the PRG to regain control of the island—a coup attempt. The likelihood of its success, had it actually occurred, was minimal, but police investigations indicated that the man behind the plotting was Gerhard Jonas. Jonas, who had been assisting the CIA, had moved to a remote house over a kilometer from the road at St. Pauls village. The police report stated that he had become a double agent and was now determined to free and reinstate his erstwhile comrades. He and a small group of agents intended to activate former PRA personnel, armed from caches still undetected, to launch an attack on the night of October 3–4, 1984. There was talk of large sums of money being available as bribes. Prominent individuals such as Sir Paul Scoon were to be seized, and the night bus carrying U.S. students between the campuses was to be ambushed, with the occupants being taken to either Calivigny or Grand Etang caves as hostages. Certain key targets were selected for blowing up, such as the prison, the U.S. helicopters parked on the Grand Anse playing fields, and the Barbadian policemen's housing in St. George's. The death list was long. At the top was Commissioner Maloney, closely followed by Inspector Watson and the other Barbadian CID noncommissioned officers.

Several former PRG members, including St. Bernard, Justin Roberts, and Gahagan, were cited as plotters. They had been recently freed on bail or for lack of evidence. Suspicions had hardened at an incident on the morning of October 3, outside the Grenville courthouse, where a number of accused had been arraigned before the magistrate on torture charges. Those involved included Layne, Redhead, James, Cornwall, and Bartholomew. As the vehicles carrying the prisoners with their escort of Jamaican soldiers moved away, an ex-PRA officer cadet, Ronnie Spooner, threatened and assaulted a Jamaican Defence Force corporal. There was nearly a shooting incident, but this was prevented, and Spooner was arrested and searched. This revealed a letter intended for Cornwall, which was to have been smuggled into the prison. One thing led to another, as Spooner, and later Ronnie Bubb, who had been beaten up in prison by Layne and Abdullah because they suspected him of leaking information, revealed much of the plot. Eventually Jonas was expelled from Grenada back to East Germany, where his fate is unknown.

‡   ‡   ‡

On December 4, 1986, over three years after Urgent Fury, the special courtroom situated inside the grounds of Richmond Hill Prison was hushed. For the first time in many weeks during the eight-month trial, the court did not have to be cleared of shouting and jeering accused. Outside, the tightest security ever imposed on a court building in the Caribbean was in place. Every vantage point was sealed off; public and journalists alike were subjected to rigorous body searches with electric scanners, and guards with automatic weapons ringed the building.

After hearing that the jury of seven men and five women had reached a unanimous guilty verdict on the eighteen prisoners, the Kittitian-born acting chief justice, Dennis Byron, asked each convicted person whether he or she had anything to say before sentence was pronounced. Those convicted of murder, or conspiracy to murder, knew what was coming. The chief justice was obliged by law to pass only one sentence: death by hanging.

Coard, in a gray jersey with black stripes, fidgeted with his glasses as he replied, "A man who is innocent of a crime cannot be made guilty of a crime he had not committed by any unconstitutional court, run by paid mercenaries." His wife, Phyllis, responded, "I stand here confident that history will confirm my innocence and condemn this Kangaroo Court."

Former army chief Austin flashed a brief smile at the jury before ending his protestations of innocence with the words, "I will die with grace for a crime I did not commit."

Abdullah, Bishop's executioner, remained true to form, shouting obscenities at the chief justice and yelling after sentencing, "How much Yankee dollars you get to do that? I will die fighting. Let them put it on record. All those who frame me up, let them know that."

James claimed, "I have been framed because of my political outlook. . . . The American government has run this show using black-faced guards."

Layne, a convinced revolutionary to the end, shouted, "My entire life to this country has been dedicated to the Grenada revolution, making it and defending it. That's the reason I stand here waiting to be condemned."

The three members of Bishop's execution squad under Abdullah —Mitchell, Joseph, and Richardson—who had actually fired their machine guns were found guilty of multiple charges of manslaughter. Mitchell and Joseph each received forty-five-year imprisonment sentences, and Richardson collected thirty years since he had been found guilty of only eight counts instead of eleven. It was a long time to spend in Richmond Hill Prison.

The lucky one was Nelson, who alone among his former comrades had not disrupted the court proceedings during the lengthy trial but remained in the dock. He was acquitted on all charges. He had good reason to thank his fate that had put him in the third APC that afternoon over three years before. He appeared stunned as he was told he was free to leave. He walked to the center of the court, where he embraced his mother, and they both wept. Before departing he shook hands with Prime, who had sat beside him in the dock, then gave a thumbs-up sign and clenched-fist salute to his former fellow defendants.

Fourteen were sentenced to hang: Austin, the Coards, Bartholomew, McBarnette, James, Layne, Stroude, Prime, Cornwall, Strachan, Abdullah, Redhead, and Ventour.

Originally there had been twenty accused. St. Bernard, the former police commissioner, had been present at Fort Frederick when the Central Committee had ordered the assault on Fort Rupert; indeed he had waved the APCs out of the gate. At the preliminary magistrate's hearing, however, he had managed to slip through the net. The evidence was not considered strong enough. The second man to avoid a murder charge was ex-Sergeant Gabriel, who had finished off Fitzroy Bain. Because he had feared for his own life if he had refused to obey Abdullah, because he was not in the firing party, and because he turned state's evidence, the charge against him was not proceeded with.

The long legal proceedings had been fraught with problems. This had been the most sensational trial ever held in the Caribbean, brought about by traumatic events. There had been a preliminary hearing before a magistrate in 1984, followed by another, lasting months, before the former chief justice, Sir Archibald Nedd. There had been endless legal delays, many contrived by the team of Jamaican defense lawyers who claimed the Grenada high court had no jurisdiction to try the case.

In fact the defense made little effort to defend the accused at all, merely claiming that the court was unconstitutional. The defense lawyers eventually withdrew from the case completely, leaving the defendants virtually on their own, to continue to disrupt the proceedings by shouting, singing, and stamping, which led to their removal from court, with the hearing continuing in their absence. Ian Ramsey from Jamaica, who at one time led the defense, was himself tried in Grenada in his absence in July 1987 for contempt of court. He was sentenced to three months in jail. It was alleged at this hearing that Ramsey had instructed the accused to carry out the persistent disruptions. According to Gabriel, Ramsey had said, "The judge will be obliged to stop the trial, and that will be victory number one."

The irony was that Coard and his followers were objecting violently to being tried by a court they themselves had set up. The Grenada Supreme Court was established under People's Law No. 4 of 1979 and stipulated that the jurisdiction, which was formerly exercised by the West Indies Associated States Supreme Court, was now vested in the Grenada Supreme Court. This court consisted of a high court and a court of appeal, which meant that appeals from the high court could only go to the Grenada Court of Appeal. This was fine for the PRG when they were enforcing "manners" on everybody they did not like but not so good when they were in the dock themselves. It meant they could not appeal outside Grenada; channels for further lengthy delays, ultimately up to the Privy Council in London, were closed to them. This, so they thought, was decidedly unfair and unconstitutional. They certainly did not wish to be tried under their own legal system. They knew only too well where that would end.

Epilogue

Hell no, none, zero! You can scream and shout and gnash your
teeth all you want, but the folks out there like it. It was done right,
and done with despatch.

> — White House aide on being asked if
> Grenada had any political fallout

URGENT Fury was an overall success politically and militarily.
Communist plans for Caribbean expansion had been dealt a
severe blow, ordinary Grenadians had been freed from an oppressive
regime, U.S. combat casualties were insignificant, hundreds of students
had been evacuated without a single injury, it was all over comparatively quickly, and American troops had been welcomed as liberators
by many.

Nevertheless, the operation came within a hairsbreadth of being
a military disaster. If it had been such a disaster, it would automatically
have become a political one as well. That it succeeded as it did, without
costly setbacks, was due primarily to incredibly good fortune. Despite
the dearth of intelligence, which resulted in units going into the island
blind; despite serious planning errors; despite an absence of strategic
or tactical surprise; despite the failure to achieve concentration at
decisive points; despite continuous communication snarl-ups; and
despite the lack of interservice coordination or an overall ground commander, this large-scale operation succeeded. It succeeded with fewer
deaths from hostile fire than countless platoon actions in Vietnam.

Fortune, they say, favors the brave. But for luck, the United States
would have been forced to pay a very high price for its success. There
was an inkling of what could have been in store early on October 25,

when all three of the Special Operations Forces assaults went wrong. The chaos inside the Black Hawks circling over the prison that morning was a glimpse of what to expect when tactical principles are ignored. Fortunately it was a handful of poorly trained, poorly equipped Grenadians, not Vietnamese or Cuban professional soldiers, manning sophisticated weapons.

Austin and his gang never intended to harm foreigners. Had they done so, had they taken hostages, the United States would have been in real trouble. The United States could not have prevented such problems because the participating units had no idea that students were scattered all over the southwestern corner of the island. Even the 1st/75th, whose task it was to take the True Blue campus, had no special plan to secure the students. This operation was not given any higher priority than airfield clearance in the planning or execution stages. There was never any intention of seizing the campus in advance of the main landing or drop. It was to be an orthodox operation: pathfinders, then the airfield clearance company, and then the remainder of the battalion half an hour later—not the way to ensure the safety of potential hostages, if they really thought they were endangered.

The use of Delta Force and C Company 1st/75th Rangers in their daylight, unsupported, blind helicopter charge at Richmond Hill Prison will remain a classic example of the misuse of Special Operations Forces. Why were Special Forces not tasked with the securing of the students at True Blue? Their safety was supposedly the main objective of Urgent Fury, yet the army's elite Special Force unit was tasked with setting free local political detainees, about whom the planners knew absolutely nothing and whose freedom could in no way contribute to the success of the D-day operations.[1]

The amazing good luck of the Rangers at Salines has already been emphasized. To take ninety minutes to drop 600 men in daylight onto a bare runway within a few meters of enemy positions and suffer only one broken leg is a military miracle. The leading elements of 1st/75th were even able to spend fifteen minutes driving Cuban vehicles around to clear obstacles without any casualties. Instead of a well-dug-in force of regular troops prepared to fight the moment the invasion started, the Rangers faced lightly armed, ill-trained construction workers, whose orders prevented them from shooting until they were themselves attacked. A unique situation.

The marines on the ground had their share of good fortune. Circumstances prevented their assaults at Pearls and Grenville being simultaneous; in fact E Company was able to go in only a platoon at a time. Their landing at Grand Mal was unopposed, and it too was a piecemeal, single-company insertion, without the benefit of the commanding officer to control it. At that stage, a Cuban battalion was thought to be north of St. George's. The 2d/8th BLT ended up controlling two-thirds of the island and assaulting Carriacou, but they did so against feeble or nonexistent opposition. During their entire time in Grenada, the marine infantry had no combat casualties, either killed or wounded. Their casualties were confined to helicopter crews.[2]

In war, both sides have a share in good fortune. Plans seldom survive the first shot in their entirety, errors are made, the unexpected happens, and victory often goes to the side that makes the least number of mistakes. After Urgent Fury, perhaps understandably, the operation was proclaimed to the public as a flawless triumph of American arms. The president announced that the armed forces were "back on their feet and standing tall." Metcalf declared, "We blew them away"; and the army chief of staff, General John Wickham, calling the operation "superb," was confident that it demonstrated the military was back "on the right track."

Certainly the United States had won a victory, but what did it prove? The United States had deployed units from the majority of their elite formations. Special Forces, Rangers, marines, and the 82d Airborne had provided the equivalent of some nine infantry battalions by the time hostilities were officially declared over. They were supported by a carrier battle group complete with dozens of ground attack aircraft, naval gunfire, air force and helicopter gunships, army artillery, and all the massive logistical support from the MAC and XVIII Airborne Corps needed to keep the forces functioning. Arraigned against them were, at most, 750 PRA-PRM troops of questionable morale, without any air or naval forces, no tanks, no artillery, and only a few long-outdated, second-hand AA guns. To these must be added the 600 or so Cuban civilian workers. The outcome was never in doubt, but the price of victory was.

Castro was infuriated that the imperialists had paid so little for their victory. He court-martialed the officers he considered responsible. The Cubans had, in all probability, killed only one American (Reitz) in the actual fighting (it cannot be established whether Yamane

was shot by the Cubans or the PRA). The workers had quickly surrendered when faced with aerial attack or after heavy bombardment.
Neither the Rangers nor 2d/325th had mounted anything bigger than
a company attack on the Cuban positions. No infantry assault was
necessary against Little Havana, the defenders capitulating after prolonged bombing and shelling. Most subunit operations were at the
platoon level. As many participants will admit anonymously, Urgent
Fury did not test the fighting abilities of the infantry. Considering
the confusion and muddle during the planning, it is probably just
as well it did not. Schwarzkopf was later unusually frank: "Even
though higher HQ screws it up every way you can possibly screw it
up, it is the initiative and valor on the part of small unit leadership
that will win for you every time." The fact that the United States
military had won their first clear-cut success since the Inchon landings in Korea over thirty years before was used as a smoke screen to
conceal the unpalatable truth that it had been "screwed up." If ever
the military had asked for a bloody nose, it had been in Grenada.

Their most unforgivable blunders had been in intelligence: in knowing nothing about the 400 or so students outside True Blue, in having no proper maps, and all this despite Grenada's having been the
center of communist activity in the region for over four years. This
horrendous failure on the part of the intelligence community, particularly the CIA, meant that the troops were badly briefed, had no
tactical information, and were led to believe it would be a walkover.

But unlike Castro, the U.S. commander in chief exacted no retribution; nobody was fired or even disciplined. The director of central
intelligence, William Casey, shrugged it off and bumbled on to the
next fiasco—the illegal sale of arms to Iran. The problem was that
to punish anybody for failure meant acknowledging that the operation had gone badly wrong, which the administration steadfastly
refused to do for reasons of self-esteem.

For some reason, the contingency plan for Grenada was not used;
neither was the designated headquarters. Instead a naval command
without adequate staff was given the job, with only a few days to
put together a highly complex invasion plan. Even then they were
obliged to give a role to every branch of the armed forces; even each
service's Special Operations Forces had to have a piece of the cake.
The imposition of stringent security did not achieve tactical surprise
but served only to ensure that participating units planned in isolation and fought in ignorance of what others were doing.

Atlantic Command was obliged to submit a report on the lessons learned from Urgent Fury to the JCS chairman. McDonald's staff held a "hot washup," that is, a staff and commanders' meeting to discuss the operation to identify problems, lessons, and remedial action necessary to improve competence. On February 6, 1984, McDonald signed the report, which began, "The outcome of this military mission reaffirmed the outstanding professionalism, dedication, and flexibility of all the forces involved in this effort." If this was really the case, it is strange that the after-action reports submitted by participants for future reference, and retained by the Analysis Branch of the Center of Military History in Washington, D.C., have never been officially released or declassified outside the military. All the criticism, all the speculation, that surfaced in the months following Urgent Fury could have been dispelled or confirmed quickly. The difficulty was, and still is, that the after-action reports highlight instances where "outstanding professionalism" was sadly lacking. Many of the uninformed allegations had gone uncomfortably near the mark.

It was perhaps asking too much for the commanders and units who participated to be wholly frank about their own shortcomings to the JCS chairman. Nevertheless, McDonald did mention some of the difficulties. He agreed there was confusion with the insertion of the Caribbean Peacekeeping Force; air assets were "not always properly controlled"; "helicopters are highly vulnerable to well aimed ground fire"; emphasis in the future should be given in training on the "protection of private property"; "medevac operations at night became a great concern because Black Hawk pilots had not been trained to land on seaborne helicopter platforms and were denied permission to land." The report mentioned the lack of understanding of interservice close air support procedures, the confusion caused by the lack of gridded maps, the need for senior liaison officers from all commands at the controlling headquarters, the lack of equipment and preplanning to deal with prisoners of war, and the weaknesses experienced with the communications systems. While admitting that the three separate locations of students were unknown, McDonald could not bring himself to admit that the lack of detailed tactical intelligence had been inexcusable. His comment was, "Available basic intelligence was generally adequate for overall planning purposes" and that the estimate of enemy strengths "was within an acceptable range of uncertainty." A polite way of saying nobody had the faintest idea.

Even allowing that some sections of the original report had been blanked out, there was no mention of how and why the operation had come so close to catastrophe. No mention of the failed Special Force missions. No mention of the lack of surprise or the failure of the D-day plan to secure most of its objectives. No mention of why it had taken so painfully long for nine elite battalions of U.S. infantry, backed up by overwhelming firepower, to defeat one weak battalion of third-rate Grenadians and another of half-trained civilians.

As in most other battles, courage and cowardice were present on both sides. With both Cubans and Grenadians, resistance crumbled quickly in the face of sustained heavy fire, but a number of Grenadian AA gun crews stuck to their posts despite their exposed positions and gave a good account of themselves in or around St. George's. As the Rangers acknowledged, the forlorn APC counterattack, without any support, at Salines on the first afternoon was courageous, as well as foolhardy. Prime's men, who chased away the SEALs from Beausejour, were another instance.

Outstanding examples of gallantry on the U.S. side were displayed mainly by helicopter crews. It was they who had to face the brunt of enemy fire on the first day, often without the benefit of supporting aircraft. In particular, the crews of the four Marine Corps Cobras and the nine Black Hawks of TF 160 had to fly into concentrated AA fire at low levels. They did so time after time without wavering.

The same cannot be said of the air force pilots carrying B Company of the 1st/75th over the drop zone at Salines on October 25. At least two aircraft aborted their mission because they did not like the look of the tracer rounds coming their way. This failure to carry out their mission was responsible for Taylor's being virtually on his own on the ground for so long. Had the Cubans been more active, this failure could have jeopardized the entire drop. There were suggestions after that some army officers wanted to press charges but were "counseled" out of it. It would have spoiled the image of professionalism.

The January 1987 *Military Review* article on the overloading of troops in Grenada cites further examples of alleged cowardice, this time by Army helicopter crews. One soldier is recorded as stating;

> The . . . crews [created] a high level of stress. They didn't know what they were doing. They were in the way. . . . They used casualties as cover. . . . It really helped to get [them] out. [When they left], they didn't [want to] take any casualties with them, they kicked them off to make room for themselves.

In another case,

> An army unit reported that pilots refused to deliver some vehicles containing equipment and ammunition. Consequently, the unit fought its heaviest combat without its full complement of equipment. Another interview revealed that "the [perceived] reason they could not get our equipment in was crew rest. Peacetime safety regulations would not permit the crew to fly any more." This report, even if merely secondhand hearsay, is most damaging to trust.

At the tactical level, the well-known inclination of the infantry to depend on overwhelming air and artillery support before attempting to advance against even light opposition was noticeable. A Cuban officer, present at their mission headquarters, commented, "The U.S. troops have a lot of training and very good support in terms of hardware, but their morale is based on might alone. . . . Their tactic is to destroy everything with their planes and artillery first and see what's left." The most glaring example of this was the use of the A-7s on October 27 to try to destroy snipers in a house, which resulted in the tragic strafing of Silvasy's command post.

Few observers were impressed with the 82d's small-unit tactics or battle procedures. Considering that, as far as the paratroopers knew, there were still plenty of Cubans around, their appearance and actions did not reassure even civilians who saw them. Often they were bunched together, obviously feeling the effect of the heat and their enormous loads, sometimes sprawled at the side of a track with equipment strewn all over the place, and no proper security precautions being taken. U.S. troops never dug in in coordinated defensive positions when they halted, and there was never any attempt at a night advance by the infantry in the south. A young Grenadian woman who lived not far from Grand Anse thought the 82d troopers looked young and inexperienced. She thought it strange that they "camped in the middle of the lawn, totally exposed . . . set up a mortar in the open, and just sat around and relaxed. . . . Their searching was poor as they didn't bother to go into the bush, but stayed on the roads only."

Afterward the military was to claim that its tactics were restricted by the need to prevent excessive civilian casualties. This may have been in the orders, but it was not obvious in practice. There was extensive use of the Spectre gunships, A-7s, and naval gunfire into areas with many private houses where enemy positions were suspected. Calliste village, the built-up area around Grand Anse campus, and the mental hospital suffered under heavy air attack. To attack small pockets of resistance or snipers in such areas with bombs and rockets is not a discriminate way of killing bad guys and sparing good guys. But for the last-moment intuition of the marines' commanding officer, the Venezuelan embassy would have been flattened.

What is of lasting concern is whether people learn from their experiences. Many officers within the U.S. military are well aware that Urgent Fury was "screwed up." But officially it remains a flawless operation, which demonstrated the competence of all services.

The U.S. military seems forever wedded to the erroneous belief that battles can be won by technology, that the human element gets progressively less crucial to victory. Human intelligence, which could have provided exactly the sort of information needed by the planners of Urgent Fury, was totally lacking. As always, reliance was placed on satellites and aerial photographs. Unfortunately, these are only aids to intelligence; they do not tell anything about people or their capabilities and intentions.

To the outside observer, the catalog of U.S. military failures since World War II points unerringly at fundamental faults in their system. In all their undertakings from Korea, Vietnam, and Iran, through to Grenada, the United States has fought with enormous technical superiority, particularly in the air. But this has not brought victory. The U.S. military malaise stems in part from the cult of management replacing leadership, from a huge bureaucracy whose aims are often, as foreign policy analyst Jeffrey Record, put it "career advancement, maintenance of an orderly flow of paper within the system, and protection from outside disturbance. The result, obvious in Vietnam, has been a pernicious inability to distinguish between management and leadership, efficiency and effectiveness, and technology and tactics."

It is saddening for a soldier to see the undermining of respect for the military brought about by the ludicrously indiscriminate distribution of medals or the court-martialing of soldiers who brought a few rifles home, while those who failed to face hostile fire continue their careers. Regrettably operational failure seems no longer to be a punishable offense in the U.S. military. Major General James Vaught, the Joint Task Force commander of the Iran rescue disaster, later received his third star, and those responsible for the monumental security failure at Beirut's airport were apparently never brought to account.

‡ ‡ ‡

Four years after Urgent Fury, little remains to remind visitors that Grenada witnessed modern warfare across its beautiful beaches or in its tranquil hills. Coard and his fellow prisoners languish in their condemned cells, striving to find a legal loophole in the judicial system they rejected, to save themselves from the gallows. A memorial to those who died has been erected on the grounds of the Grand Anse campus; Butler House remains a ruin; Fort Frederick is deserted, but Fort Rupert has reverted to its original name, Fort George. Now the rebuilt operations room houses the police headquarters. The wall at which Bishop died has been painted over, but bullet holes still scar the basketball post. Mangled masonry and rusted, broken equipment are all that remain of Camp Calivigny. The only wreckage of combat that has not been cleared away is the heap of twisted metal that lies atop Amber Belair hill. This is all that is left of Captain Keith Lucas's UH-60, lying isolated and inaccessible in the scrub with the rotor blades in the rocks at the bottom of the cliff, still washed endlessly backward and forward by the tides.

In 1987 President Reagan said of Eugenia Charles of Dominica when she was presented with the first James Monroe Memorial Award at a State Department dinner, "Because of the strength and determination she has shown in defending democracy in the Caribbean, I can think of no one more deserving of such recognition." As President, Monroe espoused the doctrine that the United States has the right to take whatever action may be necessary to protect its backyard from the intervention of foreign powers.

Urgent Fury was such an action. For all the errors, for all the confusion, for all the suffering, Grenada and its people remain grateful to those bold enough to launch the operation and those bold enough to undertake it. Let the words of Theodore Roosevelt be read again by those who are still there, those who were there, and those who mourn:

It is not the critic who counts, nor the man who points out how the strong man stumbles, or where the doer of the deeds could have done them better. The credit belongs to the man who's actually in the arena, whose face is marred by dust and sweat and blood, who strives valiantly, who errs, and comes short again and again, because there is no effort without error and shortcoming, but who goes actually to do the deeds, who spends himself in a worthy cause, but at best knows in the end the triumph of high achievement, and who at the worse, if he fails, at least fails while daring greatly, so that he plays fairly, never to be with those cold and timid souls who know neither victory nor defeat.

Appendix A

T HE former defense adviser to Senator Gary Hart, William Lind, (referred to in the introduction), was highly critical of operations in Grenada. The press coverage of his allegations was partly responsible for demands for a congressional investigation, which was forestalled by General Vessey's written response to Lind's report. This appendix sets out Lind's allegations and Vessey's replies; hopefully the reader will now be in a better position to judge the accuracy of both.

Analysis of the Lind Report by the Joint Chiefs of Staff

Allegation

"The United States required seven battalions of troops, plus elements of two other battalions, to defeat fewer than 700 Cubans and a Grenadian Army that hardly fought at all. . . . By way of contrast, the British defeated more than 11,000 Argentines with just eight infantry battalions in the Falklands."

Facts

The size of the US force used in Grenada was determined based on an analysis of the military mission, enemy forces, US forces available, and the terrain. The principal military mission was to rescue US citizens and other foreign nationals. In order to achieve this objective, it was determined that Cuban and Grenadian forces would have to be neutralized and a stable situation on the island achieved. US intelligence sources identified the Cuban strength on Grenada to be approximately 700. Grenadian forces included 1200–1500 members of the People's Revolutionary Army and 2000–5000 members of the Territorial Militia. During the planning period for the rescue operation, there was no way of determining how much of the enemy force would fight. Therefore, US forces had to be sized to meet worst case conditions. An additional planning consideration was to minimize civilian casualties and damage to civilian property while accomplishing the mission. This consideration dictated a deliberate and constrained use of force.

All US citizens were rescued without injury and major military operations were completed within the first four days of the Grenada operation despite determined resistance. Cuban resistance reflected thorough military training. Some Grenadian forces also fought well, especially those manning anti-aircraft weapons. US forces used during this four day period consisted of a Marine Amphibious Unit (battalion size), two Ranger battalions (-), some Special Forces, and a brigade from the 82nd Airborne Division, which deployed during the 25 through 27 October period. An additional brigade of the 82nd Airborne Division closed Grenada on the 28th to participate in mop-up operations which lasted another three days.

The British mission in the Falklands was to defeat an Argentine force. The Falklands conflict was protracted over several weeks and consisted of naval engagements, anti-submarine warfare, air and anti-air warfare, unconventional warfare, a conventional amphibious operation, and ground combat. The eight infantry battalions were part of a larger operation and did not operate under constraints in place in Grenada. Additionally, the Argentine force, which was rapidly deployed to the Falklands, did not possess in all cases a high level of training, and this contributed to the Falklands outcome.

Comments

It is inappropriate to compare Grenada with the Falklands operation due to differences in mission, enemy, troops available, terrain, time available, and rules of engagement.

Allegation

"Deficiencies in planning seem to have been part of the reason the Cubans did so well, relative to the odds against them. The plan did not reflect an attempt at a coup de main, in which overwhelming force is used to seize all the critical junctures in an enemy's system at the outset. Instead, a few small teams of specialized forces were sent against a few of these junctures, while most of our forces were put into two airfields on the island's peripheries. As a result, the opponent was able to form and maintain a fairly effective defense."

Facts

The plan to rescue and evacuate US and other foreign nationals, neutralize opposing forces, and stabilize the internal situation in Grenada reflected a coup de main. The plan called for the capture of the two airfields on Grenada to include the immediate neutralization of Cuban forces at Point Salines airfield as well as the near simultaneous seizure of several key targets, and the rescue of US citizens. Control of these objectives would lead to paralysis of the military command structure on the island.

The surprise airborne assault on Point Salines airfield by the Rangers effectively neutralized Cuban forces at the outset, and led to the capture of several hundred Cubans despite stiff resistance. Capture of Pearls Airport by the Marines, as well as their successful amphibious operation in the vicinity of St. George's on the 25th led to the capture of Fort Frederick, the Grenadian command and control headquarters, the next day. Successful execution of US plans on the 25th and 26th led to cessation of organized enemy resistance. Remaining isolated pockets of resistance were eliminated by the 28th.

Comments

US forces planned and executed a coup de main by neutralizing Cuban and Grenadian key installations as a first priority. Thereafter, Cuban and Grenadian resistance was uncoordinated and sporadic. US forces conducted operations in such a manner that civilian casualties and destruction of civilian property were minimized.

Allegation

"Interestingly, one early plan for the invasion, reportedly developed by the Atlantic Fleet headquarters, would have produced something much closer to a coup de main. That plan called for the use of only Navy and Marine Corps units, and proposed that the main effort be a landing at Grand Anse beach followed by a quick move across the peninsula to cut Salines airfield off from the capital of St. George's. This would have isolated the Cubans from the rest of the island and made any defense on their part meaningless."

Facts

In responding to initial JCS requests for planning for the evacuation of US citizens from Grenada, USCINCLANT developed several courses of action, including an option utilizing only Navy and Marine Corps units. This option was discarded by CINCLANT even before he presented it to the JCS because of the importance of simultaneously seizing Pearls airport on the east coast and multiple targets in the southern portion of the island. The number, size, and location of the various objectives exceeded the capability of a single Marine battalion.

Comments

Point Salines airfield was, in fact, isolated from St. George's immediately in the operations and the Cuban force contained in the southern part of the island in the area of Point Salines airfield.

Allegation

"The Army was anxious to give its Rangers a piece of the action to justify its request for a third Ranger battalion and a Ranger regimental headquarters, while the overall command for specialized, commando-type forces wanted a chance to show what its units could do. So in what seems to have become the standard JCS approach to military operations, one that turns them into a pie-dividing contest among all the Services, we ended up with a plan that allowed the enemy to put up a reasonably good show."

Facts

Forces used in URGENT FURY were chosen based on their capability to fulfill the mission of protection/rescue of US citizens, neutralization of enemy forces, and stabilization of Grenada in view of the expected opposition. The Marine Amphibious Unit (MAU) was used because of its proximity to the area while in transit to Lebanon and its combat capability. The Rangers and other Special Forces were chosen because of their unique capability to secure airfields, rescue hostages, and attack selected point targets. Based on the enemy situation (presence of 700 Cubans, 1200 Peoples Revolutionary Army personnel, and numerous militia) the 82nd Airborne was included to ensure an adequate combat power ratio and permit early redeployment of the Special Forces and the MAU to fulfill pending commitments.

Comments

Forces used in URGENT FURY were strictly chosen based on a military analysis of the mission, enemy capabilities and the type of forces required, as well as rapid availability.

Allegation

"The [specialized forces] command's SEALs undertook three, possibly four missions, only one of which was a success: the rescue of the Governor General, Paul Scoon."

Facts

The SEALs executed two missions on D-Day. All other missions were designated as ON-ORDER to be executed as the situation dictated. The D-Day missions were the seizure and control of the Governor General's house to protect Governor General Scoon and his staff and the seizure and control of Radio Free Grenada (RFG). ON-ORDER, ST-6 was to seize and control the St. George's diesel power plant.

Comments

The mission into the Governor-General's house was successful. The facility identified as RFG was successfully assaulted, seized, and disabled. One classified mission was not executed successfully.

Allegation

"Press reports that the Governor General and the SEALs were besieged in the Governor's residence under heavy fire were not correct; they detected enemy forces in their neighborhood but came under little or no fire."

Facts

The SEALs that assaulted into the grounds of the Governor's house took heavy automatic weapons fire during the assault. No SEALs were wounded.

Comments

During the ensuing 24 hours until the linkup with a USMC element, the team experienced numerous sightings of enemy personnel and vehicles who appeared to be moving to surround the Governor's house. This caused HQ elements to direct close air support for the team. One probing APC type vehicle was destroyed immediately outside the mansion's perimeter fence.

Allegation

"A second SEAL mission failed in the ocean with a tragic loss of life. Poor weather forecasting seems to have been the primary reason for this failure, although some questionable techniques employed by the SEALs may also have contributed."

Facts

The weather was as forecasted.

Comments

None.

Allegation

"The third mission, to knock Radio Grenada off the air, also failed. The SEALs got into the compound where the radio was located but attacked the wrong building."

Facts

There was only one building in the compound. It was the transmitter site for Radio Free Grenada, and it was rendered inoperable.

Comments

None.

Allegation

"Delta Force personnel were brought in to take Richmond Hill prison. They attempted to do the job by landing near the prison, by helicopter, in daylight. Hostile forces in or near the prison took the helicopter under fire and drove it off, inflicting casualties on our troops. Delta then repeated exactly the same tactic with another helicopter the next day! The result was predictable; they were again driven off, with casualties, this time by a force of just three Grenadian prison guards."

Facts

The assault of Richmond Hill prison was conducted at 0615L [6:15 A.M.] The prison was heavily defended and our troops took heavy fire from small arms, heavy automatic weapons, and anti-aircraft weapons. The force was unable to complete the assault. It did not conduct a second assault on Richmond Hill prison.

Comments

The assault on Richmond Hill prison was understood to be a high risk mission but was undertaken in an attempt to prevent the prisoners from being used as hostages.

Allegation

"The 82d Airborne Division was brought into the planning very late, which created a degree of uncertainty and confusion."

Facts

The rapidly deteriorating political situation resulted in the expansion of military planning on 21 October to require rescue of US citizens, neutralization of enemy forces, and stabilization of Grenada. On that date the 82d Airborne Division received a WARNING ORDER for possible operations in Grenada. On 22 October liaison personnel attended a planning conference at USLANTCOM Headquarters and thereafter began planning for the division's part in the operation. The 82d Airborne Commander attended a JTF 120 sponsored planning conference at Norfolk on 24 October.

Comments

Planning time for operation URGENT FURY was limited for all participants, and the 82d Airborne Division had essentially the same preparatory time as the other participating units.

Allegation

"Second, the 82d seems to have followed the traditional American practice of building up a substantial force and logistics base before moving out."

Facts

The first C-141 transporting elements of the 82d Airborne Division landed at Point Salines airfield at 1405 on 25 October with one battalion closing on the 25th. This unit came under fire upon landing and deployed to assist in providing airfield security. The buildup of 82d Airborne Division troop strength was relatively slow due to the single airfield, Point Salines, which had a single, under-construction runway and very limited ramp area. As a consequence, aircraft had to be unloaded while on the runway which precluded rapid buildup of personnel and supplies. The second battalion closed early on the 26th, and the third battalion closed on the 27th. By the end of the 28th, there were six battalions in Grenada. In addition to airfield security, the 82d was required to handle some 600 Cuban prisoners by the 26th as well as many Grenadian detainees and refugees. On the 26th, the 2d Brigade (–) attacked to the east and seized the Calliste village complex, killing 16 Cuban soldiers and capturing 86 others. Also on the 26th, the 82d Airborne Division was the command and control headquarters for the rescue of 224 students at Grand Anse.

On the 27th, the 2d Brigade conducted combat operations toward St. George's and the airmobile assault at Calivigny Barracks.

Comments

By the 28th, when the buildup of 82d Airborne Division combat forces was at its peak, all important objectives had been achieved and only mop-up operations remained.

Allegation

"Third, the Army command on the scene seems to have had some difficulty adjusting to the situation as it unfolded, leading it, among other things, to believe it was opposed by as many as two battalions of Cubans. As noted earlier, there were fewer than 700 Cubans on the island. The overestimation of enemy strength seems to have led to great cautiousness by the Army units then engaged."

Facts

Initial intelligence estimates stated Cuban strength of 700 on Grenada which included approximately 600 "construction workers," some 50 Cuban military advisors, and other personnel. The 600 construction workers translates to approximately a battalion-size unit. On 26 October, when US forces captured Fort Frederick and recovered military documents, the figure of 1,100 Cuban "construction workers" present on the island surfaced. This information later proved to be not accurate and did not result in excessive cautiousness in combat operations by Army units. On the 26th, the 82d Airborne Division and the Rangers conducted an airmobile rescue of 224 US students at Grand Anse. On the 26th deployed units of the 82d Airborne Division conducted ground combat operations against Calliste village, killing 16 Cuban soldiers and capturing 86 others, and on the 27th, the 82d Airborne Division and the Rangers conducted an airmobile assault to seize Calivigny Barracks, a Cuban base.

Comments

Information collected during combat operations initially indicated there might be two battalions of Cubans on the island. This information did not restrict or hinder the aggressiveness of combat operations conducted by US forces.

Allegation

"The fourth and perhaps most important cause of the Army's slowness was that both the Rangers, in their initial battle on and near the airfield, and later the units from the 82d Airborne, seem to have used a frontal, linear approach to the Cuban defense."

Facts

1. Both the Ranger airborne assault at Point Salines airfield and subsequent operations of the 82d Airborne Division reflect numerous flank attacks as well as many instances of initiative and ingenuity.

2. Some examples of Ranger unit flexibility include:
   a. Ranger plans for the assault of Point Salines airfield called for airborne or airland operations based on the situation. As aircraft approached the runway, they came under heavy anti-aircraft fire, necessitating an airborne assault. The decision was made to jump from 500 feet versus the normal 1100 feet to limit exposure and vulnerability of the paratroopers, resulting in no combat casualties and only one jump injury. The assault took place at approximately 0530.
   b. Ranger forces cleared the runway of obstacles while under fire from snipers, automatic weapons, and anti-aircraft guns. The runway contained obstacles including approximately 25 barbed-wire fences, 55-gallon drums, and heavy equipment such as rollers and bulldozers. Rangers hotwired the in-place bulldozers to assist in clearing the runway. By 0630 the runway was cleared.
   c. B Company, 1-75 Rangers, on the western flank of the runway, started rolling up the flank of the Cuban defensive position from west to east by 0700. The company first sergeant led a three-man team to assault a Cuban position, killing two Cubans and capturing 28 more. B Company rolled up the Cuban defenses until they reached the main Cuban camp. Ranger snipers took Cuban mortar positions under fire and killed or wounded 18 Cubans at ranges of 600–1000 meters.

d. A Company, 1-75 Rangers, assembled on the east end of Point Salines airfield and attacked the Cuban camp from east to west. The Rangers captured a Cuban ZPU anti-aircraft weapon which they used to take the Cuban camp under fire. Also, A Company Rangers seized a Cuban bulldozer and assaulted a Cuban position using the bulldozer as a "tank."

e. Rangers considered an airstrike on the Cuban camp to reduce resistance, but the mission was not flown because it could not be determined if civilians were in the Cuban camp. Instead, the B Company first sergeant sent a Cuban worker into the camp with instructions for the camp to surrender in 15 minutes "or else." Approximately 175 Cubans surrendered.

f. By 1600 hours, the Ranger units were relieved in place by elements of the 82d Airborne Division.

g. On 26 October, the Rangers executed an airmobile assault at Grand Anse campus behind fortified enemy positions to rescue and evacuate 224 US students. The entire operation took 26 minutes. When mechanical problems grounded a helicopter, 12 Rangers remained behind enemy lines to make seats available for students. The small Ranger unit conducted escape and evasion operations, captured a boat, and escaped to sea under cover of darkness.

Comments

The above actions are only some examples of the initiative and flexibility shown by US forces during the Grenada operation. Operations on the flanks and to the rear of enemy defensive positions were the norm. The initative displayed by US forces of all the Services and at all levels was one of the key factors in the US success.

Allegation

"The Army's doctrine of maneuver warfare would appear to have called instead for an attack using infiltration tactics, in which our forces would have filtered through and around the Cubans, collapsing their whole defense from the rear. Reportedly, the terrain and the positioning of the Cuban defenses made such an attack possible. But instead, both the Rangers and the 82d seem to have taken pride in attacking and destroying each and every Cuban position—a very slow process. This more than anything else seems to have enabled the Cubans to fight as long as they did."

Facts

Cuban defenses were concentrated in the vicinity of Point Salines airfield. The Rangers' airborne assault of this airfield, in fact, isolated most Cubans from the remainder of the island. An analysis of Cuban defenses and the Ranger attack show that the attack was made at the flank of the main Cuban defense. Other operations such as the airmobile rescue of 224 students at Grand Anse on the 26th and the airmobile operation at Calivigny barracks were made to the rear of Cuban positions.

Comments

Facts do not support the contention that the Rangers and the 82d Airborne Division took pride in attacking and destroying each and every Cuban position. Moreover, an attempt to correlate the Grenadian operations with a conventional assault is specious; the mission required that all hostile armed elements be neutralized.

Allegation

"Second, some units of the (82d Abn) division seemed to have experienced a breakdown of discipline. Some eyewitnesses report looting of Grenadian property. Some discipline problems can be seen in films of the action, which picture troops wearing machine gun ammunition as bandoliers. This is not just a cosmetic issue; carrying the ammunition this way gets it dirty and can bend the links, both of which can cause the gun to jam."

Facts

Reported looting and mishandling of Grenadian civilians and their property was fully investigated by staff officers and field commanders concerned with Army operations in Grenada. Wearing machine gun ammunition as bandoliers is not the standard in the 82d Airborne

Division. There were isolated instances of this happening during the Grenada operation. The 82d Airborne Division is taking corrective action.

Comments

None.

Allegation

"First, the training given to all these units (special operations, Rangers, 82d Abn Div) may be too rigid. It may be geared towards perfection of every detail within the framework of a set plan in which everything is predictable. In contrast, most combat is characterized by uncertainty, surprise and rapid change. Training must center on free-play exercises, and commanders and trainers must strive to inject the unexpected into each training situation."

Facts

There were innumerable examples of initiative and flexibility on the part of US forces in Grenada. The flexibility shown by the Rangers during the airborne assault under intense anti-aircraft fire was a key factor to the success of the entire operation. The ability to adapt captured enemy equipment to our use contributed to our success. Use of enemy anti-aircraft weapons for our own fire support and use of enemy bulldozers as "tanks" in support of our ground maneuver are two good examples. The immediate decision by 12 Rangers to remain behind during the rescue of US students at the Grand Anse campus on 26 October as well as their subsequent successful escape and evasion reflects superb initiative that is gained through realistic training.

Allegation

"Second, these units may be affected by the 'cowboy syndrome.' The 'cowboys' are people who believe machismo is what defines a competent soldier. The 'snake eater' image of some of our specialized forces and the elite image of the paratroopers tend to make these units magnets for 'cowboys.' In combat, the 'cowboy' tends to fight the enemy even when he can go around him—as some of our forces seem to have done on Grenada—and also to 'come unglued' when faced with the unexpected."

Facts

This is a superfluous assertion with no basis in fact.

Comments

None.

Allegation

"The Marines' good performance on Grenada should not be seen as a statement on the overall condition of the Marine Corps. The Marines' maneuver warfare effort is centered in the 2d Marine division, and maneuver warfare ideas and training are seldom found outside that division."

Facts

As previously noted, the attempt to use the Grenadian operation as a basis for supporting the concept of maneuver warfare is fallacious. Maneuver warfare philosophy or training is not confined to any particular Marine Corps unit, but is shared throughout the Marine Corps. For example, the tactics and techniques of maneuver warfare are an integral part of the training program at the Marine Corps Combined Air Ground Training Center at Twenty-Nine Palms, California. Moreover, amphibious operations are the essence of maneuver warfare.

Allegation

"Out of approximately 100 US helicopters used on Grenada, nine were destroyed and a number of others were damaged. These numbers include helicopters involved in accidents, but accidents are also a cause of losses in war and must be considered. A loss rate of 9% in three days against an opponent with no anti-aircraft missiles, only guns (which can be highly effective), is not easy to pass over. What does it suggest our helicopter losses would be, for example, in a war in Europe?"

Facts

Aircraft		Number
UH-60	(Army)	32
UH-1	(Army)	9
AH-1	(Army)	25
OH-58	(Army)	19
CH46E	(Marine)	12
CH53D	(Marine)	4
AH1-T	(Marine)	4
UH-1	(Marine)	2
Total		107

Battle Damage

1	UH-60 Destroyed
1	UH-60 To be Repaired at AVIM
4	UH-60 Require Depot Repair
1	CH-46E Destroyed
2	AH1-T Destroyed
9	Total

Damage Assessment

- Impacts indicated the threat was 7.62 mm in size, possible 12.7 mm.

- Most of the hits were to the cockpit, cabin, aft fuselage, and tailboom. A few hits were noted on the main rotor head, none on the engine although there were several on the inlet and exhaust shrouds, none on the main rotor controls above the cabin, and relatively few on main and tail rotor blades.

- In summary, with the exception of one fuel cell that did not selfseal, the damage to flight critical components is consistent with results of previous ballistic testing and vulnerability analyses of prototype hardware. The fuel leak may be attributable to nonperfect sealing mechanics rather than an unexpected ability of the projectile to cause damage.

Comments

Army

a. In Grenada the new helicopters were able to withstand anti-aircraft fire. One BLACK HAWK had 45 bullet holes, punctured fuel tanks, holes in the tail and main rotors, much of the control instrumentation destroyed, and five people, including the pilot, wounded. Yet the crew completed their mission.

b. All combat damaged BLACK HAWKS completed their missions.

c. Ten BLACK HAWKS received combat damage with only one loss.

d. The BLACK HAWKS met or exceeded survivability and crashworthiness design specifications.

Marine Corps

One of the primary concerns in Grenada was to minimize casualties to the civilian population. Rules of engagement reflected this concern. The first Marine AH-1 lost had been engaged in an attack mission in place of fixed wing and artillery in order to avoid collateral fragmentation and blast damage. The second attack helicopter was lost providing cover to the first aircraft. The CH-46 was damaged during an assault on Grand Anse to rescue medical students. In all three instances different rules of engagement would have played a major role in the outcome of the helicopter losses. In the case of the AH-1s, a different means of supporting fire would have been employed. In the case of the CH-46, suppressive fire support may have eliminated the anti-aircraft fire.

Allegation

"When the services give briefings to justify their heavy investment in helicopters, a line is usually drawn on a map. Our forces are on one side of the line, the enemy on the other. The helicopters can stay over friendly lines while transporting troops or shooting missiles at enemy tanks. But in most real combat, there is no neat line. Friendly and enemy forces are mixed together, often to a considerable depth."

Facts

Military doctrine calls for suppression of enemy air defense weapons with artillery or tactical air support while conducting operations over enemy territory. Nap of the earth air movement techniques limit the time that helicopters are vulnerable to air defense weapons and are an integral part of flight training.

Comments

It is recognized that there will not be a neat line in combat. Also, it is recognized that helicopters cannot simply fly over enemy air defense weapons without placing themselves at great risk. Although helicopters have distinct limitations on a nonlinear battlefield, they provide essential firepower and mobility. Limitations apply to all weapon systems and are compensated for by tactics. Helicopters, therefore, are employed in concert with other parts of the combined arms team to include ground forces, tactical air support, and artillery. In Grenada, we took measures to reduce civilian casualties and therefore did not support helicopter operations with suppressive air and artillery fire to the extent we could have. Helicopter pilots performed bravely under these conditions throughout the operation, and equipment performance was outstanding.

Appendix B
Organization of the People's Revolutionary Armed Forces, 1983

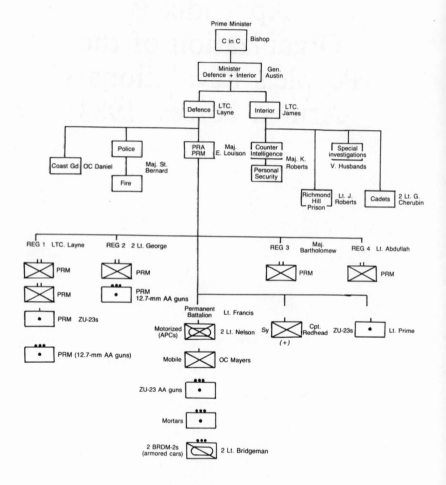

Appendix C
U.S. Order of Battle
for Urgent Fury

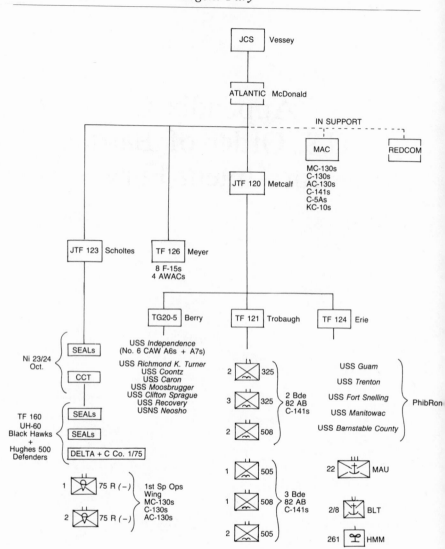

Appendix D
Letter from the Governor-General of Grenada to the Prime Minister of Barbados

Date: October 24, 1983 [backdated]

Dear Prime Minister,

You are aware that there is a vacuum of authority in Grenada following the killing of the Prime Minister and the subsequent violations of human rights and bloodshed.

I am therefore seriously concerned over the lack of internal security in Grenada. Consequently I am requesting your help to assist me in stabilizing this grave and dangerous situation. It is my desire that a peacekeeping force should be established in Grenada to facilitate a rapid return to peace and tranquility and also a return to democratic rule.

In this connexion I am also seeking assistance from the United States, from Jamaica, and from the Organization of Eastern Caribbean States through its current chairman the hon. Eugenia Charles (Prime Minister of Dominica) in the spirit of the treaty establishing that organization to which my country is signatory.

I have the honour to be,

Yours faithfully,

Paul Scoon,
Governor-General.

Notes

Prologue

1. The Mongoose Gang was so named because it was originally formed from a group of layabouts employed in a mongoose eradication project but who were quickly diverted to the eradication of opposition to Gairy.
2. Arthur Grimble was a well-known British colonial civil servant who made his name as a district commissioner in the Gilbert Islands early this century. His books, *Pattern of Islands* and *Return to the Islands,* later became compulsory reading in many British schools. He rose to become governor of Grenada in the 1950s, finishing his career as governor of the Seychelles in the Indian Ocean.

Chapter 1

1. Most Grenadians are seldom called by their proper name but rather use a nickname. These nicknames frequently appeared in official correspondence. For example, Prime Minister Bishop, when sending a written note to Lieutenant Colonel Layne, would address it to "Headache."
2. Innocent Belmar was one of the most detested of Gairy's police officers, who was forced to resign as a result of the Duffus investigation just before independence. He immediately became a GULP politician, was elected and appointed a minister. The next day he was shot dead. Bishop successfully defended the accused, much to Gairy's fury.

Chapter 2

1. All Central Committee or Politburo members carried Makarov pistols at all times, including at official meetings. Central Committee members also had twenty-four-hour personal protection from men of the security service.

Chapter 3

1. Sandhurst is the British equivalent of West Point.
2. These were prophetic words. Mayers himself had then only some two hours to live.

Chapter 4

1. There is no clear evidence that Prime went to Fort Frederick with the others, but he may have. I was not permitted to speak to Prime or the other condemned persons in prison after their trial. Prime was certainly present at the execution and was eventually sentenced to hang on the ground that he had conspired with the others to kill Bishop, although he did not apparently actually shoot anybody.
2. At the subsequent trial, Beverley Ann-Marie Charles was to claim that Redhead went forward after the shooting to slit Bishop's throat with a knife and to cut off his ring finger. Nobody else corroborated this, but it may have happened.
3. This gesture could be taken as supporting evidence that Bishop's throat was cut, but equally it could have indicated that he had been killed.

Chapter 5

1. In fact the running water supply had ceased to function since shortly after Bishop was shot. The students at True Blue constructed their own field latrines at the end of the runway. Later a prominent notice stating "We Survived So Far?" was displayed outside.
2. It is quite likely that neither of them knew about the Special Forces mission to get into Grenada thirty-six hours in advance of the main invasion.

Chapter 6

1. Five years afterward, George Bush was still endorsing the rescue of citizens in danger as the primary objective of Urgent Fury. In an election campaign interview with *Reader's Digest,* in response to a question about the use of U.S. armed forces overseas he stated: "But Grenada is a good, clear example. American lives were at risk. . . ."
2. Poindexter retired prematurely as a result of his involvement with the sale-of-arms-for-hostages deal struck with Iran and the subsequent misuse of these funds to assist the contra rebels. He faces criminal charges on these matters.

Chapter 7

1. It is often asked why the intelligence community knew so little about what was going on in Grenada. Certainly their ignorance in the circumstances reflected adversely on their competence. The usual tendency to rely on technological intelligence gathering rather than human sources on the ground played its part. But this is not the full story. It doesn't explain the lack of maps or the fact that information was actually to hand—it was there for the asking. Hundreds of U.S. citizens had children on the island, hundreds of Grenadians lived in the New York area, and the telephone lines still worked—but still intelligence agencies were caught napping. Probably the answer lies in general incompetence within the bureaucracies. Given more time, they would have come up with more and better information, but there was no time. Urgent Fury had to be conceived and executed within a few days, insufficient time for the intelligence system to catch up.

Chapter 9

1. North, like Poindexter, subsequently resigned from the marines in 1988 over the Iran arms-for-hostages deal. He faces serious criminal charges over the misuse of government funds.
2. The mission of these two special helicopters remains uncertain. They were variants of the Hughes 500 Defender aircraft, specifically built and equipped for a wide variety of tasks. They could be employed for reconnaissance or as attack helicopters, for command and control, or to insert small parties of men covertly behind enemy lines. After Urgent Fury had been under way for several hours, both were seen on the island, parked at Salines, and rocketing a target at Amber Belair on the afternoon of D day. Their presence in Grenada has always been denied officially despite the evidence of photographs and film. It is likely they had a supporting role to play with the Special Forces operations or that they were part of a last-minute attempt to get somebody into Grenada just prior to H hour. Both aircraft were seen landing at Union Island, north of Grenada, late on the afternoon of October 24, at the same time that a chartered yacht from Barbados with two CIA agents was at the island. I have been unable to unravel this story.
3. With the death of Adams in 1985, it has proved impossible to obtain a copy of this photograph.
4. Casualties were inflicted on both sides at the Beausejour action, but it has proved difficult to obtain precise details. Including the ambush, at least five or six PRA soldiers, and possibly more, died. Twelve or so were wounded, which included some of the PRA captives in the transmitter building when it came under fire from the APC. Fear of repercussions prevented former PRA participants from being more forthright in their accounts to me.

   The number of U.S. casualties is grossly exaggerated by Grenadians, and no American bodies were ever produced. Local opinion is that this is because the Americans had a special chemical, which they used to destroy all traces of their own dead that they could not remove.

   It is quite possible there were no U.S. deaths at Beausejour. The much more prolonged operation at Government House produced no SEAL casualties at all; no bodies were found, and certainly the SEALs retreating from Beausejour, and swimming for hours out to the *Caron,* would not have been able to take seriously incapacitated people with them. One SEAL is reliably reported to have been wounded in the arm, and possibly several others were lightly injured, but until the U.S. authorities are less secretive about Special Forces casualties, an accurate count is impossible.
5. Much previous speculation on the activities of the Special Forces, including the Rangers' drop at Salines on D day, was based on Richard Gabriel's account in his book, *Military Incompetence,* published in 1985. Gabriel admits he had no access to after-action reports, so his version of what happened is largely guesswork. He guessed wrong in most instances, although he was correct that much did not go according to plan that morning. His contention—that Delta dropped at Salines prior to the Rangers and became involved in a firefight with numerous losses and that this alerted the defenders—has no basis in fact. He has been confused

by the pathfinder drop in advance of the Rangers, by members of C Company of the 1st/75th, of which he seems unaware.

6. Captain Lucas was later awarded the Distinguished Flying Cross and the Purple Heart, posthumously, for his gallantry that day, as was Chief Warrant Officer Price.

Chapter 10

1. These two deaths have never been officially acknowledged; nor has the use of pathfinders. I have included the story of their use on the basis of a number of factors. First, using pathfinders is the usual tactical technique in this type of operation, and the plan for the seizure of Salines was an orthodox one. There was really no special plan for the Rangers to rescue the students at True Blue. Second, several Grenadian witnesses claim to have seen them dropping well before the main body. Third, a source within the Special Forces told me pathfinders were used in Grenada. And fourth, I was informed by a reliable military source that he had been told personally by a senior Ranger participant that two pathfinders were lost in the drop.

Chapter 11

1. The recently formed Grenadian Special Service Unit took over the new camp at Little Havana for its base after Urgent Fury, thus inflicting on itself the same tactical disadvantages the Cubans suffered from. If the surrounding hills are not secured, the location becomes untenable.

Chapter 12

1. Captain Giguere posthumously received a Bronze Star for his efforts in getting the helicopters of his squadron to such a peak of readiness for combat. From July to October 1983, he had been the assistant aircraft maintenance officer with special responsibility for technical and crew training. He had carried out these duties with exceptional enthusiasm and effectiveness.

A further eight Bronze Stars were awarded to marine officers and noncommissioned officers for their efforts during Urgent Fury. Similarly twenty-six Purple Hearts went to Marine Corps personnel. It is difficult to reconcile this figure with the number of marines killed or wounded. According to the official medal eligibility regulations, a Purple Heart is given "for wounds or death as a result of an act of an opposing armed force." Well, three marine officers were killed (Giguere, Scharver, and Seagle), while after-action reports and first-hand accounts reveal only one wounded in combat (Howard). This leaves twenty-two Purple Hearts unaccounted for. The marines acknowledge that four others were injured (during the off-loading of a CH-53 on D day and two more in a jeep accident on October 27). One must therefore assume that these awards were also made for noncombat accidental injuries and that there were at least another eighteen of these or other wounded never mentioned in any accounts of the marines' operations on the island. This latter seems highly unlikely; their accounts of even minor patrol actions are very detailed and never mention any wounded at all. The conclusion on the evidence available must be that of the twenty-six awards made, twenty-two were for minor noncombat accidents—an extraordinary situation.

2. Lieutenant Colonel Smith was fairly outspoken on several aspects of the operation. An article about Urgent Fury in the *Providence Sunday Journal* on the fifth anniversary of the operation quoted Smith as twice complaining, while on the *Guam,* about army tactics, and even directly to General Vessey when he visited the island. The *Journal* quotes Smith as saying to a Marine Corps historian, "I told my guys more than once that I was a hell of a lot more concerned of the 82d Airborne than I was the People's Revolutionary Army. And I meant it." Perhaps not surprisingly, awards and promotion do not seem to have come Smith's way in the years that followed.

Chapter 13

1. It was from a house on this hill that Buxo had used his telescope so effectively on October 19 to peer into Coard's house.

Chapter 14

1. In most accounts, the crash of the second Black Hawk has been attributed to hostile fire. This is possible but unlikely. There was no defense of the camp as such since all the PRA troops had long since departed. If a few administrative personnel had been left behind, they would not have stayed once the bombardment started. If they had, at least one or two would have been killed or wounded, but no evidence of casualties was ever found at the camp or in the surrounding area. Even supposing a few rounds had been fired, the Black Hawks have a tremendous capacity for absorbing hostile fire and surviving. There were no AA guns at Calivigny, and small arms fire would be most unlikely to have caused the crash. It was more probably a pilot error, with the rotor blades striking a building or some other obstacle.

2. Luketina's mother later complained bitterly about her official notification of her son's injuries. It was not until five days after the incident that she was told the extent of his wounds and five days after that that they were the result of friendly fire. She claimed, "First, they told me he had stepped on a hand grenade or an antipersonnel device. Then they told me his feet were blown off. It was only much later (about five days) that I found out he had lost his legs because a Navy plane had shot up his position."

3. This was the most serious friendly fire incident during Urgent Fury and was the subject of a detailed investigation. It proved impossible, or inappropriate, to apportion blame. One report later castigated ground fire-support elements generally for inadequate target descriptions, saying, "Needless to say a target brief that says 'your target is the white building on the green ridge' just does not hack it when there are thousands of white houses on thousands of green ridges." As far

as the particular incident on October 27 is concerned, this is unfair; the chief warrant officer on the ground gave a much clearer description and a bearing. Despite this, the pilot fired on a building that had a different-colored roof and did not meet the other features given him. All that can be said is that this method of dealing with the odd sniper is cumbersome, complicated, and confusing.

4. Major Van Huss (now a lieutenant colonel) received a Gold Star, in lieu of a second award of the Bronze Star, for his performance during Urgent Fury. His citation reads, in part, that he "demonstrated remarkable skill as a tactician in planning and supervising the execution of several major assaults on the islands of Grenada and Carriacou. . . . He provided invaluable counsel to the Commanding Officer, and demonstrated outstanding ability in coordinating efforts between Marine, Navy, and Joint Task Force commands."

Chapter 15

1. This is the only reference to Cubans outside their camps in the southwest actually participating in the fighting. A substantial number of Cuban technical advisers worked with various ministries in Grenada, including that of Agriculture. It is possible that either these two or three Cubans were civilian workers at the nearby hospital or agricultural station or, less likely, because all military personnel had been assembled at Salines, that they may have been military advisers to Military Region 2, whose headquarters was at Mt. Horne.

2. The suggested disappearance of Bishop's body is an intriguing mystery. It was said at the time that the U.S. authorities had removed his remains to the United States, not just for identification but to ensure that he could not be buried in Grenada, with his grave becoming a national shrine. The story of no heads or hands, and nothing being discovered pertaining to Bishop, was allegedly just a cover put out by the United States to justify their not returning his remains. Although I have no specific evidence, this story has a ring of truth about it.

   Certainly no Grenadian witness to the execution or burial ever claimed that hands or heads were cut off before burning. If they had been, somebody would assuredly have mentioned it during the following months or at the trial. Abdullah had no reason to do so; he was convinced that burning the bodies thoroughly was more than sufficient. When the Americans excavated the grave, no Grenadian or Caribbean Peacekeeping Force representatives were allowed near; the plastic bags were filled and flown out immediately. Until somebody who was actually involved reveals what happened, the probability is that the United States deliberately kept Bishop's remains and put out the story to explain their not handing them back to Grenada or Bishop's relatives, who clamored for them for a long time afterward.

3. In the November 1984 issue of the *Air Force Times,* Lind quotes General Vessey as saying to Trobaugh: "We have two companies of Marines running all over the island, and thousands of army troops doing nothing. What the hell is going on?"

Chapter 16

1. This is a most extraordinarily worded citation. It makes it look as though Urgent Fury was mounted to save hundreds of U.S. citizens from imminent death and to restore Maurice Bishop's PRG.
2. It is interesting to compare the United States system of awards for Grenada with that of Britain after the Falklands campaign. If one discounts the American AFEM and its British equivalent, the South Atlantic Medal, and looks only at awards for gallantry or distinguished service, the figures are startling. The United States, in an operation where the actual fighting lasted three days, awarded some 15,000 such medals. Britain, which fought a well-armed enemy of over 13,000, supported by an aggressive air force, for 25 days, awarded 682.
3. Michelle Gibbs, who was married to a Grenadian, was later expelled from Grenada to the United States.

Epilogue

1. Commander Rick Butler, whose knowledge of Grenadian waters was so useful to 22d MAU just prior to the operation, later told a Marine Corps historian that "This business of rescuing the students out of this place was almost a sideshow. . . . It was something that just happened. It turned out wonderfully, and it will now be the central event of the whole Grenada evolution. But in the context of the time, it was just a sideshow that was put together [on] a wing and a prayer. . . ."
2. See note 1 in chapter 12 for comment on casualties among the marines and the award of twenty-six Purple Hearts.

Bibliography

L ISTED below are the main unclassified sources consulted. A substantial number of classified documents were also examined, including after-action, intelligence, police, and prison reports, together with relevant papers, letters, and the operation log of the Barbados Defence Force.

Books

Adams, James. *Secret Armies*. London: Hutchinson, 1987.

Beckwith, Col. Charlie A., and Donald Knox. *Delta Force*. New York: Harcourt Brace Jovanovich, 1983.

Editorial de Ciencias Sociales. *Grenada: The World against Crime*. Havana, Cuba, 1983.

EPICA Task Force. *Grenada: The Peaceful Revolution*. Washington, D.C.: Ecumenical Program for Inter-American Communication and Action, 1982.

Gabriel, Richard A. *Military Incompetence*. New York: Hill and Wang, 1985.

Luttwak, Edward N. *The Pentagon and the Art of War*. New York: Simon & Schuster, 1985.

O'Shaughnessy, Hugh. *Grenada*. London: Sphere Books, 1984.

Quarrie, Bruce. *The World's Elite Forces*. London: Octopus Books, 1985.

Rottman, Gordon L. *US Army Special Forces 1952–84*. Elite Series. London: Osprey, 1985.

Russell, Lee E., and Albert Mendiz. *Grenada 1983*. Men-at-Arms Series. London: Osprey, 1985.

Sandford, Gregory, and Richard Vigilante. *Grenada: The Untold Story*. New York: Madison Books, 1984.

Thorndike, Tony. *Grenada–Politics, Economics, and Society*. London: Francis Pinter, 1985.

Valenta, Jiri, and Herbert J. Ellison, eds. *Grenada and Soviet/Cuban Policy*. Boulder, Colo.: Westview Press, 1986.

Woodward, Bob. *Veil: The Secret Wars of the CIA, 1981–1987*. London: Simon & Schuster, 1988.

Zerneman, Andrew J. *In Bloody Terms*. Indiana: Greenlawn Press, 1986.

Documents

"Bulletin from the Political Department of the PRG on 20th October 1983." Broadcast account of the attack on Fort Rupert, October 19, 1983.

Communiqué of the Government of Cuba. St. George's: Cuban Embassy, November 1, 1983.

Cuban Armed Forces and the Soviet Military Presence. Washington, D.C.: International Communication Agency, 1982.

Grenada: A Preliminary Report. Washington, D.C.: U.S. Department of State and Department of Defense, December 1983.

Grenada: Background and Facts. Washington, D.C.: U.S. Information Agency, 1984.

Grenada Documents: An Overview and Selection. Washington, D.C.: Department of State and Department of Defense, September 1983.

Grenada Occasional Papers, No. 1: Maurice Bishop's "Line of March" Speech, September 13, 1982. Wasington, D.C.: U.S. Department of State, 1984.

Grenada-United States Relations Part II: October 12-27, 1983. Dennis Conway. Universities Field Staff International, 1983.

Hearing before the East Caribbean Subcommittee, Foreign Affairs Committee, U.S. House of Representatives, November 1983.

Hearing, The Situation in Grenada, before the Committee on Foreign Relations, U.S. Senate, October 27, 1983.

Leninism in Grenada. Jiri and Virginia Valenta, Miami, 1986.

Lessons of Grenada. Washington, D.C.: U.S. Department of State, February 1986.

Letter to Members of the Central Committee and Party from Vincent Noel. St. George's: October 17, 1983.

National Broadcast on Radio Free Grenada by Maurice Bishop, June 19, 1980. St. George's: Government Printer, 1980.

Operation URGENT FURY Report, from Commander in Chief U.S. Atlantic Command to Chairman, Joint Chiefs of Staff, Norfolk, Virginia. February 1984.

Second Report from the British Foreign Affairs Committee Session 1983-84 on Grenada, Observations of the Secretary of State for Foreign Affairs. London: June 1984.

Soviet and Cuban Involvement in Grenada as Reflected by the Grenada Documents, 1979-1983. Angelo J. LaBarro and Robert Kennedy. U.S. Army War College, Pennsylvania, 1985.

Soviet Military Power. Washington, D.C.: U.S. Government Printing Office, March 1983.

Statement by Langhorne A. Motley, Assistant Secretary for Inter-American Affairs, before the Armed Services Committee, U.S. House of Representatives, January 24, 1984.

The Real Story of October 1983: Maurice Bishop and October 19th 1983. St. George's: Martyrs Foundation, 1984.

Journals

All Hands (May 1984).

Armed Forces Journal International (March 1984; July 1984; May 1985; June 1986).

Army (June 1984; October 1986; November 1986).
Army Times, January 30, 1984, November 5, 1984.
Bajan (Barbados) (November 1983; December 1983).
Caribbean Challenge 28, no. 80 (1984).
Covert Action Information Bulletin, nos. 10, 19, 20 (1980–1983).
Defence: Helicopter World (August–September 1986).
Defence Update International, no. 46 (1984).
Economist, March 10, 1984; January 11, 1986.
Everybodys (November 1983; March 1984).
Field Artillery Journal, USA (March–April 1985).
The Grenada Massacre (Jamaica) (1983).
Gung-Ho (May 1984; October 1984).
Institute for the Study of Conflict No. 177, 1985, Grenada and East Caribbean
    Security by Stanley Arthur.
In the Spirit of Butler (St. George's) (1982).
"Is Freedom We Making." (St. George's) (1982).
Jane's Defence Weekly, April 4, May 2, 1987.
Military Logistics Forum (July–August 1985).
Military Review (January 1987).
New Breed (April–May 1984).
Newsday, August 13, 1984.
Proceedings/Naval Review (May 1984).
Reader's Digest (February 1984).
Soldier of Fortune (January 1984; February 1984; April 1984; October 1985).
Time, November 7, 1983, January 13, 1986.
US Marines in Grenada 1983, Lieutenant Colonel Ronald H. Spector, USMC,
    History and Museums Division Headquarters, USMC, Washington, D.C. 1987.

Newspapers

Barbados Advocate, October–November 1983.
Grenadian Voice, May–July 1986.
Informer (Grenada), January 9, 1987.
Nation (Barbados), October–November 1983.
Nation (Barbados), supplement, "The Bishop Killers," December 1986.
New Grenadian (Trinidad), May 1984.
New York Times, October–November 1983.
Sunday Telegraph (London), November 25, 1984.
Sunday Times (London), October 30, 1983.
Times (London), October–November 1983.
U.S. News & World Report, November 7, 1983, November 3, 1986.
Wall Street Journal, October 27, November 15, 1983.
Washington Post, October–November 1983.
Weekend Nation (Barbados), December 5, 6, 1986.

Index

About the Author

M AJOR MARK ADKIN was born in Bedford, England. He was educated at Bedford School and the Royal Military Academy Sandhurst, from which he was commissioned as an infantry officer into the Bedfordshire and Hertfordshire Regiment. After service in Germany, Malaya, Mauritius, and Aden, he left the British Army to join the overseas civil service in the Pacific. For many years he worked as an administrative officer and district commissioner in the Solomon Islands and Gilbert Islands (now Kiribati). For over five years he served in the Caribbean as a staff officer with the Barbados Defence Force, and as such participated in Urgent Fury. He has now returned to live in Bedford.